Robin Barratt is probably one of the best-known nightclub bouncers and bodyguards in Great Britain. He started his career in security and protection in the 1980s on the doors in his home town of Norwich and went on to work the doors in London, Manchester and even in Paris, France. He then attended a six-week close protection training course in Hereford, England, and ended up travelling the world looking after the rich (but not so famous). He eventually became the International Director of Training for the Worldwide Federation of Bodyguards up until the year 2000 when it was sold in to an Icelandic subsidiary of Securitas.

Robin started writing in 2002 and published his first book *Doing the Doors*, which is now a genre bestseller. For a while he also published and edited *Protection News* for the close protection community, *The Circuit*, an online magazine for the British Bodyguard Association, and *On the Doors*, the only quality magazine in the world dedicated exclusively to door supervision.

Robin is currently living in Bahrain where he still writes, as well as occasionally providing security and protection consultancy services in the Middle East.

D0064607

Also by Robin Barratt:

Doing the Doors
Confessions of a Doorman
Maria's Story
Bouncers and Bodyguards
Respect and Reputation (co-authored with Charlie Bronson)
Street Smart

Recent Mammoth titles:

The Mammoth Book of Casino Games
The Mammoth Book of Travel in Dangerous Places
The Mammoth Book of Best British Crime 7
The Mammoth Book of Bizarre Crimes
The Mammoth Book of Apocalyptic SF
The Mammoth Book of New IQ Puzzles
The Mammoth Book of Alternate Histories
The Mammoth Book of Regency Romance
The Mammoth Book of Paranormal Romance 2
The Mammoth Book of the World's Greatest Chess Games
The Mammoth Book of Tasteless Jokes
The Mammoth Book of New Erotic Photography
The Mammoth Book of Best New SF 23
The Mammoth Book of Best New Horror 21
The Mammoth Book of Great British Humour
The Mammoth Book of Threesomes and Moresomes
The Mammoth Book of Drug Barons
The Mammoth Book of Scottish Romance
The Mammoth Book of Women's Erotic Fantasies
The Mammoth Book of Fun Brain-Training

THE MAMMOTH BOOK OF TOUGH GUYS

EDITED BY ROBIN BARRATT

RUNNING PRESS
PHILADELPHIA · LONDON

Constable & Robinson Ltd
3 The Lanchesters
162 Fulham Palace Road
London W6 9ER
www.constablerobinson.com

First published in the UK by Robinson,
an imprint of Constable & Robinson, 2011

A copy of the British Library Cataloguing in Publication
Data is available from the British Library

UK ISBN 978-1-84901-367-3

1   3   5   7   9   10   8   6   4   2

First published in the United States in 2011 by Running Press Book Publishers

US Library of Congress Control number: 2010925958
US ISBN 978-0-7624-4099-3

Running Press Book Publishers
2300 Chestnut Street
Philadelphia, PA 19103-4371

Visit us on the web!
www.runningpress.com

Printed in the EU

CONTENTS

INTRODUCTION

By Robin Barratt

OVER TWENTY OR SO years living in a tough and often violent world as a doorman, bodyguard and trainer of bodyguards, and then later as a writer, I have met and mingled with some real hard men. I don't mean averagely tough men who are big fish in their relatively insignificant pond, but *"for fuck's sake"* tough, hard bastards who would take on just about anyone in any situation, anywhere in the world, and who have certainly made me feel a wave of nervousness and trepidation at that very first meeting, and a few nervous gulps at the first introduction and handshake.

And I don't get intimidated easily.

Whether a renowned martial artist, bare-knuckle fighter, doorman, bodyguard or gangster, I have found that there is something quite unique and unusual about a real hard man; he stands out in a crowd, he somehow looks different, he acts different, he has an air of self-confidence that "normal" men just don't have. Of course, not all hard men look hard; not all have battered faces and missing teeth, tattoos and shaved heads, but from my experience most do have something very peculiar about them that oozes toughness, confidence and authority. The celebrated former British gangster Dave Courtney once said to me: "You can see naughtiness in a man; you can smell if someone is capable of it. Say you are gay and you go into a nightclub, you can usually spot another gay. If you are a heroin addict, you can pick out someone else who uses straight away. And if you are a naughty man, you can pick that out, too. You can pick up the mannerisms. They say the eyes are a window to the soul. I know if someone is fucking handy from their eyes. I know if they can hurt me, or if I can beat them, from their eyes – nine times out of ten. Some of the naughtiest men I know look as though they couldn't harm a fly, but they have it in their eyes. And some of the scariest-looking fucking creatures you have ever seen in your life are like fucking kids." And I can't help but agree with Dave, there is definitely something unusual and unique about a real hard man.

I have, because of my work and the things I have done, also become good friends with some real hard men; mercenaries, bare-knuckle champions, Special Forces soldiers, bodyguards and, of course, some really fucking hard doormen. And yet surprisingly very few of these men have an "attitude", very few boast or brag or bully. They know *who* they are and they know exactly *what* they are capable of. Cross them at your peril, but otherwise these tough men generally have respect and regard for those around them and they rarely have to prove anything with arrogance and bad attitude – unlike the thousands of "wannabe" hard men out there. For example, I remember working as a doorman at the Rectory, a pub in Wilmslow, a small upper-class town in the county of Cheshire on the outskirts of Manchester, England. It was an extremely popular posh venue that attracted the affluent and often extravagant "Cheshire set" of models and footballers, local young entrepreneurs and business people. On that particular Friday night the Rectory was full fairly early and we had a "one in and one out" policy and strict face control, with a queue lined up waiting to come in. Walking down the queue, chatting amicably to the customers while they waited, I noticed a local hard man with a few friends waiting in line, along with everyone else. He was a locally known gang "head", a "main man" and someone you just didn't mess with, yet he was queuing to come into my venue! I recognized him immediately, said "hello", shook his hand and ushered him and his small, tough-looking entourage past the queue and straight into the pub. He knew who he was, everyone around him knew who he was, but he was still willing to queue up and wait with everyone else. He didn't walk straight pass the queue and into the pub with a "do you know who I am?" attitude. People didn't think he was a prat for queuing either; he respected those around him and because of that, people respected him. And the fact that I recognized him and let him in then made him a friend and someone whom I came to rely on in a rather difficult situation a few months later when a large pack of "wannabe" hard men stormed the door after I refused them all entry.

Real tough men rarely need to prove it.

It is a fact that some people are born great. Some people stand out in a crowd, some people look good and some people can "handle" themselves in aggressive confrontations with little or no formal training. The opposite is also very true; some people are definitely not great at all, disappear in a crowd, look pathetic and will run a mile at any confrontation. Yes, you can poke your arse with steroids and turn yourself from a 150-pound weakling into a 300-pound muscle-head, but if you are naturally afraid of confrontation, having strength and muscles won't change a thing. Nor will learning a martial art make you into someone you are not; you may study for years and have great technique but on the streets in real-time aggressive and violent situations, even the most skilled martial artists can be quickly overwhelmed. This was also highlighted to me in Wigan, northwest England, when my friend "one-punch" Neil floored two boasting, arrogant black-belts with just the one punch on each (but what mighty punches they were!). These two idiots were playing up, boasting and bragging and causing trouble yet, even though they had trained in martial arts for many years, they quickly came a cropper against the mighty fists of Neil. At six foot two inches and almost 240 pounds of solid muscle, Neil is a monster of a hard man yet is humble, thoughtful and quiet and during the day works with people with mental disabilities.

There are also many, many men that try to make themselves look hard and tough, and act as bullies and intimidators, but in reality are not and I have seen this time and time again; men that look really scary and as though they can handle almost anyone, yet invariably would run a mile in an aggressive or violent encounter. One so-called hard, tough giant of a doorman whom I worked with on the doors in Standish, a tough mining town in Lancashire, England, hid in the gents' toilets while the mightiest of all fights was going off inside the nightclub. With a shaved head, tattoos across his neck and muscles where muscles didn't really belong, he made himself look hard in order to try to intimidate, scare and bully. He may have thought that he was a hard man, he may have made himself look like a hard man and he may have liked the idea of being seen as a hard man, but in his heart he was a coward. And another time during the Balkans conflict when, for a short while, I was tasked to pick up international mercenaries from Zagreb airport in Croatia and transport them to the front-line for training, the hardest-looking, broken-nosed, tattooed, shaven-headed, boastful brag-garts would fall apart at the first mortar shell screaming overhead or AK-47 bullet whizzing by. They would (quite literally) shit their pants where they stood – or rather cowered – and we would take many of these "so-called" hard-men back to the airport the follow-ing week, broken and embarrassed (and unbelievably many would then later boast to their friends back home that they worked as a mercenary in Bosnia!). However, there were calm, thoughtful ones who said nothing to nobody and sat quietly reading or doing *The Times* crossword on the coach as it slowly made its way towards the front-line, and would then silently go out into the field for months and months on end doing God only knows what. And they never said a word about it to anyone; they never boasted or bragged or lied about what they did or didn't do. In my mind, these are the real hard bastards.

The simple fact is that you cannot change your genes and you cannot change who you really are; sure, you can change certain things about you, but not who you fundamentally are. It isn't the technique or the skills you have gained, or even the knowledge that are important: it is who you are and, conversely, who you are not. Without doubt it is the people who are not particularly hard (but think they are) that tend to show the most disrespect, care little about those around them and who cause the most problems. These are the ones that are responsible for much of the violence in today's turbulent, troubled and violent world. For sure, there are also a few really hard men who don't give a fuck about the world around them, but thankfully most of them are either dead or serving long prison sentences. But generally I have found that the toughest of the tough rarely have to prove anything to anyone: many of today's genuinely hard, tough men are humble, polite and modest, and show respect to those around them, and in return they get respect. However, show them disrespect and you get that too, heaps of it. And this book profiles some of these unique and undeniably fasci-nating men.

It is certainly true that a great many hard men are, or have been, gangsters and criminals, only because their lifestyle and upbringing has made them into who they are. Undoubtedly, many hard men come from tough backgrounds, often with dysfunctional families and tough, violent, callous fathers, and so they have grown up to be hard bastards themselves. Really hard men generally do not come from middle- and upper-class families. Hard bastards usually come from a hard world.

But not all.

What makes someone a hard bastard? I am not a psychologist or sociologist and so have not studied this phenomenon from a desk at some university somewhere; my experience, my perception and my understanding of this phenomenon comes solely from the streets, from working the doors and as a bodyguard, and from living in some of the most violent, aggressive and intimidating places in the world, places like Bosnia during the war, Russia and Africa. Having worked alongside and socialized with some immensely tough people, time and time again I have witnessed that the critical factors in defining real toughness are: firstly, the absolute willingness to fight anyone, anything and anywhere; secondly, the ability to be incredibly and uncompromisingly violent; thirdly, the lack of any real fear; and, lastly, the inability to give up, even when the odds are insurmountable and there is a real risk of serious injury or even death. It is a fact that we all have a basic fight or flight instinct. Most people flee in a difficult or violent situation. Some fight but eventually end up fleeing if the odds are too much against them. A very rare few will fight and fight and fight, no matter what the odds or the outcome. These few are undeniably the hardest of the hard.

Although I have worked and lived in a violent world, I am not a hard man – there are many, many people who are much tougher and much better fighters than me, and who could undeniably destroy me in seconds. However, I earned a bit of a reputation while I was on the doors and as a bodyguard, not because of my fighting prowess or my attitude, but because I always stood my ground, no matter how much the odds were against me. In all the violent situations I have come across I never once backed down. But would I battle to the very end and to the death if necessary? Would I give up this life and everything I love in order to have a reputation for being a truly hard bastard?

Definitely not.

But there are many people in this world that will, some of whom I have featured in this book.

While putting this book together I didn't want to focus just on gangsters and criminals but to look closely at a variety of other astonishingly tough, hard men (and one woman) who inhabit this globe as well. I have tried to be as diverse as I possibly can and to profile amazing martial artists, reputed bodyguards, prizewinning boxers and wrestlers, notorious debt-collectors, respected doormen and champion bare-knuckle fighters, all of whom are (or have been) undoubtedly some of the world's hardest. I have also included a couple of unusual tough bastards, including a regular citizen caught up in a life-threatening situation and a tough policewoman working on one of America's toughest reservations. Moreover, I did not want to concentrate solely on the famous or "infamous" either – there is already plenty written about the more celebrated and well-known hard men – but instead have included many people that don't particularly court publicity or infamy, that few people know about and who have kept their head well under the "radar". However, just because they are not famous doesn't mean they are not some of the toughest, hardest bastards on the planet.

This book is made up of previously published articles and book chapters, as well as many wonderful and fascinating contributions specially written for this publication. Where appropriate I have also included a brief introduction and/or biography of the person featured.

Although this book is not meant to showcase or condone violence in any way whatsoever, because of the subject matter I have sometimes had to include a violent period in a particular person's life, or have focused on a particularly violent episode or incident. But in other chapters I have included a general piece about that person and what made them into who they are, and in a few chapters the whole piece is a short biography of the person featured.

I hope you find all the people featured and their stories as interesting and as intriguing as I have.

Stay safe,

Robin Barratt (www.RobinBarratt.com)

GEOFF THOMPSON (UK)

Former British Nightclub Bouncer and World Famous Martial Artist

---

Introducing . . . Geoff Thompson

UNDOUBTEDLY, WHEREVER YOU go in the world, the nightclub doorman has been both feared and loathed; even the term "bouncer" ominously refers to being "bounced" out of a nightclub for some misdemeanour or other – or maybe for nothing at all. However, it must be said that over the past few years the role of the doorman, especially in the UK, has changed significantly and that doormen are no longer represented as muscled, tattooed hard bastards standing menacingly on the doors, intimidating and bullying, but as fully trained and licensed security "supervisors" with defined roles and responsibilities. But before training, security licensing and accountability, "old-school" doormen were a select, elite and isolated bunch of hard men living on the fringes of "normal" society, who kept themselves to themselves, who trained hard in the gym or the dojo during the day in order to equip themselves for the frequently violent and often criminal world of nightclubs, bars and discotheques at night. No one became a bouncer by applying for a job in the newspaper or employment centre; bouncers were almost always referred or recommended by other bouncers, often because of their awesome reputation and their ability to fight and frighten. Old-school doormen were undeniably hard men and they certainly didn't come much harder than the first of several phenomenally tough doormen I feature in this book; former nightclub bouncer now BAFTA award-winning writer Geoff Thompson.

Although Geoff Thompson now spends the majority of his time in his calm and sedate world behind his computer desk writing best-sellers, film scripts and self-help books, he was – and probably still is – very much one of the toughest men in the United Kingdom and deserves his place at the head of this book with this compelling and powerful story describing some of the events that ultimately led him away from his life as a bouncer.

Geoff Thompson was born in Coventry, England, in 1960, where he has lived for most of his life. Now one of the highest-ranking martial arts instructors in Britain, until the age of thirty he worked through a number of menial jobs, from glass-collector in a bar to a floor-sweeper at a factory. He then spent almost a decade working on the doors in Coventry, undeniably one of the toughest cities in the United Kingdom.

Once polled by *Black Belt* magazine (USA) as the number one self-defence instructor in the world and voted by the same magazine as the "Number One" self-defence author in the world, Geoff was twice invited to teach for the well-known actor and martial artist Chuck Norris in Las Vegas, USA. He originally began his training by learning the more traditional martial arts, including karate and kung fu, but, as a nightclub doorman, he soon realized that these were pretty much inadequate and ineffectual in the harsh, hard and often violent world on Coventry's club doors. He veered his training towards more practical, full-contact, street-style martial arts and combat sports including boxing, kick-boxing, judo and freestyle wrestling, where he most definitely excelled.

Geoff eventually turned instructor and currently holds the highest-level coaching awards for wrestling, the Amateur Boxing Association instructor's certificate, as well as a first dan in judo and sixth dan in Shotokan karate.

It was always Geoff's ambition to write and, proving that not all bouncers are uneducated, illiterate and ignorant, Geoff finally left the world of the doors and became a full-time writer. He has so far written over thirty published books and was on the *Sunday Times* bestseller list with his autobiography, *Watch My Back*, about his years working as a nightclub doorman.

His first film, *Bouncer*, a ten-minute short for the UK Film Council starring Ray Winstone, was nominated for a BAFTA in the 2003 awards. *Bouncer* was also nominated at the Edinburgh Film Festival in the best short category and it was also highly commended at the Raindance Festival. On top of all that, *Bouncer* was also chosen by the British Council to be part of the Britspotting tour; it was screened worldwide and shown in Birmingham, England, prior to every screening of David Cronenberg's *Spider*. Due to its success, Ray Winstone agreed to executive produce Geoff's second short film, called *Brown Paper Bag*, which was nominated for a RTS Award, invited to film festivals in the USA and Europe, and won the BAFTA 2004 for best short film.

Geoff's first feature film for cinema, *Clubbed*, based on his book *Watch My Back*, was released in 2009 to worldwide acclaim. In this utterly compelling, funny yet ultimately moving film Geoff chronicles his mad and violent life on the doors and what finally took him away from this aggressive, brutal world to follow his dream of becoming a full-time, professional writer. Geoff was certainly one of the hardest and toughest doormen and martial artists of his generation.

BOUNCER
By Geoff Thompson

"Where's Johnny Steen? I've come for my ear!"

The man at the nightclub door had a bandana of crêpe wrapped around his head and a face etched in pain. Blood issued through the bandage at the point where his right ear should have been but patently was not.

"Johnny's not in. Hasn't been here all night." I replied, trying not to stare at his injury.

"He bit my ear off." He continued, fingers dabbing tentatively around the wound as though checking his ear had really gone.

He wandered off to the next club in search of his missing body part.

Grapevine gossips later informed me that the missing ear – bitten off in a grudge fight at the local park – had been harpooned by its new owner to a dartboard in a busy pub and auctioned off to the highest bidder. The ear of a name fighter was quite a trophy in Coventry's lower echelons.

The seller got twenty quid and the buyer got to wear his prize on a key ring – a grotesque talking point.

In my former incarnation as a nightclub bouncer I had my life threatened more times than I care to remember. I was shot at, stabbed, glassed, punched, kicked, scratched, bitten, spat on, vomited over and trampled. I fought in pub bars, car parks, chip shops, restaurants and once at a friend's christening: he'd asked me to have a word with a rowdy relative not realizing that his interpretation of "a word" was entirely different to mine.

Three friends were murdered during a decade of madness and mayhem. Another, depressed and grossly over-exposed to violence, tried to end his life – alone in a ditch – by swallowing a bottle of bleach. Many more were sent to jail, and a few ended up on the psychiatrist's couch. Nearly all – myself included – found the divorce courts before salvation found us.

Ironically, I only took the job to face down my fears. I became a bouncer in the late 1980s because I'd inherited my mum's nerves and as a consequence was plagued by debilitating depressions and irrational fears. Standing on a nightclub door was little more than a pragmatic experiment in growing courage.

Bouncing was not my first course of action; it was a last chance saloon. ·

The first port of call – the doctor's surgery – left me disappointed. Medicine had not evolved much, it would seem: I hoped that working as a bouncer might prove a little more inspiring than a sympathetic smile and a course of Prozac.

It did, but the price was high.

Friedrich Nietzsche said that we should be careful when hunting the dragon not to become the dragon. It was a prophetic warning, one I wish I'd heeded sooner.

The Coventry club scene dished out violence as thick as it did fast. It was mostly unsolicited and it was always heinous. But for a lad looking to quieten his fears with a heavy dose of desensitization there was no better place to be.

I only intended to stay in the job for a short while: ten years and many broken bones later I was still there. My fears had been trounced and the depressions a distant memory, but the reflection in my bathroom mirror was no longer of a man I immediately recognized or particularly liked. The soft youth of yesteryear had become a hard man who used violence as a problem-solving tool. Those that stepped into my world looking for a little contact were dealt with quickly, brutally and always without demur.

Not surprisingly this placed me on bad terms with the law, but then policemen and bouncers have always shared an unholy alliance. We loved to hate them and they loved to lock us up at any given opportunity. Silly, really, when you consider the fact that we were both trying to do the same job: protect the good majority from the bad minority and the indifferent from themselves. That is not to say there were no exceptions. When it suited them the police could be very accommodating. After separating a local hard man from his teeth and his consciousness I found myself in a police cell facing a charge of Section 18 Wounding With Intent, which carried a possible five years in prison. My immediate future was looking pretty bleak until it was discovered that the man in hospital had a long list of previous convictions for police assault. In light of the new information the arresting officer found a sudden and healthy respect for me; he dropped all charges, leaving me with a clean record and an unofficial pat on the back.

The police look after their own.

The camaraderie on the door was equally strong. We had our own rules and those that broke them did so at their peril. Anyone who attacked a doorman or a member of staff was taken – usually dragged – somewhere quiet and taught the error of their ways. Our reasoning was simple enough; you have to slaughter a chicken to train a monkey. Brutal perhaps, but then standing over the open coffin of a workmate who had paid the ultimate price was no picnic. Noel was one of the three friends who found their young names in the obituary column. One took a baseball bat over the head on a Saturday night and died on the Tuesday. Another upset a local gangster with Manchester connections and paid with a bullet in the head as he sat in his car. The third – Noel – forgot the Musashi (Samurai) code that all bouncers live or die by; after the battle tighten your helmet straps. He was attacked as he left the nightclub at three in the morning, a vulnerable time when most doormen switch off as they head for home. He was stabbed through the heart by a man with a head full of grudge and a skin full of strong lager. He was dead before his head hit the pavement. Noel was a wonderful man who didn't read the signs. And there are always signs. The rituals of attack. The pre-fight twitches of men with bad intentions and no fear of consequence.

Knives may be the tool of choice for the career criminal but I found to my cost that people are nothing if not inventive when it comes to finding and using expedient weapons to bash, slash and pound each other. A man called Granite Jaw once tried to demolish a concrete dustbin using the top of my head; I had to bite the end of his finger off before he'd let me go.

Doormen regularly face a multiple of offensive weapons in the course of duty; guns, coshes, bats, bars, crutches, craft knives, carpet cutters and cars – a maniac called Tank once drove a Ford Cortina through the front doors of a busy Coventry club to enact his revenge after being barred by the doormen. On another occasion a troublesome youth who threatened that he was going to "shoot you bastards!" was gambolled from the club with a bitch-slap and a challenge; "Go'n fetch your gun." Of course we never thought he would. Five minutes later he was back in a white Merc with a rifle – trained on us – poking through a gap in driver's side window. Before he could fire, myself and three other "brave" doormen hit the deck and scurried – on our hands and knees – for the safety of the club.

Even people can be used as implements of pain when an equalizer is called for. An infamous 290-pound doorman and former wrestler called Bert Assarati found himself before a judge after hospitalizing several men, one of whom was in a particularly bad way, outside a London nightclub. The judge asked Assarati, "What did you hit him with?" Assarati deadpanned, "His mate." Apparently he'd picked one man up above his head and used him to bludgeon the other.

Given the chance, people will even attack you with their bodily fluids: blood, sick, spit, shit – nothing is sacred. One drunk and incapable man was so angry when I asked him to leave the club that he unzipped and pissed all over my trousers. It was very embarrassing. I could smell the vapour for days. Another man who I'd caught stealing cash from the bar till smashed his own nose on a table edge and machine-gunned me with a gob full of blood; he later told the police that I had beaten him up for nothing and invented the whole robbery story just to cover my tracks – and the police believed him!

Without question the most dangerous weapon by far was the one handed to every customer that stepped across our welcome mat; a beer glass. Even the uninitiated in a second of drunken madness can end a life with the speared edges of a broken glass. And the girls were often the worst offenders. Especially when another female stood between them and their man. I had to administer first aid to a beautiful twenty-something after a love rival cracked a wine glass on the edge of the bar and rammed it into her face. She hit her with such force that two inches of the glass stayed buried beneath her cheekbone. It took six hours of reconstruction to fix her face. The psychological damage would take more to repair than a surgeon's stitches.

Dealing with women was not always so violent, but it was often tricky. I had my fair share of sexual come-ons from scantily clad beauties with a penchant for large men in tuxedo suits. The door is a seductive trade offering local celebrity, free beer and loose women to those with a weak will and a strong libido. I was married at the time so I should have abstained, and most of the time I did, but I can't say that I didn't occasionally succumb. In my defence – and to my shame – my indulgences were infrequent and never without a post-coital dose of guilt and remorse. Personally, I found more profit in light flirtations than full-on promiscuity. For instance, an off-the-cuff compliment about the splendid condition of a customer's bottom once earned me months of pleasure. The lady in question thanked me by lifting her skirt and flashing a frilly pair of pink knickers that clung Kylie Minogue-tight to the neatest little bottom I have ever set eyes on. I was the envy of every man in the club. It became a Saturday night ritual that never failed to please. Sadly, it ended the night she turned up on the arm of a man with a face like ten boxers. I don't think he would have appreciated her generous spirit. Still, it was good while it lasted.

Some women wanted more for their money than a bit of sexually charged banter. For several weeks I complimented Lala on how nice she was looking. I mentioned her hair, her shoes (girls like that) and how nice her perfume was. I badly misread the situation. What had been an innocent flirt for me was patently a red-hot come-on for her. I realized my folly the night she wedged me – using her ample bust – into a dark corner of a busy nightclub and whispered in my ear, "I'd love to take you home with me, I'd massage your whole body in baby oil, then I'd get Victor out." I raised an eyebrow into a question-mark and asked, terrified, "Victor?" She made a yummy smile, snaked her hand seductively down my chest and said, "Victor the vibrator." I made a few hasty excuses and spent the rest of the night hiding in a cloakroom.

Not all of the women I encountered were so enamoured by me. A rather irate lady once tried to decapitate me with the stiletto end of her right shoe while I wrestled her boyfriend from the club. He'd ordered drinks and refused to pay for them so he had to go. She was having none of it. Each time her shoe bounced off my head she screamed, "Violence is not the answer!" Hypocrisy, it would seem, holds no bounds.

I was lucky. Another doorman was stabbed in the ribs by a maniacal mother with a pair of nail scissors when he tried to stop her daughter – the bride-to-be – from having live sex with a hen-night strip-o-gram.

Personally, when dealing with women, I always recommend restraint. There is rarely cause to be physical. A keen eye and a quick wit is often all you need. The mere mention of large bottoms, flaccid bosoms and a hairy upper-lip are usually enough to send a body-conscious female scurrying for safety. We refused a rather large lady entry to a club one night because she was violently drunk and scaring the other customers (and the doormen). She wasn't happy. Intimating that she would return to the club with a bit of canine back-up, she bragged, "I breed Rottweilers." My mate Tony, a master of observational put-downs replied, "Well, love, you've definitely got the hips for it."

Violent men and frightening women are bad enough, but at least you know where you stand with them. It is when the gender is ambiguous that confusion can trigger sheer terror. Tuesdays at Busters nightclub was alternative night, which meant a culture dish of gays, geeks, goths, punks and trannies. Nothing too bad in that, you might think. I felt the same way until the night a pretty little girl who had given me the eye on the way into the club followed me into the gents' toilets, hitched up her plaid skirt, took out her manhood, smiled and then proceeded to relieve herself in the urinal next to mine.

Nightclub toilets were also the favoured hidey-hole for criminals and vagabonds. Bag thieves used toilet cisterns to dump stolen and fleeced handbags, whilst muggers regularly attacked and robbed their unwitting victims when they were at their most vulnerable; unzipped at the urinal or de-bagged on the can. Messy but effective. And it was the doormen who had to clean up afterwards. Equally unpleasant was the mess left when too much partying resulted in a vomit fest.

Escorting the ill and the infirm from the premises without getting a jacket full of sick yourself was tricky, if not impossible. It was definitely my least favourite task. Some people at least had the courtesy to wait until they'd vacated the building before shouting "Hughy!" One gent retched and heaved his way out of the club, sat down by a wall, threw up again and then proceeded to pass out. Whilst he lay unconscious in a pillow of regurgitated chicken korma I propped a sign by his head that read: "I bet he drinks Carling Black Label."

Druggies, similarly, used the multi-purpose space of the club loo to inject, roll, swallow, sniff and deal chemical highs. Occasionally, and disappointingly, those on the make were the doormen themselves, though, despite suggestions to the contrary – and certainly from my experience – this scenario is rare. A good door team would not be seen dead dealing drugs. They are constantly on the lookout for dealers and users, both of whom get short shrift and a fast exit from the club if they are caught. No moral crusade, I can assure you, just part of the job description.

People are fixated by the evils of drugs and there is little doubt that for those who deal and those that take there can be no undamaged escape. But as an empiricist I would argue that if drugs are evil then alcohol is the devil incarnate. Not only is it more damaging and deadly than Class A drugs – it kills and ravages tens of thousands more per capita than any other substance – it is legal, socially acceptable and it doesn't even carry a government warning. And the deadly trilogy of stress, booze and nightclub ambience is all the ingredients you need to turn even the nicest people into despicable creatures.

Alcohol has always been linked with – and often blamed for – many of our societal ills, not least the burgeoning growth in unsolicited violence. No doubt there is a link between binge-drinking and bar-fighting, but the former is surely a trigger and not the root cause. Pubs and clubs are brimming over with angst-ridden folk looking to displace a bad day, a bad week or a bad life in a good night. Perhaps that would explain why the violence – often heinous, sometimes fatal – is completely disproportionate to the triggering stimuli. Accidentally spilling another man's beer in a club rammed with bodies hardly justifies a cross word, let alone a broken glass in the neck and four pints of red on the beer-sticky carpet. But, in the buzz of a busy nightclub it is just one of the many reasons people will find to enact atrocities on each other. If a spilled beer is going to cost you four pints of blood, never make the mistake of chatting up another man's date; it may well cost you all nine lives.

After a decade of standing under nightclub neon and nearly losing my faith in human nature I had the growing realization that violence was not the answer. It is a cruel and ugly language, the parley of ignorant men, but a means of discourse none the less and, when you are dealing with the hard of thinking, sometimes a quick punch in the eye is better understood that a lengthy over-the-table negotiation. Some people – even despots and dictators on the world stage – will listen to nothing less.

Witnessing man's inhumanity to man is enough to turn even the hardiest stomach but my personal renaissance only began after I nearly killed someone in a car-park fight. I won't insult your intelligence by glazing over my actions with the egg-wash of weak rationalization. The situation – one that should have found a negotiable solution – started innocently enough. A local man and martial artist of some repute was consistently and blatantly challenging my authority and testing my patience by refusing to drink up at the end of the night. For three months I tried to be nice, laced my requests to drink up with politeness and respect, all to no avail. He obviously mistook my politeness for weakness and one late Sunday evening – in a fit of arrogance – he barged into me when I was collecting glasses. It was the final insult. My hat tipped, I invited him on to the tarmac.

The fight was short and bloody. Although my opponent was a black belt he was ill-prepared for the pavement arena.

When the paramedics were called I knew that I had gone too far, and my capacity to inflict hurt had astounded even me. I felt sure that he was dead when the ambulance took him away under a wool blanket and a flashing blue light. The veil disappeared and for the first time I could see exactly what I had become – or, more specifically, what trading in violence had made me. At home I contemplated a bleak future where the here-and-now promised only prison and the hereafter threatened a purgatorial darkness that I could not even begin to imagine. In bed I stroked the warm face of my sleeping wife. I could not believe how beautiful she was; she felt like silk. I got down on my knees and unashamedly prayed to God. "Give me one more chance," I begged. "And I promise that I will turn my life around."

It was the longest night of my life, with plenty of time for introspection. There is nothing like the threat of prison and eternal damnation to give you an honest perspective on liberty and life. I realized that I was blessed; a great wife, gorgeous kids and freedom. It doesn't get much sweeter. And I was risking it all for a bastard trade that I had come to hate.

The next day I heard that my sparring partner had pulled through. My prayer had been answered. I kept my part of the bargain and shortly afterwards I left the doors for good.

I found a few things during my ten-year sojourn into the dark, often criminal, world of the bouncer: my courage – fear can be beaten by those with the moral fibre to face it; my destiny – success and happiness are a choice, not a lottery; and my limitations – we all need some form of invisible support when what we know as real starts to collapse all around us.

Perhaps ironically and more notably I discovered the futility of violence.

I also lost a few things, my first marriage and the innocence of youth to name but two.

Luckily – unlike many of my peers – I did not forfeit my sanity, my liberty, or my life.

Oh, and I got to walk away with both ears.

THOMAS SILVERSTEIN (USA)

The Most Feared Convict in the USA

Introducing . . . Thomas Silverstein

BECAUSE MANY HARD, tough men are also extremely violent, many are, by their very nature, criminals and convicts. And most extremely violent men end up living the majority of their lives alone behind the bars and the concrete walls of maximum security prisons; for if you choose to lead a violent life prison is inevitable. Fewer in the US are said to be more dangerous or more violent than Thomas (Tommy) Silverstein, the first of a number of "infamous" prisoners featured in this book. Born 1952 in Long Beach, California, Silverstein has spent the majority of his life behind bars and at the age of just nineteen he was first sent to San Quentin Prison in California for armed robbery. Four years later he was paroled, but shortly after leaving prison he was arrested once again – along with his father and his cousin – for three more armed robbery offences and was then sentenced to fifteen years. Silverstein could have been a free man today but while inside he was then convicted of four separate murders (one of which was overturned) and since 1983 has lived alone in solitary confinement (he is on record as the prisoner held longest in total solitary confinement within the US Bureau of Prisons). Prison authorities describe Silverstein as a brutal killer and a former leader of the Aryan Brotherhood prison gang. His earliest theoretical date of release is 2 November 2095.

The first murder of which Silverstein was accused was that of fellow prisoner Danny Atwell in 1980, but this conviction was later overturned as it was based on false testimony from prison informants. A year later Silverstein was then accused of the murder of Robert Chappelle, a member of the D.C. Blacks prison gang. While Silverstein was on trial for Chappelle's murder, Raymond "Cadillac" Smith, the national leader of the D.C. Blacks, was "conveniently" moved by the prison authorities from another prison to a cell near Silverstein's and from the moment Smith arrived, prison logs show that he had tried to kill Silverstein numerous times. However, using improvised weapons, Silverstein, with the help of another inmate, killed Smith and then dragged his body up and down the prison landing for other prisoners to see. For this murder Silverstein received a life sentence.

On 22 October 1983, after being let out of his cell for a shower, Silverstein killed prison officer Merle E. Clutts by stabbing him several dozen times with a shank (a shiv or makeshift knife), claiming that Clutts was deliberately harassing him. Following the murder of Clutts, Silverstein was transferred to a special "no human contact" cell in Atlanta, Georgia.

In 1987, following a prison riot, Silverstein was moved again to Leavenworth Prison in Kansas and placed in a secure underground cell. When Leavenworth was downgraded to a medium-security facility, Silverstein was then moved to ADX Florence, a supermax facility in Colorado.

Undeniably one of America's most violent prisoners, in this compelling piece written especially for this book, writer Randy Radic gives his own creative account of a period in Silverstein's violent life.

AMERICA'S MOST DANGEROUS PRISONER
By Randy Radic

Thomas Silverstein, whose nickname was Terrible Tom, was America's most dangerous prisoner. When asked for his professional opinion about Terrible Tom, one prison psychiatrist laughed and shook his head, "There is no applicable term for him. He's way beyond any textbook definition." The doctor thought for a moment, then said, "I'd call him a psychosocial killer. Murder is the way he makes love to other human beings. It's like sex for him."

Silverstein wasn't Tom's real name. His real name was Thomas Conway, Junior. He grew up in Long Beach, California. When Tommy Junior was four years old, his mother divorced Tom Senior and married a guy named Sid Silverstein. Sid legally adopted Tom Junior, so he became Thomas Silverstein, but the boy hated the name Silverstein because it was so Jewish. And he hated coming home from school every day, because his mom and his "dad" fought like two cats in a bag. His parents considered screaming, slapping, punching, kicking, throwing dishes and demolishing doors normal behaviour.

Socially, Tom was a catastrophe that kept on happening. Timid Tom would have been an appropriate nickname for the young Tommy. Because he was shy and withdrawn, Tom didn't fit in at school; he had no friends, only enemies who were bullies and saw easy pickings in Tom. To top it off, everyone thought he was Jewish, which made him more of a pariah than he already was. Every day he came home from school either frightened or beat up, some days both.

His mom called him "Tragic Tom", because she said, "Your life reminds me of one of those Greek tragedies, where everybody walks around wretched, saying 'woe is me'."

One day he arrived home, crying. "What's the matter?" asked his mother, setting down her cigarette. She took a sip of her gin and tonic. She had intended to do some cleaning that day, but had fixed herself a drink instead. One drink led to another and pretty soon she didn't feel like cleaning. So she switched on the television and lit a Chesterfield.

With blood oozing from the corner of his lip and a bruise on his cheek, Tom just looked at the floor. He sniffled.

"You pathetic little cry-baby!" yelled his mother. "Tell me what happened or I'll give you something to really cry about."

"I – I got hit," said Tommy, starting to whimper.

"Did you fight back?"

"No," whispered Tommy.

"What did you do, you little wimp?"

Tommy couldn't answer because he knew that his mother already knew what he had done. He had run. If he said it, she would hate him.

"You ran! Didn't you, you little piece of shit?" screamed his mother.

Tommy began bawling. He tried not to, but it just came out.

His mother leaned forward, taking a huge puff of her cigarette. "Look at me, cry-baby," she commanded, as smoke curled out of her mouth and nose. "Look at me!"

Tommy looked up. His mother's face was sharp. "The next time you come home crying because some boy beat you up . . ." She paused for another drag on her cigarette. "I will whip you myself. Two beatings instead of one," she snarled.

Tommy wiped his nose on his sleeve. "I'm sorry, Mother. I'm so sorry."

"Get out of my sight, you sissy," she hissed. "You make me sick."

Tommy ran to his room, where he collapsed on his bed, curling up like a foetus. He sucked his thumb and cried himself to sleep. No one came to check on him. No one called him for dinner.

Tommy was eleven years old.

Years later, Terrible Tom Silverstein recalled, "That's how my mom was. She stood her mud. If someone came at you with a bat, you got your bat and you both went at it."

Tom's sister, Sydney, said, "We were taught never to throw the first punch, but never to walk away from a fight. My brother started getting into trouble because he was running away from a violent environment at home. Then he got into drugs, and he became a brother I never knew."

Three years later, when he was fourteen years old, Tom Silverstein was sent to a California reform school. In 1966, reform school was a nice-nellyism for "gladiator school" because the only subject they taught in this kind of school was violence. And the learning process was unsentimental and hands-on. Tom came away with a nuts-and-bolts approach to brutality. Like a wolf in the coldest of winters, "kill or be killed" became Tom's slogan, his religious song.

But a wisp of human smoke remained in Tom. Starved for affection and approval, Tom wanted to feel plugged-in. He wanted to connect with other human beings. So he started hanging out with his real father, Tom Conway, Senior, who used people until they were of no more use. Then he brushed them off, and moved on. Tom Senior robbed banks. At least that's what he told people. The truth was that Tom Senior was a petty thief, and not very good at that. He was a wannabe.

When the two Conways hooked up, they spurred each other on. Tom Senior told bigger lies about himself and his accomplishments. He even gave advice to his son on how to be a bank robber. Tom Junior listened carefully and then applied what he learned from his old man. Dropping out of school, Tom made a choice. He became a professional criminal. He started out small, hitting convenience stores and corner gas stations. Sometimes he got away with only a few bucks, other times he made hundreds of dollars. Whatever the amount, he split it down the middle with his dad. Although Tom Junior was doing all the work, taking all the risks, they were a team and Tom felt a loyalty to his blood-father. Things were looking up.

It went to hell in 1971. Tom Junior was nineteen years old. Walking into a 7–11 store late on a Friday night – when there would be lots of cash in the till – Tom stuck his gun in the cashier's face. "Take all the money from your drawer and put it in a paper bag," he ordered.

"Sure, man," said the cashier. "Just don't shoot me, man. Okay?" The cashier groped at the money, jamming it in a bag. Then he handed it to the robber.

Tom pointed his gun at the guy's nose. "Say anything to the cops and I'll make it my business to come back and kill you," he stated matter-of-factly. Then he walked out.

The cashier didn't say anything. He didn't have to. Surveillance cameras caught the whole thing on tape. Caught in dazzling cinematic detail as he performed, Tom was quickly identified by the cops. A warrant was issued and the hunt was on.

Ignorant of all this, Tom was arrested the next afternoon as he left a hamburger joint, where he had a cheeseburger and a chocolate malt. Tom had a thing for chocolate. For some reason, chocolate soothed the beast within him. The cops cuffed him and carted him off to jail.

Because of the surveillance tape from the 7–11, Tom's public defender advised him to cop a plea. "If you take this to trial, you'll need to find a new lawyer," the public defender told him. "Because

I won't be part of any legal suicide." He looked at Tom. "They got you dead to rights on that tape."

"Fuck you," replied Tom.

Tom knew the lawyer was right, so he copped a plea bargain. He pled guilty and in return they promised him a reduced sentence. Instead of ten to fifteen years, the judge sentenced him to three to ten years. He was shipped off to San Quentin Prison.

Being a new fish at San Quentin was like dying and going to hell; a place of edicts, torchings and infestations. Only this particular hell wasn't divided into levels based on sin. The hell that was the "Q" divided itself based on skin colour. Blacks over there, whites over here and Hispanics over yonder. Which was not surprising. Tom had experienced racial bigotry while in grade school. As everyone thought he was a Jew, he was a "kike", which meant he was less.

One good thing about the "Q" though, nobody cared if he was Jewish or not. They just cared if he was white or black or brown. And Tom figured out real fast that if he wanted to survive, he needed to hook up with a gang. If he didn't marry into a white gang, he'd be nothing but a "bitch". And bitches didn't last long.

Tom decided not to be a bitch.

Tom met a guy on the yard one day. Big white guy, with a shaved head and muscles on his muscles. Tom was on the bench press, struggling to get one final rep, when two hands the size of hams helped him get the bar up and racked. Sitting up, Tom wiped his forehead with the tail of his T-shirt. "Thanks, man," he said. "I was about to drop that fucker on my chest. Would not have been pretty." Tom stood up.

The big guy laughed. "Leave a big dent in your chest," he boomed. "Mind if I work in?" he asked. Without waiting for an answer, he grabbed two 45-pound plates from a nearby stack. Sleeving them on the bar, he reached for two more and put them on. Then he slid on to the bench and gripped the bar.

"That's more'n four hundred pounds, man," said Tom.

"Yup." The guy racked the bar off and did ten reps, easy.

"Jesus, Mary and Joseph," exclaimed Tom. "You're strong as an ox."

"Moose," said the guy.

"Well, I guess, if you say so," agreed Tom. "Moose are pretty strong, too, I guess."

The guy gave Tom a funny look. "Moose is my name. Moose Forbes."

"Oh, right."

Moose got up and added two more plates to the bar. "New fish, huh?" he asked Tom.

"Yeah," nodded Tom. "Got three to ten for armed robbery."

Moose wasn't impressed. "You hooked up?"

"No," said Tom. "I want to, but I don't know what the protocol is."

Moose squinted at him. "The what?"

"You know, the protocol. The correct way of going about it," explained Tom.

Moose laughed, shaking his head. "You talk like a college boy. Where you from?"

"Long Beach. An' I ain't no college boy."

"That a fact?" said Moose, baring his teeth. "This ain't Long Beach, it's the 'Q'. And there ain't no protocol, cuz there ain't no applications to fill out. It ain't a fucking country club, college boy."

Tom took a step back. He gazed at Moose and waited.

Moose couldn't believe it. Didn't this little fuck know who he was? If he wanted a dogfight, he'd come to the right dog. Moose loved the shit. Moose took a step forward.

As if by magic, a shiv gleamed in Tom's hand. Tom stood waiting. Moose charged, his arms reaching out.

Tom slipped to the side. Then, as Moose passed by, the shiv licked out and kissed Moose's ribs.

Moose pulled up and turned to look at Tom, who stood waiting. Moose lifted his shirt, looked at his ribs. Blood welled from a six-inch gash in his side. Pulling his shirt down, Moose looked around. The other inmates went about their business, talking, pumping iron, laughing, smoking. It had happened so fast, no one had noticed.

Moose stared at Tom for a moment, then turned and walked away.

Tom shrugged and went back to lifting weights.

The next day a guy who called himself Spots waved Tom over.

Because of his many tattoos, Spots looked like a leopard. Spots told him that the Aryan Brotherhood had accepted him as a prospect.

"The who?" asked Tom. He'd only been there a week. He didn't know the names of all the gangs.

Spots did a double-take. "Shit, man," he said. "You know, the Brand."

Tom shrugged. "Never heard of 'em."

Spots rolled his eyes. "Fuck me, man. The Brand runs this place. Drugs, guns, pruno, all of it."

"If you say so. What do they want with me?"

"They reaching out, man," explained Spots. "You know, you can hook up. Be part of the Brotherhood. No one fuck with you. An' if they do, the Brotherhood got your back."

Tom thought about that. "Sure. What do I have to do?"

Spots smiled. "Nothin'. Everythin'. Whatever they tell you. After you earn your bones, then you in." Spots clenched his fist in front of his chest.

"Okay," said Tom.

Spots nodded in approval. "You be sponsored by Moose. He be telling you what's what."

"Okay."

Spots walked off.

Later, Tom learned that Moose, rather than being pissed off, had been impressed with Tom's fury and willingness to jump in the shit. Blood in, blood out. And Tom had already spilled Moose's blood. So Moose had sponsored him, telling the Aryan Brotherhood that "The little fucker's faster 'n greased lightning."

Tom was in. Within a year he took the pledge and was branded. Being branded was okay with Tom, because he knew it was a rite of passage. It was expected. He'd read about it. Ancient warriors, like the Babylonians and Sumerians, would mark themselves with the blood of their enemies. Tom enjoyed the camaraderie he found in the Aryan Brotherhood and he appreciated the protection it provided, but he never got the rush from it the others did. Most of them were adrenaline junkies who loved the ideas of terror and power. Their drug of choice was violence. Being in the "toughest prison gang" gave them an emotional high, a kind of exalted state, where they believed they were invincible mystical warriors of some pagan religion.

In Tom's opinion, the mystical warrior stuff was bullshit. Tom simply wanted respect. He didn't hate violence. He didn't love violence. He found it inevitable. To get respect, sometimes he had to become violent. That's just the way it was.

Tom spent four years at the "Q". Then the powers-that-be paroled him. And Tom once more hooked up with Tom Senior, who had hooked up with Tom Junior's uncle, Arthur. Nervous and skinny, with lank hair and bad personal hygiene, Arthur was into nose-candy – cocaine – and needed lots of cash to pay for his habit. Plus, Arthur thought of himself as a badass and loved playing the part. He had a regular arsenal of guns in his trashy apartment on the third floor of a rent-subsidized complex, along with a freaky girl-friend who mainlined heroin, and a Siamese cat that Arthur always forgot to feed.

Tom didn't think much of the whole arrangement. In his opinion, Uncle Arthur was a goof. But he went along with it because they were family. His Dad said they had to stick together. So they did. They hit three convenience stores over the course of three weeks. Tom Junior insisted on masks because of the surveillance cameras which had tripped him up before.

Only Arthur didn't want to wear a mask. Because he used his nose to suck up copious amounts of coke rather than for breathing, Arthur spent a lot of his time writhing in twitchy paranoia. Wearing a mask gave him extreme claustrophobia, which gave him the heebie-jeebies and left him gasping for air.

So the two Toms, Junior and Senior, wore masks and Arthur went maskless. Which didn't work out well at all, because the cops identified Arthur and then followed him around for a few days, during which time they made up a list of his "known associates": Tom Junior, Tom Senior and a young female who "looked like death warmed over", according to one of the cops.

After the third robbery, the cops moved in and arrested every-body, recovering most of the cash from the robberies, which was $1,300. The cops took the money and the robbers, whom they booked and tossed into jail. The trial was a fiasco. Twitchy Arthur couldn't keep his mouth shut. He was going through withdrawal and more paranoid than ever. So, pale and sweating, he rolled over on his nephew and brother without really meaning to.

"Tommy was the leader. We just did as he told us," chirped Arthur. "Me and his dad was just taking orders. Tommy's a smart boy. He was the brains."

Arthur got five years in prison. Tom Senior got five to seven years and Tom Junior got fifteen years. He was twenty-three years old. The Feds shipped Tommy off to Leavenworth, which was a maximum-security prison in Kansas. Called the Hothouse because of its heat and humidity, Leavenworth was a hellish place. Murder occurred regularly; drugs were everywhere. To control the lucrative drug trade, gangs fought ongoing, vicious wars on the battlefield of Leavenworth Prison. The place was awash in blood.

The Aryan Brotherhood ran horse, and controlled the supply in and out of Leavenworth. Horse was prisoner slang for heroin, which was number one on the narcotic hit parade in the late 1970s. Since Tom was already branded, he immediately hooked up with the Brotherhood members in Leavenworth. It was business as usual: get the drugs in, via mules or corrupt guards, distribute it, collect money owed, and, above all, keep an eye on the competition. Other gangs tried to move in all the time. When they did, the Brotherhood took care of business.

The horse business depended upon mules. Mules were convicts who transported drugs in condoms, balloons, small tubes, or sometimes even in saran wrap, which they inserted into their rectums or swallowed and later retrieved from their toilet bowl. Horse was smuggled in by girlfriends, wives and visitors, who transferred the drugs to the inmate, who either swallowed it if it was in a balloon, or excused himself to the bathroom, where he quickly keistered it. After the visit, the mules would deliver the drugs to the Aryan Brotherhood. For their efforts, the mules received a "cut", which was a fee for their services. Usually the fee was a portion of the horse.

Danny Atwell was not branded. Nor was he a prospect. He didn't want anything to do with that shit. He just wanted to do his time and get out, and meanwhile got regular visits from his wife and family members. But the Aryan Brotherhood wanted Danny to go mule. Even though he was scared to death, Danny refused. He didn't want his family members dragged in the sewer.

Danny had signed his own death warrant.

His name "went into the hat". Allegedly, Thomas Silverstein and two other Aryan Brotherhood members were assigned to "take care of business". The initial accusations suggested that they caught Danny coming out of the shower and stabbed him to death. It only took about five minutes.

Tom and the other two Brothers were charged with murder. They all pleaded not guilty, because what happened in prison stayed in prison. No one saw anything, so no one would say anything. They thought.

Somebody forgot to tell the snitches. They came out of the woodwork to tell their lurid tales of drugs, mules and contract murder. Singing like rock stars, the snitches played their usual game. They said what they knew the prosecutor and the jury wanted to hear. In the end, Tom was convicted and sentenced to life in prison.

The names of all the snitches "went into the hat". Like elephants, the Aryan Brotherhood had long memories. They would not forget.

To this day, Tom Silverstein says he didn't kill Danny Atwell. He now admits to two other murders, but not that one. Indeed, the conviction for murdering Atwell was later overturned due to false witness testimony.

The Feds moved Tommy to the United States Penitentiary in Marion, Illinois. At that time, USP Marion was the latest supermax prison and claimed the dubious distinction of being the most violent prison in America. It was the ultimate in waste management, the place where they dumped the human waste called "gang leaders" and the nutcases who killed because they liked it.

In short, Marion was the supermax supermarket of psychopaths. Tommy fitted right in.

They put Tommy in a control unit, which was a new-fangled term for the Hole. He got out one hour a day and ate in his cell. Isolation made Tommy creative. He had to do something or go bonkers from boredom. So he started reading and drawing. As Silverstein put it, "I could hardly read, write or draw when I first fell. But most of us lifers are down for so long and have so much time to kill that we actually fool around and discover our niche in life, often in ways we never even dreamt possible on the streets. We not only find our niche, we excel."

Redemption wasn't part of Tommy's niche. There was a D.C. Blacks member in the control unit. Robert Chappelle was his name.

The only thing Chappelle hated more than whites was whites who were Jewish. To him, Silverstein was "a kike – one of them what four-pointed Jesus on the cross".

Tommy felt Chappelle didn't respect him. And in Tommy's world disrespect was more than flesh and blood can bear. So Tommy decided to take care of business. One day when he was let out for his hour of exercise, Tommy passed by the cell of another Aryan Brotherhood member, Clayton Fountain. Fountain reached into his crotch and pulled something out: a thin length of wire. He slipped the wire into Tommy's hands. As Tommy continued his exercise walk around the tier, he passed Chappelle's cell, where Chappelle was asleep. As luck would have it, Chappelle's head was near the bars of his cell. Tommy poised the wire above Chappelle's throat. The powder-grey wire looked like chrome against Chappelle's black skin.

Eyes narrowing with malice and delight, Tommy looped the wire around Chappelle's neck and began strangling him. Tommy was caught up, held almost, in those few moments. He found ease. Moving through it the very edges of his strength were sharpened like the blade of a knife. Chappelle's struggles diminished into shadow and continued to recede until there was nothing at all in the world, but death.

The murder of another human being took less than five minutes this time.

Tommy left the wire wrapped around Chappelle's dead throat, and went on walking. The next time he passed Fountain's cell, he smiled and gave Fountain a thumbs up.

"Vengeance is mine, saith the Lord," said Fountain, grinning. "I will repay."

Tommy nodded and kept walking.

Like most criminals, Silverstein and Fountain overcompensated for their lack of self-esteem. In other words, they couldn't keep their mouths shut. They had to brag about their crimes because that was the only thing they had to brag about. Soon the two Aryan Brotherhood members boasted to any inmate who would listen about how they had snuffed Robert Chappelle. Murder gave them status, elevated their reputations.

Prison officials charged Silverstein and Fountain with Chappelle's murder. A trial took place. The inmates to whom Silverstein and

Fountain had boasted played the snitch game, telling the jury of the grotesque deed. The jurors cringed in horror, then found them both guilty of first-degree murder. The judge sentenced both men to life in prison. Which meant Silverstein now had to serve two consecutive life terms. Which meant his life was over.

They couldn't execute him because at that time, 1981, a federal death penalty for one inmate murdering another inmate did not exist.

Once again, Silverstein maintained his innocence. He didn't kill Robert Chappelle. He declared that federal officials framed him, because they hated him. In the next breath, he blamed the D.C. Blacks.

It wasn't too long before the Bureau of Prisons moved the D.C. Blacks leader, Raymond "Cadillac" Smith from another prison to USP Marion, where Tommy was. They put Cadillac in a cell near Tommy.

Cadillac Smith was a drug pusher and cop-killer from Washington, D.C. He hated "honkey red-neck motherfuckers". Robert Chappelle had been his friend. Now he was dead. And Tommy had done it. Cadillac Smith was a religious man. He believed in tit for tat. His motto was "Dirty deed for dirty deed". Tommy had done a dirty deed. Therefore, Tommy had to die.

From his cell, Cadillac Smith could see Tommy's cell. "Goin' kill your white ass, Jew-boy," announced Cadillac.

Tommy pressed his face close to the bars of his cell, looking down the way toward Cadillac. "Look, Cadillac," said Tommy. "I didn't kill Chappelle. I mean it, man. I did not do it."

Cadillac gave an untamed laugh. He stuck his arm out between the bars of his cell, holding his fingers in a V-shape. "White boy speak'n with forked tongue," he said. "I'ze gonna kill you, Jew-boy. Real soon."

Cadillac tried to keep his promise. First he tried to stab Tommy, but Tommy was too quick – "faster 'n greased lightning" – and got away. Then Cadillac got his hands on a zip-gun smuggled in by another D.C. Black. Zip-guns were beautiful in their simplicity: a telescoping car aerial with a .22 calibre bullet clamped into its fat end. Collapsing the aerial acted as a firing pin and discharged the bullet. Neat and effective. The only problem was accuracy.

One day Tommy was on his exercise walk and passed Cadillac's cell. Cadillac took aim and slammed the aerial shut. Bang! The bullet missed Tommy by a foot or more, ricocheting off the opposite wall. Tommy stopped and stared at Cadillac.

"Motherfuck!" shouted Cadillac. He tried to reload but couldn't. The fat end of the zip-gun had mushroomed and wouldn't hold the bullet in place. A pair of pliers would remedy that, but of course he didn't have any pliers.

"Strike two, you stupid shithead," snarled Tommy. He took a step closer. "Game over cuz there won't be a third time." Tommy walked away.

Three days later, Tommy and Clayton Fountain were in an exercise cage, where they did push-ups and ran on the spot. While the two white Brothers did callisthenics, Cadillac Smith was escorted to the showers by a guard. "You got one hour to get beautiful," the guard told Cadillac. Then the guard left to get some coffee.

In the cage, Fountain pulled his pants down, bent over and pulled a hacksaw blade and a shiv from his rectum. Tommy carried a shiv in his rectum, too. He eased it out with care, because he didn't want to slice his sphincter. Using the hacksaw blade, the two inmates cut their way out of the exercise cage and scurried toward the showers.

Cadillac Smith had just finished lathering himself up, when Fountain and Tommy jumped him. "Bye-bye, Cadillac," hissed Tommy as he plunged his shiv into the man's flesh.

"Yeah," chimed Fountain, goring his shiv into Cadillac's stomach. "Say hello to Chappelle for us." With diabolical energy he thrust again and again.

They stabbed Cadillac Smith sixty-seven times.

The Medical Examiner said, "The man was probably dead after the first dozen wounds, many of which were fatal."

The other white inmates at USP Marion started calling Silverstein "Terrible Tom". They whispered his name in awe. In the subculture of prison, Terrible Tom became a demi-god. Like a rock star, his notorious reputation preceded him.

Again, there was no death penalty at that time for one inmate murdering another inmate. Already serving two life sentences in the Hole, it seemed Terrible Tom would get away with murder yet once more. Prison officials couldn't execute Tom, but they could sure make him wish he was dead. So they withheld his mail and shook down his cell every time he turned around. Three guards escorted him everywhere.

Officer Merle Clutts didn't like Terrible Tom. In fact, Clutts thought Tom was "the spawn of Satan". So did a lot of the guards. Still, Clutts was a professional. He did not torment Terrible Tom. But the rules were the rules and Clutts enforced them by the book.

During a shakedown of Tom's cell, Clutts discovered contraband material, so he confiscated Tom's art supplies. "You'll get them back when you earn them," Clutts said. "By following the rules like everybody else."

Flaming with righteous energy, Terrible Tom wanted to rip off Clutt's ears and piss in the wounds. He made a promise to himself that he would. And soon.

Seething inside, Terrible Tom plotted his revenge. He communicated with Aryan Brotherhood members in USP Marion, arranging for weapons and help. On 22 October 1983, Terrible Tom had just finished his shower. Shackled, handcuffed and freshly scrubbed, he was being escorted back to his cell. Merle Clutts was one of his three escorts.

As the group passed an exercise cage, an inmate inside the cage said, "CO Clutts, need a hand here." Clutts strolled over to see what the inmate needed, while the other two officers walked on with Terrible Tom.

"Permission to speak with a friend, sir?" asked Tom, pausing in front of a cell. The cell belonged to Randy Gometz, who was an Aryan Brotherhood member.

"Sure. Go ahead," replied one of the two guards. Guards often allowed prisoners to chat on their way to and from the showers.

Terrible Tom grasped the bars of Gometz's cell and began talking. Gometz pulled a stolen key from inside his mouth and unlocked Tom's handcuffs. Tom reached through the bars and pulled a shiv from Gometz's waistband. Turning, Tom ran as fast as his shackled legs allowed toward Clutts.

Dumbfounded, the two guards hesitated. Then they took off in pursuit.

As he neared Clutts, Terrible Tom shouted, "This is between me and Clutts!" Tom slammed into Clutts, stabbing him with extreme ferocity. The shiv plunged in, blood flowed out.

While he perforated Clutts, Tommy said, "I felt wickedly angelic, like the Angel of Death descending on Egypt."

Finally, the other two guards pulled Clutts away, leaving a smear of red as they dragged him to safety. Lying senseless in puddles of his own blood and drool, Clutts died within minutes of his rescue.

Three hours later, Clayton Fountain pulled the same stunt. Another inmate, who also had a stolen key and an easy-to-reach shank, unlocked Fountain's handcuffs. Like a rabid dog, Fountain turned and attacked all three of his escorts, fatally wounding Officer Robert Hoffman.

When asked why he did it, Fountain thought about it and shrugged. "I didn't want Tommy to have a higher body count than me," he said with a smile. Hoffman's blood was still caked on his hands.

Terrible Tom was moved to another prison because he was growing too famous at Marion. Fellow inmates regarded him as someone special, like a saint. His exploits were incredible, the stuff of legend. Inmates worshipped him. Prison officials shipped Terrible Tom to USP Atlanta, where he was placed in a maximum-security isolation cell. It was 1984.

The shit jumped off in 1987. A bunch of pissed-off Cubans, who were being detained at USP Atlanta while the Feds decided what to do with them, rioted. In this case, a "bunch" meant hundreds of Cubans, all of whom were brash, dangerous criminals who had nothing to lose since the Feds, more than likely, would end up sending them all back to Cuba, where they would be lined up against a wall and shot as traitors. The Cubans took over the penitentiary, capturing and holding hostage a hundred members of the prison staff.

The Cubans unlocked every cell door at the prison, including Tommy's. All the animals in the zoo were free, but they were still trapped in the prison, which was surrounded by the FBI and elite soldiers from Delta Force. Tommy didn't care. He was just happy to be out of the Hole. It was like taking a vacation. Terrible Tom roamed willy-nilly inside the prison walls, wearing shower thongs and carrying a bottle of tequila, taking it all in like a tourist from a cruise ship.

The tequila came courtesy of one of the Cubans: a big, black guy with a shaved head and a Fu Manchu moustache, whom everybody called Blind Boy because of a cast in one eye. His real name was Roberto Messia.

When the rioters had opened Tom's cell door, they grabbed him and led him out into the yard. He squinted at the brightness. After his eyes adjusted he took a look around. The yard looked like they'd fought World War III there. Part of the prison had burned to the ground, leaving a blackened, smouldering skeleton.

The rioters led him over to Blind Boy Messia, who carried a shotgun, taken from one of the guards, in his right hand and a bottle in his left hand.

"So. Terrible Tom," said Blind Boy. "What should we do with you?" He waggled the shotgun casually.

Terrible Tom did a double take. Blind Boy did not sound Cuban. He had a high British accent. "You don't sound Cuban," said Tom.

Blind Boy laughed. "You don't look so terrible."

Terrible Tom smiled and stood waiting, as Blind Boy gazed at him. Reaching a decision, Blind Boy tossed the bottle to Tom, who caught it. Glancing at the label on the bottle, Tom raised his eyebrows. "Now we're living," he enthused.

"We don't have time or patience for any inconveniences," Blind Boy advised. "So stay out of the way." From the look on his face, he expected a reply.

"You won't even know I'm here," said Terrible Tom.

Blind Boy gave a little nod, then said, "Enjoy yourself."

And that was that.

Negotiations began between the Cubans and the Feds and lasted for seven days. And the Feds knew Terrible Tom was there.

"As a gesture of good faith, you need to give us Thomas Silverstein," the Feds told the Cubans. The Cubans thought about it then talked it over. Soon afterwards, a bunch of Cubans jumped Terrible Tom in the prison yard. Pinning him down, they handcuffed him and shackled his legs. Then they turned him over to the Feds, who turned him over to US Marshals, who pushed him into a transport vehicle and whisked him off to a nearby airport. The marshals loaded him on to a plane and flew him to Leavenworth, Kansas. Other than the marshals, Terrible Tom was the only inmate on the flight.

At USP Leavenworth, the Feds had a special room ready for Terrible Tom. Resembling a large zoo-like cage, the room sat in an isolated wing of the prison – Range 13. The "range" term came from the fact that the wing was "out there in the middle of nowhere". And the number "13" referred to the floor numbers used in skyscrapers. There is never a 13th floor, because it is considered bad luck. The 13th floor is there, but isn't acknowledged. Just like Range 13 was there, but no one admitted it.

Prison officials jokingly nicknamed the special room "the Hannibal Room" because it resembled the cage in the movie *The Silence of the Lambs*. But the joke contained more than a little truth, for the Hannibal Room was truly hell on earth. Whoever lived in the Hannibal Room endured constant surveillance, had no human contact and the lights were never shut off. There was no day or night in hell – only the steady, sickly emanations of florescent bulbs. There was no one to talk to, no one to hear, no one to touch, no one to hate, no one to love. Mechanical eyes stared from every corner – all the time. Big Brother was watching!

They put Terrible Tom in the Hannibal Room in 1987.

In 2002, fifteen years later, the goon squad showed up at the Hannibal Room. US Marshal Clarence J. Sugar led the way. Behind Marshal Sugar tramped fifteen deputy marshals. Next to the marshal walked five officers of USP Leavenworth, who wore helmets with full-face masks, like motorcycle helmets, and who carried what looked like cattle prods along with a whole spectrum of weapons, including mace, pistols and billy clubs. The cattle prods turned out to be just that, Tasers mounted on the ends of poles.

Marshal Sugar marvelled as he looked at the cattle prods. They looked like something wild animal trainers would use in a circus.

"Technically, it's Range 13," one of the officers told Marshal Sugar. "But most call it the Hannibal Room or the Silverstein Suite."

Marshal Sugar nodded.

"He watches a lot of TV," said the officer.

"Who?"

"Terrible Tom," replied the officer. "Likes reality shows. 'Survivor', 'American Gladiator' – that kinda shit."

Marshal Sugar gave the officer a sceptical glance, as the platoon of armed men moved relentlessly toward Range 13.

"Spends a lot of time drawing, too," added the officer. "Really talented. I can't believe some of the shit he does. Like he's professional or something, ya' know? The way he shades stuff with just a pencil is hard to wrap your head around it's so good."

Marshal Sugar thought the guy sounded like a tour guide. A guide that was definitely captivated by his subject, which seemed to be the myth and legend and living habits of Terrible Tom.

The officer continued, "There's all sorts of weirdo collectors who would pay top dollar for any of his drawings. But he won't sell 'em." He looked over at the marshal. "Even if he did, the money wouldn't do him any good." He paused. "Too bad though. Cuz they sure are good. Wait'll you see 'em."

The marshal didn't say anything.

"Wait'll you see him," said the officer, raising his eyebrows.

"What do you mean?" rumbled Marshal Sugar.

"Long, wild-man hair, white beard down to here," explained the officer, touching the edge of his hand to his chest. "Looks like that movie actor guy – Donald Sutherland – dressed up like some weird Santa Claus. Course Terrible Tom's Jewish, but you know what I mean."

Marshal Sugar frowned to himself.

"The reason his hair is so long," clarified the officer, "is cuz he's not allowed scissors or a razor. Too risky."

"Suicide?" asked Marshal Sugar.

The officer chuckled, shaking his head. "Nah. They're afraid he'll do a Clutts. You know, kill another guard."

Like everyone else associated with the federal prison system, Marshal Sugar had heard of Thomas Silverstein, aka Terrible Tom. From what this officer had just said it sounded like the guy was a regular Chinese puzzle. Or plain insane. A talented artist on one hand, and on the other hand a crackerjack killer, who looked like Donald Sutherland in a ZZ Top beard.

Some years ago Pete Earley had written a book called *The Hothouse*, which was based on unprecedented access to the inmates and guards at USP Leavenworth. Marshal Sugar had read it. He considered it a good book, but one with an agenda – to diss the penal system, which, Sugar readily admitted, had its problems. Earley's book almost, but not quite, lionized the inmates, especially

Terrible Tom, who was the star of the show. In the book, Earley portrayed Tom as intelligent, rational and downright normal. And the fact that the prison officials kept him locked up like an animal in the Hannibal Room made *them* look like the monsters. Like they were kids, pulling the wings off flies and bees, then roasting the insects under a magnifying glass they got out of the bottom of a box of Cheerios.

When he finished reading the book, Marshal Sugar, half-convinced that Earley was right, had done a little research. The author had a website on which it was possible to listen to some of the prison interviews with Terrible Tom. Marshal Sugar listened to them. Silverstein babbled on and on about his demons, who, at a guess, were the guards and how they delighted in tormenting him. Then he went off into a stream-of-consciousness description of his hellacious killing of Merle Clutts, which included mimicking the dying man's screams and Tom's grunts as he plunged the shiv into the guard's flesh. Silverstein even described how it feels to stab a man, relating the squishy sound flesh makes as it takes the knife.

The guy was a whacko. His insanity stood out like a pile of steaming cow flop on an inflatable raft floating on a backyard swimming pool.

The platoon of marshals came to a halt. A massive steel door stared at them. On this side of the door was USP Leavenworth; on the other side of the door was Range 13. One of the guards unlocked the door and they entered another world. The air was different than on the other side of the door – heavier and without any odour, as if it came from a bottle. Overhead lights burned brightly, making everything clearer, like in high-definition.

In the middle of the room stood a giant rat cage. Inside the cage, a figure sat in a chair. As the marshals entered the room, the figure stood up.

Shoulder-length grey hair and a white waterfall of a beard made the figure look like some crackpot biblical prophet just back from forty years in the desert. A real ding-a-ling thought Marshal Sugar. Then he noticed the eyes, which burned acetylene torch blue. Marshal Sugar changed his mind – a very dangerous ding-a-ling.

Terrible Tom smiled. "Good afternoon, gentlemen," he said.

"What an unexpected visit." He laughed. "In fact, it's the first one I've had in fifteen years. Come in, come in."

"Okay," said Marshal Sugar, turning to his deputies. "Secure the prisoner. Gather up his personal belongings and bag 'em. We got a plane to catch."

Terrible Tom popped a Hershey's Kiss in his mouth. "Anybody want a kiss?" He grinned. "Unfortunately, they come to me without foil wrappers or little flags. I miss that part." He shook his head sadly. "Kind of ruins the experience."

The marshals moved forward in a standard formation. The Leavenworth officer unlocked the door of the cage, saying, "Tom, these are US Marshals. They're here to transfer you. No one wants a fuss, so your cooperation would be helpful."

Terrible Tom gave a big laugh, one that he had cultivated over the years. "Your wish is my command. Complaints? No complaints from me. I wouldn't miss it for the world. I'm looking forward to it." Then Tom peeked to see if his act was really coming off.

Marshal Sugar stepped forward. "I'm glad to hear that. Now, if you would please turn around, lie down on the floor and place your hands on the top of your head."

Terrible Tom did as instructed. Marshals swarmed over him, cuffing him and shackling his legs. Then they stood him up and patted him down. One of the marshals carefully passed a metal detector over his body. Stepping back, the deputy said, "Please do three deep-knee bends."

Terrible Tom squatted all the way down and all the way up, three times. Four Tasers pointed at him as he did.

"Okay," said Marshal Sugar. "Let's go."

The Leavenworth officers led the way, followed by three marshals. Then came Terrible Tom, with a marshal on each side and one right behind him, like three three-dimensional shadows.

Back outside, the marshals loaded Terrible Tom into a special van, where he was chained to steel rings that reached up from the floor. Six marshals took their seats in the van. As the parade of vehicles drove off, Terrible Tom gazed out the window. He hadn't seen the world in fifteen years and was enjoying the view. Hard across the way he saw storm clouds in the distance fast approaching. He'd almost forgotten about weather . . . and the billboards and signs.

It was like going to Disneyland.

At the airport, the marshals escorted Terrible Tom on to the plane. As he clinked and clanked down the aisle, he looked around. All the inmates on the plane stared at him. Not a sound.

The marshals seated him and triple-cuffed him, adding another set of shackles to his legs. Terrible Tom looked to his left. He saw a familiar face.

"Tom," said the Baron (Barry Bryon "The Baron" Mills, leader of the Aryan Brotherhood), smiling.

"Hey, Baron."

"Tell me about it," urged the Baron.

As the two killers talked quietly, Terrible Tom felt the plane rolling. It accelerated, pushing him back in his seat. The wheels left the ground and started to retract into the plane's belly.

Terrible Tom daydreamed for an instant. Maybe they really would go to Disneyland.

SEAN REICH (UK/ AUSTRALIA)

Doorman and Martial Arts Expert

Introducing . . . Sean Reich

Ask anyone working the doors in Liverpool in the 1970s about Sean Reich and they will reply along the lines of "simply the hardest and toughest bastard around". Everyone knew Sean, and Sean knew everyone. There was no one tougher on the doors at that time.

Sean Reich was born in Milwaukee, USA, on 9 August 1951. His parents separated and his Irish mother brought him to Liverpool, England, where he grew up. Reich became interested in the martial arts in 1970 and started training as often as he could. By 1973 he was working full-time as a nightclub doorman where he spent almost seven years working the doors in the roughest, toughest city in the UK.

Reich received his black belt, first dan, in Goju Kai karate in 1974; his second dan in 1978; and his third dan in 1980 in the world headquarters of Goju karate situated in Tokyo, Japan. Whilst there he trained under three of the highest graded experts in the world: Gogen Yamaguchi, Motokatsu Inoue and Meitoku Yagi, all tenth dans. He emigrated to Australia at the end of the 1980s where he became a professional karate instructor and one of the top-graded instructors on the continent.

The magazine *Australasian Fighting Arts* ran a ten-page article on Reich. Titled "Applied Karate", it highlighted some of his harrowing experiences in the security field. Reich believes this article to be the first of its kind on the subject. His first instructor, the infamous, now deceased Gary Spiers, was so inspired by the article he did a worldwide self-defence workshop using the title.

Sean has now retired from both security and karate to focus on being a husband and father of four, and to try to be a dedicated Christian. Reich now finds it very hard training. This is his story, taken from his forthcoming book *A Long Walk Home*, about his very early days on the doors in Liverpool.

THE DOORMAN – INTO THE FIRE
By Sean Reich

The iron-ore in the heat of the blast furnace thinks itself senselessly tortured
but the tempered steel blade looks back and knows better.

Old Japanese proverb

Liverpool, England, 1972

"In, in, in . . . Attack, attack, attack!"

"Get into it . . . That wouldn't put my grandmother away!"

Fifty sweating bodies, eyes glaring or shamed by Gary the instructor's rebuke, step back, readying to initiate contact again.

"Hajime [Go]."

The karate dojo resounds with the "Kiai" screams and the snap of the canvas karate-gi training suits as the killing blows are delivered to within a hairsbreadth of a vital point on the neck of the opponent.

"Yame [Stop]." The dojo walls run with condensation. The air is heavy, the atmosphere electric.

"Mo ichi do [One more time]." This is the hundredth.

"Last time, best time. Look, it's like this. Come out here big fella." The biggest student trots out in front of the class.

"Right, so blocking the punch, in you go. Same hand blocks out the eyes. Other hand cocked – lay it into the carotid artery . . . lay it in, lad." The big student tentatively lays the strike into the Sensei's neck.

"Harder." Pulling back, he lets go again and a whack of flesh on flesh is heard by all.

"This time like you mean it," glares Gary at his student.

WHACK. "Yeah, that's better. Oh! Yeah! That one hurt! Good one, lad."

Gary pats the student on the shoulder, walks calmly to the edge of the class. The student's deflated eyes go wide and he shakes his head.

That blow should have killed him, he thinks.

Gary shows the class his red twenty-inch neck.

"Now, how would you like someone like me on your doorstep one night? Coming to play with your mother or wife or daughter?"

"Richter [as Gary called me] . . . I want better than your best out of you, digga, right?"

I looked at my large opponent glaring down at me, and dropped my eyes on to his cheekbones. Now he's just a slab of meat.

"Yoi [Get ready] . . . In, in, in. Attack, attack, attack!"

"SAAARRH!"

Liverpool, 1956 – Sixteen Years Earlier

I peed my pants in class on the first day of school. I tried to get the teacher's attention but it was all just too exciting for my bladder. In the cold, sunny Liverpool autumn it was going to be a long John Wayne Walk home in shame. My Auntie Mae, who came to pick us up, could tell something was wrong by the kids dancing around me, jeering.

"What happened, Johnny?" she asked in her soft Irish brogue.

"Ah! The roof was leaking on me chair an' they all thought I'd peed meself."

"Shame on them! Never mind, c'mon then, an' I'll buy you and Ryan an ice-cream."

Three months younger than me, Ryan and I traded glances. He was my poles-apart cousin. His look said, "I know the truth and I could tell Mum."

My look said, "If you tell, I'll cut the head off your rubber ducky."

We got the ice-cream and "Donald" was saved.

I put my head down as we walked past the Catholic church . . . five years old . . . sin-laden already.

We lived in a big, old home. "Denbigh Villas, 1892" was on the front wall, along with about twenty bullet holes and pieces of shrapnel from when "Jerry" had dropped by in 1940 to say hello. It was a three-storey place with five bedrooms, shared by Auntie Mae, two uncles, two cousins, my Mum and me, and a cranky old brown dog. None of us got on. My mum and me (mother and I) were unwanted tenants. One of my uncles, John, was an ex-regimental sergeant major who had fought in Africa during the Second World War. He kept to himself but had a soft spot for me. The other uncle, Bert, Ryan's dad, was a Burma campaign veteran. Mum and her two sisters went through the Second World War nightly bombing of Liverpool. Because of the shipping and docks, at one stage the city was top of the Luftwaffe list . . . at night you could see Liverpool burn from 40 miles away. On one occasion they had all the front windows blown in. Others nearby weren't so lucky.

Mum met and married my dad, an American air-force pilot stationed just outside Liverpool at Burtonwood. She went back to the States with Dad in 1949, where I was born two years later. The marriage dissolved and she brought me back to Liverpool where I grew up. We left behind beautiful Menomonee Falls, Wisconsin, on Lake Michigan. For some reason she never changed my nationality.

And so I was to live in Denbigh Villas for the next seventeen years. A low-light of this was the coexistence with Ryan, my dear cousin, and his tell-tale sister. We never became Cain and Abel, but it was close.

Ryan always got what he wanted: "Give me the swing, I want it now."

"Yeah, right, here . . . "

Hurl . . . WHACK! . . . Ryan laid out in the playground, eyes back in the head and a big lump on the forehead. I took him home spread out on my go-cart, a few bits of wood and pram wheels acting as an ambulance. "Ee-aw, ee-aw . . . "

"WHAT HAPPENED?" Whack, whack.

"Give me the darts. I want them now."

"Yeah, right, here . . . "

WHUMP! . . . A dart in the middle of the forehead!

"WHAT HAPPENED?" Smack, smack.

Ryan and me playing at the public park lake with a toy yacht.

"Get the yacht back. I want it now."

Seven years old – the only water I'd been close to was the weekly bathtub. I leaned over and fell in. Drowning, I looked up and all I could see was my saviour – Ryan. I reached up from under the water, seeing his smiling face, grabbed the lifeline of his sweater . . . and pulled . . .

The nightly national news: "The policeman who saved two little boys from drowning today . . . "

"WHAT HAPPENED?" . . .

Ryan eventually went on to college and university and became a lawyer. It was probably to stop "no-hoper" kids like me stealing his pocket money, when we were fourteen, for half a bottle of port for the dance at the YMCA and to get a Domestic Violence Restraining Order out on me to stay right away from him. I bear no ill will.

The four men sat in the back of the Liverpool hackney cab, psyching each other up. They were high on amphetamines and anything else they could get their hands on. They sat smiling at each other in the ambient light with glazed eyes and plastic grins. One fingered the knife, kept inside the back of his watch band with the handle resting comfortingly in his palm. Another had his hand over a cosh in his pocket. The knife merchant had only been released from prison a week before for stabbing a police officer, for which he'd been king of the "poop pile"! Tonight he was looking forward to showing he was back. Eight years of hitting the prison weights and punch-bag and all the tricks he'd learnt inside, combined with the anger he felt at society, plus booze and drugs, and this guy was "Mr Indestructible" on the night. He was really looking forward to carving up a young little fella on the nightclub door where they were heading.

"There's only a little pip-squeak on the door lads, he's a joke. My Uncle Pete checked it out last night. The little sod tripped him at the top of the stairs. Bruised him right up he did. So tonight we'll really do the business on him. The owner'll be a walk-over, got no connections; the club'll be ours in a month by the time we finish with him and his family."

The taxi pulled up outside the club. "Just wait till we're inside, pal."

They stood before the black door and banged for attention.

I began learning judo when I was twelve, after seeing Alan R., the smallest guy in our class, give Hendo, one of the big, fat, school bully boys, a lesson in the finer points of the art. Poor ole Hendo, he had more bounce in him than a Dunlop tyre! This was years before the public became awakened to the martial arts. The only thing known in those days was James Bond's karate chop. These were the days when Bruce Lee was probably starting to kick the crap out of his school bully boys and pocketing their rice money.

With what I saw that day with little Alan R., I was hooked.

"Sign me up for some of that, mate."

I instantly became Alan's new best mate. Previous to this I had been the most unprepared kid for defending himself. I was the original Tonto, getting the poop kicked out of me every time I went into town without the Lone Ranger.

Something had to change before I really wound up on someone's menu.

At seventeen I began a serious study of karate: five nights a week, three hours a night.

At twenty-one, I was probably the smallest, youngest, most inconsequential-looking guy to ever work a nightclub door anywhere. I was a "doorman", a "hinge", or a "caretaker" (taking care of the business). The word "bouncer" was defined by us as: "A woman jogger not wearing a bra". The first altercation came one week after starting on my first door. I found out later my boss had arranged this to see if I was worth the extra money he was paying me than the last guy. He apparently offered free drinks if they got past me.

A father and his two big sons had put their "wobbly boots" on after drinking hard in the pub round the corner. They wobbled their way around to the club and banged on the door. I opened the door in my nice black suit, white shirt and black bow-tie. "Good evening gentlemen – are you members?"

One of them became the spokesman and answered like he had a mouthful of pebbles.

"Sorry, fellas, not tonight."

I went to shut the door and it was "on".

The three of them launched themselves against the door. I was two steps up on the staircase, the door opened to the left and you went straight upstairs to the right. As the first one came on, I slammed his head into the door-frame and pushed him back into the wide alleyway outside the club. The other two followed . . . there was a bit of jostling, then I was outside the club. The owner shut the door behind me.

The first one came running at me, both hands ready to grab. I did a double-hand inside hook-block, grabbing the insides of his forearms and spun, launching him into the boss's Mercedes parked just outside. He went straight into the motif and knocked himself out. He's probably still got the emblem tattooed on his forehead.

The second one came in swinging: same hooking block, and in a millisecond I got a "counter" in – I did this a million times: block and counter, block and counter. He careened off me, spun his face into the wall and put himself out cold, too.

The third one, the old fella, ran in and pulled all the buttons off my shirt, backed off, danced around like Ali, then realized he'd got his wobbly boots on and fell over.

I walked back to the door, knocked, went in and quietly shut it.

A little while later there was a banging on the door.

"We don't want you, John [the owner] or you Mike [the manager] . . . Just send out that little Chinese bastard!" (I have no Asian origins.)

There were a lot more experiences like that, none quite so easy, including some bloody "Demonstrations" that had to be done to show why I was where I was. I hate violent and/or rude people – the ones who just love to hurt people and dress up: shirt, trousers, shoes, razor – compared to the innocents who are just out for a nice night. So yes, I'll stand on the door on your behalf. I'll do everything I can to protect you. None of these scumbags will get in while I'm on post. And if they are in, they'll deeply regret hurting you if they do.

I earned the respect of all who frequented this nightclub except for a bunch of "hard cases" from a new housing estate nearby. I knew it was only a matter of time until we would have a serious disagreement. The boss tolerated them because they were big drinkers and always there. Unfortunately, the solid members no longer sat out where the disco and live music were, feeling safer in the cocktail lounge and restaurant areas. These young thugs were gradually dominating the dance-floor area. I didn't like it one bit. There were a couple of fights, but nothing major. That changed one night.

One particular guy used to give me "the once over" and smirk every time he came in. This particular night he showed what a hard lad he was by shoving a beer glass into some young innocent guy's face. When I heard the glass smash (you tune in to certain sounds of trouble above the music), I went racing up the stairs. It was closing time so the lights came on. The first thing I saw was this poor young lad's face, covered in blood. The next thing I saw was the guy who caused it – "Hardcase" himself. He took one look at me and charged. I dropped one leg back into a strong stance and took him front on, did a double hook-block, grabbed and pulled him straight on to the top of my forehead.

Whack. It was a perfect "Liverpool kiss" . . . night, night. He dropped like a stone.

This had been coming for a while, so I was "lit up" now, but there were no "number two" takers tonight. As I went to attend the young lad, I told scumbag's mates to get him out and that he was barred from the club. That was the Friday night.

Next night they were all cheerfully back, minus one. They were here for some fun tonight – and I was to be the fun.

It got to around midnight. All quiet. I secured the door and went upstairs to check around. As I walked in, thirty pairs of eyes all turned to stare.

"Uh oh!"

I wandered back out. They'd never congregated like this, so something was definitely up. I told the boss to go and take a look – he'd been the one letting them all in. He came back pale.

"What are we going to do? They look like they're going to smash the place up."

"Can I use your phone?"

Gary, my instructor, was working the biggest nightclub in the city. It housed three discos of various kinds of music, plus a live-band ballroom that could take up to 2,000 people. The security team was fifteen.

"Sensei, sorry to bother you . . . " I explained my situation.

"Stay out of the light, digga. We'll be right up."

"I'll be right here."

Well, if I was going to get "done" tonight, it was going to take thirty of 'em to feel comfortable enough to do it.

Twenty minutes later, a light knock on the door. I opened it and a shiver went through me. Gary had brought up four friends and an aura with them.

Gary was 250 pounds, with a twenty-inch neck, bench-pressed 350 pounds and was fourth dan Goju karate. He had fifteen years' martial arts experience, the last two spent in the world headquarters of karate in Japan. He was absolutely lethal, having been involved in the security field for over ten years.

Terry was six foot two with sixteen years working nightclub doors. He had been British karate team captain (of the only team to beat Japan), with lightning-fast kicks, deadly with everything; fifth dan black belt, Shotokan karate.

R.C. was five foot six of steel wire; ex-British Special Air Service; seventh dan ju-jitsu; third dan karate; and the All-Asia weapons champion. A living legend whose glare alone would stop you breathing.

Richie was a six foot three ex-mercenary – Congo, exploits "classified"; second dan. He had a shaved head, goatee beard and a big earring . . . We called him "Shazam". He had the original look of so many in the security field today.

Jimmy was a five foot ten natural street-fighter/survivalist with a solid build and piercing black eyes. If you put Jimmy and a cougar in a sack and dropped it in the river, my money would be on Jimmy coming up, wearing a new fur coat – my best mate.

And of course, lil' ol' me.

I explained the situation and they told me what to do.

I went inside to see Mike, the manager, and got him to turn the lights on early and shut the music off. This caused a groan from the crowd. Next, the waitresses were pulled back behind the bar. The metal roller shutters then came crashing down over the serving hatches. At this sound the double-doors into the dance-floor crashed back against the walls. The six of us walked in and spread out round the dance-floor where this big team had gathered. It quickly became evident that my friends weren't here for a drink.

You could have heard a pin drop.

Thirty pairs of eyes took on the look of lambs . . . as the wolves gathered.

Standing with my back to the bar I removed my watch in front of them. I always liked the psychological effect that had on people.

Terry started a walk around the dance-floor. The others were either pacing back and forth or just glaring at them. Terry walked toward me, giving me a small smile and a nod of encouragement. As he walked past me, all I saw, for a split second, was the sole of his shoe going up past my nose and the wind of the fastest, strongest side-kick I've ever been in front of. It gave a blow-wave to the front of my hair. Terry didn't even break stride, just kept walking. I nodded and smiled. I looked at the gathered gang, all standing there gobsmacked.

Terry sauntered back over to me and quietly said, "Just go and tell them nicely to leave now, John. We're closed."

"Enjoy your night, lads? Time to leave now," I said, with a friendly smile.

"Yeah, yeah, we're goin'. Listen, who are these guys who just came in?"

While I discreetly pointed each of them out, and their credentials, the mob went pale.

"I was told to tell you that if this EVER happens again [pause for effect], then there'll be the greatest practical demonstration of martial arts you'll ever see. Goodnight now."

This episode we called, "The art of fighting without fighting."

That's the way we worked the doors back then – interlocking, all for one.

The four men stood before the black door in the wide alleyway. The hackney cab waited at the corner, its diesel motor running.

On the other side of the door, four of us waited.

I knew something serious was going to go down by the perform-ance from the night before when two large, mature strangers had rocked up on a quiet Wednesday night. The boss had been down, talking to me, and he'd let them in. The look of them and the smell of hashish off them sounded big warning bells in my head as I saw them swagger up the stairs. "I shouldn't have let them in, should I?" says the boss."But it's a quiet night so it should be OK."

I just shrugged.

About thirty minutes later the sound of screams and smashing glass had us charging up the stairs into the club itself.

One of these thugs had just KO'd a young woman because she wouldn't dance with him.

I grabbed, spun and leg-swept him. Grabbing the back of his jacket, I dragged him through the double-doors to the top of the stairs.

As he tried to get up I jumped on top of him and tobogganed him down the stairs, banging his head as often as I could on the way down. He was out cold when we stopped at the bottom. I dragged him into the alley for some Afghani soccer with my steel toe-capped shoes. I can't stand men who hit women – lowest of the low in my book.

His mate came bowling down the stairs, looking worse for wear, thanks to several of the locals. He was screaming that we were all dead and that they were going to trash the place, mentioning the name of my playmate as though we should all know it. He came back with his car and loaded his pal in. They took off, screaming and cursing. "I think we'd better take this one seriously," says the boss.

So here we were, the four of us; Gary, Jimmy, Rolo (another mate) and me. Stand by, stand by . . .

My earliest memories were of sexy Auntie Fran, Mum's other sister, who also lived with us for a while until she got married. She was a big-busted, hip-swinging, red lipstick, suspender belt and nylons with black lines running up the back kind of woman. And I loved her for it . . . I was three at the time!

I used to sit under the table while she had her breakfast, sucking my thumb, with my hand up her skirt, playing with her suspender nylon fastener! At first, of course, she tried to stop me. But looking under the table into my big, brown, loving eyes, she couldn't say "No".

It became a ritual, sitting down for breakfast, not looking under the table.

"Morning, Johnny."

"Morning, Auntie Fran."

"Happy down there, Johnny?"

"Ummm."

"That's good."

Things started to get out of control, though, when she wasn't around. I was standing at a bus stop with Mum. Another young lady came and stood next to me. She looked down and smiled. I smiled back and put my thumb in my mouth. As she looked away my hand just went naturally up her skirt, looking for the "sussi" belt. The scream nearly turned my hair grey. It took a week to get my eyes back in my head.

I can still remember the look of shock/horror on Mum's face. Profuse apologies followed from Mum, with sideways glares at me. The young woman had an amused look on her face. It seemed like I'd won another lady over with an innocent look and a soft touch.

My happy habit was brought to an abrupt end, however, when I got separated from Mum while shopping in a big department store in the city centre. I thought I'd just wait for her in the shop window, with one of the mannequins. They found me in the usual pose of thumb in mouth, hand up skirt, all in front of an amused crowd of onlookers. Poor Mum went home in shame again and tied a pair of gloves on me, and that was the end of that little avenue of pleasure.

The bangs on the door weren't the usual polite knocks. I looked back at the others. "This might be it, all ready?" I opened the door enough to see out.

I'd made three phone calls after the visit by the two thugs. The first call was to Gary, at work. He was a New Zealand Maori, winner of literally hundreds of bloody episodes, who told me once that his introduction to white people was his grandfather giving him an ankle bone to chew on! He was cool, calm and deadly in violent events. He also had a wicked sense of humour. One night a huge black guy, who was a known troublemaker, came to the door that Gary was working. Gary refused him entry.

"You're only not letting me in 'cause I'm black."

"Look mate, I'm not racially prejudiced, I like Al Jolson!" Gary replied.

This huge man blinked, mouth opened, shut, turned and left, nowhere to go but home.

Second call was to Jimmy. My best mate. Gary had introduced us and got Jimmy a job on my door, back-stopping me on the weekends, though sometimes it seemed the other way round.

On the first night we worked together alone after the "gang of thirty" night, I was politely explaining to four inebriated young fellas why I wasn't letting them in. Jimmy was on the next stair up from me, against the wall. As they were arguing/pleading/ threatening, Jimmy leaned over the top of me and, wild-eyed, screamed "FUCK OFF!" at them and slammed the door. Just before it slammed I witnessed four gobsmacked guys who'd died in the arse.

I was rolling around inside for ten minutes trying not to laugh out loud. He looked like Charles Manson, or the other way round, bigger and scarier to look at, with a wicked sense of humour. "You gorra have a laff in this game, lah, or you'll go rats!" says Jimmy, with a grin.

Gary told me that legends abounded about him. He was a seaman when he was younger. Whilst in a bar in South America he'd stabbed seven locals who weren't keen on seeing him leave the place alive. He was jailed for mutiny in Spain and when in New York he'd had a T-shirt made: "Mug me I dare you."

Nobody touched him.

First time I saw him in action we'd finished for the night and gone to where Gary was working. As we entered, Gary asked if we'd stay loose in the foyer – trouble brewing inside – no problem. A few minutes later Gary and Terry go through the double-doors into the disco. The next thing – BANG – this guy comes flying through the doors, like Clark Kent who hadn't had time to put his Superman costume on.

I straightaway side-stepped, dropped into a good strong stance, guard up, good to go, while Jimmy side-stepped the other way, with his coat still over his left arm. His right hand caught the back of this guy's head and, while still in the air, ran it straight into a poker machine behind him. The guy was unconscious before he hit the ground and Jimmy's heart rate wouldn't have increased one beat. That's a natural. I learnt many things from ol' Jimmy.

My third phone call was to Rolo. Ultra dependable Rolo. Gary had introduced us a year before and he'd become a firm friend. We'd shared a real bloody night on his nightclub that really bonded us. Back-to-back, we'd come through a nine-on-two encounter with some visiting soccer supporters from Manchester. Two minutes full-on action – bodies dropping at our feet, till we were rescued by a police riot squad, who fortunately were nearby.

"Yeah, John, I'll be there for you mate."

The most beautiful girl in the world came into my life when I was four. She lived on the next block to me and her name was Gillian. She was two months older than me, so she was always more mature. She had short black curly hair; round thick clinical glasses; and big teeth that she always tried to hide by not smiling. And she had a mum and dad from Dublin, just like my mum. For me, it was love at first sight. Our destinies were sealed.

Real manly things were performed by Yours Truly to get her attention, like leaping off park benches and breaking my arm and stuff – she was real impressed, although she just never showed it. Oh yeah! There was that one time when we were playing "footy" in the park and she got me down and bashed me with a big rock that doubled as a goalpost. What-a-gal!

Every year I'd send her an anonymous Valentine's card. Her mum and my mum worked in the same shop that sold the cards. They'd make that little shoulders-up smile to each other; "Yeah, they'll be together."

We'd spend Sunday afternoons listening to The Beatles and The Rolling Stones, and she'd show me these wonderful drawings of clothes designs and things she'd done. She was the one for me all right. I just knew it.

A fair bit of preparation went into this coming encounter. It had a heavy feel to it.

I went down in the afternoon and got a real short haircut so there was nothing to grab on to, did about an hour's loose training . . . loosening up . . . loosening up . . . had a sauna, went home and got my gear ready.

The nunchaku is an Asian lethal weapon. Made of

hexagonal-shaped hardwood, it has two pieces about a forearm's length and joined at one end intricately by a strong, thin nylon cord or chain. It can kill or maim an opponent with short-term practice. I had been training with them for two years.

I cut a horizontal slash across the inside lining of my jacket, about twelve inches above the bottom on the left-hand side. It was about six inches wide and I sewed both sides of the cut to strengthen it. I then snugly fitted a set of Japanese oak nunchaku into this holster. They were joined by nylon cord, much quieter than the set that Bruce Lee demonstrated with the chain. You don't want people saying later that they "heard a chain noise clanking around the head of the victim, Your Honour". I wrapped them carefully with black electric tape.

In America in the 1970s, when this weapon came to the public's attention and everybody started making their own, police officers were authorized to use lethal force if confronted by them. They'd been around since the sixteenth century, being used by the Okinawan farmers to flail rice in the paddies. Someone then had the great idea of using them on people.

I cut up pieces of an old tyre and softened them to give my kidneys some protection and wrapped all my middle with bandage. If I got slashed by a knife or Stanley knife – also called "a Liverpool credit card" – then I might be able to get to a hospital without my guts hanging out for all to see. I put on my groin protector box and belt, bandaged my wrists for support and protection, put a square piece of steel in both my top and inside pocket against knife-thrusts and polished up my steel toe-capped dress shoes. Lastly, I taped a switch-blade to my ankle.

Checking myself in the mirror: black suit, white shirt, bow tie . . . polished dress-shoes.

"Good evening, sir . . . ladies . . . Have a nice night."

Losing is not an option when you work a nightclub door.

"Stand by . . . stand by . . . Here we go . . . "

The door crashed open and it was "on".

We saw there were four of them, muscling together, to storm up the stairs. We needed space quickly, so being the front man, standing two stairs up, I zeroed in on the third guy, back right. Our eyes met and I knew straight away that this was "The Guy", this was the one that I'd been waiting for since I started this job, the one that was going to do me like a dog's dinner.

Well, you'd better go hard, mate. "In, in, in. Attack, attack, attack."

I dived off the second step over the front two and grabbed his lapels, managing to pull him out of the doorway into the alley. I got pushed from behind, so while I still had hold of him I did a sacrifice throw, pulling him over the top of me and into the ground next to me. There was a sudden mêlée of legs round us, shouting and cursing, so by the time I sprang up he was up, too.

I went straight at him with a spinning elbow strike to the head, guaranteed to put his lights out, my favourite technique. (First night I was shown this special technique by Gary, I accidentally KO'd four other students, one after the other, while "light" sparring, 'cause I couldn't control the spin.)

BANG. I felt like my elbow had hit a telegraph pole. He just shook his head, backed off and said, "C'mon in here, Sunshine, I've got something for you."

I saw a quick glint of a knife as he pulled it out of his watchband.

Looking back, I think if I hadn't got him with that elbow strike he would never have let me see that knife. A knife-man is a very dangerous person. Forget the movies, usually you won't even see it before it's in you. If he's right-handed the knife hand will now be palm up, close to the body, bottom of the ribs. The left hand will come over the top to hide and shield it. Left elbow points at target. Left hand will quickly sweep away any guard you've got up. Knife goes in . . . bye, bye. It's quick, sudden and lethal.

The left hand went over the blade . . .

The 1950s were good in Liverpool, but the 1960s were even better: the "Mersey Sound" music with the Beatles and a host of other groups; the comedians – Jimmy Tarbuck, Ken Dodd and others; the soccer – Liverpool and Everton . . . It was a great place to be. The clubs were playing Motown and soul from the US, too, brought back by Liverpool sailors.

By 1962, Ryan had passed the exam to go to a private college, with its own swimming pool and sports field. His mum and dad were real proud of him. I failed the exam, so got to go to the concrete jungle high-school round the corner, no pool or field. The boys and girls went to separate schools next to each other.

All sorts of ruses were employed to gain access to the girls' school: bribing teachers, hot-air balloons, tunnels. Many a young man went blind in those tunnels, I can tell you.

I managed to do quite well in History, Maths and English (tho u woodn't no it . . .) and was doing OK in Science until one of my team (I'd never dob a team-mate in, Jimmy Golbourne, if ever you read this) put sulphuric acid in the teacher's pet fish tank! Goldfish started behaving like piranhas in a feeding frenzy. We managed to save one and it became the school mascot. We called it Moby Dick. Everybody loved it. We gave it fish food, then sandwiches and sausage rolls, but I think it was the curry that killed it.

Our team all got an "F" for our Science project. We got our own back on the last day of school, though. We super-glued the teacher to his chair and put a dead toad sandwich in his lunch-box. He was a horrible man; I did feel sorry for his fish, though.

There was no way I was going to let this guy get within arm's length of me. Our eyes locked and we both knew this was going to go all the way. I reached with my right and found the comfort of the "nunch". I pulled them, sprang back and we were "into it".

This mongrel has to go. I try a classic "S" strike with the nunchaku. WHOOF – forward swipe catches him on his left ear and cheek, opening it to the bone. Recover and WHOOF – back swing to the right elbow. Must have hit the funny bone; he lets out a howl and has to drop the knife. Recover and WHOOF – strong forward swipe on to his left knee-cap – "GAAARRH!"

Blood is pouring down his face, right arm hanging by his side, useless, and he's still limping towards me making guttural animal noises.

"I'll 'ave you now . . . I'll 'ave you now, yah bastard!"

He dives in on me, grabbing on with his left. I still have the nunchaku in my right, too close to use. I would have tried a judo throw but I panic, the flail frozen to my hand. Anyone else would have been right out of the game but not this fella. This is my introduction to the drug-crazed ones. I come too, drop the nunch and grab him back. His breath is on my face, trying to grab hair that isn't there now. I feel his mouth on my ear, slobbering on it, trying to get the breath to bite it off.

"I've fucking got you now, you little cunt. I'll fucking kill ya!"

"No, you won't!" I scream back at him.

Grabbing on tight, I draw back and head-butt him twice, as hard as I can. His nose explodes into his face. I push back off him and put two groin kicks into him, in once, then bounce the ball of the foot, in again. "ARHHH!"

More noises come out of him, bent over double, unbelievably still up. I am so scared, I'm going mad. I grab him now by the hair and run his face into the wall, spin him round, knee him under the heart, step in and hip-throw him – he's down, but still not out. I'm off the planet. I set into him. No way was he getting up again.

On Sunday mornings we'd all go to nine o'clock mass. I used to watch out for Gillian just so I could walk near her. I just loved everything about her. There was this inner beauty and strength that exuded out of her.

The ten o'clock mass was the most popular in our parish because it would finish around the time the pubs opened. All the Irish-Catholic men would pat their broods on the head outside church. They'd give them a couple-o-bob for holy water – usually spent on lollies – and off to the pub till 3 p.m. closing. Certain suburbs of Liverpool were like the second capital of Ireland. The single men would then wander off to the park for drunken "footy". The married ones would come home to a big roast meal then upstairs for a cuddle with the wife. This worked very well for the Catholic Church's "Withdrawal method" policy (at the point of climax – withdraw). The O'Reagans had ten kids, the O'Briens eleven and the Delaneys twelve.

The church was bursting at the seams. "Oh well! If you can't convert, go forth and multiply."

The blood was splashed over the white wall in the alley. I looked down at the glistening stains on my trouser legs. My shoes, as well, had a wet look to them. My hands face and shirt had blood all over them.

I walked back down toward the door. There was another one of the four, sitting down in the entrance way, head down, legs splayed. He was unconscious and sounded like he was snoozing. The fingers of his right hand were grotesquely bent. A cosh lay next to him. His face was mincemeat. I looked around for the other two. One was sitting down on a small wall on the end of the alley, Gary and Rolo standing before him.

He put his hand up in submission to them, then put his head in his blood-covered hands, and gobbed out a mouthful of blood and teeth. He was shaking his head to get rid of the galaxy in front to his eyes. Both his cheekbones were done, eyes closing up, blood running down his face, dripping on to the pavement.

The taxi was still there, the driver frozen.

Where was the fourth one? I walked down to the taxi, door open, and looked in. Number four was sitting in the back, wide-eyed, grinning and rocking. He'd run away when the night didn't go the way it was planned. That wasn't fair. Grabbing both sides of the cab opening I put a front snap-kick on to his chin as he leaned forward. CRACK . . . He slumped back in the seat, eyes open but no one home. Steel toe-caps can have that effect on people.

"Fucking 'ell, lah, that was a cracker!" said Jimmy, looking in and seeing the result.

Gary and Rolo were heaving the carcass of "Snoozy" into the taxi, which was now the four men's transport to a hospital. I walked back up to where "Mr Indestructible" was. I looked down on this piece of shit that would have killed me if he could. His chest was making a death rattle, and there was what looked like a pink-blood-spume coming out of his gurgling mouth. Grabbing the back of his jacket, I dragged him down to the taxi.

The conscious one, still stuffed, sitting on the wall and trying to focus, looked at me and said, "We won't forget this . . . "

I grabbed him by the larynx and the back of his hair, lifting him, face into face.

"Good. Look at it, remember it well. Don't come back."

The sight was a bundle of arms and legs and bloodied bits and pieces, making memorable noises.

The school occupational advisor (SOA) came round to our

school just before we finished. There was no graduation party for the likes of us, just a kick in the arse and a "don't come back" . . . as if.

"So," the SOA says to me, with a Rolodex full of job vacancies, "and what would you like to do when you leave school, sonny?"

It might have gone down better if I'd sat on his knee and he had a red suit and a white beard.

"Well, I'd like to be a soldier. No, a fireman. No, an engine driver . . . a brain surgeon?"

"No, no, none of those. Look, it says here you're good at art. How would you like to be a painter?"

A big soap bubble appeared over my head. I could see it all now, standing in front of the Eiffel Tower, canvas and easel, brush in hand, one in the mouth, beret on, women falling at my feet . . .

"Hold me back – Yeah, sounds great," says I.

"Done," says he.

Next week I started as a painter in a Liverpool dry-dock painting the bottom of a huge cargo ship. I was covered from head to toe with red lead paint from using a big paint roller.

"Don't worry, son. It'll wash off. There's a bucket of diesel over there, you can wash your hair, face and hands in that."

"Oh yeah, thanks, boss."

I did buy myself a black beret though, just to make me look "windswept and interesting", as Billy Connolly used to say . . .

We found out later that the cab driver was a friend of the two thugs from the night before.

"Mr Indestructible" was their homecoming champion and cousin. He needed resuscitating three times that night. Emergency surgery put several plates in his head; corrective eye surgery was needed; he had a heap of stitches to the face; his nose needed resetting for breathing; his right elbow was reset; he had several broken ribs and a punctured lung that had to be drained; ice packs were put on his swollen testicles, which had gone black; and he had a knee-cap removed. And then there were the other three . . . busy night all round.

They told them at the hospital they'd crashed their car but couldn't remember where.

There was not a grain of sympathy or remorse for any of them. I was just glad it wasn't me or the innocent patrons in the club, or the boss and his family.

After everybody had gone home, Jimmy and I went to the hospital to "have another word" with them. We don't like being threatened. It was a nurse that saved them. We told her we were "concerned relatives". She took one look at us, a wild-eyed skinhead and a big woolly Mad-Manson and shooed us out, locking the door. They owe their future well-being to her – we'd have made sure they stayed there for a long, long time. That's how psyched up we were.

After the fight, the boss and I really showed our appreciation to Gary and Rolo – the boss with two envelopes and me with an "eye to eye" handshake. There was no hugging in those days. "Anytime," was all that was said.

They left me smartly in case the "Ee-aw, ee-aw" boys arrived. It left me and Jimmy on the door. The boss disappeared. Jimmy suggested I get cleaned up.

Up in the Gents, trying to get myself back in order, I noticed guys were shrinking away from me. Looking in the mirror, the effect was definitely a first. The person that looked back at me was hardly recognizable from the one I'd seen two hours ago; mad eyes, full of adrenaline, a face splashed and smeared with blood. A shirt that was bloody and torn. The bow tie was interesting though – halfway round my silly neck!

I did the best I could with myself and noticed I hardly had a scratch on me. What had happened felt like an hour's event. I went back down to Jimmy and took my spot.

Another banging on the door, same as before.

I looked back up at Jimmy; his black eyes are scary. He put his hand on my shoulder. I took a breath, Jimmy was with me, we're pumped to go again. I opened the door a fraction . . .

"POLICE! . . . Who had the nunchakus?"

My poor Mum. There wasn't much to make her proud of me. After I'd nearly drowned Ryan and myself, she got the bright idea of getting me swimming lessons, three years later mind.

I took to it like the proverbial duck. Inside three years I was the school backstroke champion. Ha ha! Things were starting to look up. So when the Inter-schools Swimming Championships came up I invited her to come and watch her champion son, and along she came, proud as Punch. When the backstroke event was called I came out, threw the towel off my skinny little shoulders, arms spinning round like propellers, dancing like I was Ali at a boxing match.

"Yeah, that's right, bring 'em out. Where's these kids I'm going to cream?"

This kid walks out and stands next to me. I looked around. You've got to be kidding right? You've heard of David and Goliath? This kid was about eight feet tall! His hands dragged along the floor, his feet looked like huge flippers painted pink. Evolution's Missing Link?

Another kid came out, smaller than me. Ha! – I had his number. Three other kids ran away.

"Take your marks."

BANG – we're away. That was the last we saw of the Missing Link until halfway up the first lap of three when he passed us, twice. The crowd went mad – a new schools record.

I managed to finish second, about half an hour later. Only Mum and Gillian clapped. I think the third kid drowned, in the dark.

"Never mind, John, God loves the little dodo bird as much as the golden eagle."

"Yeah, thanks for that, Mum." She had a wonderful way of putting things, Mum.

Two detectives stood in the club's doorway. Being "the little fella" I was standing on the second stair going up, again. The older one had a torch in his hand and shone it on my trousers and shoes.

"Well, what have we got here?"

"Er . . . I painted a friend's fence before I came here tonight."

"Come out here with me, son."

He shone the torch in the alleyway – there was blood everywhere.

"Been 'painting' here as well, have you? What's your name, Jackson Pollock or something?"

"No, sir, who's he?"

"What do you do – karate or something?"

"No, no. I'm just minding the door for the night – the bouncer's sick." Jimmy slipped away upstairs.

"Who had the nunchaku?"

"What's that?"

"So you don't know these martial arts, eh?"

"Nope," shaking my head in wide-eyed innocence.

"YES YOU DO!" he screamed in my face.

My bodyweight dropped into stance, eyes came out of my head with adrenaline. One hand went for his larynx. I was nearly inside his shirt before I realized it.

He took one look at me, snorted a laugh and said, "Yeah, right," as he walked back down the alleyway.

I came back up, defeated, put my hands out ready for the cuffs.

"Come over here, son," the wizened detective encouraged with his hand. I walked over to him.

"Do you know who that was tonight?"

I shook my head, "Not really."

"That was two of the Bainnets, one of the three worst organized crime families in Liverpool."

"Oh!"

"Yeah, 'Oh!' Welcome to the underbelly world of Liverpool, son. Lad, if you don't want to wind up in pieces in the Mersey, I would strongly suggest that you cease employment here tonight and go somewhere where nobody knows you because these people *will* find you if you stay here. They've got their fingers in nightclubs, pubs, prostitutes, taxis and I'm ashamed to say a certain couple of police officers. They are the vermin of society – they're from the sewers and they won't stop looking for you, for what you've done here the last couple of nights. We heard what happened last night, so we sat across the street in an unmarked car. We saw everything, and we saw nothing. You understand?"

I nodded.

"That gobshite that you put down is only just out of jail for stabbing one of 'Ours'. All he did was eight years, so we're very happy with your evening's work. So we'll cover this for you, up to this point, but that's all – right? We've got the nunchakus. You won't be needing them because you don't know what they are – right?"

"Thank you. Thanks a lot."

"Take my advice, son. Leave before it escalates. This garbage won't stop. You're known now. You've shown everyone they're not as hard as they think they are. Leave while you're still a winner."

As we walked away from each other he turned and said, "Hey! You know you guys had all that stitched up in about two minutes flat?"

"Yeah?"

"Damnedest thing I've ever seen. Wished I had a movie-camera, wouldn't mind seeing that again."

"Not me – once'll do me, I think. See ya."

'I hope not, son, I hope not."

My only real regret those last four years of high-school was that Gillian – the love of my life, the girl I'd known and the only one I wanted – well, she went and rose right out of my league. She'd been a duckling when I fell in love with her and now she'd gone and turned into this beautiful swan.

You could always tell the boys from our school: they all had the indents of two lines running down their faces from being pressed against the school railings as she passed by.

I had mine for the rest of my life.

CHARLIE BRONSON (UK)

Britain's Most Violent Prisoner

Introducing . . . Charlie Bronson

TAGGED BY THE British press as Britain's most violent prisoner, in contrast to triple murderer Thomas Silverstein, Charles (Charlie) Bronson has actually never murdered anyone. Neither is he a rapist or paedophile. However, because of his relentless and continual violence towards prison staff and other prisoners, like Silverstein, Bronson has managed to keep himself locked away in solitary confinement for most of his adult life.

Bronson was born Michael Gordon Peterson on the 6 December 1952 and grew up in the working-class town of Luton. His aunt, Eileen Parry, was once quoted as saying, "As a boy he was a lovely lad. He was obviously bright and always good with children. He was gentle and mild-mannered, never a bully – he would defend the weak."

Peterson first started getting into trouble when his family moved up to Ellesmere Port in northwest England and in 1974, aged twenty-two, he was first imprisoned for seven years for a bungled armed robbery attempt at a post office in Little Sutton, a suburb of Ellesmere Port, during which he stole just £26.18 (US$45). After having his sentence continually increased for bad behaviour, he was eventually released on 30 October 1988, changed his name to Charles Bronson and started a short-lived career as a bare-knuckle fighter in the East End of London, where he became an associate of another notorious hard man, Lenny McLean. However, Bronson only spent sixty-nine days as a free man before being arrested and imprisoned again for robbery. Released again on 9 November 1992, this time he spent only fifty-three days as a free man before being arrested once more for conspiracy to rob.

Since 1974 Bronson has spent a total of just four months and nine days out of custody and his sentences have been repeatedly extended for crimes committed while inside, including: grievous bodily harm, criminal damage, wounding with intent, wounding, false imprisonment, blackmail and threatening to kill. Bronson has also been involved in a large number of hostage-taking situations dating back to the early 1980s including a forty-seven-hour rooftop protest at Broadmoor in 1983, causing damage estimated at £750,000 (US$1.2 million). In 1994, whilst holding a guard hostage he is alleged to have demanded an inflatable doll, a helicopter and a cup of tea as ransom. Two months later he held Deputy Governor Adrian Wallace hostage for five hours at Hull prison, injuring him so badly he was off work for five weeks. In 1998, Bronson took three inmates hostage at Belmarsh Prison in London and told negotiators he would eat one of his victims unless his demands were met. On that occasion he demanded a plane to take him to Cuba, two Uzi sub-machine guns, 5,000 rounds of ammunition and a cup of beans. He told staff: "I'm going to start snapping necks, I'm the number-one hostage taker." In court, he said he was "as guilty as Adolf Hitler".

Another seven years were added to his sentence.

His violent and dangerous behaviour has meant that he is continually moved and has spent time in over 120 different prisons, including Broadmoor high security psychiatric hospital. All but four of his years in prison have been in solitary confinement.

Bronson is currently in HMP Wakefield where he remains a Category A prisoner. For the past ten years has occupied himself by writing poetry, for which he has won numerous international awards, and producing pieces of art which are collected worldwide. He has also written a large number of books, one of which is called *Solitary Fitness*, detailing his extreme fitness regime involving over 3,000 press-ups and hundreds of sit-ups each and every day.

Both feared and respected by almost everyone, Bronson is definitely one of the toughest and hardest men in the UK, and he was once one of the most violent. However, Bronson's intentions are now to serve the rest of his time as peacefully and quietly as he can in the hope of spending his last few years as a free man. This distinctive contribution from his book *Loonology* highlights the violence of his life behind bars, coupled with the anger and sexual frustrations of being locked away on his own for so many years.

THE LION AND THE PUSSYCAT
By Charlie Bronson

It's been said that I'm Britain's most violent prisoner. Am I? Am I bollocks! How can I be? It's just a label. So how did it come about? Why? I'll tell you. I was naughty. A little bit naughty. I've done things most only ever dream of doing. I do your dreams. I live out your fantasies. My dreams I turn to reality. If I don't like somebody they sure know about it, and I don't give a flying fuck about it. Just stay out of my space. Live and let live I say. But some prats don't know how to keep out of your face.

I remember one time I was being escorted over to the hospital wing to see a dentist in Wandsworth. Ten screws were taking me "cuffed up". As we got to E Wing I clocked a con cleaning the stairs. It was a filthy grass I'd known in Scrubs. I just acted on impulse. I legged it over to him with the ten screws chasing me, blowing a whistle and shouting. I made it to the cleaner and kicked him at least six or seven times before I was restrained. Not bad, eh, considering I was cuffed up?! Eat your heart out, Rambo!

Who remembers the Cambridge Rapist, going back to the early 1970s? That little toe-rag raped a dozen women. He used to creep around Cambridge with a leather zip-up mask with "rapist" written on it. He was only five feet nothing; a horrible scumbag that looked like a little rat. He was into wearing women's clothes. He had also done a spell in Broadmoor.

I remember when he turned up at Parkhurst in the 1970s. He was a cocky little fucker; arrogant. He started poncing around in women's clothes. I thought to myself, of all the jails to send him to they put him in Parkhurst. This jail at the time was the No. 1 jail, full of proper villains, real cons. Is it any wonder I wrapped a steel mop bucket around his fucking crust? Little bastard. I'll teach him to walk down the landings in his see-through panties and silly pink shirt. Crack! Cop a hold of that. He would've got more but some prat rang the alarm bell.

And who remembers the "Guernsey Beast" Beasley. Sounds a lot like beast. It's probably why I remember the toe-rag. He got thirty years for sodomizing little boys. A right ugly fat bastard. Sadly I only got to see him through a fence in Albany and a couple of times through a window in Parkhurst. He served his time on Rule 43 with all the other nonces. He actually served twenty years (that's one good thing) but, believe me, when these monsters all get together on a little unit, or wing, they party. They get through pots of KY Jelly. They all have a funny walk. Their arses must be red raw.

I used to stick razor blades in bars of white Windsor soap and throw them over the fence where they walked by, hoping maybe one would find its way into one of their pockets and a nice little accident would happen in the shower (one can wish). I also used to throw sweets in wrappers over the fence after I'd contaminated them with shit. I wonder how many were ever eaten? If only one, then it was a result. Personally, I'd sooner punch them up.

I just can't be having a serious nonce around me. Can you? Could you live next door to a nonce, let's say a paedophile or child killer? Well could you? No you couldn't. Well why should we in prison live with them? I'm just not happy with them monsters near me. They should be in "special jails", away from the proper cons. Let me say now, I'm a believer in punishment. I actually believe in the birch. I think prison should be hard. It's all we deserve. I'm not into a soft regime. But why should some get it easy and some hard? Let's all get it hard. Let's stop playing silly games. All this psychological crap, it don't work, it's a joke. Prison is for punishment; to teach us a lesson, not to treat us like a load of muppets.

I just read in the paper that Ian Huntley has just bought a bed rug as the prison rug is too rough. He should be sleeping in a black hole with the rats. It all makes me feel sick. But that's how it is today. It's all crazy and if you don't go along with it then you become like me: the dangerous one. You end up in a solitary cage. Yeah, for real. You end up in a fucking big hole that sucks away your light. This is the end of the line. The crematorium awaits. Mine's a bacon roll with mushrooms. Fuck the Rice Krispies. Give mine to the muppets. In fact . . . sling it in the bin. Don't spoil the fuckers.

Hey, did you know that bulletproof vests, laser printers and windscreen wipers were all invented by women? I thought you might like to know that. Fuck knows why, but it's just historical facts.

"*Tostum*" is the Latin word for scorched or burning, thus cometh toast. Hey, I love cheese and tomato and spring onion on toast with a nice mug of tea! It's years since I had a treat like that. I'm fucking hungry just thinking about it. I can almost smell it. Why do I have to torture myself with these beautiful memories? Maybe I'm just a masochist! I probably am.

In the early 1970s the toughest jails were places like Winson Green, Strangeways, Armley and Wandsworth. These were known as the POA (Prison Officers' Association) Power Houses. Trouble-makers were sent to these seg. (segregation) blocks for a good kicking. Make no mistake about it, it was brutal and you got fuck all. My life, my world, was in these blocks. I was kicked around from pillar to post. I would arrive naked in a body belt and the treatment would kick off from day one. These blocks were run by a fist of steel, always by the biggest and ugliest screws in the jail, not one of them under six feet. All were ex-military; men you would be proud of on a rugby field. They loved nothing more than a good old-fashioned ruck. Some – most – were vicious, vindictive bullies. They loved the power and used it to the full. The black cons got it the worst in Wandsworth block, as at this time there were a lot of National Front screws, all proud to display their member badges. Also the Irish got it bad. As for me, they just loved me every time I turned up there. On my first spell in Wandsworth block back in 1975 I attacked three screws within a week. My life was forever in the strongbox in restraints. I used to do anything and everything to fuck up their regime. Regularly I used to walk across the infamous steel-rimmed centre. It's sacrilege to step on that centre. Every time I did that I was jumped on and carted off back to the box black and blue.

That's how it was. You either behaved or you suffered. I was labelled a prison activist. I would climb the roof, smash the place up, shit on it all. Shit up. Nobody knew what I would do next – not even me.

Incidentally, the only two other cons I knew of who used to walk across Wandsworth centre were Frank Frazer and Frank Mitchell. Apart from them I don't know of any more. For 99 per cent of cons it's just basically head down, do your bird peacefully and get out fast.

Every jail has nasty screws; evil fuckers who are set to make your stay a bad one. In the 1970s the two worst screws I knew there were Ryan and Beasley. Beasley was a giant of a man with a seriously nasty streak and he would nick you for a button undone. I chinned him and told him, "Next time I'll cut your throat." That cost me 120 days' remission, 56 days' punishment and a £5 fine. Five quid was a lot in the 1970s – about two months' wages for me. But that's what you get when you attack authority. You have to take the consequences.

Strange enough, Beasley wasn't so bad to me after that. I think he respected me. Bear in mind that I was only a young man of twenty-three at the time and he was well into his forties. But he was a giant of a man; a hard man. Rumour had it he'd been out in the Middle East snapping necks in some special force. That could be shit, but with him I wouldn't doubt it.

Ryan was a different kettle. He was a little vindictive fucker. Even the screws despised him, as he was always causing unnecessary trouble. He worked on D Wing, the long-term wing. D Wing was a little easier owing to the sorts of cons it held: lifers Cat A and Cat E; all sorts of high-risk inmates. Most had just got their sentence, so it was very tense in there. The screws sort of kept a back step. But Ryan was a total cunt. I mean it – a cunt. Slamming doors, shouting abuse, pushing it all the time. Like all Irishmen he loved a drink. You could always smell it on them. Him and me just had to get it on. He was in my face all the time. It happened in the mail bag shop on the end of D Wing. I just felt that's it, I've had my lot of him, so I hit him with a right hook (that's all, I swear). The alarm went and in rushed the mob to take me off to the block for a good kicking. I could hardly walk for a week afterwards as one of my balls had swollen to the size of an orange, but that's showbiz.

There was one old screw there who told me privately, "You done us all a favour there. It got rid of the Irish prick for a spell." There was an old screw there in his sixties. I used to chat with him coz I liked his style. He was one of those screws that just did his job, and he treated the cons with respect. All the cons respected him. He used to stop a lot of trouble by using his own ways of dealing with problems. "Come on, son. Cool down. Go behind your door. You don't need this shit. Come on, do yourself a favour. Think of your family." Nine times out of ten his way worked. When he was on duty it was always a treat to see him. Other screws did not react like him. Incidentally, he was a screw in the hanging days. The stories he told me were amazing. He actually witnessed them. He spent time in the death cell with the condemned prisoner. I told him that when he retired he should write a book.

By the way, did you know that most hangings literally shit themselves? The bowels just burst open and that was it. Piss and shit just pours out. I bet that's put you off lunch.

I met all the faces in Wandsworth: anyone who was anyone. It was a breeding ground for criminals over the years. Real villains come out of Wandsworth: men like the Krays, Richardsons, Freddie Foreman, Frank Frazer – all the legends; good old-fashioned armed robbers like Danny Alpress, Terry Smith, Ronnie Easterbrook, Wayne Hurren, Roy Shaw and Ronnie Brown. They all passed through Wanno. Wanno was the stepping stone for Parkhurst or Dartmoor. It's like an apprenticeship of crime. You have to get the experience. That's what it's all about. To be a criminal you will one day get porridge. You will fall eventually. So expect what you get and plenty of it.

My true advice would be: don't do what I've done. Do your bird easy and get out fast. You only win by walking out or going over the wall. Freedom is the ultimate goal in life inside unless you are a complete institutionalized moron. After all my years inside I still hate prison life and prison life hates me. I can never become institutionalized. It's against my philosophy.

Some of my best years were in Wandsworth – crazy years, but memorable. I was just born to rock the boat and rock it I did. I almost escaped from there, I cut people there, I chinned people there, I got on the roof there, I shit up there, I met some of my best buddies there, I slept in the cell next to the condemned cell there, I taught myself to play chess and bridge there (out of books), I spent a good four years in solitary there, I was on hunger strike there, I chinned a doctor there, I chinned several governors there, I attacked a good dozen screws there, I smashed up dozens of cells there, I attacked many nonces there and I met some decent screws there. They weren't all bad. There's always some good everywhere. One in particular was a gentleman. He'd done a lot for me over the years. Over the last thirty-four years I've probably been back there twenty times, if not more, and he was always there. I watched his hair go grey. He watched mine fall out. That's how life is inside – a fucking journey of madness. I'll leave you with a funny story on Wanno. You'll love this one . . .

Lord Longford – Frank to me – used to visit me all over England from as far away as Durham all the way to Parkhurst, the Isle of Wight. He was one of my favourite regular visitors and we had some bloody good laughs. He also helped me a lot with advice, etc.

My first visit with Frank was in the block in Wanno years back. He came to see me over my long years in solitary and he wanted to interview me for the book he was writing called *Prisoner or Patient*. Our visit had to be held in the Governor's Office in the block (the Adjudication Room) as I was considered too unpredictable to be escorted over to the visiting area. Plus, going to the visiting area would mean passing the centre, and they didn't want me walking over it. So the visit would be in the block. The Adjudication Room was quite large with a portrait of the Queen on the wall. So, ten screws unlocked me and marched me to the room. Frank had been told it was not safe to see me alone, but he responded, "Charlie won't attack me. I wish to see him alone." I walked in to see an old man with bottletop specs. I gave him a hug before we sat down to chat. The door had a plastic glass in it so they could look in on us. I said to Frank, "Look at them nosy fuckers." He smiled and said, "They're only doing a job." So we had a good chat. He was a really nice fella to talk with: very clever; very helpful. He asked me what I did all day in my cell. I told him press-ups. How many, he asked. So I told him: between two and three thousand. As we spoke about my press-ups I said, "Look, watch this." I got on the floor and told him to sit on my back while I did a quick hundred. To my amazement he did, but he fell off. As I went to help him up, the screws rushed in. They thought I'd hit him! It was so bloody funny. Then Frank showed me his press-ups. He managed about five, which for an old man is great. He put all this in a wicked book he did called *Longford Diaries*. He was a brilliant old fella and I really liked him a lot, although we did have some heated arguments about Brady and Hindley, as my thoughts were anti and always will be. A lovely man. He's another one I'll not be having a pint with, but he remains in my heart – respect.

My prison records date from 1974 to 2008 (I was inside 1969, 1970 and 1971 for short spells – a shit and shave as they call it):

Risley: Chinned about five screws; attacked a good ten nonces; attempted a roof protest; got wrapped up in the barbed wire; cut a grass.

Walton: Took the roof off; smashed up the block; chinned the Governor; shit-up on a couple of screws; attempted escape; half a dozen fights with cons.

Armley: Attacked the riot mob; took off a cell door; a shit-up; assaulted a governor and screw.

Full Sutton: Took a probation officer hostage; attacked six screws; attacked the riot mob; assaulted several governors; set fire to a cell with a grass in it; half a dozen fights with cons; smashed TV sets.

Durham: Chinned two screws; kept in specially constructed cage.

Gartree: Chinned four screws; alleged stabbing; alleged scolding of a nonce; smashed up four cells.

Long Lartin: Attacked five screws in one day; chinned nine screws.

Whitemoor: Hunger strike; attacked riot mob; shit-up.

Lincoln: Chinned Deputy Governor; assaulted two screws; shit-up.

Leicester: Got on roof; took cell door off; two assaults on screws.

Woodhill: Took library screw hostage; smashed up special unit in stand-off riot.

Highdown: Chinned Governor; three assaults on screws.

Bullingdon: Took solicitor hostage; smashed up cell.

Bristol: Assaulted Governor; shit-up.

Albany: Smashed block up; assaulted two cons; chinned one screw.

Camp Hill: Attacked four screws; hunger strike.

Parkhurst: Certified insane – liquid cosh (drug control); stabbed con; assaulted five screws; chinned two screws; cut one screw; stabbed-up myself multiple times; several fights with cons; smashed up wing; got on roof; alleged arson to workshop.

Winchester: Got on roof; smashed up block; two assaults on screws; one assault on con.

Hull: Took Governor hostage; got on roof; took teacher hostage; cut a con; three assaults on screws; two shit-ups on Governor; attempted escape; once put in restraint and ankle straps and moved out in wheelchair; liquid cosh.

Wakefield: First con in Britain to be pepper-sprayed; attacked riot mob; smashed up three cells.

Norwich: Shit-up.

Strangeways: Assaulted two screws.

Oxford: Chinned a screw.

Ashworth: Cut a lunatic; asylum; attacked four screws.

Rampton: Attempted strangulation of a lunatic (paedophile); attacked four screws; liquid cosh.

Broadmoor: Three roof protests; attempted strangulation of a nonce; attacked three screws; attacked four lunatics; attempted escape; hunger strike; liquid cosh; smashed up lots of cells.

Winson Green: Attacked four cons; stole Michael Samms's leg; took doctor hostage; attacked riot mob; smashed up three cells.

Belmarsh: Attacked two cons; took three hostages (Iraqis); assaulted Governor; smashed up cell.

Scrubs: Smashed up seg. block; attacked riot mob; assaulted two screws; attacked Governor.

Pentonville: Shit-up; smashed up cell; assaulted two screws.

Do you know, this is only half of what I did? It's not even counting my disciplinary charges or verbal threats and abuse or bad behaviour. Fuck me, I really was a nasty bastard. How I've changed. It's now seven years since I was in any serious trouble. I've actually learnt the hard way. I'm just not the same man nowadays. I'm now anti-violence and anti-crime. This record is my past, thanks. Fuck, it makes frightening reading and it's only a small summary of my past behaviour. Now you know me better. Maybe you now hate me or you believe I should die inside, but bear in mind that I have paid the price. I have been punished severely. People do change. I'm the proof of it. I could actually help a lot of youngsters stay out of jail.

I will never glamorize crime or violence. One thing's for sure – my body is now paying the price for my violent life. I'm a walking scar and the arthritis is kicking in. My eyes are going. My mind wanders. I feel shell-shocked. I suffer with post-traumatic stress disorder. I'm the old ghost . . . Did I ever tell you about the time I carved a gun out of a bar of carbolic soap and then spread black boot polish over it? I stuck it in a work screw's face and said, "Give me your fucking keys now, you cunt!" Fuck me, he nearly had a heart attack. The Governor wouldn't accept that it was only a prank, so that cost me three months in chokey with no canteen and no bed. They just can't take a joke these people! Hey, it did look like a real gun though. You see, in jail you have time to think, time to pass. You can do anything if you're determined; well, anything within reason.

In one jail I was in, which I'll not name for obvious reasons, I made a kite. Yeah, a fucking silly kite. I got hundreds and hundreds of yards of cotton and flew it over the wall from my cell window. Why? Use your head! Let's just say I never went without for a good brew. It's easy if you're 100 per cent determined, but you have to believe in yourself and have contacts outside. Nowadays they smuggle in mobiles. Every week in jail there are hundreds found and confiscated, especially in the low category jails. Times change. How nice it must be to call your girl up, in private, and have an hour or two's dirty talk. Why not? In one jail I was in the lads were passing around a blow-up doll with a real fanny hole. It cost 3oz of baccy a night. You'd be amazed at who was shagging that doll. It's more like who never shagged it! Okay, I had a go. I put a load of margarine in the hole and went for it. Fuck me, I never kissed it! Then rock band Procol Harum came on the radio with "Whiter Shade of Pale", so we had a slow dance. Then I bent her over the bed and did her doggy style. Sure it's mad, but that's how jail is – mad! You can't get through it without being mad. Luckily I covered up the door spyhole, or I'd have ended up in the padded cell! The screw ended up knocking on the door at 2 a.m.

He shouted, "Take down the cover so I can see you, Bronson."

I shouted back, "I'm having a shit!"

He yelled, "What, since nine p.m.?"

"Fuck off!" I shouted as I cuddled up to the doll.

"You're nicked, Bronson."

What's new! The next night some other hot-blooded stag had a go. Now I'm not making this up, but in one jail they had a sheep, a fucking blow-up sheep . . . and no, I never!

There's a whisper here that some have blow-up dolls with cocks on. Now that don't amaze me with all these filthy nonces, so it's probably true. It's fucking loonyology, total insanity gone mad!

I've only ever had one fair fight with a screw in thirty-three years and that was in the seg. block in Wandsworth back in 1976 – or was it 1975? One of them years. He was a Geordie screw; a big lump, in his early thirties. He loved a drink and a fight. What Geordie don't?

Anyway, one thing led to another and a confrontation broke out. He took off his keys and ran into my cell. That was it. A real fight began, toe to toe. Crack, bang, wallop! It was a good fight. That's how it should be sorted, not ten on to one. Men don't need ten behind them. So Geordie got my respect. Even though some of his mates ran in to break it up just as I was getting the better of him, it was a proper scrap that we both wanted. It cleared the air.

You gotta understand that men are born to fight. In my walk of life you can't but fight. Prisons are a volcano of violence just waiting to erupt. It don't take a lot to work out why: we are men; frustrated; anxious; fed up; bored. We are sick of it all. Why can't the system wake up? Let us have a good old-fashioned fuck every once in a while; a bit of pussy juice. Let us do what we are put on the planet for. That's unless a guy is satisfied wasting his life away. I'm not. That becomes boring.

Hey, I should have been a psychologist! My way would clear up all prison violence. I would make our prisons safer places – with common sense! Work the cons hard, with lots of discipline, but every so often let the girls in to bring in some loving. Sweet and tender loving works! Wake up you prison officials. My way would stop all the pain!

SWEET AND TENDER LOVING
Games of the mind . . . a tortured soul
Loveless and empty
A body full of pain
No release
No smells
No sweet smells. Nothing but doom
Sweet and tender loving
Roll it my way
I'll have some of that in a slice of bread

Toasted and hot and juicy
Without love there is no hope, no life, no dreams
It's a fucking pit of despair
A cage of snakes
Ripping out your lungs
Squeezing your strength
A dead man breathing
A fucking pile of shit
Dehumanized . . . Brutally destroyed
Bloodless . . . All dried up
A faceless, boneless person
A number for a name
Close the coffin lid and fuck off!

Over the years I've had some memorable visits from all walks of life: family, biz and pleasure. I've even had a fuck several times. Difficult but it's possible.

Kelly Anne was one. We got it on in Albany and Hull jails. She was one crazy bitch but a good visitor. At Albany on the Isle of Wight I was forever in the seg. block and all my visits were in a room meant for solicitors' visits. Screws used to sit outside the door and it also had CCTV, so you would think it impossible to have a shag. Yeah, so would I. Plus we were supposed to sit at either side of the table. This was the rules. This was the late 1980s. This is what happened.

I arrived at the visit with an escort of eight screws, as I was on a seriously heavy unlock these days as my world was a crazy journey. I was so unpredictable. I sat down at the table waiting for Kelly Anne to come in. In she walked with a tray of orange juice and chocolates. She had a wicked smile. She was up to no good. I always knew when she was being naughty. Then she undid her coat. Fuck me, she had fuck all on and it was winking at me. What she'd done was slid into the ladies, taken her clothes off and stuffed them in her pockets! I couldn't believe it. I really couldn't. I had a raging hard-on and said, "Right, let's do it."

She came around my side of the table and sat on me. It slipped right up her. I just could not fucking believe it. We was fucking. Her coat was still on, so all the screws could see was her sitting on my lap. It was mental.

One screw came in and said, "Come on, Charlie, that's not allowed."

What could I do? What would anybody do?

I said, "Look boss, she's a bit upset. Give it five minutes."

And it worked!

He said, "Five minutes or you'll get me in trouble."

As she bobbed up and down there were screws looking in. It was fucking brilliant. Hot, wet, sticky and bloody lovely. But, as usual, Kelly can't behave. She just goes over the top.

"It's supposed to be a secret fuck," I whispered. "Slow down, you're putting it bang on me there."

But she kept bouncing up and down and making the noise that's only ever used when you're alone.

The screws came back in. "Come on, Charlie, you'll have to let her sit on her side of the table."

As he spoke I shot my load right in her. The screw must have known as I was truly hazy.

"Yeah, okay boss, no problem."

Kelly got off and went to the toilet to clean up, but most of it was all over me. My jeans were drenched in pussy juice and come. When she came back we just started laughing. It did me the world of good. All my stress and anxiety had vanished. I felt human again. It was brilliant.

After I ate some chocs and drank some orange Kelly then gave me a good old-fashioned wank under the table. I swear the screws could see. There's no way they couldn't but see. She wasn't playing chess under the table. Her body was shaking as she wanked me off. It was so funny. A bit strange, but again I shot my load. Most went on the floor, but she must have got some on her hand as she licked it off. Kelly Anne was to me sex on legs. What a visit that was – very memorable.

Another time was in Hull Jail. Looking back I guess she's an exhibitionist. She loved getting men at it. It's her scene but it all turned nasty with Kelly. It's all in my other books so I won't bother going into it again. I've no real bad feelings on the matter, I just move on in life, bury the hatchet so to speak. But marks out of ten for sex with Kelly would be ten-and-a-half. It was brilliant. She was bloody crazy and that's how I like my women: a bit mental, dangerous, unpredictable. She took a gamble and it paid off. It could've turned nasty, but it truly was a brilliant fuck to remember. That shag in Albany must go down in history.

She must've been so up for it, as it just slipped in. It was the hottest fanny on the planet. It's the danger that does that to a woman: the dare, the gamble. She had planned it down to the split second – all the way from Luton to the Isle of Wight. She was gagging for it. She wanted to give me something to behave for. It was her way of saying, "Be good, behave and get out fast and you can have a lot more of this. It's waiting for you. Come home."

But life don't ever work out like that. I don't believe in fairy tales. Never have done. Life is reality. Kelly Anne knew it too. She had other plans for me. Plans that I knew fuck all about but I was sure to be dragged into them, and I was. The rest is history.

The moral to the story is: the cat that gets the cream is not always a happy cat. Some cats are greedy, selfish fuckers!

I also had a blow job in Parkhurst Visiting Room. I'll not say who by. My reason for that is simple: I don't wish to. Some women don't deserve to be exposed; in fact most don't. Most to me are ladies I respect.

This blow job was not planned. It just started off as a kiss and a bit of fondling. A screw did come over and say, "Cool it, Charlie," and that was that. The visiting room was quite full, so there was a lot of noise and I just enjoyed the company. For a laugh I pulled out my dick under the table and grabbed her hand and put it on it. She laughed and gave it a few pulls. Then she disappeared under the table. I was having a fucking blow job in the middle of the visiting room! I could not believe it. Remember, it's months and months with no sex. So it don't take long to come, and come I did. I couldn't stop coming. Another memorable visit. But, believe me, these sorts of visits are very few and far between. It's why you can never forget them.

Talking of pussies, the nicest pussy I can remember was Jan Lamb's, and I say this with the utmost respect as she's a proper lovely lady, solid. Anyway, it's no secret that she's proud to have had me in the sack. I'm still in touch with Jan all these years later. We practically fucked ourselves silly. She done things with my cock I never thought possible. There's shagging and there's shagging.

This was SHAGGINGGGGG. Fuck me, my dick was red raw. We never stopped. If we'd videoed it, it would've sold a million copies overnight. People just don't understand, but when a man's gone without pussy for so long it just takes him over. Jan Lamb was a very lucky lady meeting me. Someone had to help me back to sanity and it was Jan. Hey, make no mistake about it, she's a lovely sort and a respected woman amongst my firm, my circle, my special haunts, my world. The Krays loved Jan as well. Both respected her. But my memories of her are special. We'd never laughed so much in our lives – so much were crying: a pool of sweat and tears. That's how sex should be: raw and mad. When a bloke shoots his load he's gotta let it fly: hit the fucking ceiling, shoot it in the face, over the tits, then rub it in and start all over again. Fuck till you drop. With Jan we loved it doggie style, growling and barking. It's fucking fantastic. I've got a hard-on now just thinking about it.

Well, I love a good woman and when that woman becomes a part of my journey she becomes "special". So when we fuck, we fuck with our souls, we enter the unknown. It's fucking wicked, beautiful. Jan had those special piss flaps that sort of wrap around your cock like a foreskin. Do you know what I mean? Maybe you've not all seen them. Let me explain if I can. The flaps sort of feel like bits of liver – nice. Anyway, she had lovely flaps that have stayed in my memory. I study things like that. I'm a bit of a studier on the quiet; an analyst. I like to see how the human body works. There's nothing quite like our body. It's unique in every sense of the word. So look after it. It's yours. Don't let nobody ever abuse it. Love yourselves. Love your body. Reach in and love it too. My cock is still erect. I'm ready to rumble. I'll leave it at that.

Who remembers their first fuck? Come on, you must do. That first time you felt that hot, wet, sticky pussy and you thought: fuck me, does it bite? Was that first time scary or what? That first time she grabbed your cock and slipped it in the honeypot. We all remember it. Awesome. It don't make no difference if you reach a low, you always remember it. That first-love fling when your whole world was lit up with rainbows. Dreams come true. You just cannot get enough of it. No sooner had you shot your load, you was ready again. You fucked till your dick was red raw from hour after hour of grinding away. Who says dreams don't come true?

The teenage years was just one long fuck. I had my share of pussy but my greatest memory was with a half-caste chick. She will remain nameless as it's not my thing to embarrass women – unless, of course, they're evil bitches – plus by now she would be a granny.

I met her at a party and we just hit it off. I was seventeen and she was twenty-four. She had a flat she shared with her mate, who I actually knew. She worked at a factory that I once robbed. Anyway, something mental happened that night that's never happened before to me. I think it was a one-off, a miracle. Call it what you will, but it was mental; it just happened.

We were naked in the bedroom and I was giving her some serious fucking doggy style, really banging away big time. My balls were slamming into her like the birch and we was doing it in front of a mirror so we was both looking at each other. I shot my load and something weird happened – my dick stayed rock hard, it never went limp. It was mental. I kept pumping away and thought no more of it till I shot my second load. I still never went limp. This time I actually pulled out just to check. I was rock hard and all my come was trickling out of her. It blew me away. It didn't make any sense. Even she said, "Don't you ever stop?" That night was weird. I came five times before I went limp. My dick was really sore for days after. I've never forgot it. I never will. Would you? I bet she hasn't either!

There's no explanation for it. It's spooky, but we've all been there as teenagers. Was it good or was it good? Come on, how good was it? It was brilliant: the music, the style, the parties, the speed of living. We was always fast living, but the pussy was something else.

Why is it that black girls are so sexy and hot? Can a black girl move, or can she move? Have you ever seen them move on the dance-floor? Come on, you must've done! The way they move that arse is lovely! They're just sex on legs. You can't take it from them. They're just oozing with sex – and they know it! I wouldn't mind dying of a massive heart attack in bed with a beautiful black girl, say about twenty years old. What a way to call it a day! What a way to leave the planet! The ultimate dream! Here I go again. My dream would probably end with a Colt 45 in my mouth and my brains all over the pillow. She would probably be an escaped lunatic, a right psycho, crazed bitch. Come on, we all love a sexy hot bird, don't we? You can shag your wife or husband for forty years, but you can't tell me you don't dream of a sexy young bird. Yeah, you know it too. We all know it. That tight little hot, sticky, sweet-smelling pussy. Come on, you know it's your dream. Or, for your old lady, I bet she's sick of your shrivelled-up dick with your baggy bollocks all wrinkled and heavy and your bad breath or your bald patch or beer belly. She wants a good stiff cock with tight balls and a nice firm arse to grab hold of. And if she don't then she's not normal. It's everyone's fantasy. It's why so many mid-life crises happen. They all want that last big fuck to prove they haven't lost it. There's nothing wrong with it – just don't get caught! Live out your dream and enjoy it. When I hit out, every day will be a dream come true for me. Believe it! I'm sure you do.

Love will be the making of me! But am I gonna have a sore dick? Or am I? I can't fucking wait. I really can't. Whose gonna love me to death? Who's gonna shag me to death? Whose gonna kill me with love? I fucking can't wait to die! Just kill me slowly. Torture me with kisses and tongues! Smother me in pussy. Yahoooooooooo! Yippeeeeeeeeeeeee! It's gonna be soooperdoooooperrrrrr.

LOVE IS . . .
Love is robbing a bank and getting clean away
Love is finding a wallet of £50 notes
Love is waking up with a beautiful pussy in your face
Love is bumping into a rat who grassed you up years ago
Love is a giant plate of apple pie and cream
Love is driving a Roller in the rain
Love is riding a Harley on a summer's day
Love is walking out of prison
Love is leaving school for the last time
Love is seeing your mother smile
Love is finding a lost treasure
Love is swimming with a dolphin
Love is on top of the world
Love is health and fitness
Love is being loved
Love is a beautiful vision of loveliness
Love is art

Love is poetry
Love is helping a child to win in life
Love is being respected
Love is being wanted
Love is buying an old car and doing it up
Love is your first shotgun and sawing the barrel down
Love is having a dog
Love is nice clothes
Life is love and love is life!

Everything is love if you want it to be! There's nothing that can't be loved. We all love something, or somebody. What's your greatest love? If it's me, you're fucking mental!

Hey, I loved that Tina Turner in her heyday. What a lovely arse she had. And what about Suzi Quatro in her leather trousers?! Or Joan Collins in *The Stud*? There's been some hot chicks over the years. She's a handful that Dolly Parton. It's a wonder she don't lose her balance. What a lovely singer though.

Love is a box of Dairy Milk chocolates and a good video and someone to share it with. That's what love is all about: being free to do it all. I loved it when Robert Stroud found some love with his birds. For those who don't know of Robert Stroud, well he was "The Birdman of Alcatraz", You may've seen the film starring Burt Lancaster, who played Stroud. It was brilliant. Let me tell you the story. He killed and robbed a bar worker back in 1909. He started his sentence on McNeil Island in Washington State Penitentiary. There he turned into a vicious and violent inmate, stabbing and cutting anybody who crossed his path. He built up a serious reputation as a prison activist, so they sent him to one of the toughest penitentiaries in America at that time: Leavenworth in Kansas City. Make no mistake about it, Leavenworth was a tough old jail, built and designed to break a man down slowly. The screws were a hard bunch and kept on top of the cons by sheer brute force. Stroud made a tool and stabbed a screw to death in the mess hall, witnessed by a thousand convicts and a hundred guards. He'd just dug his own hole. Mysteriously he was reprieved and committed to a life sentence. They built a cage for him in Leavenworth where he remained in solitary for almost thirty years, and that's where he became the Birdman. It all began the day he found an injured bird out on the exercise yard. He put it in his pocket, smuggled it back to his cell and treated it. The prison governor heard all about this kind act and the system allowed him his own birds, mostly canaries. And the rest is history! He bred them, wrote books on them and became a bird expert!

Now get this. It may shock you. The Birdman was moved to Alcatraz in 1942, where he was put straight into solitary and denied his birds. For the next six years he remained in Alcatraz seg. block alone – a purely vindictive move. For thirty years he'd kept sane and made some good out of all the bad. He'd become a living legend in US prison history. Sure he killed a screw, but thirty years in the hole was not long enough for him and they wanted more. Bear in mind that he's now knocking on in age. After six years in the Alcatraz hole they then moved him to the hospital wing, where he spent the next eleven years. All believed he would die there, and no doubt he believed that too. Then in 1959 he left Alcatraz a very old man to go to Springfield Medical Centre in Missouri. He survived till 21 November 1963, dying at the ripe old age of seventy-three. He'd spent fifty-four years in prison. For me, I think it's a tragic story. But it's one of many from that era. It's why they made so many films of these legends. So next time you hear about "The Birdman of Alcatraz" you can say, "Yeah, he was the Birdman but he had no birds in Alcatraz." Really it should have been "The Birdman of Leavenworth". Well, now you know the story. This is one Birdman who never flew the nest. He actually died the day the screw died.

Let's be honest with ourselves, those manic sex-romping years are long gone (for us oldies). Imagine even trying to live it now! You couldn't last a week. You'd burn out in no time. Your dick would get you down. Fannies dry up. Tits sag. Teeth fall out.

How the fuck do people stay married for forty, fifty, even sixty years? How do they do it? Is it love or is it more a weakness? Nag, nag, nag. It's like a prison. It's not a real life is it? Where have you been? What time is this? Who do you think you are? Do the garden. Clean the car. Don't wear that. Do this. Do that. Gimme all your money. Does my bum look big in this? Honey, your arse looks like a hippo. Yap, yap, yap. Bunny, bunny, bunny. Nag, nag, nag. Pass the aspirin.

How does a man remain a man living like that? Is it love? What is love? I believe marriage is a form of torture! I really do. You've gotta be a nutcase to survive it! I also believe a man becomes broken, weak and manipulated. It ends up like a mother/son relationship. You become the boy all over again. That sweet, hot, wet, juicy pussy actually becomes your soul; a fucking big black tunnel of darkness. Crazy, eh? Loonyology at its best.

Enjoy the teenage years, coz that era soon flies by. No sooner are you shooting your load than you're shitting in a colostomy bag! Hey, don't old folk smell? Stale piss, B.O., smelly feet, bad breath and they fart a lot. They creak when they move, their hair's white and their skin's flaky and flabby and their eyesight's not good. The pussy is like a dried-up fig and the dick shrivels to a maggot. Fuck me, it's horrible! And then there's some nasty nurse giving you a slap to behave and if you're extra unlucky you end up with a Dr Shipman! How mad is that for an ending?

I'll say now to all you old folk: don't die a shell; if you're gonna go, then go out in style. Go get a nice hot, wet, pussy and pay her to bring a dream ending. Die with your heart and dick pumping some love. Or if you're an old woman, go get a young stud. Have one final orgasm of life. Scream the house down. Spend all your savings. Go out happy. Fuck the lumbago away. Shag the arthritis away. Enjoy the dream all over again. At the very worst you can always act it or die with a "69" – a sweet, hot pussy in your face or a big stiff cock in your mouth. Housey-housey – bingo!

Fucking sex toys – do me a favour. I am the sex toy and this is how it is with us birdmen. We are starved of sex, hungry like a loon, and then we fly out and become greedy. What do you expect? We are hungry men, desperate for a fuck, and the ladies love us. It's true. Line me up with a dozen normal men and I guarantee that if we were all bollock naked with hard-ons the ladies will choose me. Even if some are in their thirties they'll still choose me. Why? It's simple. The ladies love a bit of rough and I'm the roughest diamond you'll ever get hold of. The only problem is, you could never keep me. I'm unkeepable. I soon get bored, fed up and need some action, some excitement.

Let me explain. If I was on a seaside pier and a big fish was swimming below – let's say a shark or a whale – and hundreds of people were looking, I'd dive in, just to say I did it. Now that's a rare gift. If the fish don't eat me then it's a story; historic; something to be remembered for.

There was one black lunatic in Broadmoor who had a cock on him like a hosepipe and he loved showing it off too. He liked to walk down the corridor with it hanging out of his dressing gown. It was fucking gigantic – terrifying. It almost touched his knees. It swung like a giant pendulum and he always had that sick smirk and those beady eyes saying: cop a load of this. He got on my nerves in the end, so I hit him with the fire extinguisher. Flash bastard. I hate flash cunts. A laugh's a laugh, but every day he did that. Well, it soon stopped after I cracked him. Fucking lunatic. Blimey, I've some breaking news: I've just farted. I've gassed my cell out!

Talking of farts, that's what Fielding done when I cut him down the boat in Wandsworth in 1977. Fucking rat. He fucked my escape up. I was doing well on it. I had six bricks out of the back of my cell wall. They were crumbling out and that prick grassed me. That cost me 180 days' remission with fifty-six days' solitary: no bed, no canteen and a fucking good kicking to go with it. That's how it was in them days. It's all part and parcel of life inside. Grasses have been around since day one. These weak, gutless Jesus people. Fielding actually believed he'd got away with it. He thought I didn't know, but the daft bastard made one mistake. I clocked him at the spyhole in my door. My spyhole had a pinhole in it through which I could see light. I happened to notice no light so I rushed to the door and saw him walking away. Five minutes later the riot mob came rushing down the landing and my door crashed in. I was bang to rights: a fucking big hole in my wall, twenty feet of sheet-knotted rope, a steel chair bent as a grappling hook, and I had £100 and a black coat.

My feet never touched the floor all the way to the chokey block and I bounced off some walls on the way there. Fielding done me up like a kipper. Three months later I hid behind a cell door and cut the rat from his left eye to his jawline: "Stripe". So every time he looks in a mirror he will be reminded that he's a filthy grass. That's thirty-one years ago but he's still the grass. I've always said a grass is born a grass. You don't wake up one morning and say, "Oh, I think I'll be a grass today." It don't happen like that. You're always a grass.

Some may hold it back in the good times, but it always slips out. Some are that stupid they even grass themselves up. How mental is that?

I'll always remember Fielding's face the second he knew it was bang on him: the "Oh God please help me" look. Well, he will tell you himself that there is no God's help in hell. That prick destroyed a brilliant escape plot. In the war he would have been shot as a traitor. You may laugh and say that's a bit extreme. Well, it is extreme, as my freedom was stolen from me.

I remember once in Wandsworth block when it used to be down on H1. Our exercise yard used to be at the back of the laundry. Four screws used to take me on my own and stand in a circle whilst I walked round. One day a lorry come up. Bear in mind that there's a fence and a wall. A security screw and a dog handler opened the gate in the fence. That was it for me. I made a run for the lorry. I only had seconds, but it was worth a try. I jumped on the bonnet of the lorry, and as I went to scale up it a screw was on my legs. All hell broke out. I kicked, punched and nutted for my life. All four were on me with sticks, and even the other two joined in with the dog. By the time I got back to my cell my clothes were drenched in blood. My head had swelled up like a melon! The things we do to go home! I was very spontaneous in them days. I just acted on impulse.

That's how it was with me. If the gate of opportunity arises, then jump at it. Fuck the consequences, coz if you don't act on it you may live to regret it. It's like walking down a street and you see a security van pull up outside a bank and a hatch opens and two bags of loot are slung out. There's just you, one guard and two bags of loot. What do you do?

Years ago I'd have chinned the guard and done a runner with the two bags. I'd have been a mug not to! Now I've no need to do that, but then I wouldn't have hesitated. It's a golden opportunity that 99 per cent of guys only dream of taking. They dream their boring lives away. Me, I'm what you call an opportunist. I'm just born lucky or unlucky, whatever side of the wall I'm on. It's a prisoner's duty to escape isn't it? I'm not so sure nowadays. Maybe it's just old age and the thought of forever being on the run. I guess I prefer to "walk out" the right way, simply as my crime days are well over.

Believe me now, you can't relate to my world. It's fucking crazy, inhabited by crazy people, and I love 'em all. I've grown up with loonyology. It's in my blood, in my brain. I eat it, shit it, sleep it and I'm in control of it. Nothing or nobody can ever drive me over the edge again. I'm now the driver on this journey. You have to trust me. So put your tongue into my mouth in the dark. Will I or won't I? Trust me . . .

Right now my last seven years have been closed visits. I've not had a hug for over seven years. I actually feel dehumanized. I probably am. I no longer feel human. I feel different, not the same. Bear in mind that I'm forever in isolated conditions. Hey, people shout about human rights, well let me tell you something: human fucking rights don't exist for Bronson. I'll tell you now. I don't have animal rights let alone human rights. It's a fact.

I'm a born poet but yet to be discovered. I'm a philosopher but silent within. The late Lord Longford told me I'm a genius. How? Why? Don't ask me. I don't know. I'm an artist. I'm an author. Me. So how the hell does my label stick to me like shit to a blanket? Somebody tell me before the hearse arrives. Tell me before my bones crumble. For God's sake fucking put me out of my misery.

WALKING ALONG THE EDGE
A tightrope
No net
No harness
Just you and the drop
The bottomless hole
Black as the night
No stars, no moon
Only shadows
Have you ever been there
Well?! Have you?
Have you felt that sweat drip down your spine
The stinging of the eyes
The tremble of the lips
That's looking at hell
You can smell it
You can taste it
It's in your veins

The big rush
Like a volcano in your heart
Just waiting
Throbbing
Pulsating
Bubbling away
Have you been there?
Come on . . . tell me
If you're afraid to say then whisper
You're safe with me
Trust me
I'm one guy you can trust
I know how it is
I've lived on the edge all my life
A fingertip job
Hanging on, holding on for the hell of it
Laughing all the fucking way
I've laughed so hard I've shit myself
It's crazy
Everything is so fucked up
It's unreal
A giant circus
Forever on the road
I can't get off
Of course I tried
Many times
It don't work
It's in your blood
You are what you are
Accept it
The sooner you accept yourself
The sooner you laugh
Tears turn to laughter
Fear turns to pleasure
Pain becomes a thrill
Join the circus
The Bronson Loonyology Tour
Grab a midget

And throw him as far as you can
Yippeeeeeeeee!
Look at the little fucker fly
Look at the bearded lady
The lizard man
The two-headed dog
We love 'em all
I mean them all
Monsters in human form
Men and women from the unknown
We loved the Elephant Man
We love an ugly bastard
Don't you?
Political correctness
Kiss my arse
You fucking wimps
Keep away from the tents
It's not for wankers
Seeing is believing
Believe or fuck off
Faith and hope and ugliness
Bring it on
Wicked
Pukka
Magical
It's my old woman all over again
The Queen of Tarts
The local bike
Don't forget to pay the bitch
No freebies
And wipe your shoes before you go in
And don't wipe your dick on my towel
Why?
Coz I'll rip your head off
That's why
So what's it gonna be, buddy?
My way or your way
Sheep or lion

Butterfly or maggot?
Make up your mind, you sad bastard
It's your life
Your journey
Your crash
It's not if . . . it's when
But you're gonna crash
We all crash in the end
One way or the other
Fast or slow
It don't make no odds
Your time will come
Until it does
Go kick some butt
Kick it black and blue
Keep on kicking till you die
Die kicking
Kick it till the light goes out
Smash your way out of this ugly world
Don't crawl out, OKAY?!

DAVE "BOY" GREEN
(UK)

Former British and European Welterweight Boxing Champion

Introducing . . . Dave "Boy" Green

THIS IS THE first of two contrasting interviews by writer, actor, martial arts expert and former doorman Jamie O'Keefe. An undeniably hard man himself, in this interview Jamie talks to British and European Welterweight Boxing Champion Dave "Boy" Green about what really makes a tough man tough.

David Robert Green was born on 2 June 1953 in a small fenland town called Chatteris in Cambridgeshire, eastern England. He took up boxing in 1967, joined the Chatteris Amateur Boxing Club, and in 1969 won the National Federation of Boys' Clubs championship. Dave trained under the watchful eye of Arthur Binder who had also taught Eric Boon, another famous local boxer. Before Dave turned professional in 1974, he'd had 105 amateur fights and won about eighty-two.

As a professional boxer, under the guidance of his manager Andy Smith, Dave won the British Light Welterweight championship against Joey "The Jab" Singleton of Liverpool on 1 June 1976. A few months later, on 7 December 1976, Dave also won the European Light Welterweight championship. Three months later at Wembley, as a final eliminator to challenge for the WBC (World Boxing Council) title, Dave "Boy" Green fought former WBC World Champion John H. Stracey and won, earning Dave a shot at the WBC title.

Dave's first WBC welterweight bout was on 14 June 1977 at

Wembley against Carlos Palomino of Los Angeles. "I was winning the fight right up to the tenth round when my eye closed up and he knocked me out in the eleventh. Full credit to Palomino, it just shows you what world champions are made of," remarked a humble Dave. It was the first time Dave "Boy" Green had been floored as a professional.

Andy Smith got Dave another fight for the world title against Sugar Ray Leonard on 31 March 1980 in Maryland, USA. He was knocked out in the fourth round and respectfully says of Sugar Ray; "That man was the best man I have ever seen in my life. I honestly believe that even if I had trained for twenty-five years I would have never beaten him."

Dave "Boy" Green's final bout was on November 1981 at the Royal Albert Hall against New York-based Reg Ford, a one-time sparring partner to Thomas Hearns. Smith retired Dave in the fifth round with cuts and closing left eye. It was the correct decision to end Dave Green's formidable career as one of Britain's most popular and exciting fighters.

Dave still lives Chatteris, runs a successful business, takes part in charity golf events and is a respected member of the local community. His success can be summed up by Sugar Ray Leonard: "Dave was a brave fighting man who never gave less than 100 per cent whenever he put the gloves on. He is a warm human being who does tremendous work for charity, and I'm thrilled he has made such a success in business."

The reason for including two Jamie O'Keefe interviews in this book is to show the complete contrast in beliefs, thoughts and philosophies between a trained and professional boxer, who is not a criminal and has never been to prison, and, later in the book, a champion bare-knuckle street-fighter who has served many years inside. In their professions both are, unquestionably, some of the hardest and toughest men on the planet, but for each toughness has manifested itself in completely different and contrasting ways.

A CHAMPION
By Jamie O'Keefe

Jamie: Dave, we have known each other for over fifteen years now. We also worked for a year together on a project, giving us plenty of time to get to know each other. At the time, we were both proficient in our own fighting arts. Yours being boxing and myself with martial arts yet even then when things became a little strained or we clashed on things, neither of us ever resorted to physical solutions or attempted to use our art to resolve things. For me personally, I was in awe of you and your achievements in boxing and had bundles of respect for you but I don't think you ever recognized it as such. From my perspective, you were bit of a tough guy who had a heart of gold. I truly admired you. Many people took to you as their boxing hero and would certainly regard you a tough guy. What are your thoughts on that?

Dave G: Well as you say, at the time you knew more of me due to the TV coverage than I did of you as a martial artist but the word that really comes to mind is respect! And that's what it's all really about. You knew that I worked very, very, hard to get where I got and the word respect is what it's all really about.

Jamie: Do you feel that some people are naturally more respectful than others though, because there are a lot of disrespectful people around.

Dave G: Oh yeah! There is definitely. But I think that people respect you for different things. If you're in a pop group and have a hit, some people respect you for that. If you are a boxer and make it to the top, some people respect you for that too. If you're a politician some people respect you for that. It's all down to the effort you put into something that makes people respect you for that particular thing.

Jamie: Do you think that discussing a problem is much better than resorting to violence? Because you fought Sugar Ray Leonard and many other boxers, over 105 amateur and forty-one professional fights, so being physical and using your fists to solve a problem would have come easy.

Dave G: Yeah, but that's not the answer. It never finishes there does it! It just goes further and further and adds more people into the world of violence, including your family, etc.

Jamie: So you much prefer the discussion approach to the fighting approach!

Dave G: Absolutely! Every time.

Jamie: If I were to ask you what you feel makes tough guys tough, what would your answer be?

Dave G: Well to me, I think you're born with it. It's a mental attitude, it's determination, you're either tough or you're not tough. I do think it helps, as well, coming from a rough background, although I'm an exception to the rule. I did not live in a rough area, my parents always loved me but you find that a lot of rough fellows come from rough upbringing.

Jamie: But that wasn't the case for you?

Dave G: Not at all. My father had a farm; he was a farmer. I think I just had the determination to get to the top.

Jamie: Do you think you would have succeeded in anything that you went into?

Dave G: Well my manager Andy Smith said to me that I should go into business when I finished boxing and he was right. I've proved again that I can be successful. I have a company and factory that has been distributing to all the major banks since I left the ring, I have six houses, timeshares in Florida, a couple of Cash Converter stores, stocks and shares, and so on. I'm not saying this to be flash. I'm just trying to make the point that it was in me to succeed in whatever I went into.

Jamie: Your success is not that common for retired boxers, is it?

Dave G: Definitely not. In fact it's not that common for sports people in general. When I turned professional and got married I had absolutely nothing! All my money came afterwards. I had a very good manager who looked after me and made sure I looked after my money and taught me the right ways to do it. I think whatever you do in life, you need somebody above you to look after you and make sure you do the right things. I was very lucky in that aspect because Andy Smith was like a father figure to me. He made me realize that boxing only goes on for so long, maybe six, eight to ten years. Mine was only seven years but he made me realize that there is a lot of living to be done afterwards and I'm pleased I took his advice.

Jamie: Yeah, I suppose you could have ignored his advice and stayed in boxing and ended up with nothing.

Dave G: Absolutely, that's why he was such a good manager. I had won two British titles, two European titles and fought twice for the world championship and I was never going to be in the position to fight for a world title again so I took his advice and got out and did something else while I could.

Jamie: So to put it into a nutshell, you were born with that ability, and didn't go and actually learn how to be tough.

Dave G: No, I don't think so. I've always had it in me. I used to play a lot of football, then progressed to boxing, but was always aggressive with everything I went into. I would always put 120 per cent into everything I did, no matter what it was I was doing. It's determination.

Jamie: I believe that anyone can go to a class and learn the physical, psycho motor skills, the physical movements, like taking a young lad through the movements of boxing, karate, etc. Also, I believe you can teach them how to think. For example, if a certain type of punch is thrown to bob, weave, duck, whatever. You can teach them to do certain combination of punches which draws on the cognitive thinking side like, but I do not feel that you can learn the feelings, attitudes, emotions, and values that you get from affective learning, which I believe can only come from your upbringing and life's experiences, making you what you are, be it tough or soft, bully or victim, etc. What is your view on this?

Dave G: I think you're born with it. You're either an aggressive person, or have the will to win, toughness, call it what you want. You just can't put that into someone; you've either got it or you've not got it.

Jamie: Toughness sounds a silly word but it's convenient to use for the purpose of my research.

Dave G: Yeah, but I understand what you're trying to say. Toughness comes in many different ways.

Jamie: Of course, but many people have watched people like yourself, Mo Hussein, Terry Marsh, etc. in the ring and want to be like that. They want to know what makes you that tough.

Dave G: I'm not tough in the world. I'm just as friendly as anybody else in real life. But when I put a pair of gloves on and got in that ring, my personality changed.

Jamie: That's the same thing Mo Hussein said to me when I approached him for an interview; "I'm not tough." It appears that all the guys that are tough in their own arena are also very modest and humble and try to play down their aggressive, tougher side. If I was the most passive person on this planet, afraid of my own shadow, could I be trained and converted into a tough guy, afraid of no one?

Dave G: Again I would say no! You're born with it, you just can't teach people to be tough.

Jamie: You're well known for your boxing ability and obviously you have had exposure to boxers of all levels. Does a boxing title mean someone is tough? If not, what does it represent?

Dave G: It represents many different things to me. It means some people are very skilful, some have got loads of heart, a person like myself has lots of determination but it doesn't mean that they are tough. I've met some great fighters who are very skilful but they are not tough.

Jamie: Could you put all the tough guys you know of into any sort of category, i.e. are they mostly from the Forces, or mostly from broken homes, etc.?

Dave G: No, not really, because I come from a good family. I'm not saying that my father had loads of money, but he was comfortable. I think, generally, tough people come from rough areas like Liverpool, Newcastle, the East End of London, places where things are generally tougher. But there are always odd people like myself who are successful or tough from other areas.

Jamie: If, as you say, you cannot make somebody tough, is it all to do with how you're brought up? What is the nearest you can get them to what you consider as being tough?

Dave G: You can't make anybody tough, you have either got it or you haven't. That's my own personal opinion on it.

Jamie: As a young lad I had a pal, who was a tough and brilliant street fighter who was rarely defeated. I met him fifteen years later and he was a shadow of his former self, practically flinching if anyone came near him in a threatening manner. It was like his spirit had been broken. Do you think a tough guy can be made to be un-tough?

Dave G: No, I just think it's approach and a different attitude to life. He was a tough little guy who doesn't think it means anything to be tough now.

Jamie: What, like he has matured?

Dave G: That's it, he's matured. When he was growing up he probably thought he had to be tough to be noticed, but now it's no longer important to him. You're not going to believe this but when I was at junior school, the best fighter in our year was a girl; it certainly wasn't me. She was the toughest one in our year.

Jamie: Do you think it is possible to sense that someone is tough just from the way they carry themselves?

Dave G: No, not really. I think people do try and act tough but you just can't tell. I've seen ordinary fellows who are bloody hard as nails. You just can't tell.

Jamie: You don't think you can just sense it when someone walks into a room?

Dave G: No! Because I've seen some great boxers who have won championships who don't even look tough at all.

Jamie: Is it possible to act tough without really being tough?

Dave G: Yeah! Anybody can act tough, can't they? It's easy to act tough, but it's about being able to handle yourself at the end of the day.

Jamie: Most of us have had to do it sometime in our life, right back to school days, to stop ourselves getting beaten up.

Dave G: That's right, and we don't want to take that chance of fighting in case we lose so we act tough, hoping that this will win the fight without fighting.

Jamie: I think this is a major time in our lives, no matter what age we are, that we must cross the barrier of acting tough to actually having that fight and taking our first step towards being tough.

Dave G: Absolutely, but even if you have that first fight, be it in the ring or the street, it's the one that has toughness inbred within them that will go on to be tough whether they win the first fight or not.

Jamie: How would you deal with a tough guy who is in your face, prompting you to kick off with him? Have you ever had that situation?

Dave G: I've had it a couple of times even when I had my title in boxing. My message to everybody is run like hell, get out the way. As I've always said, if you're in a pub and someone wants to fight you, there's no promoter there to give you money afterwards. You could end up getting a good hiding for nothing. So you might as well just get away. There are plenty more pubs to drink in.

Jamie: We touched on this next question earlier regarding the girl in your junior school, with regards to the toughness of male and female. Would you be happy to let women take the place of men on the front-line of pubs and clubs?

Dave G: I don't think so. I believe it's men for some jobs and ladies for other jobs. You can't do that.

Jamie: Some would regard that as bit of a sexist viewpoint.

Dave G: No, no. I mean, like boxing, I've seen the ladies boxing in Las Vegas. It's terrible, horrible. You see a lovely pretty girl with a bleeding nose, to me it's just unbelievable, I don't believe in it at all. What do you think?

Jamie: Well morally, I would not feel comfortable sitting in a factory packing bullets while the women were out there fighting in the front-line.

Dave G: How can anyone sit indoors looking after the kids while the wife is out earning the living as a professional boxer? It just doesn't sound right, does it? Mind you, we could be better looking then, ha!

Jamie: I don't think that would help us, though. I think we're beyond saving!

Dave G: I don't think many women would want to carry broken noses around. Also, even in your days as a nightclub doorman, it was naturally a male-dominated profession and it just wouldn't have looked right having a woman on the door.

Jamie: Why?

Dave G: Because you want to feel you're secure. You're better off with a six-foot-four chap standing there and ready to deal with any problems, who can sort it out very quickly.

Jamie: So are you saying that men only feel secure being looked after by other men who look tough.

Dave G: Absolutely.

Jamie: What do you feel the role of boxing has in making tough guys tough?

Dave G: Well, it's very difficult to say. I just think it's dedication, ability, training, you've got to believe in yourself. I just can't really pinpoint one thing. It's many things but for me, I've got to say, before I fought Carlos Palomino for the world championship, which was my twenty-fifth fight, having been unbeaten twenty-four times I really believed I was unbeatable. But when you do get beat, it takes something away from you. It's no different to being in the street. It just takes something away from you. Did you ever experience that?

Jamie: Yeah, I must admit. As a young black belt I thought I was unbeatable in the street. Whether through luck or skill I was winning fights with ease, but the biggest awakening I had was when one guy pulverized me. He didn't give a toss as to what belt I was. He kicked my arse. It was the biggest favour anyone had done for me. I changed the way in which I train from that day on. The sad thing, though, was that up until that day I loved karate but losing that fight took that away from me. I have never enjoyed the art since. Silly really, because it wasn't karate that lost the fight, it was me. Same as it was you that were beaten on your twenty-fifth fight and not the fault of boxing.

Dave G: I think it proves to everybody that you never stop learning. That's what it's about.

Jamie: When you first took me to your house, I saw a picture on your living room wall of Sugar Ray Leonard. You had so much respect for him and will never be able to forget your fight with him. Do you regard him as being tough?

Dave G: I regard him as being a complete boxer, really. He could fight, he could box, he could move, he was a very intelligent fellow. I think he's perhaps the nearest we have ever been to the most complete fighter in the world. Not because he beat me. Everybody thinks I'm biased, but I thought that Muhammad Ali was the greatest fighter ever. But I regarded Ali as lacking one thing, the big punch. Ali was not a big puncher at all. He beat people by a combination of punches but Sugar Ray could do everything that Ali could do, but he could punch as well. That's why I think I have so much respect for him. I also think it was very nice of him to have respect for myself to come over to England to see me. I think that's what you get in sportsmanship, really, in all sports.

Jamie: But even with all you've said about Sugar Ray Leonard, you still haven't answered my question. Do you think he is tough?

Dave G: Oh! I think he's tough. I think he's tough, definitely tough. Even though [Roberto] Duran beat him on points, in the next fight he made Duran look like a bit averse with Duran retiring in round five.

Jamie: I can also remember a time around twelve years ago when you were watching videotapes of Sugar Ray. I was watching videos of you and your son was watching videotapes of me doing my martial arts. Do you think that toughness is more in the eye of the beholder rather than the holder, meaning that we always regard others as being tough rather than ourselves?

Dave G: I still have those tapes; the twins watch them now. Yes, I do think toughness is seen more in the eye of the beholder. I often say, "Christ, he's a bloody tough guy" when talking about someone that is not connected to fighting in any shape or form. Then someone will say to me, "You've got to be joking, you're twice as tough as him," but we don't see it in ourselves, do we? We definitely see it more in other people.

Jamie: I can remember once sitting in your Mercedes waiting for you, when a group of lads came over to get a glimpse of you. Although you weren't there, they spotted your number plate DAV 8OY, which looked like DAV BOY (Dave Boy). We began chatting and it took me a while to convince them that I was not a boxer. They decided that I must be an East End gangster purely because of the way I speak and look, and that I must be your driver. I mention this because I know many people associate toughness with areas like the East End, Glasgow, and so on, and many boxing fans actually thought that you were from the East End, which you're not. Do you think that areas or accents have any bearing or connection with being tough?

Dave G: I've still got the personalized plate but the Merc's gone. I've had one or two Mercs since then. As for accents, I do definitely. If someone comes from Glasgow and you hear that Glaswegian accent, you think Christ, he's from Glasgow. I had the greatest time of my life in Glasgow; I came back in stitches. Ha! But seriously, the East End has a reputation for being hard, Glasgow, Liverpool, and you get a lot of good fighters from each of these places. I am just a one-off from the Fens but tough within my art as you are with your martial arts, but you also have the East End accent to go with it. My accent doesn't conjure up the image of toughness. So I would say that accents do have a connection with toughness but more so because you are exposed to many people who are tough that have the same regional accents. I would say toughness is in you, regardless of your accent, but some accents make you less likely to becoming a target for a bully. I certainly think that the East End accent is a tough accent.

Jamie: Can you be tough and still be nice?

Dave G: Look at Brian Jacks! I did the TV show *Superstars* with him about ten times and what a lovely guy he is, but boy is he tough – but a very nice man. There's different ways of being tough. When he was fifteen his father sent him to Japan to train. He couldn't speak a word of Japanese and that toughened him up as well. What a tough man. He stayed out there for two years to learn the business properly. In fact, I played golf with him last week. I was also chatting to Glen Murphy from the TV show *London's Burning*. He's a mate of yours, isn't he?

Jamie: Yeah, I know Glen. His dad ran a pub called the Bridgehouse in Canning Town, East London where we all grew up. Glen went into boxing and I went into martial arts. Later on he came to train with me along with Terry Marsh to gain their black belts in my New Breed training system. Glen had to give up due to a back injury and Terry could not get leave from Brixton prison to come and train, so both came to a natural end. Dave, thanks for answering my questions.

Dave G: You're welcome!

JOHN BRAWN (IRELAND)

Ireland's Leading Self-Defence Instructor

Introducing . . . John Brawn

BORN IN 1961, John Brawn grew up in Westport, County Mayo, Ireland, where he still lives, and is Ireland's leading self-defence instructor and recognized internationally as an expert in both self-defence and security. Humble, polite, respectful and a father of two, John is also undeniably one of the toughest men in the country.

Having started his martial-arts training in the early 1980s, John was appointed as a coach with the Irish Amateur Boxing Association in 1989 and three years later became a black belt in karate Kyokushinkai. In 1993 he became an instructor with the Association and Register of Self Protection Instructors. In 1995 he reached second dan black belt with the Irish Karate Kyokushinkai and started his successful security company providing security and close protection (bodyguard) services, as well as teaching practical self-defence and self-protection techniques worldwide. That same year he earned his Certificate of Completion in Advanced Learning Technologies for Close Combat and became an instructor with the US-based Rape Awareness and Prevention Organization.

John is currently the Irish director for several of the world's most advanced self-defence and protection techniques such as the Blue Maxx and Bulletman. He is also an exponent of kettlebell techniques of fitness and organizes regular seminars in Ireland and worldwide.

Living up to his surname, this chapter – written specially for this book by Irish writer Barbara Preston – is part biography of John

Brawn, Ireland's toughest man, and part anecdotal tales from his sixteen years working the doors.

A HARD MAN IN A QUIET COUNTRY
By Barbara Preston

There are many excellent, tough security professionals, martial arts experts and instructors out there; so what qualifies John Brawn to be included in a book about hard men? A quietly spoken man with a shy smile, John is modest and self-effacing about his abilities, but says that when it comes to security and protection "the smile sucks them in and then the explosion happens". It isn't looking or acting tough that's important, it's knowing how and when to *be* hard that matters.

The small town of Westport on the shore of Clew Bay, County Mayo, produces more than its fair share of Ireland's poets, artists and musicians, but it's not the kind of place where you'd expect to find one of the hardest men in the country – but John Brawn is exactly that. Recognized worldwide as an expert in both self-defence and security work, Geoff Thompson (award-winning writer and martial-arts expert) describes John as "one of the most powerful strikers and experienced martial artists I have ever had the pleasure to work with".

John Brawn grew up in the 1970s, attending the local Christian Brothers' school. Those were the days when heavy-handed teachers and playground bullying were the norm and John wasn't one of the bigger boys in his class. Around the age of twelve he decided that he needed to learn to take care of himself. With little opportunity to join a club, he got some Bruce Lee videos and some weights, hung a punch bag in the shed and started to train. It didn't take long to work out that he needed a more methodical approach to reach his goal of being good at self-defence so he bought a book on karate and began his life-long love of martial arts.

After a couple of years training on his own John wanted more. There was no karate club in the town so he joined the (now famous) local boxing club, St Anne's, to further his training. He says he was a mediocre boxer without the psychological edge to do well in tournaments. He would lose bouts on split decisions, or find himself matched against the eventual championship winner, but John is proud of the fact that he was never knocked out in a championship and only hit the canvas once! He did win the title of Best Boxer in one tournament, though.

Boxing did improve his physical fitness and ability to look after himself, and, more importantly, helped enormously with his self-confidence because during his teens he needed to grow up fast. His father died when he was only fourteen and, being the eldest of five children, he had to help his mother and work in the family butcher's shop. He continued his training when he went to college in Dublin for a year but his boxing career came to an end at the age of twenty-five when he had his appendix removed. By the time he had recovered from the surgery, the boxing club was on summer break so John joined the newly formed Shotokan karate club in the town and never boxed again. From then on martial arts were to become the cornerstone of his life.

In 1987 the Westport Kyokushin karate club was founded – the first Irish Karate Kyokushinkai (IKK) club outside of the capital – and John was quick to join. He had made contact with (now) Shihan Kevin Callan of the IKK Dublin branch, who came down with some of the other members to help with training. John was delighted to be able to train in full-contact karate at last and, at the end of the first year, got his second kyu, later going on to become one of the first Kyokushin karate black belts outside Dublin along with his friends James O'Malley and Ger Dawson. Local interest in karate was growing and John and his two friends were not only training hard but teaching big groups of youngsters as well. In 1992 John set up dojos in Clifden and Letterfrack (County Galway), and he, James and Ger were also running successful summer camps in the Westport area and Connemara.

Brawn ran the family business until he was thirty, but after fifteen years he decided it was time to break out on his own. To earn a living he began to work on the doors of local pubs and clubs. He was getting more and more offers of door work and this led to him setting up his own security company – JB Security. He was regularly covering at least three nightclubs and seven pubs as well as festivals and race meetings. A year after getting his black belt, John became an instructor with the Association and Register of Self Protection Instructors and, besides teaching IKK, started training as well as employing doormen. In those years there was no formal training of any kind for the doors so he started his own programme and began giving courses on door security.

After reading Geoff Thompson's book, *Watch My Back*, John realized that he had found the next step forward to develop his skills for working in the security industry. He travelled to England and over the course of a few years trained with Geoff Thompson and Peter Consterdine, joining the British Combat Association and even bringing Geoff and Peter over to Ireland to train the guys he was working with. John also studied close-quarter combat techniques with Marcus Wynne and Dennis Martin, which he says was a life-changing experiencing for him: "In one day I learned more than I had in over twenty years of traditional martial arts. He was using NLP (Neuro Linguistic Programming) to instil the techniques and I came away with a high level of skill. It was fantastic. There was a lot of edged weapons training and we were starting to come up against this more and more on the door so the relevancy was very high."

The practical self-defence training made all the difference on the doors and his security company became highly regarded for its professionalism and service.

During the 1990s John completed about thirty courses in Britain, including Peter Consterdine's Body Guarding Course, as well as his driving and surveillance courses, and Close Quarters Battle Training with Dennis Martin. Brawn incorporated all that he learned in practical self-defence into his work and his training courses for doormen. Currently, as well as the security training, John runs fitness and kick-boxing classes, gives private self-defence and kettlebell training, and has made three DVDs on power-punching.

Years of dedication and training have made him highly skilled and incredibly tough. Here's a day in the life of the Irish hard man.

The Longest Day

In John Brawn's sixteen-year career as a doorman, one day stands out as the perfect illustration of his stature as one of the hardest men in Ireland.

The day started off with a trip to the next county to give a karate demonstration at the dojo he had set up. It was a great success and went down really well with the spectators. John was on top form and upped his game to break two one-inch roof tiles with a single punch. However, despite his conditioned knuckles, he came away from the event with an injured, swollen hand and had only a few hours before he was on duty at a well-known nightclub.

As Brawn arrived at the venue for work, he saw two guys arguing with one of his team on the door. To have people causing trouble early on in the night wasn't unusual so John quickly manoeuvred himself past the men, noticing that one of them was already blind drunk and the other, was "nasty drunk". As he was now standing closer to them than his colleague, he started to talk to them, taking on the "good cop" role to try and diffuse the situation. Generally an effective technique to avoid trouble, this night it wasn't working. The two troublemakers still tried to push their way into the club, one using the body of his drunken mate almost as a riot shield. Both doormen were at a disadvantage where height was concerned and, thinking that John's "nice" approach was a sign of weakness, the more dangerous of the two men pushed his friend into John and started raining blows down on him. No more Mr Nice Guy! Brawn grabbed his attacker by the front of the hair, leaving the other man for his partner, and intended to move him round to the side of the building. A thirty-foot drop around the corner meant an instantaneous change of plan so John quickly slammed the man on to the ground and gave him three or four rapid punches to the head, with a chop to the meridian line on the back as the *coup de grâce* – the would-be tough guy "lost all interest in fighting after that", remembers John. Turning to help the other doorman, he saw that drunk number two was down but trying to get up. After such a start to the night John was in no mood to take anything from the second guy but, thankfully he says, his partner stopped him before he lost the plot altogether as he'd have "taken his head off!" The last the two doormen saw of the men was them crawling on their hands and knees twenty yards down the road and round a corner.

It was a quarter past eleven. John looked up and saw that there was a full moon and thought to himself, "This is going to be a long fucking night." He told the other doorman that it was going to be a "shit-house" and laid out the plan – Martin (not his real name) would man the inside door, John would stay outside, and they would watch one another's backs. The nightclub had hired only six doormen for the night (two of them Brawn describes as "toilet attendants" – likely to hide in the bathroom if a fight broke out!). Brawn would have brought more if he had known what the night had in store for them.

With the earlier karate demonstration keeping him busy, John had forgotten that in addition to the usual weekend revelries, the Irish soccer team had been playing that day and, unexpectedly, had lost to a much weaker team. This had meant that many of the punters out on the town had been in bad humour and, fuelled with drink, they were spoiling for a fight. Just to make matters worse, in a venue with a capacity of 650, complimentary passes had swelled the crowd to over 750 – basically, a recipe for trouble.

The club was filling up but the next thing John had to deal with was a couple coming up to him and asking him if he had seen a fight outside the club earlier. John said he hadn't but they were insistent, saying that two of their friends were in hospital after being badly "beaten up". As he was physically involved, Brawn could truthfully answer that he didn't "see" a fight but that only served to enrage the man, who started screaming abuse, calling Brawn every name under the sun. Before anything could kick off, the door of the club burst open and a brawling fight spilled out from inside. John excused himself (in very impolite terms) and said he had to get to work. The doormen pulled the fighters out of the entrance and dumped them out on the street where they quickly lost interest in fighting. Quickly, the team went back inside and were met with what Brawn describes as a "scene from the Somme". There was broken glass all over the floor, blood everywhere, people lay all round the place and there was an all-pervasive ugly mood in the air. And the night was only starting.

A man staggered towards John and Martin, blood streaming down his face from where he had been glassed in the toilets. He was taken to the first aid station for treatment and the team headed back into the mêlée to get those responsible and eject them from the club. From then on, until about three o'clock in the morning, Brawn spent the night fighting. He and his team were constantly moving through the crowd to where the latest fight had broken out, circling the protagonists, and then pushing, pulling and, if necessary, punching them through the room and outside. They worked in pairs, John and Martin targeting the ringleaders, watching each other's backs. Brawn reckons he punched more people in that one night than the rest of his career on the doors. "Anything that came into your zone you punched it . . . elbowed, kneed it, whatever way it was. It was a fight for survival," he recalls.

As the night drew to a close and the music was finishing, the crowd was still milling around on the glass-strewn dance-floor and finishing up their drinks at the bar counter and tables. Brawn was walking through the room, hoping that things would now quieten down, when he witnessed one of the worst acts of violence of the night. A man took a run at a girl and kicked her squarely between the legs, leaving her screaming in agony on the floor. John couldn't believe his eyes but went instantly into action. He grabbed the man in a headlock but, unfortunately, he was so slick with sweat that the hold didn't take. When one of his mates grabbed John's arm, the man got out of Brawn's grip and landed a head-butt on the side of his face. This is where all the training and experience came into play. Brawn wasn't going to take any chances so he changed to a trachea hold, gripping tightly along the nerve pathways so that his opponent had to stop struggling or lose his windpipe. The girl was still screaming in pain and Brawn was in no mood to be gentle. Following a swift head-butt, he started towards the main door, knocking and bumping the assailant against all the stationary furniture they passed. He got him as far as the entrance, slammed him against the door and then outside, where he gave him six more head-butts. As the man was sliding to the ground, lapsing into unconsciousness, another doorman had to stop John before he found himself up on a murder charge!

Then all hell broke loose at the door. Somehow the team had to get the doors shut, and get everyone else who was fighting out and keep them out. This wasn't easy because the door opened outwards which meant John had to lean out into a crowd that was punching, kicking and wrestling to grab the door and pull it closed. At the same time, the other doormen were pushing, punching and manhandling those fighting inside out through the same door. It was complete mayhem. At one stage Brawn remembers seeing something coming at him out of the corner of his eye. He instinctively ducked and felt a kick going along the side of his head. If he hadn't moved he would have been seriously injured or even knocked unconscious. That would have been disastrous because once he was down he would have been used as "a can of coke".

Finally, the door was closed with all the fighting now on the other side. Brawn turned round and lo and behold, there was the club manager! He didn't get a chance to say a word. The danger and tension of the night had Brawn incensed; feeling as if he was a foot off the floor with adrenaline, he lambasted the manager for overcrowding, lack of sufficient doormen to control the crowd and goodness knows what else. John says he didn't know what he looked like at that moment but he certainly felt like another person altogether.

The exhausted team then went into the club and surveyed the effect of the rolling maul that the night had turned into. There was an inch-and-a-half of glass covering the floor and so much blood that it might have been used as a slaughterhouse. Brawn could now feel the effects of the head-butts, punches and kicks he had received over the past four hours but at least the night was over. It dawned on him that he was lucky not to be one of those taken away by ambulance that night. This was one night the team had a drink together before heading home. It was the most violent night of John's life and he says the whole thing was a blur. He compares it to boxing in the ring. "When you are in a boxing match you don't know how well you've done or badly you've done, but when you look at the tape afterwards you realize you did a lot better than you thought," he says. "The four hours were like that." He never worked in any venue that was as violent as that one, with so much anger in the crowd from losing the football match. He and his team may have looked in bad shape but none had more than superficial injuries; in another town on the same night a doorman had to have twenty-two stitches to his face after he had been glassed by a well-known football fan.

As Brawn drove back to Westport, "feeling like an eighty-year-old", he swears he saw the Man in the Moon laughing at him!

After this incident, Brawn developed a zero tolerance policy when it came to running security at a venue. His company would be hired in to clean up clubs and pubs where violence was the norm and regular troublemakers needed to be removed. He insisted that once he was responsible for maintaining order, his rules must be applied. When a person was thrown out, they stayed out, barred for life. The last thing a doorman needs is to be walking through a crowd in poor lighting and someone with a grudge shoving a glass in his face! A few weeks afterwards, JB Security was working the same venue when Brawn noticed that the man who had kicked the girl was back in the club. He got his team together and walked out. Even if it meant losing business, the safety of his team was paramount. None of his staff was ever hospitalized when working for him.

Thankfully, not all nights on the doors are like that. There could be a thousand routine, quiet nights but every doorman has to expect the worst as it *will* happen and Brawn says that if you're not fit to do the job you will be seriously injured, or even killed. This is why Brawn is so insistent that doormen are trained properly, not just in the classroom to get a licence, but also in self-defence as well as combatives to counter the current trend of troublemakers carrying knives. Not just trained, but they also must keep up a fitness-training programme to make sure that they are ready for the bad nights.

JB Security was wound up in 2007. Brawn says he wouldn't work the doors in the overly PC world of legislation and red tape. Times have changed a lot since Brawn started working in security. Fights at clubs and other venues used to be sorted by the bouncers and nobody would dream of calling the police if they got a hiding for starting trouble. Now all doormen and security personnel have to be licensed and wear badges, and CCTV watches their every move. He has strong feelings about the lack of protection and proper training for doormen, who, if the official training course to get a licence is anything to go by, are expected to do nothing but try and talk their way out of trouble. As John says, "They might as well walk around with 'Target' on their back and someday a doorman will pay the ultimate price for that."

Brawn takes the training of doormen very seriously and runs special courses to pass on his skills and experience to them. He says that for street fighting you need to use everything you've got – elbows, knees, head-butts – and you have to perfect your techniques for the time you need to use them. You also need to build up strength for when you have to pull or push people out of the door and do anaerobic training, because fighting is an anaerobic activity.

Brawn would always try to calm down a situation by talking to potential troublemakers, and most of the time a composed, professional attitude is enough to keep a situation in hand. However, the "nice guy" routine won't always work and, if an assault on a customer or doorman occurs, it's time to get physical; control and restraint techniques, including the use of pressure points, are valuable skills to have when minimal force must be used to prevent being sued when irate punters sober up. Sometimes, though, serious fights do break out on the doors and the security staff are often the targets, so self-defence is as important, if not more so, than protecting the clients at venues. As John says, you have to be prepared to use the maximum force necessary to keep things under control and for that you need to build up a skill set and train hard. You also need to develop a mindset so that, faced with a violent opponent, you must not only make the right decisions but also be 100 per cent committed to following through.

John Brawn attributes much of his success to the Neuro Linguistics Programming he learned from Marcus Wynne. Not only does it help with physical training, it has also given him techniques that he uses to help prepare for action. He uses triggers, something like a ritual, which ensure that he is in a state of awareness before work and also help him to wind down afterwards.

Brawn doesn't think that it is necessary to project a hard image; he knows what he is capable of and when to go into action. Being hard, for him, is the ability to switch it on when necessary, even when not feeling great or carrying an injury. He has only been attacked once when not working the doors – when he had a leg in plaster from ankle to thigh and was using crutches. As he was manoeuvring on to a bar stool to have a quiet drink in his local, he felt a flying punch swing past his head. Thinking it was one of his mates having a bit of fun, he turned and realized that the man beside him was trying to coldcock him while he was in a vulnerable position. Brawn didn't hesitate – he hit him in the throat with a crutch and, while the man was choking, threw him out the door – on one leg! Hard or what?

"PISTOL" PETE ROLLACK (USA)

New York City Gang Member

Introducing . . . "Pistol" Pete Rollack

R ANDY RADIC TAKES a look at a period in the life of "Pistol" Pete Rollack, notorious because of his tendency to shoot first and ask questions later. One of America's most feared men, he was the leader of the formidable and incredibly violent Sex, Money, Murder (SMM) gang, which was at the heart of the gang culture in New York.

By the time he was just twenty-four years old, Peter Rollack had personally committed four murders and ordered two other murders. By 1994 his gang SMM had several thousand members, all of whom were heavily armed and involved in murder, robbery, heroin and cocaine use, possession and distribution, and dealing in firearms. They were undoubtedly one of the most feared and toughest gangs in New York at the time. In 2000, when Rollack was twenty-seven, he was sentenced to life in prison without parole for the murder of six people and drug-trafficking in three states. In addition to life, the judge also sentenced Rollack to a further 105 years in prison. If Rollack had not pleaded guilty at his trial, he would have been executed.

SEX, MONEY, MURDER
By Randy Radic

Soundview is a low-income residential neighbourhood located in the south-central section of the borough of the Bronx in New York City. Most of its population of 80,000 people, primarily

African-American and Hispanic, live below the poverty line and receive whatever public assistance they can get their hands on. Poverty, disease, drugs and violence are a way of life. In short, Soundview is hell on earth.

There's no hope and no way out.

During the 1960s, youth gangs became part and parcel of the landscape. The first and most famous gang was the Black Spades, originating in the Bronxdale Houses, a public housing project of twenty-eight, seven-storey buildings in Soundview. The Black Spades sprouted out of the Savage Seven and rapidly achieved renown. They dominated the area, controlling every housing project in the neighbourhood. Members of the Black Spades "bopped" through the streets, carrying boom boxes (ghetto blasters) on their shoulders, which blared music that eventually became known as "hip-hop". Through sheer barbarity, the Black Spades became the most feared gang in New York City. By 1978, the gang had mutated into the Zulu Nation, which was strongly rooted in African ancestry and not as brutal.

Sex, Money, Murder (SMM) came on the Soundview scene in 1987. SMM was one of the sets (gangs) of the New York Gang (NYG) Alliance, which was a loose coalition of African-American gangs. Because of an ongoing power struggle, where each gang wanted to be number-one, SMM flipped. They left the NYG Alliance and became a sanctioned set of the Bloods.

The Bloods started in 1993, when many of the leaders of the various African-American gangs were doing time on Riker Island's George Mochen Detention Center (GMDC). GMDC, which was also called C-73, was where problem inmates – those who were extremely violent – were segregated from the rest of the prison population. Which meant that GMDC resembled a war zone. Battle was being waged as the Latin Kings – a Hispanic gang – targeted the African-American gang members. To protect themselves, the African-American gangbangers banded together. They called themselves the United Blood Nation (UBN), which was a direct reference to their African heritage and the oneness of their blood. Once they were released from prison, the UBN leaders went back to their respective "hoods" in New York City, where they retained the Bloods name and began recruiting members.

Initiation into the Bloods involved a "Blood-in" ritual. Which meant the new member had to draw blood from a victim. This ritual usually took place during robberies, when the new member would viciously slash the cheek of his prey with a razor blade or knife.

To distinguish themselves from the Bloods of Los Angeles, the United Blood Nation adopted the official name of East Coast United Blood Nation. East Coast Bloods exert their identity by means of colours, clothing, symbols, tattoos, jewellery, graffiti, slang and hand signs. The colour of the Bloods is red. They prefer to wear athletic clothing, especially Starter brand jackets from the San Francisco 49ers, the Phillies and the Chicago Bulls. Their number is five, and is reflected in the five-pointed star. Blood gangbangers refer to each other as "Blood" or as "Dawg", and a dog-paw tattoo is favoured among them – three dots burned on to the member's shoulder by means of a cigarette. Blood gang members are called "soldiers", and these soldiers are highly committed and radically brutal.

At this time, Peter Rollack was the unchallenged leader of Sex, Money, Murder. Because of his tendency to shoot first and ask questions later, Rollack was nicknamed Pistol Pete. And usually, Pistol Pete didn't bother with the questions.

Under Pistol Pete's generalship SMM spread like a cancer to other locations. SMM found willing recruits in the South Bronx, Bedford-Stuyvesant, Brownsville and East New York. In no time at all, SMM soldiers numbered in the hundreds. So eager were black youths to join SMM that the gang soon had lines (local chapters) in Trenton, Newark and Camden, New Jersey, with others in Philadelphia and Baltimore. By 1994, SMM's soldiers numbered in the thousands. Each soldier was indoctrinated, swore everlasting allegiance and was heavily armed.

Some of the lines included: the Viewside Line, which was out of the Bronx Projects; the Hillside Line, out of the Castle Hill Projects in the Bronx; Killerville, which came of the Van Dyke Projects in Brownsville and Brooklyn; Murderville, which was in Paterson, New Jersey; the Omega Line, which hailed from Jersey City, New Jersey; Murder City Mafia, from Philadelphia, Pennsylvania; Paper Boys, from Trenton, New Jersey; and Slug Line, which also came from Philadelphia.

Each one of these lines, operating under the leadership of Peter Rollack, proudly traced their Blood roots and were "right", which meant they banged correctly. Correct banging involved murder, robbery, heroin and cocaine use, possession and distribution; and, of course, the carrying and use of firearms.

By the time he was twenty-four years old, Peter Rollack had personally committed four murders and arranged two other murders that took place in the Bronx. The two Bronx murders occurred on Thanksgiving Day in 1997. Rollack ordered the killings from his prison cell in North Carolina, where he was waiting to face federal narcotics charges: the dead men were two SMM members who were scheduled to testify against him. According to Rollack, "all snitches got to die".

The reason Pistol Pete was imprisoned in North Carolina went like this. In the early 1990s, he was really building a reputation for himself. SMM was going strong, making noise, getting noticed. Naturally, other heavy-hitters were attracted to his crew. One of those who joined up with Pistol Pete and SMM was Savon Codd, aka "Yaro Pack", who had a rep as a money man who could move a lot of weight. "Moving weight" was gang-slang for smuggling, distributing and selling drugs. When Yaro Pack joined SMM, things really started happening. Almost overnight, SMM became a major distributor of cocaine and crack cocaine.

Then in 1994, Yaro Pack and his associate David Gonzales huddled with Pistol Pete in the Bronx. Gonzales informed Pistol Pete they could "score some big-time cash" down in North Carolina. The demand for cocaine in North Carolina was "scandalous". All they had to do was move the coke down south. So Pistol Pete and his SMM crew began making trips to North Carolina in a leased Nissan Quest, which was packed to the gills with drugs. The trips were very, very lucrative. And Pistol Pete and his crew became "hood rich". The more coke they moved, they richer they got.

Pretty soon, SMM was transporting huge amounts of narcotics up and down the East Coast. Pistol Pete's drug empire was growing larger every day. He was the McDonald's of drugs. SMM was everywhere. And if they weren't there, they soon would be.

By the summer of 1994, SMM had become major players. They were an event all by themselves. Rock, who was a friend of Pete's back in the day, said, "When he was out there, dude was a million-aire when he was nineteen."

Pistol Pete wasn't only swift to shoot, he was also a quick-draw thinker. Sex, Money, Murder's business was transportation inten-sive, meaning it depended on cars to get the coke where it needed to be. Which gave Pete an idea. He took the letters SMM and added a C – SMMC. Then he formed a corporation that went by those four letters. SMMC, Inc. was a front company used to lease a fleet of luxury cars from a company in Pittsburgh. SMMC, Inc. quickly became the leasing company's bread and butter and it made it possible for SMMC to obtain cars by means of prepaid leases, which made everyone happy, because when a lease was paid upfront there were no background or credit checks to worry about. Simply drop a bundle of cash and drive the cars off the lot. Besides that, the leasing company camouflaged outright purchases of vehicles made by some members of the gang. By means of forged paperwork, the company made it look like these purchased cars had also been leased.

Whether the cars were leased or purchased outright, they all had stash boxes (secret, invisible compartments), which were used to transport drugs, money and guns. Many of the leased vehicles were minivans, which were easily modified with stash boxes, and didn't attract much attention because they were prevalent and usually driven by law-abiding family-types. But boys being boys, SMM also had a number of Hummers, Mercedes and BMWs just for fun.

As one former SMM member said, "When Sex, Money, Murder rolled, they rolled in style. They were doing it for sure. Their shit was bubbling."

Then it all went to hell.

Yaro Pack, Gonzales, Pistol Pete and a fourth SMM member called Leadpipe left New York in a leased minivan, which carried Pennsylvania licence plates. It also carried ten kilograms of coke, both powder and crack. When the van got to Pittsburgh, they deliv-ered six kilograms of coke and collected payment, which was $22,000 per kilo. Which worked out to $132,000. Then they drove to Lumberton, where they picked up money owed for previous deliveries. After taking care of business in Lumberton, they headed for Rockingham, where they were to pick up $90,000 from a dude named Darius Covington.

Darius Covington was a small-time drug pusher who was trying to go big-time, only things weren't going as planned. Darius had a problem. He didn't have the whole ninety grand. He only had part of it. Pistol Pete was aware of Darius's problem, but wasn't buying it. Pistol Pete didn't do instalment plans. His motto was "get mine or be mine". Darius needed to pay up or he needed to die.

When the van pulled up to Darius's favourite haunt, which was a broken-down billiard parlour, Pistol Pete tapped a pistol against his own forehead and said, "Yo, I'm goin' in there and murda him."

Gonzales wasn't as hardcore as Pistol Pete. Pistol Pete was all about rep, respect and revenge. Gonzales believed in granting grace periods, because he was in it for the money. And, like he said, "Dead bodies don't pay up." Corpses also made a mess and attracted cops. So Gonzales made a short, passionate plea to give Darius more time to come up with the money. In the end, Pistol Pete agreed to a twenty-four-hour stay of execution. Darius had one more day to get the money.

Gonzales got out of the van and went inside, where he told Darius the facts of life, according to the Gospel of Pistol Pete. "We got business in Charlotte," Gonzales said to Darius. "After it's taken care of, we'll circle-jerk back here tomorrow. Have the money, dude. Cuz tomorrow Pete'll be the one ya' talk to, not me. Ya' understan' what I'm sayin'?"

Darius licked his lips, nodding.

Back in the van, Gonzales headed the vehicle toward Charlotte, where the four gangbangers planned on attending a concert, then making a delivery. There were still two kilos of coke and some guns in one of the two stash boxes of the van.

After the concert, they drove to Wilmington, North Carolina, where they made another delivery of cocaine. They crashed for a few hours, then headed back toward Rockingham to meet up with Darius.

On 21 October 1994, as they approached the city of Rockingham, Gonzales stopped the van at a pay phone so he could make arrangements for the meeting place, and agreed to meet Darius at a local Burger King.

When they got to the Burger King the gangbangers went inside, ordered food and sat down to eat while they waited to collect their money. Darius never showed, because while he had been on the phone with Gonzales, he had told him he didn't have the money. Gonzales had suggested he leave town if he didn't want to learn why Peter Rollack was nicknamed "Pistol Pete".

Not showing was not cool. As far as Pistol Pete was concerned, Darius was as good as dead. Pistol Pete didn't let nobody get over on him.

"Look, Pete," said Gonzales. "The dude didn't show cuz he's scared. You got a bad rep, man. Darius, he knows that. He's probably down in Florida by now, man." Gonzales laughed. "Ya'll go on home, back to New York. I'll stay here an' see if I can't find Darius and maybe collect the money."

"Fuck that shit," snarled Pistol Pete. "Ain't nobody going to live in this world who owe me money."

Gonzales held out his hands and shrugged. "I don't know what to tell ya', man."

"Take me over to Darius's house," ordered Pistol Pete. "Because I'm going to murder his wife and kids. I ain't playing."

While Gonzales stalled, looking for a way out, the shit hit the fan. A bunch of cops popped up like Jacks-in-a-Box and proceeded to detain the gangbangers.

An anonymous informant had tipped the police that a burgundy Nissan Quest, with Pennsylvania licence plates, carrying four men, was transporting illegal narcotics into North Carolina. The anonymous informant was, of course, Darius Covington, who had decided it was better to be a live snitch than a dead drug pusher.

The police officers escorted the gangbangers out of Burger King to the burgundy Nissan Quest in the parking lot and asked permission to search the van. Yaro Pack nodded, handing over the keys. He also signed a written consent to search the van.

While two officers searched the van, other officers questioned the gangbangers, who gave phony names. Yaro Pack told the police officers that his name was Corey Hines. Gonzales gave his name as David Richards, and Pistol Pete identified himself as Nathaniel Tucker. Leadpipe said his name was John Adams.

The two cops searching the van couldn't find anything. But they didn't give up. They called for help, requesting drug detection canines. When the drug-sniffing dogs arrived, they quickly picked up the smell of coke and alerted the officers that there were drugs somewhere in the van. The cops immediately called for a tow truck and had the minivan taken to a police garage. They also got a search warrant.

With the help of a Nissan mechanic from a local car dealership, the cops proceeded to take the van apart, piece by piece. The SMM gangbangers stood nearby, watching. Beneath the front seats of the van, the cops located one of the two stash boxes. Inside, they found nothing. Undeterred, the cops continued dismantling the van. The existence of the empty stash box gave the police grounds to seize the vehicle and to hold the gangbangers for seventy-two hours.

The Sex, Money, Murder crew were handcuffed and transported to the local police station, where they were booked under their alias names. A few hours later, after posting bail, Pistol Pete and his crew were released, but their van had been impounded and was still being searched. This meant they had no wheels and, after posting bail, no money. The bulk of their money was in the second stash box in the van.

Yaro Pack wanted to get out of town as fast as possible, because he knew that when the cops discovered the other stash box – which also contained guns and coke – the game was over. He made a suggestion. "I ain't liking the way this feels. Let's get the fuck outta here, go on over to Charlotte. From there we can catch a plane back to Zoo York."

"Fuck that shit," said Pistol Pete. "We'll hang here until the van is released. Get our shit back."

"Man, didn't you see them po-lice taking our van apart?" asked Yaro Pack. "Sooner or later, they gonna' find our shit. Then they gonna' put our ass in a sling. We need to blow this Ma and Pa town, man."

"Sheeit," scoffed Pistol Pete. "These country-ass po-lice so stupid they ain't findin' nothin', man."

Pistol Pete was wrong. Even as he and Yaro Pack were arguing, the police found the second stash box. This one wasn't empty. It contained the guns and coke and a pile of money.

The SMM gangbangers walked to a pay phone and made a collect call to New York, informing their members back home of their predicament. While they were on the phone, the police arrived and arrested them again. This time their bail was high. The gangbangers made their phone calls and lingered in jail, waiting to be redeemed.

A few days later, George Wallace, who was a friend of Pistol Pete, and Yaro Pack's cousin arrived with bail money. Once they were released, the gangbangers got out of town as fast as possible. There was no way they were hanging around this podunk town to face the music. Sooner or later the police would match their prints to their real names, which meant their problems would escalate geometrically.

Pistol Pete decided not to take any more risks. He stopped taking trips. Instead, he stayed in New York and ran his empire from there, telling his crew where to go and what to do.

His tendency to resolve business disputes with his pistol caught up with him in late 1995. Karlton Hines, who was a basketball star at Syracuse University, owed Pete some money for drugs. Karlton decided not to pay what he owed. It was a bad choice. One day, Pete spotted Karlton standing outside a stereo shop on Boston Road. Karlton was with a friend of his named Carlos Mestre. They were waiting while Karlton had a new stereo installed in his car. Pistol Pete opened fire at the two men, killing Karlton and wounding Carlos. Pete didn't mean to hit Carlos, but his policy was to spray lead everywhere, which meant Carlos got hit because he associated with the wrong people.

Two months later, Pistol Pete finished the job on Carlos Mestre. Pete had nothing against him personally, but Carlos's status had changed. Now he was a witness to the murder of Karlton Hines, which meant Carlos had to die. As Carlos walked out of a Bronx hip-hop store called Jew Man, Pistol Pete gunned him down.

The police got a tip and arrested Pete for murder a few days later. The tip came from David Gonzales, Pete's old drug-running buddy, who was pissed off at Pete because he had been shaking him down for money. When Pete was arrested, as usual, he had a gun on him. Possession of a gun demanded a mandatory eight-month jail sentence, which Pete served at the Rikers Island Correctional Facility. When the eight months were up, his mother bailed him out so he could walk free while he awaited trial for the murder charge.

Because there were no witnesses to the murder of Carlos Mestre, Pistol Pete was acquitted. However, instead of walking out of court a free man, he was remanded to custody. Gonzales had fixed Pete's wagon but good. While Pete was sitting through his murder trial, Gonzales had told the Feds about Pete's activities in North Carolina, back in 1994. After Pete beat the murder rap, a federal narcotics indictment out of the Western District of North Carolina was waiting for him. The "country-ass po-lice" indicted Pistol Pete for the guns, coke and money they had found in the stash box of the van.

Pistol Pete was moved to the Charlotte-Mecklenburg County Jail in Charlotte, North Carolina, where he would be held until his next trial began.

It was 1996. He was twenty-three years old.

Pistol Pete kept up a good front. He had a rep to live up to, so he pretended like he didn't care. "A true player will accept the hand he is dealt simply because he did not live a lie," said Pete.

The Feds went all out in their case against Peter Rollack, aka Pistol Pete. They hit him with the RICO Act (Racketeer Influenced and Corrupt Organizations Act), charging him with drug trafficking, conspiracy to distribute drugs and ongoing conspiracy. The charges portrayed Pistol Pete as an interstate high-profile drug-trafficker, who was the leader of a Bloods gang involved in drug-smuggling and murder.

During the trial, it came out that Darius Covington was an informant for the Rockingham Police Department. Covington testified that he had been a paid informant for years, and that he had purchased drugs from Peter Rollack, watching as Rollack removed the drugs from a secret compartment in the Nissan van.

The jury was informed that after impounding the van, the Rockingham Police Department had thoroughly searched the vehicle. The search process had involved completely dismantling the van. When the police finally opened the second stash box, they discovered unregistered guns, two kilos of cocaine and $250,000 in cash.

Yaro Pack and David Gonzales also testified for the prosecution. Both men stated that Pete accompanied them on the trip to North Carolina, and that the primary purpose of the trip was to deliver drugs and pick up money due for past deliveries of drugs. Yaro Pack stated that Pete acted as the group's enforcer. In return for their testimony, both men received immunity. As soon as the trial concluded, Pack and Gonzales entered WITSEC, the federal witness protection programme. This was necessary to protect their lives. During the trial, Pistol Pete had put out death contracts on both men. He had written letters in Bloods code from his prison cell, ordering the members of Sex, Money, Murder to kill Yaro Pack and David Gonzales. According to Pete, they were snitches and deserved to die.

One of Pistol Pete's letters ordered SMM members to kill David "Twin" Mullins and his brother Damon Mullins, along with Efrain Solar. Pete believed the twin brothers and Solar posed a problem. They could testify against him, and even if they didn't, the possibility was enough to require their deaths. Sex, Money, Murder carried out the order from their boss. They killed David Mullins and Efrain Solar. However, the connection between the letter and the murders was not made until after Pistol Pete's trial.

As the trial progressed, Pete's letters were introduced as evidence. Pursuant to a federal search warrant, all Pete's mail had been intercepted, examined, copied and then allowed out through the mail. A handwriting analyst testified that the letters had been written by Peter Rollack. The letters validated the testimony of the government witnesses and indicated Pete's active participation in an ongoing conspiracy.

As one SMM member said, "The letters that they got fucked Pistol Pete up. A lot of shit rode on the weight of those letters."

On 9 January 1998, the jury found Peter Rollack, aka Pistol Pete, guilty of conspiring to possess with intent to distribute a quantity of cocaine and cocaine base, and of knowingly using and carrying a firearm, and of aiding and abetting such conduct in relation to a drug-trafficking crime.

He was sentenced to forty years in prison.

One month later, on 10 February 1998, the headline of the *New York Times* read: "Imprisoned Gang Leader Ordered Killings at Neighbourhood Football Game, US Attorney Says."

It happened like this. On 27 November 1997, thirty people from the Soundview and Castle Hill projects were enjoying a game of touch football in a local park. A group of men, allegedly SMM gangbangers, swaggered into the park. Pulling weapons, they opened fire. Dozens of shots rang out. Then the gangbangers left, reloading their weapons as they walked away. Five blood-soaked bodies lay on the ground. David "Twin" Mullins and Efrain Solar were dead. Three other people were seriously wounded.

Sex, Money, Murder members Robinson "Mac 11" Lazala and José Rodriguez were arrested and charged with murder and attempted murder. As the Feds investigated the case, they discovered other murders that SMM had allegedly perpetrated. The emerging pattern of evidence pointed directly back to Pistol Pete. The pattern included racketeer activity, drug sales, robberies, acts of intimidation, acts of violence and murder.

In February 1998, Pistol Pete and ten other SMM members were indicted for nine murders and for trafficking in cocaine and crack in Pennsylvania, New York and North Carolina. A separate indictment against Pistol Pete charged him with narcotics trafficking, RICO violations, five actual murders, two conspiracies to commit murder and witness tampering, and with committing these acts for the purpose of maintaining or increasing his racketeering enterprises. The witness tampering charge referred to the murders of David Mullins and Efrain Solar.

The Feds were asking for the death penalty against Peter Rollack aka Pistol Pete.

And the prosecutors had plenty of witnesses lined up, including Yaro Pack and David Gonzales, along with SMM members Brian Boyd and Emilo Romero.

Pistol Pete's attorney argued that "the witnesses are willing to admit anything and say anything. If they don't, they will go to jail for a very long time. The government's case rests solely on the uncorroborated testimony of cooperating witnesses."

The jury didn't buy the attorney's argument.

The Feds case looked like a slam-dunk. Pistol Pete must have thought so, too, because he agreed to a plea bargain. Pete pleaded guilty to federal racketeering and the murders of six people. In return, the Feds agreed not to seek the death penalty.

To this day, Pistol Pete maintains that the only reason he pleaded guilty was because the Feds threatened to incarcerate his mother for receiving drug money. In other words, as Seth "Soul Man" Ferranti put it, "The Feds put some shit in the game." Only the Feds and Pistol Pete know the truth of the matter.

In 2000, Peter Rollack aka Pistol Pete, age twenty-seven, was sentenced to life in prison without parole, plus a further 105-year sentence, for the murder of six people and drug-trafficking in three states. Conditions of his sentence were draconian. He was to be placed in special restrictive confinement and prohibited from communication or receiving visits from anyone other than his lawyers or his family members. And even these individuals had to be pre-approved by the court and the prison.

Even though Pistol Pete was out of business, SMM was not. Its members kept on banging.

In 2002, Tommy Thompson, who was the leader of SMM in Jersey City, New Jersey, established himself as a headliner. He was the biggest of the Big Wheels, moving drugs all over the East Coast and killing anyone who got in his way. Only his run didn't last very long. On 14 November 2004, an eighteen-count RICO indictment charged Tommy Thompson with conspiracy, racketeering, conspiracy to murder, robbery, conspiracy to commit robbery, conspiracy to distribute heroin and cocaine, and nine counts of violent crimes in aid of racketeering.

In short order, the Feds put Tommy Thompson out of business too.

Next to step up and try their hand at becoming the top dogs of banging were Antonio Merritt and Bobby Williams of Trenton, New Jersey. Merritt and Williams were the co-leaders of the Trenton set of SMM. Their thing was drug-trafficking, and they were good at it. From 2005 to 2007 they flourished and got "hood rich". Just like their predecessors, violence was their standard operating procedure. They killed anyone who got in their way. Which was their undoing. In 2007, the New Jersey State Division of Criminal Justice indicted them for first-degree racketeering and two counts of murder.

Merritt and Williams went out of business too.

Nevertheless, SMM continued to grow in numbers. SMM soldiers kept banging and moving heroin, cocaine, crack cocaine and crystal meth. To protect their "shit", SMM relied on unleashing hell – a rain of blazing gunfire. Sooner or later, most of them ended up in prison. In response to SMM's growth and activities – and that of the other sets of the East Coast Bloods – New York's Department of

Corrections started a Gang Intelligence Unit. The focus of the unit was to identify and mitigate the activities of the different Blood sets, including Sex, Money, Murder, the Gangsta Killers, the Concepts of War and the Nine Trey Gangstas. So far, the Gang Intelligence Unit has had little impact. In fact, staff officers of the unit have begun getting "popped" without warning, usually in drive-by shootings.

Today, Peter Rollack is incarcerated at the supermax prison in Florence, Colorado. He attained legendary status during his brief career. Even though SMM flipped from the NYG Alliance, the Alliance still throws up the number seven hand sign (gun) in his honour. And SMM uses the number code 252 or 252 per cent to represent twenty-five years to life in prison – in homage to the life sentence that Pistol Pete is serving.

SMM has extended its reach into the hip-hop world. Various rappers are known members of SMM, including Hocus, S-ONE, Lord Tariq, Peter Gunz, Took and Hussein Fatal of the Outlawz.

Today, SMM members refer to themselves in verbal shorthand as "Murder Gang" or as "Blazing Billy", because, like Billy the Kid, when it comes down to it, they blaze away with their guns. A new Pistol Pete may be in the making.

WILLIAM COSS
(USA)

An American Citizen with
Nerves of Steel

Introducing . . . William Coss

WHAT HAPPENS WHEN a fairly ordinary person doing an ordinary job on a normal day gets caught up in an extraordinary and terrifying situation? Can this turn someone who is not particularly tough into a tough, hard bastard? This is exactly what happened to William Coss, a thirty-two-year-old single father in Arizona, USA, who was living the life of a solid citizen when he had the chance to find out what he was really made of.

At just five foot eight inches and 165 pounds, average-looking with brown hair and brown eyes, Coss had joined the US Army as a paratrooper when he was a youngster. After his discharge in 2000, he returned to Arizona to live a regular life as a construction superintendent. Other than the army stint, Coss had lived in the desert city since the second grade at school when his parents had settled there. He married, became a doting father and then divorced. When the housing market bottomed out, Coss left construction and found a new career in pest control, becoming certified in "The Sting of the Scorpion", "Mosquitoes – Their Biology and Habits", "Small Fly Control Strategies" and many other components of battling bugs. In 2008 he put his new skills to work at a local pest management company where he worked a night shift alone, doing a route of commercial properties with a truck full of poisons and sprayers.

Just as Coss was starting his new career as a bug exterminator, a chain of eateries based in the western United States was enjoying phenomenal growth and announced plans to open ten new locations in the Phoenix area within six months. A few months later, on 22 March 2009, the expansion of the food chain suddenly became quite important to the former paratrooper. It nearly killed him. "Almost Out of Time", written specially for this book by Camille Kimball, is the story of how.

ALMOST OUT OF TIME
By Camille Kimball

The cold air whipped his jumpsuit into ferocious waves and whirling crests all over his arms, his shins, his trunk. The diesel and aluminium smell of the C-130 Hercules cabin suddenly seemed as comforting as a home-cooked meal. 1,200 feet below him, the landscape was tiny and distant and lethal.

He stomped a foot on the metal belly. In his mind he had visions of the squad member who had made the leap only to have the static line tangle and trap him on the exterior skin of the plane. His comrade had been "towed" for several minutes and banged about, mercilessly pinned between the rushing air and the hull, with only the snarled line holding him, very uncertainly, to the plane. The soldiers had to first keep him tethered, then battle against the 100 mph windspeed pushing the young man backwards. When he was finally hauled inside he was bruised, battered and lucky to be alive. That one had left the unit – and the army – shortly thereafter.

William Coss was remembering that incident as he hovered at the edge of the open hatch for his own first jump. 1,200 feet was such a long, long way to fall, but such a short distance for him to get safely away from the plane, orient himself, have the chute fully blossom and find the emergency cord if it didn't. If all went well, it was just twenty seconds until thudding to earth; twenty seconds isn't long to get it all right.

William's heart was racing. He felt sick to his stomach. Images of his squadmate trapped underneath the fuselage, the tangled line, the struggle to pull him in, the broken body, passed through his mind. The tiny landmarks below were so far away, the time to get there so short.

He swung his legs over and dropped.

"You got people yelling at you and everything else, you never know what will happen when you come out of that plane: you could be towed, your chute won't open, all sorts of things and you're so low to the ground you don't have a lot of time to react," the thirty-two-year-old Arizonan says. "I smacked the door and fell out backwards once. I had too much weight. The air flow pushed me back into the plane and wouldn't let me fall out. It knocks the breath out of you. I hit it pretty hard. I was nervous every time I jumped, then once you're out of the airplane all those feelings go away and then you're just amazed at everything: you go into a different world."

A US Army paratrooper with the 82nd Airborne in North Carolina, William Coss eventually made upwards of 400 jumps, but his heart raced every time and he never forgot the sight of the helpless soldier bouncing against the fuselage in the wake of four Allison turboprops throwing out over 18,000 shaft horsepower.

And Coss never forgot how to think when too much open space becomes your enemy and death is coming at you fast.

In the northern corner of Iraq there is a region that is home to one of the oldest civilizations known to history: Assyria. The giant stone monuments with the rigid beards are familiar all over the world and the name figures prominently in Bible stories. In 2 Kings 17, the king of Assyria "carried Israel away into Assyria". No wonder Jonah fled when God commanded him to preach to the Assyrian city of Ninevah and ended up in the belly of the whale for three days instead.

From Ishtar worship and other forms of paganism, Assyrians were amongst the first of the ancient ethnic groups to adopt the new religion of Christianity. This left them as a minority in Mesopotamia as Islam took over the region in the Middle Ages, on down to today's vivid conflicts. Some Assyrians fleeing the various troubles that plagued the region have collected in one or two small towns in California. In Modesto – the same small town famed for the Laci Peterson murder in 2002 and the recent Chandra Levy case – they have slowly built their own churches and amassed a social life centred on their heritage: the flavours of anise and cardamom, yoghurty soups and lamb stews, the Syriac or Aramaic language, early paradigms of Christianity, women dancing in a circle to the music of the long-necked tambura and the rhetoric of a diaspora. The Mesopotamian politics emanating from California grew so heated that the FBI in 1990 foiled a plot by Saddam Hussein to assassinate a leader of the Assyrian-Modesto community.

But, as so many immigrant communities have discovered, the struggles of the first generation and the passion for homeland lose voltage for the sons born to good fortunes. American-born in 1977, Ramsen Dadesho, nephew of the man Saddam Hussein had ordered assassinated, gained a reputation in Modesto as a high-flying rich man's son with a taste for the fast life and a family who used their power to get him out of trouble. He married within the community, but the marriage failed and a bitter custody battle pitted his ex-wife against his powerful family. Ramsen had the dark, good looks of his ancient bloodline, but at five foot seven inches did not cut an intimidating figure in person.

Everyone in the Assyrian clan in Modesto seemed to know everybody else and there was a lot of pressure on the generation coming of age in the 1990s and 2000s to marry within the community. It would not seem unusual then, that after his failed marriage Ramsen Dadesho would one day date another Assyrian girl, Sharokena Koshaba, who had already had a romance with one of his Assyrian-American friends.

That friend was Rami Merza. Rami was cherished by a family of five brothers and two sisters and he was the youngest. His father had died before he was born. A strapping fellow of six foot three with a handsome face and flashing smile, Rami found himself to be a very popular character in his community.

Rami and Ramsen grew up going to the same parties and the same churches and the same high school.

By 2009, Ramsen Dadesho was living with Sharokena in Modesto. He had no job, but he always seemed to have money. His battles with his ex-wife, involving their young daughter, sent sparks flying in the Assyrian social circles. Sharokena figured prominently in the gossip.

On the other hand, Rami Merza had left the Assyrian enclave in Modesto and was living hundreds of miles away in Mesa, Arizona.

Mesa is a suburb of Phoenix. Rami had been working at a Honda dealership but, in a clash with the manager, Rami got fired. With no job and few Arizona friends, Rami had a lot of time on his hands to travel back to Modesto. He often did so, making the ten- to twelve-hour drive in a silver Honda. The centre of gravity of his life was still there, in the Assyrian-American community and the small town atmosphere. When in Modesto, he had his mother, brothers and sisters to fuss over him. And there was the vibrant Assyrian haven for socializing.

Both Rami and Ramsen liked flashy cars and nightclubs and cash.

In March 2009, twenty-nine-year-old Rami was visiting Modesto and palling around with thirty-two-year-old Ramsen. As the weekend of 20 March approached, Rami and Ramsen left California together. They drove back to Arizona in Rami's silver Honda.

The players were now in place: the remnants of the ancient culture of Assyria, carefully fostered in California, were about to collide with the very modern 82nd Airborne, via a dark and deserted Scottsdale parking lot.

By Sunday night, 22 March, the two childhood friends were clubbing in Scottsdale. At 11.30 p.m. that night, Rami called a friend and asked for directions.

William Coss was working in Scottsdale that night, a cool evening with temperatures around 60° Fahrenheit, the skies clear, the winds calm and the air bone dry.

At 11 p.m. the thirty-two-year-old former paratrooper had pulled into a sprawling shopping centre of free-standing buildings, small strip malls and giant open spaces. He had dropped off the 101 freeway north–south, and turned on to an east–west running street named Raintree. From Raintree, he turned north into the interior of the development. He drove his white pickup truck, with its Eco company logo emblazoned on its sides, to the eastern perimeter where a small strip mall sat with its rear nestled up against the frontage road of the southbound 101 freeway.

He parked the truck directly in front of the doors of Paradise Bakery. The acres and acres of paved parking lot stretching before the cafe were vacant. Immediately to the north, across a small private side road, was another little strip mall, anchored by a Pearle

Vision Center. Stucco and lumber enclosures, discreetly masking dumpsters, dotted the Pearle Vision Center terrain.

Will had parked with his nose out so he'd have easy access to the back of his truck as he went in and out of the restaurant. Wearing his Eco uniform, he gathered up his materials, turned to the west-facing front doors and let himself in.

He turned on all the lights and began to spray.

About twenty minutes later, William had finished with the interior of the eatery. He stepped outside for a cigarette before starting his work on the outside grounds. He noticed another car was now there. It would be impossible not to notice the vehicle as it was so close to his own. It was a silver Honda Accord Coupe only six spaces away from his truck and not only were the headlights on but the engine was running and both the passenger and the driver's doors were wide open.

Two men were there, one in the driver's seat of the Honda and the other standing beside it. Will figured the men had seen the lights on in the Paradise Bakery and had assumed it was open. They were probably figuring out what to do next once they realized there was only a service truck parked at the otherwise locked front doors. William had retrieved his cigarettes from the cabin of his truck: now he walked around to the back to start pouring chemicals. The man at the driver's wheel in the Honda was quiet. The car's passenger was talking on a cell phone, carried in his left hand, and walking about.

The man with the phone crossed the short distance between the two vehicles and approached Will.

"I thought he was going to ask me for cigarettes or directions. He was within two feet of me. He just stared at me for about ten minutes and nothing was said and he kinda walked away so I just went back to doing my thing," Coss recalls. He measured, he poured. Just when he was screwing the lid back on a bottle of chemicals, he heard it.

Gunfire.

"Oooooh, yes," Coss draws in a long breath when asked if he recognized the sound for what it was, not fireworks or a car muffler. "I was only twelve to fifteen feet away. I knew somebody else was in the car so I knew exactly what had happened: somebody got shot."

Who was it?

"I sidestepped my vehicle and I looked over the top and I saw him with the gun walking away from the car . . . and I saw the person who was still in the car, too."

The one with the gun was the one who had been staring Will down, eye to eye, just moments before. He still had the cell phone in his left hand, but Will immediately spotted the silver barrel, gleaming in the moonlight, in his right.

The former paratrooper in that moment knew two things: he had heard no arguments between the two men so this had to be both a cold-blooded and a reckless act; and the man with the gun knew full well that he, Will, was just a few feet away.

Adding these two facts together, Will knew he would be next.

It was now past 11.30 at night. Other than himself, the man at the wheel and the one with the gun in his hand, the terrain was desolate.

The 82nd Airborne training came back to Will. It had taught him, he says, to be calm in "live-fire" situations.

"Not having a weapon to protect myself and definitely wishing I had one I thought, okay, what do you do next? Protect yourself: it's part of your training. Get away.

"I was airborne so I was always jumping out of airplanes and you gotta have quick reactions and think on your feet or you're dead."

Will had few options. To the west was wide-open parking lot, acres of it. Although the expansive shopping centre was carefully landscaped, befitting its Scottsdale address, it was still a desert locale. The plants were austere. There were a few spidery mesquite trees, narrow branches dusted with feathery green that was more air than substance; otherwise, there were purple sage bushes, meticulously groomed into cylinders, low to the ground, with fingernail-size silver leaves dotted with small pink purple blossoms. The development was also quite new – the few plants were still immature and small. There was very little to break up the panorama of the parking lot. He would be a clear shot at any angle.

The Paradise Bakery formed the northern tip of the little strip mall. The interior side road separated it from the Pearle Vision Center strip mall, forming a right angle or broken "L". But that little side road was wide for a pedestrian – Cass would not only be a clear shot through there but he'd be trapped by the "L".

To the south, just a couple of car lengths away, was the man with gun.

William thought quickly and came up with an immediate target destination. Around the back of the Paradise Bakery was a little bit of forgotten space between the strip mall and the 101 freeway frontage. He could hide there for a moment. He ran around the northern corner of the Paradise Bakery and headed east. He ducked past an electrical transformer and scooted behind the back wall of the building.

But he could not stay there long. If the man with the gun followed the same path – a space traversed in one or two seconds . . . he'd be cornered worse than ever as the strip mall building widened out and closed the territory to the freeway.

He needed to increase the distance between himself and that silver gun.

As he was running to the hiding place, William had used the electronic devices in his hands. With one hand, he pushed the button to remotely lock the doors on his truck. With the other, he flipped open his cell phone: but he did not dial because he was too close to his pursuer. Will wanted to use the darkness to his advantage. A lit cell phone would reveal his position.

Will organized his thoughts before he placed the call. He had to leave the shelter of the Paradise Bakery and cross the open space across the broken "L" to the next strip of buildings. "I slipped around back through the buildings then I came back around front so I could observe what he was doing. I did not want to end up in the same spot as him because I wasn't watching him. But I also did not want him to see my cell phone all lit up."

Will made it across the side road that opened on to the 101. The people in the cars that whooshed past in the darkness at 65 or 70 mph had no idea that just outside their rolled up windows a man was running for his life. The footing underneath Coss changed from black asphalt to grey concrete sidewalk and then to the crunchy loose rock of the landscaping as he made his way around the far side of the "L".

Behind the Pearle Vision Center, Will finally felt it was dark enough and sheltered enough to risk the phone call. He pushed the buttons. The cell phone connected to a 911 dispatcher at 11.40 p.m.

"Yeah, there's just a shooting over here, Raintree and Pima at the Paradise Bakery," Will says calmly, "The dude's still walking around in the parking lot with a gun."

The dispatcher looks at her screen and determines the exact address. While she does so, Will is describing the man with the gun – he's "short", wearing a black shirt, maybe around 185 pounds and is possibly Hispanic. He's also told her about the vehicle where the shot had taken place – a silver Honda.

"Okay, is it right in front of Paradise Bakery?" she asks.

"Yeah," he says, "right next to my Eco truck."

"Okay, now I've got . . . " she begins to say.

But she is cut off by the sound of a loud boom.

"Uh, there's another shot right there . . . two shots," Will breaks in. "Get somebody here quick, please."

Will is on the move. He is slipping in the shadows between buildings. He has watched the second shot. The unknown man has calmly returned to the car and pointed inside. Will has watched him do it. Will has seen the flash in the darkness.

"Okay, they're coming to you. Talking to me is not slowing my officers down," the dispatcher says. She wants to ask more questions and Will keeps feeding her information but no one is arriving yet. He is staying to the shadows, shielding the light of the phone and trying to keep an eye on his unpredictable enemy. Will has more than enough time to describe the silver car and the clothing worn and the size and complexion of the man shooting. But the dispatcher wants more description of the man. "You said he was short?" she asks.

"Yeah," Will responds but quickly moves on to the most compelling item to describe: "He has a revolver with a nine-inch barrel. It sounds like it's probably a .380 or a little bigger."

Now she wants a description of Will's own vehicle. His tension at last surfaces as he struggles for the make and model of the truck he drives every day "It's a white silver . . . uh, uh, what do you call it? Shit, 'Colorado' and it says 'Eco' on the side. It has that, uh, cover on the back . . . "

She starts to cut him off. She has bad news, "The officers . . . "

"It's backed up to the Paradise Bakery," Will finishes.

" . . . are saying," she delivers the stroke of disaster, "they don't see a vehicle. Are we sure this is the correct address?"

The fact is officers are now at a Paradise Bakery. They've got no silver Honda, no man with a gun, no bleeding victim.

The success of Paradise Bakery, building ten new stores in the area in the last six months, is on the verge of costing the young single father his life.

Officers are at the Paradise Bakery on Doubletree not Raintree. The Doubletree store is on Scottsdale Road, not the freeway. The two locations are six congested, urban miles apart.

"I don't know if you heard that or not," Will says, as he hears the devastating news.

"I heard it," says the operator.

A third shot.

"And the pop sounded like it was right there. It's pretty close," he tells her.

Will has kept on the move, ducking into dumpster shelters and behind walls to keep the lit phone from giving away his position as much as possible, but also trying to keep the man in view, "If not, then there's somebody else in this parking lot. But I saw that dude with the freaking silver revolver."

The third shot occurs at four minutes and four seconds into Will's 911 call. He has stood face to face with a murderer. He has seen a man be killed. He is in a cat-and-mouse game for his life. He has watched two more shots be discharged.

And now officers have gone to the wrong address.

Without panicking, he switches from street names, which have failed him, and gives her detailed directions to "turn first right", "after heading west" and so forth. Will looks around the far-reaching shopping centre and begins to name off any building other than Paradise Bakery. There's New York Pizza Department, he tells her, there's a Teri's Consignment Furnishings . . . "I'm trying to see what else is in the parking lot . . . Sport Chalet . . . "

"Okay, yeah I know where you're at now. That, that address I read to you, that was the wrong one so . . . "

"I'm sorry," Will apologizes.

"All the officers are on the way so just stay safe and just stay on the line with me."

Will wants to stay safe, too, but it's getting more difficult.

"Now the dude's running."

"Okay, uh, do you see the officer?"

Will sees no officers. "Um, no, which way did he come in?"

"What direction?"

But he sees the man with the gun.

"He's running. He ran towards my truck, he's gone behind Paradise Bakery or he's in my truck. I don't know. He ran towards the freeway like right between Paradise Bakery and the Pearle Vision between the freeway."

Will is describing the small side street of the broken "L", the same space he himself had to cross. The Pearle Vision Center is in the lateral strip mall, across from where Paradise Bakery caps the north/south strip mall.

"Okay."

"He's on foot and I'll tell you if I see him running to the left. I still don't see an officer – no, he's walking back to the car."

Will keeps scanning in the darkness, balancing his position between monitoring his pursuer, keeping hidden and scanning for the arrival of any help at all.

At last, "Okay, the officer is . . . here."

Scottsdale PD Patrolman Alex Dyer has arrived in a patrol car from the north. He's been told shots are fired. He sees the Eco Pest Control truck. But with the confusion from the other bakery location, Dyer is not sure what he'll find here and at first does not see any men on foot, not one with a cell phone and not one with a gun.

From the shadows, Will begins to issue play by play directions:

"I'm standing right here on the left. Tell him to go straight . . . go straight, keep driving, keep driving, keep driving . . . Now tell him to take a left. Tell him to take his left and the dude's right there."

"So he's back at the vehicle?"

"Yeah, oh, he's walking towards us right now."

"The, uh, suspect?"

"Yes, that's right. He's walking in front of a moving van."

The goods-moving van, parked for the night, is in front of the Pearle Vision Center. Will is hiding in dumpsters behind Pearle.

Officer Dyer has entered the giant shopping centre from the

north. His plan was to take a defensive position and then wait for back up. But Dyer now sees a man matching the suspect's description emerge from a dumpster enclosure near Pearle. The suspect is heading north. The officer doesn't know it, but at this location so far from the Honda the suspect can be doing only one thing: looking for Will.

"I immediately drew my weapon and began issuing commands," Dyer wrote in his report.

Will sees the man's hands go up. The dispatcher wants to know if he sees the officers with him. Will corrects her . . . he only sees one officer. He himself is still in hiding.

"He told him to get on the ground, he's laying down," Will narrates for her, "Well, he's half up, half down."

The dispatcher begins to ask Will his name and phone number, she thinks he is safe now. But Will knows better. He has kept to the shadows even though a police cruiser is on the scene. He has seen his pursuer put his hands up in the air. He has seen the officer order him to the ground. But knowing what was waiting in the silver Honda at the kerb, Will knows what this assassin is capable of. He thinks neither he nor the officer on the scene are safe.

Will is right.

"He's running now. The guy just ran."

Astonished, the dispatcher again enlists Will's secret direction: "Okay, what direction is he going?"

He tells her he's running east, he's running towards the freeway.

Officer Dyer records that he fell in hot pursuit: "I chased him on foot for approximately fifty to seventy-five feet while keeping him at gunpoint." Officer Dyer can't talk to dispatch. He's all alone on scene.

Except for his secret ally, still in the shadows.

Because Will is giving real-time information on the suspect's actions, dispatch is able to relay the information to other squad cars. One comes screeching in from the south and pulls into the west end of the side street between Pearl and Paradise. Another comes screeching in from the 101 frontage road on the east. The squad car from the 101 had been monitoring the radio dispatches for the last seven minutes but had not deployed because it was too far from the Doubletree bakery. It had been on routine patrol near the Raintree location the whole time. The other squad car has already been to the first bakery, in vain. But they are here now, lights flashing, wheels squealing. Both patrolmen jump from their cars with weapons drawn.

Now the suspect is trapped.

He goes back down to the asphalt but he's fighting and screaming. One of the officers turns on a tape recorder to capture the ravings: "I fuckin' merked him, I'm gonna fucking kill all of you, I smoked him, fool, you guys are all gonna die." It takes four patrolmen to control the suspect. Officer Dyer even sustains injuries and the suspect will be charged with assaulting an officer. The officers ask him what "merked" means. The suspect explains it means to shoot people. He continues to thrash and struggle and yell threats. When the paddy wagon comes, the suspect is still so combative, even though he is already handcuffed, he is strapped into a restraining seat.

Will later described the situation, "I was off in a corner in the dark watching him, observing him so I could run if I had to run. I knew she sent them to the wrong place when she said 'they're on site' and I said 'no, they're not' cuz I pretty much could see both directions down the parking lot.

"It was a big relief when they came," Will says with a soft giggle. "Finally there was enough cop cars there I knew they would they get him so I could come out into the open."

With the suspect finally in custody, the next officers to arrive surrounded the Honda. With weapons drawn, they called upon the man at the wheel to show his hands. He did not respond. They cautiously crept nearer. When they got close enough to see, they dropped their weapons. With one foot drooping out the door, the man's upper body stretched toward the passenger side, his head facing toward the open door. Behind that passenger door, on the south side of the Honda, was where the suspect had been standing when William heard the first shot. The man at the wheel, lifeless foot dangling out the door, had been shot from behind.

The man's brains and skull pieces were blasted all over the interior of the cabin.

As officers looked inside, a cell phone began to ring.

Rami Merza had placed a calm and innocent call asking for

directions at 11.30 p.m. At 11.40, Will's phone had connected to 911. The person calling now, as officers gazed upon his spattered remains, had no way of knowing yet that big grinning Rami would never pick up.

Homicide Detective Hugh Lockerby arrived on the scene and took over the case. "William Coss's cool demeanour played a huge role in this case," he says. "He stayed on the move in case he needed to escape more, he made his way around buildings, always keeping an eye on the suspect. He must have had an elevated heart rate, a fear for his life, probably scared shitless, any person would be, hearing a gunshot and being that close yet he was still calm enough and cognizant enough to get on the phone, keep himself alive and actually direct officers to the scene and even during that time observed the suspect going back and shooting the victim again. It was huge. It was massive."

When Ramsen Dadesho was finally taken into custody – nine minutes into Will's call – the weapon Coss had described was no longer on his person. William continued to help.

"He walked back by the silver car," he had told the dispatcher during the confusion. "He didn't get to the car but he walked back toward the parking lot . . . a little north of that behind the car. But I don't know if he walked and hid the gun and then came back out or not but that's about right when all the cruisers showed up."

At 2 a.m., Detective Richard Best found the weapon. Eighteen inches below the surface of a three-foot-tall purple sage bush, tucked down inside the cylinder shape of the plant, the gun was suspended in the darkness. He reported from the way it was positioned, it had to have been placed deliberately inside the shrub, not thrown. The purple sage bush was far out in the parking lot, just as Will had suggested.

The gun was a Smith and Wesson .44 revolver. It would have sounded like a cannon when fired at such close range, as Will screwed on the bottle cap at his truck six parking spaces north. Three cartridges were spent. Three bullets were still in the chamber.

Lockerby says without Will Coss's icy calm under fire, they most likely would have ended up with a very difficult, even unsolvable, case. "I mean, how often do you have an actual eyewitness that was completely uninvolved with the murder? If he wouldn't have done what he did, first of all officers wouldn't have been able to get there as quickly which would have given the defendant time to get away. The two Modesto men were friends, too, so without the witness, it might have been impossible to figure out the role of the suspect or who the suspect was. Even if we had figured it out, it would have been a lot harder to prove."

Without Coss's quick manoeuvring, Scottsdale Police Department may have been presented days later with two separate missing persons reports, with no connection to each other: an Eco Pest Control employee and the unemployed Modesto man with the Mesa address. They may have found two bodies in the parking lot and had to assume some kind of confrontation or relationship between them. Or they may have found one body but not the other. If Coss had not been there at all, Rami's murder may have been pinned on a mythical third party such as an armed robber who got away. In fact, Ramsen did try to sell a story of a mysterious black Tahoe with tinted windows.

But William Coss kept himself alive, got police to the correct scene and told them just who shot who, all while the body was still warm.

Detective Lockerby asked his colleague, Scottsdale Homicide Detective Pete Salazar, to fly to Modesto to find out what he could about the two men in the Honda. It was here that Scottsdale PD found themselves immersed in the ancient culture with its tiny trans-plant offshoot still thriving and, in some ways, festering in California. Salazar heard tales of love affairs, vendettas, even "hits". There was gossip that someone who was connected to a cousin of Ramsen wanted Rami taken out. A recent threat had been made that Rami would be "taken on from the back". Here the personali-ties of the senior Dadesho brothers and the fiery Assyrian exile political scene came to life against the backdrop of known assassins and the Saddam Hussein regime.

Salazar finally came to interview Sharokena Koshaba, who proved elusive in his first attempts to contact her. But when he did catch up to her, she was talkative with the detective. That is, she was talkative until she received a collect call from an Arizona jail during their inter-view. Salazar knew it was Ramsen who was phoning her. She imme-diately terminated her interview with the detective.

Subpoenaed phone records showed she had been in constant contact with Ramsen during the time of the murder and had been the one on the phone to him when he walked up to Will and stared him down at his Eco truck. A text message to Ramsen showed she was still his "girl", "no matter what you did". Another text told him she was arranging a flight for him to flee Arizona immediately. She did not know that the phone was already in possession of the Scottsdale police, thanks to Will, at the time she was texting.

As the investigation progressed, many people in the Assyrian community spoke of Ramsen's increasingly paranoid and erratic behaviour in the weeks leading up to the slaying. His ex-wife found out he had left their small daughter with his mother while he went to Arizona with his victim. It seemed like an odd action after a hard-fought custody battle.

Did Ramsen Dadesho have a specific purpose in travelling to Arizona on what was supposed to be a daddy weekend? Or did he just snap? Was there a remark about the shared girlfriend, Sharokena? Did two young men suddenly flare over insults about a lover or the loyalties of a woman?

Sharokena's last name is the same as that of the man, also from Modesto, serving time in a federal prison for plotting with Saddam Hussein to assassinate Ramsen's uncle.

Had William Coss, with his canisters of bug spray, walked into an Assyrian-Iraqi execution in progress?

Why the two Modesto men drove to the deserted parking lot, with Rami at the wheel, and why Rami calmly sat there when Ramsen abruptly killed him may be locked forever in Ramsen's own head. Ramsen's bail was set so high even the powerful Dadesho brothers from the senior generation have not been able to raise it.

Be it political assassination, love triangle, drugged rampage, soured partnership or quarrel over cash, in the United States, Ramsen is presumed innocent when he enters a courtroom. But William Coss's voice recorded on the nine-minute 911 call giving the details of the murder while it was in progress speaks for itself.

The sounds of the gunshots on the recording preserve forever the actions that ended one life, and narrowly saved another.

"Previously being around something like that," Will says, recalling his paratrooper training, "it's kind of like you're more calm. If you've never been in that position the stress overtakes you and people who've never been in that situation panic and they freeze. If you panic and freeze, you're dead at that time."

Detective Lockerby couldn't agree more: anyone who panicked would have been dead that night. "His background and his nature saved his life. He had that edge, of knowing how to play the situation when it's bad guy versus good guy, where he was outmatched and had to escape. Most people, if they thought at all, would have hid in one place and not moved. And then when he was chasing them, they would not have known what he was up to. This situation was not just rare – it was unreal."

William Coss still seems to have no idea of the magnitude of the night's proceedings. When asked about his thoughts during those lethal minutes, he says, "I just wanted to finish my work and get done with this situation."

He's not quite aware of the awe in his interviewer's voice at this revelation. "I was sitting there [after the police came] for at least a couple hours before it dawned on me. After a couple hours, then I knew my night was shot."

Coss is impatient to end the interview. He's got drywall to hang. Mom and Dad are expecting him. He's got a bunch of new accounts to service for Eco. He is very busy.

"I just try to take care of my customers," he says, "Just do the job that needs to be done."

Author's Note: Sources for this story are Scottsdale Police Department Case Number 0908001, 911 transcripts, author's interviews with William Coss, Detective Hugh Lockerby, Detective Pete Salazar, MaryAnn Carbone of Eco Pest Management, Arizona State Pest Control Board and other sources. All quotes are factual as transcribed.

VLADIMIR BOGOMOLOV (RUSSIA)

Soviet Leader's Personal Bodyguard

Introducing . . . Vladimir Bogomolov

ALTHOUGH I NEVER visited the Russian Federation prior to 1992 – when it was the USSR – I have been to Russia a great many times since and lived permanently in the capital Moscow for almost all of 2003 and again in 2005. Over the years I have worked and trained with a great many Russian bodyguards and I can say, unequivocally, that they are some of the hardest, toughest and most ruthless bodyguards on the planet. The training they need to go through and the conditions of getting a bodyguard licence in Russia means that Russian bodyguards have a particular set of skills and a unique mindset that very few other people have on this planet. I remember attending a close protection course run by the Russian bodyguard company Grant-Vymple in Moscow in the late 1990s and their close-quarter unarmed combat was like nothing I had seen previously. I was in complete awe of these bodyguards.

Prior to 1992, the Cold War left the world trembling. Russia and the West – particularly the USA – were arch enemies; spying was prevalent, and distrust and suspicion were normal. Although much is written about modern bodyguarding in Russia, it is still extremely rare to hear about the everyday lives of Soviet-era bodyguards, mainly because many have now died and the last few remaining still keep their life and their work a secret.

And so this fascinating chapter, specially written for this book by Russian bodyguard Aleksey Fonarev (in a typically Russian style of stating facts with little emotion), gives us a brief but unique insight into the life of Vladimir Bogomolov, one of the government's top bodyguards during the Soviet era.

SOVIET BODYGUARD
By Aleksey Fonarev

Translated from Russian by Inna Zabrodskaya

Vladimir Bogomolov was a second-generation bodyguard and for many years his father Viktor had also been working in the Soviet State Security Service.

Viktor Bogomolov was a man of great physical strength; he was tall and powerful, an excellent marksman and could easily overpower three or four people in traditional wrestling (imagine a man whose shirt collar size is forty-eight!). Among fellow security officers, Viktor was known as "The Rottweiler" and was one of those rare characters who were sought after and chosen to be in the personal security detail of state leaders. During and after the Second World War, Viktor served in Joseph Stalin's private security service and was awarded the Red Star Order for his work during Stalin's trip to the front in August 1941. Afterwards he served as private security officer to General Georgy Zhukov and often went to the front to protect other high-profile Soviet Army generals, as well as on secret missions throughout the USSR.

Once, when Viktor who was only twenty-six years old and was standing behind the doors leading to Stalin's office in Moscow, the head of Stalin's security came out and asked whether Viktor could play chess, as Stalin wanted to take a break from his work. As luck would have it, Viktor was a confident chess player, so he and Stalin ended up playing a few games of chess together.

When telling his son Vladimir about the secrets and tricks of being a good personal security officer, Viktor would often recall many interesting stories about his time in his service with Stalin. For example, even during heavy bombings in Moscow, Stalin liked to go outside and walk in the fresh air, much to the concern of a very nervous protection team. And once in the very beginning of the war in 1941, he turned to Viktor and said reassuringly: "Don't worry, everything is going to be all right. We will have Victory Day celebrations one day!"

During Stalin's funeral a proud and dignified Viktor Bogomolov stood beside his coffin as an honoured member of Stalin's personal security team.

From very early days it was known that Viktor's son Vladimir Bogomolov would follow in his father's footsteps as a high-ranking security officer, and would one day serve in the KGB. Indeed, Vladimir graduated from the KGB school in St Petersburg (then Leningrad) and then to a position in the department providing route surveillance and security for VIP mobile units. It took Vladimir just two years working diligently within this department to achieve the necessary experience and knowledge of the job. He developed a good reputation and proved himself to his more experienced colleagues and superiors. In December 1971 Vladimir was instructed to join the illustrious legendary KGB 9th Department; Leonid Brezhnev's personal security team tasked to look after the Soviet leader, visiting heads of state and other VIPs. Branch 18 consisted of eighteen officers, plus security for Brezhnev's city apartment and country residence. At first the team that accompanied Brezhnev on his trips around the country consisted of just three protection officers on a rotation basis, with others tasked to other protection duties as required (but in 1975 two more officers joined Brezhnev's personal team).

Vladimir had all the necessary skills and training for the position; he was an excellent runner, wrestler, swimmer and marksman, and his employment references, as well as his experience, expertise, morale and professionalism, were impeccable.

Vladimir, along with his other team members, provided security during the visit of Willy Brandt, Chancellor of West Germany (1969–74), and accompanied him all over the country, and also successfully completed an assignment to accompany the vice president of an Arab country. He was then asked to provide security to Comrade Ryabenko, which meant that Vladimir was about to start his security career as part of the personal security detail to the

General Secretary of the Central Committee of the Communist Party. This was one of the highest honours a KGB security officer could be granted in the USSR at the time.

In the mid 1970s Brezhnev started using a new Russian ZIL115 car with drivers who were not part of Branch 18, but the security team maintained a good personal and professional relationship with them, making sure the vehicles were always manned by a driver and at least two security officers, and in the winter time the engines were continually kept running in case the car was urgently required.

Up until 1977, police vehicles were not used to escort Brezhnev's vehicle until one evening, after a Communist Party reception, Brezhnev and his entourage were on their way to his country residence when suddenly a huge truck with a drunk driver at the wheel came hurtling towards them. It was only the professionalism of the driver that prevented what could have been a tragic accident. Following that incident the Ministry of Internal Affairs issued an official order decreeing that a police car should always precede the state leader's vehicle during all of his trips, and along the route policemen should be tasked to prevent vehicles crossing or entering the path of the motorcade (although years later this didn't stop a Jeep, part of Russian President Vladimir Putin's motorcade, smashing into a car that had mistakenly entered the route). Also, up to the 1970s the personal security officer accompanying Brezhnev never actually opened the car door for him; the security officer's task was solely to monitor the surroundings, looking out for any dangers, while a senior duty police officer opened the state leader's door. This was also changed.

In December 1978 Vladimir Bogomolov was involved in a terrible car accident that almost ended his life and career as one of the USSR's finest bodyguards. That year Moscow was experiencing an unusually cold winter and Bogomolov's team were heading quickly back home after completing their shift. The car's speed was around 100 mph and at a crossroads collided with a truck that had failed to stop because of the icy roads. The officer sitting in the back seat was thrown out of the car and was killed, and another other security officer was seriously wounded. Vladimir himself was unconscious for nine hours and spent two-and-a-half months recovering in hospital. Later, when Vladimir saw what was left of the car, he could not believe how he had survived the impact or how he was taken out from the squashed metallic remains; the car looked like an accordion. The only thing he said he could recollect was a white light at the end of a corridor and then darkness.

His progress was personally monitored by the head of the KGB and after Vladimir recovered he was offered a number of positions in different departments, but he refused, asking once again to be included in Brezhnev's personal security team.

In 1977–8 Brezhnev's security officers received new state-of-the-art Soviet weapons including a PSM pistol designed at the request of the KGB for their plain-clothes operatives, which is still one of the flattest pistols ever made. At close range, when the bullet goes through the body it leaves small entry wound, but the exit wound can be up to 16 cm in diameter. However, at long range they are not particularly effective. Brezhnev's personal detail was also the first in the country to receive new compact machine guns which could be hidden in briefcases and, with the help of specially made equipment, deployed very quickly. Vladimir became the quickest marksman in the entire unit.

Brezhnev loved cars and his favourite car was a black Eldorado Cadillac that US President Richard Nixon gave to the Soviet leader in 1972. Brezhnev also liked to drive his own Rolls-Royce, with his personal security officer in the passenger seat. One time, when Vladimir was accompanying Brezhnev in the Crimea, the Soviet leader almost fell asleep at the wheel after taking some sleeping pills, with Vladimir reaching over to steer the car to safety.

Another tragic accident happened during Brezhnev's visit to Uzbekistan. The delegation headed to a building plant in Uzbekistan's capital, Tashkent, where Brezhnev was going to award the Soviet Republic with the Order of Lenin. The premises were not checked and prepared in advance properly, as the visit was unexpected. All the workers gathered on the building's balconies in order to have a glimpse of the state leader when one of the balconies crashed under the weight of so many people, directly where Brezhnev and his entourage were standing. The accident created panic, with Brezhnev's security team shooting in the air as they tried to clear a path for him. Brezhnev broke his collarbone during this incident but was well enough to give a speech and present the Order of Lenin to the Republic the next day.

According to Vladimir, Brezhnev took special care of all of his personal security team and once, when the KGB decided to remove one of his team for lapses in discipline, Brezhnev insisted on his return. Following Brezhnev's orders, Vladimir himself got three new apartments during his time serving the leader, which meant a great deal during Soviet times. It is said that no other Soviet state leader was so attentive to the needs of his security team than Brezhnev.

During the summer, Vladimir would always accompany Brezhnev to Yalta, in the Crimea, where Brezhnev took his vacations. Brezhnev loved to swim and would frequently swim for over two hours in the sea along the coast. He was guarded by at least two other swimmers and other bodyguards positioned in a security motorboat. Once, in 1976, when the current was quite strong, the swimmers were pushed away from their usual swimming area, so when they finally made it on to shore they took other holidaymakers by surprise – nobody expected to see the leader of the USSR surrounded by his security team with no other protection apart from their swimming trunks! Some people immediately recognized Brezhnev, others did not. The security services had already located Brezhnev and his protection team and were waiting on the shore with towels and his vehicle. When long swimming sessions in summer became the norm for Brezhnev, it was decided to create a special team of nautical security guards. The training sessions were held according to specially designed programmes run by the best diving instructors in the Navy. Bogomolov was one of the first to pass all the tests and training, and he became one of Brezhnev's special submerged security detail with the additional benefit that he was already completely trusted by Brezhnev.

In July 1977, Brezhnev, together with his entourage, was returning by motorboat to his Yalta residence from Feodosya, where he had attended the opening of an art exhibition of works by the famous nineteenth-century artist, Ivan Aivazovsky. The motorboat captain brought the guests home quicker than usual so there was still enough time to go for a swim. Everything was running as usual with Brezhnev's bodyguards swimming alongside him. Brezhnev stopped and floated for a while; it was known that the state leader used to like float on the surface with his arms wide on both sides – his security used to call it "Brezhnev's Cross". But this time Brezhnev had fallen asleep after apparently taking sleeping pills while on the motorboat earlier. But for the prompt actions of the security team the consequences could have been quite tragic.

Vladimir Bogomolov, like many of the other security officers, spent a lot of time accompanying the state leader on different trips, both within the USSR and abroad. In 1974 it was calculated that the security team spent 276 days away from home, which was quite difficult both physically and morally. But financially his security team was rewarded quite well as during Soviet times Brezhnev's personal guards took home around 370 roubles a month in comparison to a qualified engineer's salary of only 140 roubles.

Once, acknowledging the high professionalism of Bogomolov's security team, Yuri Andropov, the head of the KGB, said that there would never be another team like it and, during Soviet times, the head of the most powerful special service in the world was always right.

According to Bogomolov, during ten years of protecting Brezhnev as part of his personal security team, they did not once permit anything (such as packages, envelopes, etc.) to be handed directly to Brezhnev by someone unknown, unlike when Mikhail Gorbachev was in Yalta on holiday and a man came from behind a statue and handed over an envelope containing a personal letter directly to the leader. In Brezhnev's time this would have been impossible.

Once, in Belorussia during an important event involving the participation of Soviet government officials, another famous Soviet bodyguard, Mikhail Soldatov, prevented an attempt to hand over an envelope to Nikita Khrushchev. One of the female performers, while walking on the stage, put her hand in the pocket of her dress at the very last moment with the intention of taking out a letter for Khrushchev. The leader's bodyguard managed to grab the woman's hand before she took it out of her dress. It could have been anything. Her expensive stage outfit was ruined in the ensuing tussle.

10 November 1982 would always remain in Bogomolov's memory. On the evening of 9 November, as usual Brezhnev's security team accompanied him to his residence. Vladimir carried

the leader's personal belongings into the bedroom and wished him good night. Next morning the security team was preparing for the usual working day protecting Brezhnev, which would start with Brezhnev taking a swim in the pool and going to the sauna. At 9 a.m. the senior security officer Vladimir Medvedev went to take his post outside the Brezhnev's bedroom door while Bogomolov checked the water temperature in the small swimming pool, prepared a lifebuoy and found a couple of minutes to smoke a cigarette. All of a sudden there was commotion, shouting and crying in the house; Brezhnev had died. He was seventy-six.

After Brezhnev's death, Bogomolov continued working as a security officer for different state officials both in the USSR and abroad. His most memorable trip was as a part of a security team in Afghanistan, working as personal bodyguard to Afghanistan's leader Mohammad Najibullah. Najibullah never trusted his own people to protect him and Vladimir received an order to shoot anybody who seemed suspicious. It was a difficult and dangerous job and Vladimir had to grow a beard and moustache so that he could blend in with the locals. Najibullah's personal security team never wore suits but ordinary clothes, hats, caps, etc. – the protocol was not important, just the security of the person in their protection.

In the last few years of his life Bogomolov taught other bodyguards and passed his skills and experience on to a new generation through the NAST Russia Bodyguard Academy, and his expertise and knowledge of working in the field became legendary among young security officers.

In 2009, Vladimir Bogomolov died. He was only sixty-four, but his vast experience will always remain in the minds of those he worked with and taught.

BOB HONIBALL
(LITHUANIA)

Martial Arts Expert

Introducing . . . Bob Honiball

I FIRST WITNESSED the awesome power and phenomenal speed of Bob Honiball when he and I worked together on the doors at a nightclub called Rick's Place in my home town of Norwich, in the east of England. It was in the mid 1980s, I was fairly new to the doors and had just started martial arts training. We were patrolling the club when a barman came over to tell us that there was trouble at one of the bars where, apparently, a group of five men decided not to pay for their drinks. Bob and I rushed over and before I had time to blink Bob had downed four of the men in a series of punches and kicks, so fast it took my breath away. He turned to me and jokingly said: "The last one is for you, Rob!" Those were the days on the doors when doormen hit first and asked questions later. Bob was a master at martial arts back then and, twenty-five years later, he is unbelievable. He is undoubtedly one of the very best martial artists I have seen and one of the hardest men I have ever met, anywhere in the world.

Bob now lives in Lithuania where he has his own dojo and teaches unarmed combat to the country's Special Forces, police and private security. Even though Bob is undeniably one of the toughest men on the planet, he is also one of the nicest people you could ever hope to meet. This is his story, as told specially for this book by Bob himself.

MY STORY
By Bob Honiball

I guess it's always best to start at the beginning as our childhood usually shapes and affects our values, and how we think and act later in life. I was born in 1952 in Liverpool, England, into a working-class family; besides my father and mother I had an older sister called Celia. Guess things were hard in those days, although being a child you don't really realize it. We lived in a property which was later to be condemned as a slum; the house had no bathroom and had an outside toilet; bathing was a weekly event as we only had a tin bath and had to boil up the water to use it, which took some time. The house was always damp, something my parents forever struggled to remedy. At the bottom of our backyard was a huge factory producing tin cans, so there was continuous noise from the machinery.

When I was about nine years old I contracted double pneumonia and pleurisy, and nearly died. Because my mother was a nurse during the Second World War, she pleaded with the doctors to let me stay at home where she could give me more care and attention than if I was in hospital. The doctors agreed. I remember the doctor popping in to check on me from time to time, and being given what seemed like bottle after bottle of penicillin; in those days there were no antibiotic tablets. I can still clearly see myself being too weak to even move and remember constantly struggling for breath. After more or less recovering I visited my specialist in hospital for the last time, and he showed me the X-rays of my lungs; both my lungs were black shadows and I remember him saying, "See son, how bad your lungs were, for God's sake never smoke as it will kill you." He scared me so much I never smoked but in those days nearly everyone did smoke so as a result I suffered greatly from secondary smoking.

In total I missed about a year of schooling and this obviously affected my education. In those days we had secondary and grammar school education and everyone had to sit an eleven-plus exam in order to be accepted into a grammar school. I failed and as a result was sent the local secondary modern school; I have never been that academic but feel the schooling I missed while ill had some bearing on my academic failure.

The school I attended was not a good learning environment; some teachers cared but there was generally little incentive to learn. Really, it was all about just doing enough in order to give the children a basic education and nothing else. Being a tough inner-city school there was also a lot of bullying; my tactic to avoid this was to keep a low profile, which for the most part worked. It was about this time that the comprehensive school system was introduced. My class, the highest one within our school, was allowed to stay on for an extra year to take exams, but in order to do this we were absorbed into the old grammar school and had to face the fact that everyone thought we were the "plebs from that other school". This helped to bond the members of our class together and we all looked out for each other. My credibility was enhanced when one day on the playing field I spectacularly threw a boy much bigger than myself over my shoulder. After that I never had to face the threat of intimidation again, although I continued to suffer with bronchial problems virtually every winter, still having to spend long periods away from school. I wanted to be good at sport, but my health affected my fitness and held me back. My uncle Sid and brother-in-law Dave tried to encourage me to get fit but it wasn't until I was fifteen that my friend Rich introduced me and another friend, Ray, to judo. It was only then that my fitness and health started to improve. However, I continued to suffer with bronchial problems right up to my mid twenties; my sister Celia has said that if it wasn't for my early judo training she doesn't think I would be alive today.

In the early 1960s most people who wanted to study the martial arts had the choice of either judo or karate. There was boxing, of course, but in those days the "martial arts" had a sort of mystery surrounding them which attracted me, so in 1967 I decided to start judo classes with my friends. I continued judo training for several years, but during this time a karate guy came to train with us and one day we asked him to demonstrate his techniques. We had never seen anything like this before; to me karate seemed mysterious, powerful and deadly, and I was sold straight away. I was introduced to my first karate instructor, Sensei (teacher) Harry Benfield and the style of karate was Mushindo Ryu. Harry used to be a street-fighter and a doorman, and the combat effectiveness of karate interested me greatly.

Eventually, for reasons I can't now remember, we decided to stop training in this style and looked for one that better served our needs. In 1971 I briefly started training in Uechi-Ryu Karate Do under Sensei Tony Christian and Bob Greenhalgh. In 1972 Gary Spiers appeared on the karate scene in Liverpool and we invited Gary to become the teacher at our dojo (club).

Gary had been invited to come over to the UK from Japan, where he had been training in Goju Kai karate, by the Sensei Terry O'Neill, who had an awesome reputation as a karate practitioner as well as through working the tough doors of Liverpool. At that time Gary Spiers was considered one of the leading lights of practical karate, introducing his version of Goju Kai karate, a no-nonsense fighting style, to the UK. I always remember the first time Gary walked into our dojo; we didn't know what to expect. In came this big half-Maori with close-cropped hair, which was unusual as in those days everyone had long hair, a nose that had been broken so many times that the bones had been removed and a scar from an old knife wound running across his face. There was definitely a feeling of trepidation that day, even amongst the real toughies in the dojo.

Gary was a technician, but the whole focus of his training methods was towards practical no-nonsense fighting. In those days free sparring was tough with no holding back in some cases; I remember Gary standing behind me screaming, "Go, go, get in there, digger, don't stop." Having what they call a combative attitude, he always pushed you to your very limit and taught you that once the fighting started you should never stop hitting until your opponent is no longer a threat. Developing this "combative attitude" was the main thing Gary taught his students. He also believed you should always be prepared to fight, no matter where or when, and on a couple of occasions on a Sunday afternoon before training, he would take me and my friend into the pub next door, slap some money on the bar and order the barman to ply us with beer until the money ran out. We would then have to spar full-out for the rest of the training session with a belly full of beer, feeling like you wanted to throw up, with no control or accuracy and knocking spots off each other. Gary was a bit crazy like that and I suppose so were we for doing it! However, he would tell us with his usual laugh that it was important for us to know how to fight, even in an inebriated state!

Even though Gary had always lived in a violent world, during all the time I knew him he only ever meted out his version of justice to those individuals who deserved it. One of the first stories I heard about Gary working the doors was not long after he arrived in Liverpool. One night while on duty, Gary was confronted by an individual who was waving a broken beer glass at him. Straightaway, Gary picked up another beer glass, smashed it and threw it at the feet of the individual shouting, "You're gonna need two of them, digger." The individual's response was to take to his heels. For me this story sums up the spirit of Gary. Perhaps in some way this also explains the ability to "fight without fighting"; if you dominate the psychology of an opponent in any confrontation you have gone a long way to winning the fight . . . or you might not even have to fight at all.

At one time Gary lived with Sean Reich, a student of his and one of my closest friends. Gary got Sean into full-time door work. I was a frequent visitor to Sean's house and would sometimes sleep over, which was an experience in itself. Being in my early twenties I was impressionable and, like so many people who came into contact with Gary, I was in awe of this larger than life character who had "been there and done it" and who certainly lived life to the full. A lot of people were afraid of Gary but to me and my buddy Sean he was like a big brother who taught us a lot about real fighting, spirit and life.

Sean worked on the doors of an out-of-town nightclub. One day he had to intervene with a bad guy who had stuck a beer glass in someone's face. The guy tried to do the same to Sean and Sean turned it back into him, making a mess of his face, a technique we used to practise over and over again. I wasn't there at the time, but when I went to see Sean at the club the following week, the friends of the guy Sean had hospitalized were in the club, "tooled up". Sean called Gary for back-up but he was working miles away in the city centre and would take a while to arrive. Luckily for us Gary turned up just in time, with Terry O'Neill and another guy who was a professional wrestler. They had run red lights to get to us and when they walked in Sean calmly approached the group of guys and said, "If you want it, let's go." Such was the reputation of Gary and Terry they just got up and walked out and there was never any trouble from them again.

Interesting events, and meeting interesting people, were always par for the course around Gary. On one occasion we travelled to Spain for a long weekend of training. Driving to the airport Gary produced an SAS (Special Forces) training manual and tossed it to us to read; things like that were not in the public domain in those days and Gary had made friends with a guy from the service who had given it to Gary to look at. It had all sorts of fascinating information, including improvised bomb-making. A few days later, after we returned to the UK, I was sitting with Sean at his place – Gary was out – when there was a strong knock at the door. When Sean answered there was a group of heavy-looking Special Branch guys standing there with a search warrant. When they entered, some searched the property while we were separated and interviewed; Sean received particular interest because he was an Irish American who had spent most of his life in the UK, and at that time the IRA was active in the country, planting bombs and making terrorist attacks. Later we found out that the raid was related to the SAS manual that "someone" had stupidly left on the back seat of the hire car in Spain. Gary laughed it off, of course.

The one time I saw Gary on the back foot was after an all-night party. The next day I was ill after consuming too much alcohol. Gary, out of the goodness of his heart, decided to drive me back to my mother's home. He knocked on the door and when it opened I staggered in. Looking back I could see my dear old mum, who was five foot nothing, looking up at this big bear of a man wagging her finger at him, telling him off for bringing her son home in such a state. It was the only time I saw Gary on the defensive, walking backwards and apologizing in the most polite way possible. A real gent!

Gary taught me how to get stuck in, to fight dirty, and the importance of fighting spirit and having a combative attitude, qualities I lacked up until then. One day Gary, who had once been a butcher, was cutting up meat; he was quite skilful and knew how to fight with a knife. While I watched I asked him how you would fight someone armed with a knife. He said, "Bob, if you want to fight anyone armed with any weapon, first get good with the use of that weapon yourself." That has always stuck with me: I have practised various weapon skills and how to counter them ever since. He also fostered in me the importance of always respecting and thinking about the reality of combat, and I've always trained and taught with this in mind.

Training with Gary was excellent but over time his attention was drawn more towards the nightclub security scene. Although Gary taught us a hell of a lot, it was felt by my senseis, Tony Christian and Bob Greenhalgh, that my direction needed to be more traditional and to go deeper into the practice of karate. After training on several courses held by Sensei James Rousseau, it was decided that I should go on to study Okinawan Goju Ryu Karate Do. During this time I trained under Sensei Morio Higaonna, Teruo Chinen and James Rousseau.

In 1978, together with Sensei Roy Flat, a friend of mine, I opened a dojo in Liverpool. A year later I then moved to Norwich on the opposite side of England and opened another dojo. I continued training with various groups including Karate Do International, based in South Africa, my main sensei being Francis Rink who was based in Rhodesia, as Zimbabwe was called back then. This was an Okinawan Goju Ryu organization headed by Sensei Hugh St John Thompson, an early student of Morio Higaonna whose main representative in the UK was Sensei Dennis Martin. Dennis was a friend of Terry O'Neill and also worked the doors, gaining an awesome reputation. Dennis went on to specialize in teaching unarmed and armed combative skills and has taught bodyguards and other security personnel worldwide, also writing extensively on the subject. I spent a month of intensive training in South Africa. Although I learned a hell of a lot from all these sensei, I decided that I needed to look for an organization with a more direct lineage to Master Chojun Miyagi's teachings.

With the approval of my dojo I decided to apply to join the Okinawan Goju Ryu Karate Do Kyokai, Jundokan. The association was then headed by Master Eiichi Miyazato, tenth dan. Eiichi Miyazato was the head student of Master Chojun Miyagi, the founder of Okinawan Goju Ryu Karate Do. After the death of Master Miyagi, it was decided by the students and family of Master Miyagi that Master Miyazato should continue as head of the dojo. This was because Master Miyazato was held in such high regard by Master Miyagi. Master Miyazato also trained with Master Miyagi for longer than anyone else, right up until his master's death; he was Master Miyagi's chief assistant both at the Okinawan Police Academy and at his home dojo. Later Master Miyazato opened his own dojo which he called the Jundokan. Since then he has devoted himself to preserving and passing on the teachings of his master. Many first-class karate practitioners have been the products of both Master Miyazato's teachings and the Jundokan. At this time the UK branch of the Jundokan was headed by Sensei Richard Barrett. Richard had been training in Okinawa at the Jundokan for an extended period, returning in 1985 to open a branch of the Jundokan here in the UK, with the permission of Master Miyazato. Richard is a very strong Karate Ka with an excellent technical ability.

It had always been a wish of mine to travel to Okinawa to experience the birthplace of karate and to train there under the masters. In 1988 my wish came true and I travelled with my student and good friend Tony Green to Okinawa for the first time to train intensively under Miyazato for a month. I also trained under Masters Koshin Iha, Nanko Minei and Tetsunosuke Yasuda. Master Iha was also one of the top students of Master Miyagi and was the technical adviser for the Jundokan. The depth and quality of instruction at the Jundokan was awesome.

When we first arrived in Okinawa we were advised not to ask too many questions, as it wasn't the Japanese way; we were to just do as we were told and to train hard. But we wanted to learn as much as possible so every day we would turn up at the dojo before anyone else and when Master Miyazato appeared would politely ask things. Sometimes he would just say, "Train more and you will understand," but for the most part he would answer all our questions – to some questions he would give us direct answers but to others he would answer in a way to make us think and try to discover the answers for ourselves. In the end though, I think he enjoyed our cheek. When I asked him about certain individuals who say that they have the secrets of karate, he laughed and said, "Bob, the only secrets are the ones you find out for yourself." Wise words.

Master Miyazato lived above the dojo with his wife. The dojo itself is spacious by Okinawan standards and well-equipped. Traditionally in the Jundokan we use specialized weight-training equipment to develop our bodies in the right way for karate – by developing the structure and muscular strength of the body. To develop our body's weapons we use conventional boxing bags and pads. However, we also use traditional equipment to condition our fists, hands, elbows and feet by repeatedly striking what is known as a Makiwara, a chest-high chamfered piece of flexible wood that is inserted into the ground. The top is covered by a leather pouch and it is then stuck repeatedly, not only to harden our body weapons for combat, but also to develop full-body power through effective dynamics. A bamboo bundle called a tou is struck with the finger-tips to develop this type of striking. There is also a tree trunk which is struck with the forearms and shins to develop blocking power, and to harden the shins for kicking and being kicked.

When a student first started training, Master Miyazato would delegate a senior to be his or her instructor. This relationship would usually last for the whole of the student's karate life. During the day there would only be a handful of people training, but during evening the numbers would increase dramatically and the range of experience and knowledge was great. Because there were no set classes you had to motivate yourself; you could be lazy, but if you had this attitude you would be left alone. On the other hand if you worked hard with enthusiasm you would usually find that a senior would take you under his wing and others would train with you or offer advice. Although everyone practised the whole system, there were senior sensei within the dojo who specialized in all the different aspects of training. This made for an excellent work and learning environment, as you could call upon the expertise of all these individuals to resolve any problems that you had.

On occasions Master Miyazato would ask us up to his living area for a little something to eat or to share a drink or two. This was a great experience; to be able to talk, to ask further questions and just to be in the company of a part of karate history.

Training in the dojo is strict and no idle chatter is allowed, but after the evening class we would usually be invited out by one or more of the seniors. This would be interesting and very informative, because away from the dojo the seniors let their guard down and opened up. In some respects I've learned just as much on these occasions as being in the dojo itself. Also, on occasions we were invited to train at one of the other dojos run by another master, which normally ended with some sort of party afterwards. Just being able to socialize with these senior masters and to ask questions about history and training was a great experience.

During this first visit we were instructed and refined in all aspects of Goju Ryu by Master Miyazato and the other masters at the dojo. We finally felt that we had trained at the heart of Goju Ryu Karate Do and were taught by some of the best in the world. This made Tony and I determined to return to Okinawa on a regular basis to gain further refinements and deepen our knowledge of karate. The knowledge you receive is pure and direct, not third or fourth hand. Based on their knowledge and experience, masters and good teachers can help to refine you and short-cut the mistakes you would normally make. I actively encouraged all my students to make the pilgrimage to Okinawa at least once in their lives.

Tony and I returned to Okinawa several times to train under Miyazato and in 1997 when Richard Barrett, the former chief instructor for the UK resigned, I was made Shibucho, Chief Instructor for Jundokan UK, by Master Miyazato. The last time we trained with Miyazato was just before his death in 1999. Although looking frailer he was teaching right up until the very end. I remember when we left for the airport he said goodbye, telling me to look after myself. I bowed and said, "No, Sensei, you look after yourself." In saying those words I think I realized I wouldn't see my sensei again.

I felt very sad when I heard about his death but also felt privileged that I'd had the opportunity to train with such a great man; I made a pledge to myself to pass on what I had learned from him.

I once asked Master Miyazato what is the greatest gift karate can give. He simply replied "humility" and this has always stayed close to me and I hold it dear. Master Miyazato said various things to me that inspired me to think deeply about my training and to refine it based on the principles he taught. He also told me, "If you're true to yourself, even if you lose a battle, you will never be defeated." In my life I've had a few people who have influenced and inspired me in different ways and Master Miyazato was one of those.

Despite Master Miyazato's death we continued to travel to Okinawa on a regular basis to deepen our knowledge and I am constantly trying to refine my own training and the way I teach based upon what I've been taught and the principles of Goju Ryu. I always tell my students that the day I stop refining is the day I give up training. Although at the time of writing this I have been training in the martial arts for forty-two years, I still strongly believe it is vitally important to seek out teachers who are more experienced and knowledgeable than me. Training in Okinawa with the likes of Masters Yasuda and Omini (tenth dans), as well as other very experienced masters and sensei, is essential to me.

Personally, I've never been particularly interested in sport karate, but I do have a great respect for those who practise it. I am not saying that an individual who practises sport karate would not be effective in a "real" situation – there have been great sport karate practitioners such as Terry O'Neill, an individual who has been top of his field, whom I greatly admire and who, while working on the doors of Liverpool, has amassed a great deal of practical experience in real fighting. Moreover, I do believe that in the West we have some of the best competition fighters in the world and I think that one should constantly look to the "modern" methods being developed by sports scientists and other individuals to improve both physical and mental performance. However, there is a Japanese saying: "Cherish the old to understand the new." Karate practitioners who wish to call themselves traditionalists must cherish the fact that their fighting tradition has evolved out of the research, training methods and fighting skills of previous masters. Over the centuries each new generation of masters has rediscovered and built upon the teachings of their masters. Therefore, the training methods, principles and philosophies of the past, which form the bedrock and essence of what we call Traditional Karate Do today, must always be studied, researched, trained in, refined and *never* forgotten. Only by doing this will people come to understand the true power and deeper meaning of karate. Karate is an important part of the cultural heritage of Okinawa and as such will always be held very dear by its people. Therefore to those Okinawans who follow the "Karate Do" or "The Way of Karate", it is a special treasure that forms a major part of their lives. One Okinawan sensei told me, "As long as I can breathe I will practise Goju." I feel that because of this strong feeling for the tradition of Karate Do in Okinawa, there will always be a concentration of experience and expertise. Personally, for me it is important to always have a sensei to look to, not only to refine my physical ability but to guide me towards a deeper understanding of the essence of karate. To me it's all about emphasis and in sport karate the main emphasis is on winning a point or having the best precision there is. The skill level required to achieve this is undeniably to be both admired and respected, but in traditional karate the emphasis is more about realistic fighting and the development of Kata (karate forms or sequences of karate techniques passed down to us by previous masters). This is not only dynamically powerful but also reflects the practical fighting principles of that style. There is a saying, "Train the way you want to fight and you'll fight the way you train." Also, on a deeper level, traditional karate emphasizes the development of character through an understanding of self. Master Motobu Choki (1871–1944), who was renowned as a practical fighter (gained through his experience of real fighting), wrote in 1927, "In seeking to understand the essence of karate, we must search beyond the immediate results of physical training and not place too much emphasis upon competition or record breaking, but rather to seek wisdom through self-knowledge and humility."

In 1992 I was invited to Lithuania to teach traditional Goju Ryu. The people I taught there were both tough and eager to learn. At the end of that visit I was presented with a sports medal from the Lithuanian army for teaching some of their self-defence instructors; in fact, I was invited by them to stay on and teach unarmed combat but at that time I politely declined. However, I was invited by a former student several times to teach seminars and many years later made Lithuania my home.

In 2007 I was invited to teach in India, which was a unique and extremely interesting experience. I am currently planning to return to help develop and promote traditional karate and the other martial arts. I stayed at my student's family house; they are Hindu and it was interesting to experience a completely different culture and religion. In India, to my embarrassment, I was called a guru; it is the custom to bow, touch the feet of your teacher and then your heart, and this happened to me many times. As gifts I gave away a couple of karate black belts from Okinawa and the students I gave them to actually prostrated themselves and kissed my feet. I was also asked to be the chief judge at a karate tournament and award the prizes. They gave me what looked like a throne to sit on to survey the tournament. I am a quiet person and don't like a lot of fuss so this was a very humbling experience for me. Unfortunately, one day my student Balaji was involved in a motorcycle accident on the way to pick me up. He nearly died and was in intensive care for the rest of my stay. Most days I was taken to visit him in hospital; although he was unconscious I was asked by his family to talk to him and encourage his recovery. Once or twice when I was with the family, the doctors would appear and said there could only be one visitor and I was told by his father to go in. I would always say no, that it was more important for a family member to see him, but they would insist, saying it was important for me to see him, being his teacher and an honoured guest. Again, this was a very humbling experience. It was touch and go that Balaji would survive but thankfully he did and now he has made a full recovery.

Because of my interest in the reality of how karate would be applied in actual combat and the fact that I was being asked to teach self-defence seminars, I decided to increase my experience of actual conflict by working on the door of nightclubs. Later, I got my friend and student Tony Green a job working with me. I felt I knew how to fight from the days training with Gary Spiers, as well as with my own training, but I wanted to confront my own fears and learn how to deal with real and violent confrontation. Having a knife pulled on you or facing multiple attackers wanting to rip your head off certainly brought home the importance of effective techniques, tactics and reality-based training. Working on the doors taught me the importance of effective awareness skills, correct body language, verbal skills, how to deal with fear and stress (flight or fight syndrome), the positive use of the adrenalin pump, and the use of the mental attributes of courage, determination and having a combative attitude. If practised correctly I do feel that all these qualities and attributes are there in karate training and in the writings of the various martial art masters, but security work has given me more understanding and insight into these particular aspects of karate. I've heard it said that Kata is only good for the development of technique and is of little use in actual fighting. My experience of working "the doors" disproves this. More often than not I would use Kata applications, or a variation of them, during an altercation.

Therefore, I would suggest that the people who hold this view have little or no knowledge of the use of effective applications in relation to the Kata they practise. Kata and their applications must be practised together in an effective way so that they become one and the same. In this way when you practise Kata you will be practising the applications and when you practice applications you will be practising Kata. If you train in Kata and applications in this manner, their use in real situations will become natural, reactive and effective.

In total I worked the doors for nearly ten years and the reason I eventually gave up was because I got ill. One day the doctor called me and said he would like to have a serious talk. I feared I had something seriously wrong but he said no, he wanted to talk to me about my lifestyle. I told him what I did; working full-time at the Post Office, training and teaching four times a week, and working the doors three or four nights a week. He shook his head and told me that if I carried on like that I would not be around much longer. Something had to go; so I gave up the doors.

I never thought of practising another marital art but on the advice of Master Miyazato I decided to try something else. I wanted something that would balance out the stronger aspects of karate training, so I decided to give Taiji a go and have been practising Yang-style Taiji under the guidance of my teacher Pete Dobson. My training in karate and my attitude, together with my knowledge of structure and body dynamics, helped me understand and develop my Taiji quicker than normal. In time Pete and I became close friends; Pete is a really interesting guy, an artist, ordained Buddhist, ex-boxer and boxing coach, and has also worked in prisons for years teaching Taiji and meditation. He has had some successes in turning some real bad guys around. He's a deep guy with a big heart and has helped me to think and better understand myself. Although in a totally different way, Pete has a similar charisma to Gary Spiers; going out with Pete and being in his company was always interesting and fun. He can engage with almost anyone and being around him I have met some very interesting people, from Buddhists to ex-cons!

One day he asked if we could stop off and see some guy he knew from his work in prison. Over the years he had done his best to help this guy sort himself out, and before Pete left to emigrate to New

Zealand, he wanted to see if he was OK. He was a big guy, a bruiser and you could tell he had been around a bit – he had been in a few Mexican stand-offs with the police and I believe the police sent in armed officers first if they wanted to have a talk with him. I had some trepidation but the guy was really friendly and polite.

Taiji has helped me in my karate training in many different ways, especially understanding how relaxation can deliver force, as well as by refining my sensitivity for close-quarter fighting where eyesight becomes less important but sensitivity to the pressure and/or energy or lack of pressure and/or energy an opponent gives you is vital. Taiji has also improved my health and has helped me to become more in touch with my mind and body. I also encouraged one of my karate students, Paul Fretter, to train in Taiji. Paul has gone on to teach Taiji and Fujian White Crane successfully all over the UK.

While in New Zealand Pete trained with Chinese teacher Mr Wee Kee Jin. Pete invited him to the UK to teach and once we had trained with him we were well and truly sold. Jin has been training in Taiji as long as I have been practising karate. His ability is second to none and he is one of the best teachers I have ever trained under as he is very knowledgeable, totally open and completely sincere. He is also very humble; a man who would never call himself a master but instead regards himself as a true student of Taiji. His lineage is also exemplary; when you are taught by him you know that you are being taught the true heart of Taiji. I am proud to have him as my teacher and over the years we have also become friends. We eventually found out that Jin was also taught Fujian White Crane by his Taiji teacher, Master Huang Sheng Shyan (1910–92) and Huang originated from Fujian Province in China. For me and Paul this was a remarkable coincidence as there are very close links between our style of karate, Goju Ryu and Fujian White Crane. In fact Master Huang had been taught by a Master Xie Zhongxiang (also known as Ryuru Ko), the same master who had taught one of the previous karate masters in our lineage, Master Higashionna Kanryo. Higashionna was taught by Xie Zhongxiang during the years he spent in China furthering his study of martial arts. This seemed like fate to us and we had to learn this fighting tradition. Furthermore, some of the Okinawan karate masters from previous times also trained in the same fighting tradition. Jin taught the whole Fujian

White Crane system to Pete, Paul and me. Jin hadn't the time to teach it in the UK himself, so he has left it in the hands of Paul and me to teach, develop and promote. However, Jin is always there to help and refine our practice and answer questions, and in turn this fulfilled the promise made to his teacher, Master Huang, to pass on his Fujian White Crane fighting tradition.

Jin is wise. When I asked him about practising different systems of martial arts he said, "You should never change one thing for another but you will find that one influences the other." I've found this to be true. The martial attitude and spirit I have developed from my years of training in karate is always there, but the principles I've learned from Jin's teachings and my practice of Taiji and Fujian White Crane have influenced and refined my practice of karate and how I teach it, without changing anything that Master Miyazato first taught me.

As mentioned, my friend Pete Dobson is also an ordained Buddhist minister and I also call myself a Buddhist. For many years I have had a keen interest in Buddhism and the relationship it has with the martial arts and it was Pete who inspired me to experience meditation practice. Zen Master Dogen (1200–53) describes Zen in this way:

> To study the Buddhist Way is to learn about oneself. To learn about oneself is to forget oneself. To forget oneself is to perceive oneself as all things. To realize this is to cast off the body and mind of self and others. When you reach this stage you will be detached even from enlightenment but will practise it continually without even thinking about it.

Zen, or Ch'an as it is known in China, has had a great influence on the martial arts. The Shaolin monks of China, together with many of the warriors of feudal Japan, believed in the importance of Zen. These warriors thought that the study of Zen was essential in order both to become an effective warrior and to overcome their fear of death. In fact modern sports psychologists and security advisers use similar methods of mind development for sport and combat survival. The Zen term "*Mushin*", meaning empty or no mind, and what sports psychologists call "being in the zone" is, to me, one and the same. The Japanese maxim "*Tatakawa zushite katsu*", declared by some masters to be the true meaning of Budo, means "Winning without fighting by overcoming the enemy within". For me, this holds true.

I also practise the Buddhist tradition known as Kokoro No Kai, which is a practical form of Buddhism involving meditation through the practice of chanting and the study of a Buddhist scripture called the "Lotus Sutra". My teacher is Sensei Hiromi Hasagawa, whom I have known for many years as he is the proprietor of the Oriental Martial Arts Centre in Norwich where I used to teach. Hiromi is a wise, generous man and a good friend, who is always there to offer me advice and guidance whenever I need it.

My life changed in 2004. I took redundancy from the post office where I had worked for most of my life, and a long-term relationship ended. My life seemed to implode and it took me a long time to get my head together. My family and friends helped me through it all and I owe them everything for that. The phrase "You know who your true friends are when times are bad" holds true for me. In re-evaluating what to do with myself and why I'm here on this planet I came to realize that training and teaching is my true purpose in life. My mother once told me that it is important to be good at least one thing in your life.

I wanted a fresh start and at first thought about going to live in either India or Lithuania, where I already had students. Then two female karate students from Lithuania turned up to train in the UK with me and I ended up marrying one of them! Her name is Simona and I now live with her in Lithuania. Everyone thought I was a bit crazy but I have my fresh start and my own martial arts centre – I am doing something I love to do. Our centre has been open a couple of years now and we are gradually developing a hard core of students, as well as teaching seminars around the country. But without Sensei Hiromi and the support of the Kokoro No Kai we wouldn't have achieved what we have so far. Our intention and ambition is to create a special place for people of all ages who want to study traditional martial arts, improve health and fitness, develop character, learn how to effectively defend themselves, and, if they wish, to follow the Buddhist path. Already people are saying that attending our centre has affected their lives in a very positive way.

We have also trained some of the instructors who train the president's bodyguards and hope to do some more work with them in the future. I have one government bodyguard attending regular classes with me and some anti-terrorist police attending my seminars. An instructor who has trained with me is one of the best combat shooters in the country; he also works for the government and teaches firearm skills to bodyguards, anti-terrorist teams and other specialist units. We have become good friends and he is teaching me combat shooting.

People sometimes ask me why I still train and I have to be truthful and say I don't really know. I think this is because over the years training has become so much a part of me, just like eating and sleeping; it's just something I do and still love. It is who I am. If you have the right attitude, training in the martial arts is like a bottomless pit which is why masters are still able to refine themselves and still be effective well into old age. The key word here is "refinement" and through refinement seeking perfection. Refinement to me means that I'm always striving to go deeper into my training, to improve myself in order to try and achieve perfection. Sometimes I feel I'm almost able to touch it but in reality it's always just out of reach. Striving for perfection is the way I keep my drive and enthusiasm alive. I still get a buzz from teaching, not only from seeing my students develop but also from seeing how training helps affect their character in a positive way. For example, I once had a thirty-year-old guy start training with me; he had been knifed in an unprovoked attack while leaving a pub with his wife and as a result he lost all confidence and found it difficult to go out anywhere. Training gave him back his confidence and self-respect, and helped him to overcome his problems. He only trained for a couple of years but every Christmas after that he would seek me out and give me a bottle of wine as a thank you. Another guy, who was an ex-con, was recommended to me. As a rule I never teach individuals who I think may abuse what they are taught, but I was assured the guy was trying to sort himself out. Training helped to give him some focus and channel the aggression he felt. He was also dyslexic, which was not recognized when he was young, so as a result he became dysfunctional at school, which in turn led to Borstal and eventually prison. I never forgot his first karate examination; this big bruiser of a man was nearly in tears when he passed – he told me that he had never been awarded anything before. Once again training helped to give him back his self-confidence and his self-respect; he has now settled down and has a family.

A good teacher is only as good as the students he produces, as the ultimate aim of any true teacher is to develop a student who excels himself or herself to refine their teachings still further. Over the years in the UK I've helped produce some excellent karate exponents who are now respected and highly regarded for their ability, and I am proud that they still consider me their sensei. I hope to do the same here in Lithuania. At the time of writing this I am nearly fifty-eight, and as well as trying to refine myself as much as possible, my main goal now is to produce good students who can carry on the traditions I teach.

DAVE WEEKS (UK)/ MIKE TYSON (USA)

Hard Man/Boxer

Introducing . . . Dave Weeks and Mike Tyson

IN THIS UNUSUAL and compelling chapter, British hard man Dave Weeks compares his abusive conduct, violent rages, anti-social behaviour and anger-management problems with those of the iconic former American heavyweight boxing champion Mike Tyson. Dave chronicles his own journey through life, his legal and illegal means of employment including debt-collecting, running massage parlours and petty crime, and compares it to Tyson's escapades in-and-out of the ring. It's also an examination of human frailties and harmful reactions to life's disappointments but told from a perspective of violence.

The author Dave Weeks was born in the town of Hornchurch, Essex, England, in 1962. An outwardly normal working-class upbringing hid the fact that Dave's father was an abusive and bullying figure who terrorized his family with his alcohol-fuelled rages behind closed doors. It was a childhood which would haunt Dave throughout most of his adult life.

Upon leaving school Dave qualified as a graphic designer but the following years were a roller-coaster ride of random job changes, verbal and physical abuse, and failed relationships, as Dave sought contentment and happiness in all the wrong places. This culminated in several failed and abusive marriages, as alcohol and violence took control of his psyche and emotions.

In 2004 Dave's father died and this event forced Dave to confront the mental demons from his past and analyse why his behaviour had virtually mirrored that of his forever-angry father. Even when trying to change and become a better person, Dave still succumbed to the lure of violence and dabbled in both debt-collecting and running a massage parlour. However, in an attempt to change the pattern of uncontrolled anger and destructive addictive behaviour, Dave began to work with people with disabilities and mental health problems, as well as qualifying as both a health and fitness trainer and martial arts instructor, eventually finding solace through his work and sporting endeavours.

Across the Atlantic, Michael Gerard Tyson was born on 30 June 1966, four years after Dave. Mike Tyson was the undisputed heavyweight boxing champion of the world and remains the youngest man ever to win the World Boxing Council (WBC), World Boxing Association (WBA) and International Boxing Federation (IBF) world heavyweight titles. Throughout his career, Tyson became well-known for his ferocious and intimidating boxing style as well as his controversial behaviour both inside and outside the ring.

At the start of his career Tyson competed at the 1982 Junior Olympic Games, where he won a gold medal. He won every bout at the Games by knockout (KO) and still holds the Junior Olympic quickest knockout record with eight seconds.

Three years later Tyson made his professional debut on 6 March 1985 in New York, defeating Hector Mercedes via a first-round knockout. During his first two years as a professional, Tyson won twenty-six of his twenty-eight fights by knockout, sixteen in the first round.

Nicknamed "Iron Mike" and tagged "The Baddest Man on the Planet", on 22 November 1986, Tyson was given his first title fight against Trevor Berbick for the WBC heavyweight championship. Tyson won the title by second-round total knockout (TKO) and, at the age of just twenty years and four months, became the youngest heavyweight champion in history.

On 7 March 1987 in Las Vegas, Tyson fought James Smith, winning by unanimous decision and adding Smith's WBA title to his existing belt. And on 1 August of the same year he took the IBF title from Tony Tucker in a twelve-round unanimous decision.

In January 1988 Tyson faced Larry Holmes and defeated the

former champion by a fourth-round knockout which was the only knockout loss Holmes suffered in seventy-five professional bouts. On 27 June of the same year Tyson faced Michael Spinks. At the time, the bout was the richest fight in history. The fight ended after just ninety-one seconds when Tyson knocked Spinks out in the first round. Spinks, previously unbeaten, would never fight professionally again.

During this period, Tyson's problems outside boxing were also starting to emerge. His marriage to actor Robin Givens was heading for divorce, his future contract was being fought over by Don King and Bill Cayton, and late in 1988 Tyson fired long-time trainer Kevin Rooney. Without Rooney, Tyson's skills quickly deteriorated.

In Tokyo, on 11 February 1990, Tyson lost his heavyweight title to James "Buster" Douglas by a knockout. Douglas unleashed a brutal combination of hooks that sent Tyson to the canvas for the first time in his career.

And then in July 1991 Tyson was arrested for the rape of eighteen-year-old Desiree Washington, Miss Black Rhode Island, in an Indianapolis hotel room. In February the following year Tyson was convicted and given a sentence of ten years; six in prison and four on probation.

Tyson served three years of his six years and after being released from prison in 1995 engaged in a series of comeback fights. He regained one belt by easily winning the WBC title from Frank Bruno by knocking him out in the third round, and added the WBA belt by defeating Bruce Seldon. However, on 9 November 1996 Tyson lost to Evander Holyfield, who at the time was given virtually no chance to win. Their rematch on 28 June the following year ended in shocking fashion as the fight was stopped at the end of the third round and Tyson disqualified for biting off part of Holyfield's ear.

Tyson's boxing licence was revoked by the Nevada State Athletic Commission and Tyson was fined $3 million, which effectively made Tyson unable to box in the United States. However, little more than a year later the commission voted to restore Tyson's boxing licence.

Legal problems caught up with Tyson once again and in 1999 Tyson was sentenced to a year's imprisonment and fined $5,000 for assaulting two motorists after a traffic accident.

In 2000 Tyson fought Lou Savarese in Glasgow, UK, winning in the first round but he continued punching after the referee had stopped the fight, knocking the referee to the floor as he tried to separate the boxers. In October of the same year Tyson fought Andrzej Gołota, winning in round three, but the result was later changed to no contest after Tyson tested positive for marijuana in a post-fight urine test.

Tyson fought only once in 2001, beating Brian Nielsen in Copenhagen with a seventh-round TKO.

In 2002, at thirty-five years old, he fought Lennox Lewis for a championship. Two years prior to the bout Tyson had made several inflammatory remarks to Lewis, "I want your heart, I want to eat his children." On 22 January 2002, a brawl involving the two boxers and their entourages occurred at a press conference held in New York to publicize the event. The fight eventually occurred on 8 June in Memphis, Tennessee, when Lewis knocked out Tyson with a right hook in the eighth round.

Despite receiving over US$30 million for several of his fights and $300 million during his career, Tyson was declared bankrupt in 2003.

Tyson finally retired from competitive boxing in 2005 after two consecutive knockout losses to Danny Williams and Kevin McBride.

Tyson began spending much of his time tending to his 350 pigeons in Paradise Valley, an up-scale enclave near Phoenix, Arizona, and, on the front page of *USA Today*, was quoted as saying: "My whole life has been a waste – I've been a failure."

On 29 December 2006, Tyson was arrested once again on suspicion of driving under the influence and drug possession after he nearly crashed into a police vehicle shortly after leaving a nightclub. Tyson pleaded not guilty. On 8 February 2007, while awaiting trial, he checked himself into an in-patient addiction treatment programme. On 24 September 2007, Mike Tyson changed his plea and pleaded guilty to possession of cocaine and driving under the influence. He was sentenced to twenty-four hours in jail, 360 hours community service and three years' probation. The judge praised Tyson for seeking help with his drug problems.

Tyson has been married three times and has seven children with several different women. At the height of his career he was one of the most recognized sports personalities in the world and undoubtedly once was "The Baddest Man on the Planet".

ROUND TWELVE – JANUARY 2002 TO JUNE 2005
By Dave Weeks

I'd met Maggie through work. We'd hit it off immediately but, at that stage, I was reconciling with Liz and Mags was with her boyfriend of three years. It seemed that we'd met at the wrong time in our lives.

However, I left Liz shortly before my fortieth birthday and Maggie finished with her boyfriend, so I moved into her flat in central London and we spent the following months "getting to know each other" properly.

Life with Maggie seemed so calm and laid-back after living with Liz. We'd both arrive home in the evening and sit and discuss our respective days. We'd chat, cuddle up on the sofa and simply love each other. There were no arguments, nastiness or disparaging comments. We enjoyed each other's company and I revelled in the loving non-confrontational lifestyle.

On my fortieth birthday, we went out for a Chinese meal and then, the following evening, met up with my family and friend Danny for a night out. All we had to do now was convince them that there was nothing wrong with the fact that Maggie was black.

Also, in January 2002, things were coming to a head between Mike Tyson and Lennox Lewis. Following his victory against Neilson, Tyson had arranged to fight the dangerous veteran Ray Mercer. This was seen as a smart move by the boxing media, who respected Mercer. He was a durable and tough opponent, who always came to fight, and had given Lewis one of his toughest battles. Lewis and his handlers, however, threatened to go to court to prevent the Tyson fight happening.

Several years previously Lewis and his management had campaigned vigorously for a Tyson bout but Mike had insisted upon adequate preparation. Finally, after his victory against Andrzej Gołota, Tyson had declared himself ready but Lewis had then elected to fight Hasim Rahman instead. One year on, he insisted that Tyson face him next or not at all. It was a thoroughly confusing scenario and hard to figure out which one of them – if either – actually wanted the fight! Certainly it was a rarity in boxing for the champion to chase his number one challenger but there was a method to Lewis's tactics.

Recognizing that Tyson was a fighter who required regular work to keep him sharp, Lewis and his camp re-challenged him now, knowing that his bout against Neilson was insufficient preparation. Preventing him from facing Mercer first only loaded all the odds in their favour.

Tyson was in a no-win situation. In January his wife Monica Turner instigated divorce proceedings – against a background of renewed rape and sexual assault slurs in the press – and it was revealed that Mike was still in serious debt. One way or another, Tyson needed to find some money quickly, both to clear his remaining arrears and to provide a financial package for his soon-to-be ex-wife and children, and so the Lewis bout increasingly made monetary if not strategic sense.

Tyson was no fool. Although boxers are amongst the worst judges of when to call it quits and seem incapable of recognizing their own physical decline, Tyson knew that at thirty-five years of age and with just one fight in over a year – against an outclassed opponent – it wasn't the correct way to prepare to face the best heavyweight in the world. However, maybe he only had himself to blame.

Following his Gołota victory, Tyson could have stayed busy, retaining his sharpness and adding a few more million to his dwindling bank account. The reality was that Mike just didn't have the desire any more. He piled on the pounds through inactivity and over-eating and ended up fighting Neilson, purely out of desperation for spending-money, twelve whole months after his previous victory.

Perhaps it was no surprise when his wife explained her reasons for wanting a divorce as Tyson's outrageous designer-clothes-and-jewellery spending sprees – despite his financial predicament – and his persistent womanizing. It certainly wasn't because he spent too much time in the gym.

Even though Tyson was desperate for money, and even after finally agreeing a date in April 2002 and signing the contracts, the fight was nearly "lost". It was just another Tyson moment.

Boxing has a long history of hyping contests. Promoters gather the fighters and their entourages together in front of the press and encourage them to swap insults and threats and generally look menacing in order to boost ticket and pay-per-view TV sales. But, as Tyson marched towards Lewis at the press conference, one of the champion's bodyguards pushed Tyson back. (Now, here's a funny thing: if you're the heavyweight champion of the world, supposedly the most dangerous unarmed man on the planet, why do you need bodyguards? Never have understood that.) Tyson swung a theatrical punch at him, which missed – "deliberately", he later claimed, stating he'd been asked to "help hype the contest". Lewis, who later said that no one had told him that Tyson had been asked to throw a pretend punch, threw a genuine punch at Tyson which landed and opened a cut above his eye. Tyson reacted in the way he was apt to when angry and stressed. He ducked his head down and bit a chunk of flesh out of Lewis's leg! (Okay, point taken: maybe Lewis did need a bodyguard.)

Everyone jumped on everyone else at that moment and mayhem ensued.

When the two camps were eventually separated it didn't end there. A member of the press shouted out, "Put Tyson in a straight-jacket", and an adrenalin-fuelled Tyson turned and exploded: "I'll fuck you in the arse, you punk-assed white boy . . . You fucking faggot. Come up here and take me on you scared coward. You white bitch. You ain't man enough to fuck with me, bitch. There ain't no one in the room big enough to take me on. This is the ultimate man. You're just scared like a little white pussy . . . I'll fuck you 'til you love me, you faggot."

This adorable little quotation didn't endear him to the boxing committee who met subsequently to discuss Tyson's actions. The Nevada board refused to allow Tyson to fight in Las Vegas because of his behaviour. The multi-million dollar super-fight was off.

A disconsolate Lewis tried to put a brave face on it but the truth was – despite his protestations about the flesh missing from his thigh and his claims that Tyson had "mental sickness" and "needs help" – Lewis couldn't make the same kind of money by facing anyone else, plus it was a career-defining bout for Lennox. If he were to end his career without having faced the most iconic figure of his era, Lewis's record would always be dismissed by some with, "Yeah, but he didn't fight Tyson, did he?"

Tyson, too, was between a rock and a hard place. He had no way to earn the kind of huge money he required without facing Lewis.

Both camps got together and searched for a solution. Eventually, the date was reset for June 2002 in Memphis, Tennessee, and, with the rape charge dropped at the last minute, Tyson was able to finally focus on the bout which could help change his messy life.

By this time, my own life was no longer messy. It was extremely happy. In fact, I couldn't remember the last time I'd felt angry about something. There were odd moments, of course. We had a new manager at the place where I worked with disabled people and I just couldn't get on with him. His personality grated with me: mainly the fact that he didn't have a personality I could grate.

Rather than allow myself to get sucked into a dark mood every time I saw him, I decided to leave and work elsewhere. There was a temporary glitch in this plan. Mags wanted me to leave the company altogether, rather than just transfer to another site, as she was still doing occasional work for them herself – although she'd now qualified as a nurse and was mainly working at a nearby hospital – and didn't feel that it was good that we work together and live together.

Glitch, part two. I developed a hernia. It was quicker than developing a photo but more painful. The constant discomfort I was in forced me to cut down on my martial arts training and the time I spent off work allowed me to consider my options. What could I do with the money I'd just received from my divorce settlement?

Well, how's this for an idea? I bought an old Jaguar XJ6. Mags hated it. She'd had a Mazda before, which you could fit inside a shoe-box. Now she had to try and park something longer than one of those bendy-buses. As a consequence of this Mags decided to kill the car one day on the motorway. I felt like crying as I watched my lovely Jag loaded on to the tow-truck. (We've had Mercedes since then and she managed to write one of those off, too, although that one was definitely an accident.)

I also used the money to take on the lease of a massage parlour in North London. I was convinced that this was the ideal way to make easy money. Men would always want to get laid and many of them were willing to pay for the privilege. Why not pay me?

Mags and I cleaned the place from top to bottom and I bought some paint to smarten the place up. Then I placed advertisements and interviewed a selection of attractive women to work there, sat back and prepared to reap the rewards of the sex industry.

All I reaped was a selection of heavy bills; money was coming out of my account to pay for constant running repairs to the place, while the locals proved to be the least sexually motivated males in the whole of London. The immediate area must have been the impotence capital of the world!

After a few months I handed the lease back and returned to working with disabilities. It was far less stressful than alcoholic prostitutes, drunken clients who turned violent when they discovered that they couldn't get an erection and the constant threat of a police raid. Plus, a stream of Eastern European women – without passports or visas – who offered me unlimited sex in return for work at the parlour were just another potential legal headache.

Before I gave the business up, I'd had to eject stroppy punters from the premises on several occasions. Debbie, who was running the place for me – and almost certainly ripping me off – suggested that I hire a doorman after I had to physically throw a young guy out when he started abusing her because he couldn't reach climax. He wanted his money refunded but I was already losing enough money on the place, without taking on extra staff.

Instead, I started arming myself with a large-bladed knife and extending baton when I went there. (If I'd owned a grenade-launcher I'd have taken it!) In truth, though, most guys were easy enough to intimidate and usually chose to leave with just a few expletives and a firm push towards the front door. Only one guy became a potential problem.

He was a Hell's Angel type: biker jacket and boots; shaved head but long beard; tattoos, etc. He arrived one day and announced that he used to be the bouncer for the previous leaseholder and wanted his job back. I told him that I didn't need a bouncer, thanks, but he just smiled and intimated that I "might do soon".

I could feel the adrenalin rising and assured him that I didn't believe so. He asked if he could come in and have a massage. Ten minutes later the masseuse came out of the room and informed me that he refused to pay her.

He claimed that the previous owner had let him have sex with the girls for free, in return for his door services. I pointed out that we didn't have such an arrangement and he walked towards me. I'd anticipated that he wouldn't leave quietly and so, as he approached, I unzipped my bomber jacket and rested my hand on the handle of the knife. He was a really big guy and going hand-to-hand with him was secondary in my list of options. I intended doing whatever was required to cause him maximum damage whilst minimizing injury to myself. I decided which areas of his body I was going to start stabbing and slashing first, and prepared for a violent, bloody scene which I knew I'd live to regret. (I could sense that prison cell looming . . . but it was preferable to my death or hospitalization.)

False alarm! He merely smiled that annoying grin of his once more and ambled out. This wasn't good. I'd been trying to move away from these sorts of confrontations but realized that I wouldn't be able to if I pursued this sordid line of work.

As much as the girls' stories of their clients amused me – the guy who wanted one of the women to put lipstick and mascara on him, whilst another girl inserted needles into his penis and foreskin till he cried, was a favourite – and as much as I loved sitting there flirting with women who constantly crossed-and-uncrossed their long stockinged legs, it had been a terrible mistake.

I was trying to change my life and temperament for the better. I was no longer angry and confrontational but this business was forcing me to adopt that persona again. I needed to get out of this place for my health, sanity and emotional well-being.

And so, I handed the keys back and got a job in a school for autistic children.

I could never be accused of being predictable. Nor could Maggie. She told me that she wanted a baby!

*   *   *

Mike Tyson versus Lennox Lewis was a huge anti-climax. The initial press conference to announce the championship match-up, which had resulted in carnage, violence and verbal abuse, was far more entertaining than the fight itself, for this was the contest which clearly exposed the fact that Tyson was past his sell-by date.

In retrospect Tyson would have been better off making a kamikaze stand in the opening minutes, throwing caution to the wind and trying to expose Lewis's less-than-concrete chin. In fact, Tyson did win the opening round but Lewis was merely sizing him up, determining how much danger and ferocity "Iron" Mike had left. Satisfied that he had nothing to fear, Lennox assumed control in the second round and it was all one-way traffic from then on. It was the quietest I'd ever been for a Tyson fight.

Whilst the likes of Julius Francis, Lou Savarese et al. might still crumble at his feet, the truly world-class boxers such as Lewis were beyond him now. This was painfully revealed to both Tyson and the watching world, as the huge heavyweight champ rammed his left jab into Tyson's steadily swelling face round after round, following it with crunching right-handers.

Even against "Buster" Douglas and Evander Holyfield there had always been the chance that a sudden savage right hand or crushing left hook could turn things around but, against Lewis, Tyson never showed that he still had the power or ability to turn the tide. Neither did he have the excuse of inadequacy in his corner this time. Respected trainer Ronnie Shields tried desperately to motivate Tyson between rounds, urging him to "let his punches go", but Tyson seemed incapable of throwing anything significant. He appeared mesmerized by the constant jab-jab-right of Lewis and obligingly walked on to the punches round after round, merely proving his ability to absorb heavy punishment.

The bout could well have ended earlier than it did if Tyson hadn't benefited from some dubious refereeing decisions. I groaned as Tyson went down in the fourth round but was then confused and delighted at the referee's deduction of a point from Lewis for holding and pushing Tyson to the canvas. It was true, Lennox had draped his massive bodyweight over Tyson but, to my mind, he was already on his way down from a punch at the time.

Then, as Lewis opened up and hurt Tyson, the referee stopped him and gave Tyson a standing eight-count, giving him a chance to recover.

It was all immaterial. I watched in stony silence as Lewis repeatedly drove his punches into Tyson's battered and bleeding face. In the eighth round a left hook precipitated the end. As Tyson lurched to his left from the force of the blow Lewis perfectly timed a following right cross. It exploded upon Mike's chin and he fell heavily to the floor, not rising until the count had reached ten.

It was the conclusion which most boxing experts had predicted, particularly in light of Tyson's woeful preparations regarding warm-up bouts and his weight-gains between contests (although he had managed to slim down considerably in comparison to his bulk against Nielson.) However, Tyson retained the ability to confuse onlookers who thought they'd summed him up. Just as Mike was garnering praise for his willingness to take a beating like a warrior and not quit on his stool, he had the media scratching their heads with his post-fight comments, in which he did everything but kiss Lewis's ass. As he stood looking up at his unmarked conqueror, dabbing at the blood leaking from his right eye, Tyson – the man who'd stated that he wanted to "eat Lewis's children" and "rip out his heart" – described Lewis as "a masterful boxer", adding, "The pay day was wonderful. I really appreciate it. If you'd be kind enough, I'd love to do it again. I think I could beat you if we tried one more time."

Let's analyse these words. He was more or less saying: "I'm finished as a fighter but I need lots more money to pay off all my debtors and fund my extravagant lifestyle. Thanks for this opportunity. Now, would you like to beat me up again, as I need much more money than you've already given me?" (And I didn't even need the Enigma machine or the Da Vinci code to crack his underlying meaning.)

I loved Mike to bits but I'd have been so much happier if he'd told Lewis he was a bum and that, if they'd met ten years earlier, he'd have "ripped his head off". Tyson's comments removed any lingering illusions I or anyone else had that he was still interested in the heavyweight title or in improving his status in boxing history. He was in it purely for the money now and this meant that he would never regain the former ferocity or "bad intentions". In which case, without that mindset and anger, Mike Tyson was just a small, ageing heavyweight.

However, luckily for him, Lennox Lewis also thought about boxing in terms of pounds-and-pence and said that he'd happily give Tyson a rematch. And so, the saga continued.

On my forty-first birthday I sat at my dad's house, preparing to let my family know that Maggie was pregnant. During the year or so we'd been together my family had welcomed Mags into their midst, almost as much because of the sheer contrast in personalities between herself and Liz as for anything in particular Mags had done to try and ingratiate herself. My dad had been the biggest revelation.

The others had been fine about Mags's skin colour from the start but my dad had taken more convincing. He'd sometimes ask me whether I felt self-conscious walking down the road with her – Yeah, right, with my shaven and tattooed head you mean? – or whether it was "fair on Jim, for his dad to have a black girlfriend", etc.

Questions such as these were raised periodically but they'd become infrequent, as Mags had won him over with her niceness. Nevertheless, it was with more than a little trepidation that I announced the news of the impending new arrival.

I told them that "something" would be arriving soon at the flat and that something would grow bigger and bigger each year until, eventually, it would be adult-size. When my mum responded, "You've got no room for a pot plant in that tiny flat," I gave up trying to be subtle and told them: "Maggie's pregnant."

My mum and sister were delighted but my dad's response sickened me: "Let's hope she loses it!"

I felt physically ill and had to force myself to keep quiet, otherwise forty-one years of bitterness towards him would've come tumbling out of my mouth. As he left to pick up the Chinese takeaway we'd ordered, mum cuddled me and told me to ignore his comments.

I'd just add them to the stack of hateful comments he'd made over the years. He and Liz would've made a fine pair!

*   *   *

In February 2003 Mike Tyson commenced his boxing rehabilitation by meeting fellow puncher Clifford Etienne. The public needed to be convinced that Mike was deserving of another bout with Lennox Lewis before they'd part with their money again and so he'd agreed to several warm-up contests which, if successful, would lead to the lucrative rematch later in the year.

Tyson blew Etienne away in the opening minute with a devastating right hand but this was incidental in comparison to the litany of incidents before and after the bout.

Before arriving in Memphis, Tyson had announced that he was withdrawing from the contest. The reasons ranged from flu to diarrhoea, a back injury to an infection in the facial tattoo he'd had done (this was a Maori design across the left side of his face that got me thinking about tattoos again until Mags said "No!"). The real reason appeared to be that Mike had thrown several temper tantrums and refused to complete his training. Trainer Freddie Roach even advised Tyson not to turn up, as he didn't feel that Mike was fit enough. Well, Tyson was physically fit enough to hammer Etienne into unconsciousness, but what about his mental fitness?

Even after all those years of competing, Tyson still struggled to control his pre-fight fear and emotions. It wasn't even the Lewises and Holyfields of the world that induced these self-doubts, for Tyson had exhibited similar nervousness and unstable behaviour before facing Julius Francis!

Lennox began to get twitchy about the prospect of banking another multi-million payday and tried to convince Mike to meet him again in June 2003, without a prior contest. Tyson, however, stuck to his guns and stated that he needed at least one more fight before jeopardizing his health again against man-mountain Lewis and so a double-bill was arranged for June, in which Lewis would headline, whilst Tyson would face the decent Russian boxer Oleg Maskaev. Then, if both men proved victorious, they would have the rematch later in the year.

So . . . this is what actually happened in Mike's crazy little world.

In May promoter Don King, who'd been circling Tyson warily from a distance for some time, hoping to ingratiate himself again despite their legal battle over King's alleged fraudulent behaviour, made his move and attempted to speak to Tyson. Mike responded to him in words beginning with "f" and – allegedly – a physical assault. However, their altercation and King's attempts at convincing Tyson that he could make far more money if he returned to Don's camp seemed to have an effect on Tyson. He suddenly refused to fight Maskaev and, with his withdrawal, any hopes of the Lewis rematch were ended. (Subsequently, Maskaev became a heavyweight champion himself and so it's a shame that we never got to see him swap blows with Tyson.)

Lewis went ahead and defeated the dangerous Vitali Klitschko and then retired, stating that the only fight which still motivated him was the Tyson rematch but he no longer believed that it would ever take place.

Tyson, meanwhile, did have a fight in June. Unfortunately, it was in a hotel, against two men who'd drunkenly mocked him. Tyson put them both in hospital and was promptly arrested.

In July 2003 I was offered the role of Disability Project Manager for young people within a London borough, and – for the first time – commenced employment which offered both job satisfaction and decent financial remuneration.

Then, in October, Mags and I celebrated the arrival of our beautiful daughter Delilah. We couldn't have been any happier but we needed to find somewhere else to live now. This proved problematic.

I didn't want to rent a property, I wanted something I could call my own, but London house prices were astronomical, so we commenced searching for an area near to London but within our financial reach. Eventually we settled upon a small town in north Essex where my mum had moved to after her divorce but, although it was green and picturesque, it was also almost exclusively white, which caused Maggie extreme discomfort and the issue of race became a constant one in our conversations.

It was apt then that, around this time, I was studying race and culture as part of my Informal & Community Education Diploma for work, as well as reading a lot about mixed-race relationships and being a mixed-race child, in order that I might understand the kind of issues Delilah might face as she grew older.

This led me to examine what our friend Mr Tyson was struggling with for years. I wanted to understand how skin tone affects people's treatment and perceptions of their fellow man. It's obviously beyond the confines of this book to examine the subject in infinitesimal detail but issues of race must have a bearing on understanding Mike Tyson, for he was born into one of the most intense periods of change in American history, involving some of the pivotal figures in black social advancement.

The battle for social equality and acceptance became an increasingly bloody one, as black intellectuals and activists fought against segregation and oppression, during the Civil Rights Movement. Much of this oppression took the form of what Frantz Fanon described as "the Colonial mentality". After decades of assumed white supremacy many black people actually perceived themselves as sub-standard, submitting to the racism and bullying of white people because they genuinely believed – due to years of having it viciously beaten into them – that they were inferior. Thus, it became as much of a battle for black activists to educate their peers as to their right to equality as it did for them to convince the white establishment of this fact.

One of the turning points was Oliver Brown's battle to overturn segregation in the American South which, for those of you who've been living in ignorant bliss for half a century, was a process of discrimination by which blacks and whites were kept apart, to the detriment of blacks, and which Brown focused upon Rosa Park's refusal to give up her seat on a bus to a white person.

The furore this caused was unprecedented and inspired Dr Martin Luther King's leadership of the Civil Rights Movement, which finally resulted, in 1964, in legislation to eliminate all discrimination against race or skin colour.

Of course, love and happiness didn't happen overnight – or even at all! – leading to the more aggressive urgings of Malcolm X (formerly Malcolm Little), the minister of the Nation of Islam who advocated meeting white violence head-on with reciprocal black violence in order to achieve parity. Stokely Carmichael (Kwame Toure) started to promote "Black Power" and coined the phrase "institutionalized racism" as a way of explaining that discrimination was deeply ingrained in all levels of the white establishment, due to centuries of supposed white supremacy.

Mike Tyson was thus born into a mid 1960s America that was in the midst of huge social change via the words and actions of the likes of the above and authors such as Maya Angelou, who vividly described her childhood in the prejudiced and segregated American South.

As a young boxing fan Tyson must have been aware of the controversy surrounding heavyweight champ Cassius Clay, who changed his name to Muhammad Ali as a rejection of his "slave name" – blacks were traditionally named after their slave masters – and aligned himself with Elijah Muhammad's movement, which controversially rejected integration with white society and fought for separation (as opposed to segregation!)

It still must have been hard though for the infant Tyson to hear songs such as "Young, Gifted and Black" or James Brown's anthem "Say It Loud, I'm Black and I'm Proud", whilst laying on his bed at night, listening to the sound of his empty stomach churning, wondering whether he would get his next paltry meal before or after another hideous beating from the brutal, disillusioned black youths on his deprived and crime-ridden neighbourhood.

No wonder then that the youngster grasped the opportunity to live in a large, rambling house in leafy Catskills with the elderly, white, boxing trainer and manager Cus D'Amato, who treated the delinquent Tyson like a human being for the first time in his life, as well as showing an interest in the teenager's opinions, spending long hours talking to him about life and its unpredictability.

However, the following years of living and interacting almost exclusively with white people would result in an ongoing confusion around race which Tyson would struggle with for years, as he sought to understand his own feelings and personal perception of "who" he was, especially when he later became surrounded by strong black characters such as Don King, who convinced him that everything wrong in his life was due to a white conspiracy to keep the black man down. (A conviction that has more than a shred of truth to it.)

In July 2004 Mike Tyson stepped between the ropes for the first time in a year-and-a-half, ending eighteen months of speculation as to what his next step would be. In that time he'd declared himself bankrupt. He had also been linked with a bout against kick-boxing man-mountain Bob Sapp (in a similar financially lucrative stunt, during his ban from boxing in 1997–8, he'd appeared in the WWF). He and Sapp had swapped insults and shoves but never actually stepped into a K1 ring together. (Tyson had often stated his love for martial arts, being a big fan of movies of the genre, and had been tempted several times by offers to fight in mixed martial arts tournaments.)

During this break Tyson had received six months' anger management counselling for his hotel assault back in 2003, not receiving a prison sentence this time because the judge had accepted he had been provoked.

The distractions were all very entertaining, but what was less clear was how Tyson was going to maintain his extravagant lifestyle without entering a boxing ring. He was thirty-eight years of age, the same age Muhammad Ali had been when first Larry Holmes and then Trevor Berbick finally ended the magic of the "Greatest", and the exact same age Holmes himself was when a young Tyson handed him his first knockout defeat. His best years were long behind him but, as Mike himself acknowledged, he "wasn't going to go into brain surgery" and so, with a sad inevitability, he prepared to wage battle again simply because he had no other option. There were still bills and creditors to be paid.

Tyson's latest comeback was different to the others in that there was no particular end product in mind this time. Whereas previously every ring return had been seen as a prelude to another assault upon the world championship, this time around no one – including Tyson himself – was under any illusions. This was all about the money. People were still prepared to pay to see "Iron" Mike in the flesh. It helped that his last contest had been a devastating first-round knockout victory. That helped erase the image of the Lewis humbling. He was an icon, a living legend and it was akin to buying a ticket to see Sinatra after 1970. You knew his voice was shot but he still retained the aura – he was still "Ol' Blue Eyes".

Anyway, a bottle of rioja and I sat up late to watch my man but Mags didn't bother. She happily watched endless Steven Seagal, Jean-Claude Van Damme and other martial arts movies with me, but she drew the line at sitting up until 3 a.m. to watch boxing. I was politely asked "not to shout too much" in case it woke Delilah. Oh, please!

Tyson versus Danny Williams was a strange evening altogether. Mike had chosen someone whom he felt reasonably certain he could dispose of comfortably and earn a few quick bucks, although at this stage of his career there were no such certainties. Former British and Commonwealth champion Williams appeared made-to-measure in that he was a decent boxer with a reasonable punch but was emotionally as stable as Judy Garland and had a questionable chin.

Williams had often threatened to emerge on to the world scene but had always stumbled when faced with opponents he'd been expected to defeat. By his own admission he was fragile mentally and thus appeared the perfect fall-guy for an intimidator like Tyson. Unfortunately for Mike, what Williams had perceived about Tyson's reluctance to enter the ring on a regular basis was true. He was completely shot and no longer capable of intimidating a half-decent young foe. And that's why Danny had been so eager to accept the bout.

Williams admitted afterwards that he'd been in awe of Tyson when he was a twelve-year-old boy watching "Iron" Mike decimate the heavyweights. That Tyson, he knew, no longer existed. Only his marquee name survived, offering a spring-board for Williams to leap into the heavyweight title picture, if he could only hold himself together emotionally under the intense pressure Tyson was still liable to provide.

In the opening three minutes Tyson's hand-speed was awesome and he blasted Williams with an assortment of hurtful punches, staggering him and causing him to lurch drunkenly from one side of the ring to another, defying gravity by remaining upright. I shouted my appreciation – Mags can't claim that she wasn't warned! – at what, so far, had been the most devastating Tyson performance since Gołota. Little did I know that he'd practically exhausted himself with that three-minute burst of non-stop punching.

Tyson hadn't taken training that seriously, believing that he'd walk through Williams based upon his erratic record and reputation. Mike hadn't foreseen that this wasn't merely a nice payday for Danny but, rather, a life-altering opportunity for him – a chance to emerge from obscurity – and so a hitherto unseen mental fortitude allowed Williams to come out for the second round and risk every-thing, matching Tyson blow-for-blow.

It was an exciting fight whilst it lasted. In the second and third rounds the two men swapped fast, damaging punches but it was noticeable that Tyson's work rate was already slowing. Instead of putting his punches together in quick-fire clusters Mike was now regressing to throwing single big shots and then absorbing Williams's rapid counters.

The end came in round four. Whilst it had been acceptable for the likes of Holyfield and Lewis to batter him, it was painfully embar-rassing to watch a lower-grade heavyweight walking forward and pouring punches into a clearly demoralized Tyson's face.

When Tyson fell backwards into the ropes and slid to the floor it saddened many boxing people to watch him simply sit there, waiting for the referee to complete his count. Mike's brave and stoic accept-ance of his pummellings at the fists of Douglas, Holyfield and Lewis had led even his fiercest critics to applaud his courage and warrior-like spirit; a willingness to go down fighting. Now, he simply gave up! As soon as he realized that Williams wasn't going anywhere and had tasted Danny's determination via repeated punches to the face, Mike waved the white flag. It was a fantastic moment for the unher-alded Williams but the latest method Tyson had conceived to further damage his standing in the annals of boxing history. FUCK!!! (Note: There's only one "fuck" to follow this defeat, symbolizing both my new-found calmness and contentment, and my realization that "Iron" Mike Tyson had long since departed. It was the bankrupt Michael Gerard Tyson who now begrudgingly pulled on the black shorts and ankle boots, echoing the image of Jack Dempsey but without his previous savagery and spirit. Tyson without the anger was impotent.)

In October 2004 Delilah celebrated her first birthday and we'd planned a party for family and friends. A week or so prior my dad had gone to my sister's for the weekend and suffered severe stomach pains and diarrhoea, which had continued over the following days. Concerned at his drastic loss of weight, his neighbour contacted the doctor and dad was admitted into hospital for tests.

I was explaining this to my friend Danny and he said he'd pop into the hospital and say "hello" to my dad the next day. None of us believed that it was anything more serious than dehydration due to days of diarrhoea and sickness, until Danny phoned me the next evening and warned me that it appeared more serious than we'd thought.

The following morning I packed a bag and spent the next fortnight at my dad's, going back-and-forth between his house, work and the hospital, and watching my dad slowly deteriorate each day.

It was a mystery as to why he was getting worse instead of better. The hospital had diagnosed that he'd been suffering from food poisoning when admitted but his condition had rapidly worsened and he was pumped full of drugs, virtually comatose, incapable of interacting with anyone around him.

Late one evening the hospital phoned me and asked my permission to operate. They didn't really know what they were looking for but stated that, if they didn't "open him up for an exploratory", he would definitely die.

I phoned around friends and family and then spent the night waiting for the hospital to ring back. When they eventually called it was good news. They'd discovered a section of "dead" intestine which they'd removed and had reconnected each end of the working intestine.

I went to the hospital in the morning and was amazed to see my dad sitting up in bed. I explained to him what had been happening for the last few days and why they'd had to operate, and told him that I'd see him later, after work. It was the last conversation we ever had. Within hours his condition had deteriorated again and, several days later, he was dead. A combination of an infection and blood poisoning had killed him. Mum, my sister Lisa, our cousin Karen and I sat around his bedside and watched the last remnants of life drain slowly away from him.

For hours afterwards I cried. I cried for myself, I cried for Lisa, I cried for our dad, but most of all I cried for the relationship we never had.

The time I spent staying at my dad's and the subsequent period leading up to the funeral gave me an opportunity to reflect upon my life and my relationship with my father and how it had affected my adulthood.

I regretted a lot of decisions I'd made and actions I'd taken over the years and wondered how much of the man I'd been back in the 1980s and 1990s had been a self-creation or the sum of my genetics and all the influences around me.

If, as I believed, this "new me" was a self-made man, made calmer by good choices, positive people around me and learning from life's experiences, then how much of my anger, resentment, depression and generally anti-social behaviour back then was down to my early life experiences. I thought of nothing but my childhood for days.

"Nature versus nurture" is an expression used to compare someone's innate qualities and genes versus their learned experiences when determining how responsible we are for our own behaviour. At this point in my life I keenly explored these concepts in an effort to better understand myself and my conflicting emotions.

Some things are definitely genetic and are personality traits or physical characteristics we inherit from our parents whilst other factors can be attributed partially to genes and partially to the learning environment we find ourselves in. For instance, my mother is artistic and thus my pursuing a career in art may be partially due to innate creativity. (That and the fact that art college seemed a great way to do bugger-all for three years whilst staring at girls.) However, art – like many talents – can be taught and there is no doubt that my basic skills were improved upon by studying the mechanics of art: proportion, tone, perspective, etc.

Again, with sportsmen whose sons or daughters follow them into professional sport, how much is genetic inheritance and how much applied technique and learning?

Personality has been proven to be genetic, although it can be influenced by external factors and people may try to model themselves upon personalities which attract them. In a series of studies, identical twins that had been separated at birth were found to have very similar personalities when later reunited; far more similar in fact than adopted siblings who were raised together.

One of the great questions about genetic inheritance controlling our later behaviour is "What about free will?" At what point do we take control of our own destiny and make decisions based around what's right for us and not based on the previous actions of others?

Genetically, certain diseases have been passed down through

generations but where does this leave addiction such as alcoholism? It's been proven that a susceptibility to nicotine addiction is genetic but debate continues as to whether alcoholism is genetic or learned behaviour from watching other people who abuse drink.

This was definitely one of the factors which intrigued me. The period when I'd drunk a crate of brandy per night in order to forget that I was married to that abusive cow Liz had left me believing that I'd inherited my dad's (and granddad's) propensity towards over-indulgence. Certainly, when I'd stayed with him we'd sit up drinking until the early hours, pouring glass after glass of alcohol until it was either all gone or he'd decided it was time to spew. (Sometimes he decided it was time to fall over various items of furniture first.)

I'd always convinced myself that I couldn't possibly be on the road to alcoholism – (just off the M4) – because I didn't feel the urge to drink alcohol every day. Often it was just weekends that I'd drink (although weekends tended to last from Friday to Thursday when I was with Liz), and so I reassured myself that I was in control. Then I read an article which explained that alcoholism was not – as most people thought – a constant craving for booze but an inability to stop drinking once you'd started. This was me!

I'd never met a bottle of red wine I didn't like. In fact I liked them all so much I had to drink them from start to finish, just to show my appreciation. Once I had "the taste" for alcohol I would not look back.

My sister Lisa was lucky. She also liked a good drink but had the capacity of a three-year-old to absorb it. Thus, she'd get drunk after three glasses and then just giggle for hours (except one night at my house when I had to carry her upstairs because she had "alcohol blindness" and couldn't see).

Anyway, maybe alcohol addiction is inherited; maybe it isn't, but either way, if you're surrounded by heavy drinkers all your life it's bound to make an impact. Perhaps more pertinent to me, though, was whether my dad's uncontrollable anger was an inherited trait or, again, learned behaviour.

Biologically anger is not actually a problem; it's an instinctive reaction to threat and part of our primitive inner selves, designed as a vital aspect of our survival mechanism. As with fear, anger triggers the adrenalin rush which gives us the energy for fight-or-flight and better enables us to defend ourselves and our loved ones.

However, in modern society it's how we behave when feeling this emotion that causes other people's perceptions and interactions with us to be negative or fearful. Shouting, violence and hurtful comments are prime ingredients of uncontrolled, damaging anger. (Although I take serious exception to sarcasm being described as a negative by-product of anger. Sarcasm, in my humble opinion, is a magnificent art-form and I will continue to use it lovingly through-out the remainder of my life!)

In today's society there are causes of anger unrelated to a Neanderthal about to club your partner over the head. Unhappy relationships, low self-esteem, exclusion, fear, jealousy, poor communication skills, alcohol, drugs and learned behaviour can all cause outbursts of anger.

In the case of my father and myself – and Tyson, let's not forget that he's involved here, due to his own well-chronicled anger-management issues – the nurture side of the equation is probably more pertinent than the genetic inheritance. Anger may well be inside all of us but it only explodes outwards in such damaging degrees in certain individuals. (And we *are* those certain individuals!)

Examining the above reasons for anger problems, it has been seen that I've endured unhappy relationships, fear and alcohol abuse but how much of that is because of my father's negative influence? (Oh, I'll go for "pretty much all of it", actually!)

I can't blame him for Liz. I need to blame my overactive penis for that one. But, I'm sure I wouldn't have married Susan if it were not for the fact that I wanted to get away from living at home with my dad and then I promptly treated her exactly the way he'd abused my mother for twenty-odd years. Well, not exactly – I didn't throw hot coffee over her head, whilst shaking the living daylights out of her and the kids – but I did shout abuse at her and talk to her as if she were retarded.

I believe now that my anger was derived from childhood fear of my father; a disappointment that my mother didn't intervene more positively when my sister and I were younger (although I under-stand that she was going through her own form of fear of my dad);

and a general bitterness that the relationship I'd seen my mother enjoy with her own loving father had not been replicated in any way between my dad and I. He was cold, bullying, abusive, angry and unapproachable, and I hated him for it.

I once put my arm around him – he hadn't been speaking to any of us for days and the atmosphere indoors was awful – and I asked him, "Why can't we just be a normal family and love each other?" He turned and laughed in my face, called me a "silly bastard" and walked off.

Ah, memories! It was like the Waltons . . . only with violence, swearing and things being thrown around the room.

As I grew older I put my bitterness to the back of my mind and got on with my life. Except that I didn't really. I now recognized that my constant anger – made worse by alcohol and general disillusionment with my life and relationships back in the mid 1980s to 1990s – was the unhappy child inside me screaming to be heard and loved. (I know . . . I've read that bit myself and it does sound like tree-hugging hippy shit! But, hey, this is me exposing myself to you and if you don't like it, tough.)

It is a recognized fact that most psychotherapy centres upon our relationship with our parents and our childhood memories. Freud placed great emphasis upon the influence of parental behaviour upon a child's developing psyche. Hey, if it's good enough for Freud . . .

My mum certainly didn't mean to damage us but, indirectly, she did through not telling my dad to "change his ways or leave" when we were small.

But, what of Tyson? Where did all of his burning anger come from? What – or who – were the emotional skeletons in his closet?

Mike's own father left when he was just a baby and contact had been minimal afterwards. (Interestingly, there is no firm evidence that a father dying or leaving a family when a child is young actually affects the child's emotional development. Usually it's only a financial impact but this can be huge, as poverty will impact upon anyone's development.)

Many observers have claimed that Tyson saw Cus D'Amato, his co-manager Jim Jacobs and Don King as successive father-figures, looking to them to fill a void in his life, but Tyson himself has always angrily denied this. Ultimately, only Mike knows the true impact of a lack of a father in his emotional development but there is little doubt that Tyson's mother's struggle to provide financially for her family and her exasperation at her son's attraction to the criminal element amongst his peers led to his estrangement from her.

Environment played a huge role in Tyson's emotional development, for it was the violent streets of deprived Brownsville in Brooklyn and the moral-free gangs which roamed unchecked that "nurtured" the young Tyson's psyche.

Every day he awoke and witnessed or participated in muggings, shootings, abuse and general anti-social behaviour. This is what passed as normal conduct in Mike's childhood and what almost certainly shaped his personality for years to come. Even when he was scaling the heights of professional boxing, hailed as a hero everywhere he went and earning extortionate amounts of money, Tyson's behaviour remained that of a brutal teenage street-thug. The anger and resentment he'd felt for the formative years of his life was all he knew. It comforted him in its familiarity, even when it was also destroying his life. Allied to his natural anger was confusion over what exact role "race" played in his ability to progress. As I well knew, anger and resentment were hard companions to say goodbye to when they've been held so closely for so long. And yet . . . it was time for both of us to move on.

I read the eulogy at my dad's funeral and, upon arriving back home, covered the walls of my house with photos of my mum and dad. He was a man full of faults but I'm sure he had his reasons. Who knows what incident or person in his own past had turned him into the insecure, bullying figure of my youth? One day, we'll all be judged by a higher power.

He'd tried hard to alter his persona and make amends over the last few years of his life and perhaps that was more important ultimately than the violence, anger and hostility he'd evidenced for the vast majority. I needed to believe so, otherwise I'd be judged for the man I'd been for the first forty years of mine.

The control and suppression of anger is a learned skill and is acquired only if an individual wants to change. I wanted to change! I'd learned what had made me so bitter and angry over the years and now I was able to put it to rest. Allied to this, the natural maturation process and the understanding that we need to surround ourselves with positive people and the tools are there for anyone to change if they really want to. Accept what made you unhappy and then focus upon all the things which currently make your life worthwhile.

So, no more bitterness and looking back with bile. I wouldn't waste any more energy on negativity. My focus now would be on the future.

Tyson's future remained as uncertain as ever. In June 2005 he faced the huge Irishman Kevin McBride, a year after the Williams debacle and a few days prior to his thirty-ninth birthday. Ever more severely in debt, nothing else had come along to offer Tyson an opportunity to earn anything approaching what boxing could garner him. So, despite the blatant evidence of his decline, he sat and watched his hands bandaged and taped once more, preparing to give the Tyson-hungry fans – who'd had twelve months to forget the Williams surrender – another taste of "Iron" Mike.

Except that he simply couldn't do it. At least against Williams Tyson had blazed briefly for two rounds before running out of gas and desire. Against the lumbering McBride – who, like Danny Williams, had been chosen to politely fall over for Mike – Tyson looked like an old man. The expected opening round barrage didn't happen. For five rounds Tyson and McBride plodded around the ring, throwing nothing of any great significance at each other.

For the first time ever, for a Tyson fight, I sat back in the chair and watched events unfold with a sense of sad acceptance. Even though I realized that his prime was long gone I'd still expected him to defeat Williams and had cheered his opening round explosion, just as I'd vocalized my ardent support so many times before. But there was a lesson to be learned from that bout.

Although Tyson was no longer a force to be reckoned with, his sheer iconic status and selling-power meant that victory over even a faded Tyson had garnered Williams a world title shot. My worry here was that McBride and his managers would foresee the potential for huge earnings and title fights if they could replicate Williams's desire and fortitude. I doubted very much that Mike would be taking this bout as seriously. If he couldn't motivate himself to train hard for the likes of Ruddock and co. when he was in his prime it seemed highly unlikely that he'd over-exert himself now that he was nearing his fortieth birthday. Champagne and loose women were far more important to Mike than punch-bags and sit-ups. (He's a very wise man, bless him!)

Even though Tyson wasn't even a fraction of his former devastating self, he still won the first few rounds but then, as his stamina visibly expired in the fifth, McBride saw his chance of glory and began to exert more pressure, pushing the pace further than Tyson was now capable of matching.

I sat and listened to the hysterical screeching of the commentators. Sensing an imminent and humiliating defeat, a weary Tyson once again panicked and reverted to street tactics, butting McBride, twisting his arm in an effort to break it and then biting him on the chest in a clinch! All to no avail.

Unlike Holyfield and all the countless others who'd stopped and complained about Tyson's illegal tactics over the years, McBride remained emotionless. He scented victory and ignored Tyson's blatant rule-breaking, bullying Mike into the ropes and then pushing him disdainfully down to the floor. Where Mike remained . . . simply refusing to get up.

The bell rang to end the round and Mike Tyson's career. Mike refused to come out for the seventh round, diminishing his reputation even more than he had against Williams. As with Nigel Benn's refusal to continue against Steve Collins several years before and Roberto Duran's infamous cry of "no more" against Sugar Ray Leonard, the boxing media attacked Tyson for not continuing. In a combat sport such as boxing, the cardinal sin is giving up before the opponent has the chance to finish you. It's a macho thing to be "carried out on your shield", presumably in the same way as Michael Watson and Gerald McClellan were carried into the nearest hospital emergency ward. (It's so easy to be brave when you're sitting on the outside of the ropes criticizing men who are damaging each other's brains for your entertainment.)

Tyson's only saving grace was that he was brutally honest with them afterwards!

When questioned about his decision to quit on his stool Tyson replied: "I just don't have the guts to do this any more!" He then added, "If I can't beat Kevin McBride, I can't beat anyone", a comment which forced his Irish opponent to counter with, "I didn't think great champions quit on their stool."

Tyson was unmoved. He realized the full extent of the dissipation of his skills and saw no reason to risk serious injury by continuing once his reserves of energy had petered out. After all, as he admitted, he was "only in it for the money".

Attempting to explain his lacklustre performance Tyson commented, "I look good. I feel good. But, when I get out there, I can't do it! I don't have the heart for fighting anymore. Not for fighting, nor for training . . . I can't beat Father Time. It's over. I'm finished."

These statements were revelatory enough but it was when Tyson then admitted that he'd been "living a lie since 1990" and confessed that losing the titles to Buster Douglas in one of the biggest shocks in boxing history had upset other people more than it had himself, as his desire for boxing was already on the wane.

He claimed that, since the early 1990s, he'd been in the sport only for the financial rewards and no longer the glory, and that when he looked back at images of himself decimating the heavyweight division back in the 1980s, he didn't "even know that guy".

As a loss of anger had effected a change in my psyche and life-style, so too did it impact upon Tyson. As exemplified against Lennox Lewis and Danny Williams, Tyson without the burning anger and resentment of 1985–9 was a less-than-devastating proposition. At one point even a mildly angry Tyson had still been good enough to destroy the likes of Bruno, Seldon, Francis, etc., but now a fully contented Tyson couldn't even dispatch a journeyman like McBride. Power of punch alone couldn't compensate for a lack of "bad intentions" behind it.

Whilst the commentators criticized Tyson's lack of desire, I poured a drink and toasted Mike. I understood his current mindset, just as I'd once empathized with his anger. I found it significant that he and his ex-wife Monica Turner had remained friends and that she was actually managing him now, helping him to bolster his finances for altruistic reasons. (Turner, apparently, waived her fee for the McBride bout.)

Anger is an emotion lying semi-dormant within all of us; it's just that it surfaces more readily in some people than others and becomes a hard animal to tame once it's reached the surface. The experience of years can teach you how to recognize the warning signs and keep the anger subdued, but the person must *want* to do so. If you're alone and depressed this can be hard but if you're fortunate enough to be surrounded by positive, loving people then you'll be motivated to examine the best method of controlling your emotions. Some can do it on their own, looking inside themselves and finding the strength, whilst for others the process can be engendered by an outside influence.

It took me forty years to believe that I was truly capable of love, simply because I had too much baggage to be able to relax and give or receive such a powerful emotion. Now that I've put my past to rest, I can finally embrace these feelings.

When asked what he wanted from his life now that his boxing career was over, Tyson considered and replied, "I just want to be happy."

Cheers, Mike! It's been one hell of a journey!!

DON MURFET (UK)

Minder to Rock Stars

Introducing . . . Don Murfet

L IFE ON THE road looking after one of the wildest rock bands of a generation is tough, hard, demanding work, and they do not come much tougher than Don Murfet, minder to Led Zeppelin, the Sex Pistols and other top international rock stars of the time.

Don came from a tough background. He wasn't born lucky, rich or ambitious and was the first to admit that he accidentally stumbled into his career as a "minder", a career that took him around the world protecting rock 'n' roll royalty and sorting out all the problems that living in an drug- and alcoholic-fuelled world brought, some of which resulted in him serving time at various British prisons.

In this chapter Don Murfet explains how he started working as a minder for Led Zeppelin at the very start of their rock 'n' roll careers, how he became good friends with Bonzo – the band's legendary drummer John Bonham – and what he and his team did when Bonzo was found dead at his home.

1963–94 LED ZEPPELIN
By Don Murfet

"Bonzo's dead," said a shaky voice on the phone. It was Ray Washbourne – the PA to Peter Grant, Led Zeppelin's manager.

The enormity of his words took a few moments to sink in. And then that cold fact took its grip on my guts. I was sickened. John Bonham was such a lovely bloke; I'd been through so much with him . . . It was a shock. But there was no time for grief – not yet. But maybe I'm starting at the end? Before going into John's tragic death, I'll explain how I came to be involved with Led Zeppelin and how I had come to be so close to that legendary band's members.

They say first impressions last – and that's certainly true of my first encounter with Peter Grant. The name Peter means "rock", and no one ever epitomized rock – in both senses of the word – like Peter. He was physically huge; an enormous hulk of a man, a former wrestler who, on a fateful night in 1964, had landed the job of road manager for the evening's show at the Regal Theatre in Edmonton, North London. With wild American blues legend Bo Diddley and the latest teen sensations, a louche and motley bunch of kids called the Rolling Stones on the bill, it wasn't going to be an easy ride. But old Peter was a rock in the face of any crowd, no matter how unruly. And, as I was to find out later, he was "rock" personified in other ways too – notably in his unrelenting passion for what became known as "rock 'n' roll habits". But more of that later . . .

I wasn't exactly uninitiated in the esoteric ways of the music business behind the scenes and I'd turned up to take care of someone else on the bill: Tommy Roe, who'd just scored a big hit with Sheila and who was represented in the UK and US by GAC, the massive American agency into which my mentor Vic Lewis had tied his own London firm. Used to breezing my way unquestioned past security to the backstage area, I strolled through the front-of-house and made my way easily to the pass door (the door at the side of the stage leading into the auditorium that was a feature of all the old theatres). There, I was accosted by this towering giant with piercing eyes and a Mandarin style moustache and beard who growled, "Who are you and where do you think you're going?"

I gave him my name and humbly explained that I was there to look after Tommy Roe. After a painfully long and, on my part at least, very tense pause, the future legend shrugged and let me pass with a gruff, "OK."

Sad to say, the strikingly vibrant Regal Theatre's days as a Rank cinema, concert hall and focus of local social life are long gone. Like so much that we took for granted as part of the rock 'n' roll life's rich fabric, it's been torn apart and now, where guitars and drums rang out almost nightly, you only hear the ring of cash registers. No longer Regal, it's now a lowly local supermarket. Thinking back on it, I and associates like Peter Grant, Don Arden, Mickey Most and countless others were incredibly lucky to have been starting out in the music business in the mid 1960s – a time now acknowledged as one of the most creative, vibrant and innovative that British rock 'n' roll has ever seen. At the time, though, like the people who saw no heritage of great import in the old Regal Theatre, we just saw every epoch-making event as another "day at the office". If only we'd known the significance of the times we were living in – and our impact on them!

It may not have seemed the most auspicious of introductions, but increasingly my life was to become intertwined with Peter's – and those of the bands with whom we both became associated. Within a year or so I found myself sharing the same London business address – 35 Curzon Street – with Peter and a whole gang of blokes whose names now read like a list of the biggest music business figures: Vic Lewis, Mickie Most, Pat Meehan, Barry Clayman, Ken Pitt, Alan Blackburn, Don Black, Barry Dickens, Irene Korf, Colin Berlin and Richard Cowley.

I was still working for Vic – and Peter was the road management supremo for another soon-to-become-legendary rock figure: Don Arden. He was one of the new, seminal breed of band promoters that the 1960s sired – dynamic, charismatic, creative and often even more outrageously flamboyant than the artists they looked after. With a fast-growing stable of the hottest, brightest stars, including the Small Faces and Black Sabbath, Ozzy Osbourne's Birmingham rockers who were to become the definitive heavy metal act, Don was something of a star himself. Incidentally, his daughter Sharon later managed and married Ozzy. And the more he shone, the more trouble gravitated towards him, wherever in the world he showed his face. Which, of course, was why he needed to be surrounded by brick shit-houses of men like Peter and his equally imposing colleague, Pat Meehan. No matter what he got up to, you simply didn't cross Don Arden – and over the years there were many who rued the day they'd tried. One hapless accountant springs to mind. He made the (almost literally) fatal mistake of mismanaging Arden's financial affairs in the early 1970s. Don and his son David weren't the types to call the cops. They called the shots.

I don't recall exactly what that poor accountant's fate was, other than that he was held prisoner for a while – but I'm sure their vengeance was swift and terrible. It was certainly illegal, because David ending up doing time for it and Don fled to the States, just out of reach of the long arm of the British law. As Arden's right-hand man, and a force to be reckoned with in his own right, Peter was a formidable character – and one you definitely wanted on your side. Although I never had any business dealings with him, I always got on well with Don Arden and found him great company.

Another nascent manager/producer saw the value of having a man of Peter's magnitude in his orbit – and soon Peter was installed at the Oxford Street offices of one Mickie Most (now sadly departed) and Ron Madison. Mickie was riding his first wave of success – and it was a big one. He was an immensely successful producer with hits by the likes of Donovan and Herman's Hermits but he was also handling seminal acts such as the New Vaudeville Band and crucially, the Yardbirds – a group whose success at this stage was to lead to undreamed prosperity in the future for Peter. Mickie went on to set up his own label, RAK Records, in 1969, and continued to work with Peter and the bands he managed.

Things were taking off for everyone around me – and by late 1965 I thought it was time I struck out on my own. I knew all about the hassles the most popular acts faced – and the three most important of them were security, privacy and transport. With my new venture I was going to solve all three it a stroke, filling what I saw as a gaping hole in the market – and, with a bit of luck, filling my pockets at the same time!

I was right. Artistes Car Services, as I christened my new enterprise, was an immediate success. The core of the idea was to offer performers a genuinely luxurious ride to and from their concerts with a minimum of fuss, total security and discretion. This proved to be exactly what the new breed of pop stars needed as their fans' adulation began to feel like persecution. That year some very big people rode in our sumptuously appointed limos, including the Beatles and Donovan among many others in an increasingly galactic list that began to read like a Who's Who of British rock 'n' roll. But undoubtedly the biggest arse to grace the seats of my fleet of cars was that of Peter Grant! From 1966 onwards he relied on us to get his fledgling acts from A to B (and often via C and D and all the way to Z!) and back again without incident or embarrassment. Of course, that meant we saw each other on a regular basis and, with so much in common, it was almost inevitable that we became close friends. What it really all boiled down to was trust. A simple thing, you might think – but a rare and valuable commodity in that exciting yet frightening dog-eat-dog time. Ultimately, Peter knew that he could rely absolutely on me – and, by association, on the team of level-headed, broad-minded, strong but utterly discreet men I employed. The old-school rule books had gone out of the window and he knew we could cope with any of the bizarre problems this new untamed form of showbiz could throw up. More importantly, he knew we could make them go away.

Nevertheless, it soon became apparent that many of these problems were actually of Peter's own making – certainly, he increasingly involved us in circumstances that had little to do with our original remit, which was just to chauffeur the artists to the gig and back again and protect them all the way. Drawn into all sorts of disputes from run-ins with the authorities to "withdrawing" illegal bootleg albums from record shops, I found myself in the dubious role of Peter's personal trouble-shooter. I suppose it was a compliment really. It showed his utter faith in my integrity – a faith that was, though I say it myself, completely justified. However, over the following years, it embroiled me in difficult personal, even intimate, situations that often I could have done without – even if Peter had convinced himself that he was merely acting in his artists' best interests. For example, if a band member lost interest in a particular girlfriend it was our job to make her *persona non grata* and ensure that she was no longer on the scene. Cast-off groupies were "cleansed" from the band's entourage with ruthless efficiency – the unfortunate girl concerned would suddenly find that the backstage doors and party venues that had once magically opened for her were now firmly closed, and often slammed, in her face. But it wasn't only people who were intimate with the band that we had to remove. Sometimes Peter simply took an instant dislike to a face in the crowd for no apparent reason. Ours was not, as they say, to question why and it was down to me to get the unfortunate owner of the face he'd taken exception to removed. Of course, I tried to elicit some sort of rationale from the great man as to what constituted a "threat to security" – but in the end it was a lot easier to just "do it" than to try and reason with him.

All the hassle and heartaches paid off handsomely. When Peter asked me to take on the road management duties for the forthcoming US tour of his new management signings, the Jeff Beck Group, it was quite an honour. Probably the first "supergroup", the band comprised four established faces (two quite literally!) who were destined for a place among the greatest in the history of rock 'n' roll: former Yardbirds, guitar hero Jeff Beck, of course; future Faces and Rolling Stones strummer Ronnie Wood on bass: new boy Tony Newman on drums; and a fresh-faced former gravedigger with a voice that sounded like it was made from the gravel he dug – one Rod Stewart. Like everything else in the music business in those days (and right up to this day I suspect) the job description of road manager was an elastic one. I imagine even the uninitiated would expect it to involve overseeing the hotel bookings, flights, shipping, trucking, setting up, sound-checking and breaking down the PA, lighting and staging at each venue. In fact, most of that would be handled by the roadies themselves – and the road manager would only get hands on when there were problems to sort out, such as equipment going astray. Less obvious are what you might call "ancillary" duties – they were often the least predictable, most onerous and prone to disaster. There were disputes and fights to settle, bills to pay, concert promoters to harangue and haggle with, and percentages of gross and "dead wood" to keep an eye on ("dead wood" was the unsold tickets, which had to be meticulously checked because they were our only means of verifying the number of tickets sold, and therefore the percentage owed to the band). And then there were services of a more personal and often illicit nature that are always in demand by a rampant rock group pumped full of adrenalin and testosterone after a great gig. I'm sure I don't need to spell out the exact nature of such missions! Suffice to say I jumped at the job and threw myself into it wholeheartedly, as always!

I'd already met Jeff Beck some years before – he'd turned up at the office in his pre-Yardbirds days several times while Vic Lewis was courting him for a management deal. Jeff had recorded a single called "That Noise" and CBS were keen to sign him, but he hesitated before signing just long enough to get another offer. As you can imagine, Vic was gutted when "the one that got away" joined the Yardbirds and began his meteoric rise to stellar status. That single never saw the light of day. It turned out that Vic's loss was Peter Grant's very lucrative gain – and it was my baptism of fire in the sheer madness and barely contained anarchy that was rife on the road in the States with one of the original hair-raisingly hedonistic rock supergroups.

I didn't meet the rest of Jeff's boys until our rendezvous at Heathrow. Like a dog urinating to mark out its territory, I knew I had to make my mark immediately – stamp my authority on the lot of them. If I didn't I might as well not get on the plane. I should explain that some of the road manager's more banal duties are also the biggest nightmares, like coaxing a hideously hungover musician from his hotel bed and getting him on to the plane/tour bus/stage on time. They don't thank you for it and a lot of the time you have to be the "bad guy". In fact, at times I felt like some kind of satanic scoutmaster!

The high jinks started almost the second that the plane levelled out at cruising altitude and the seat-belt lights went out. The boys were in a particularly playful mood, like a bunch of schoolboys on an outing with a teacher – although considerably less innocent. They seemed set on testing me; goading me to see just how far they could push me and at times it was hard to tell the playing up and play-acting from whatever would pass as normal behaviour in the unique world of a successful rock musician, which is, as far as I can tell, one gigantic amusement park. I took the wind-ups and pissing about with good humour until suddenly the atmosphere of levity dropped like a . . . well, like a Led Zeppelin. Young Rod was squirming in his seat, clearly overcome with nausea. As he clutched his stomach in agony, and gagged and heaved those dry retches that make everyone around feel sick too, a couple of concerned fellow passengers got out of their seats and rushed to his aid. Right on cue he shuddered, convulsed and spewed forth a torrent of evil looking grey vomit all over his would-be Good Samaritans. I bet that was the last time they rushed to the assistance of an unruly rocker! It turned out that the disgusting globby mess that splattered out of Rod the Mod's mouth wasn't vomit at all – just an unpleasant papier mâché of superstar spittle and the paper he'd been chewing up since take-off. Not, I imagine, that this was much consolation to the people whose clothes were soaked in it!

Unfortunately that was just the start. They got down to some serious drinking and some bright spark suggested a game of "Kelly's Eye". One of the group, sitting in the window seat (which is important) would call out weakly for a stewardess (and they were generally female in those days. Somehow the game wouldn't have the same appeal these days as there are often males in the flight crew). When the stewardess arrived and asked what was wrong, the occupier of the window seat would mumble incoherently in reply. So she'd lean forward, cocking an ear to hear what he was trying to say. He'd groan something equally unintelligible under his breath. Keen to do her duty and help an ostensibly sick passenger, she'd lean further forward, now almost prone across the aisle seat. He'd gasp helplessly. And what the hapless stewardess took to be the whimper of a seriously ill man was actually the strain of stifled laughter – because the further she stretched over, the higher up her thighs her skirt would ride and the better the view for the rest of the group, ogling enthusiastically from behind. I don't think the name of the game needs any further explanation! And from there things went downhill fast. Halfway into the flight the members of the band were considerably higher than the plane that carried them. Their raucous laughter and shouting – screaming even – were getting out of control. And it was out of order. It was time, I decided, to draw the line – not the kind of line usually associated with rock stars, but it certainly got right up their noses! Ironically, the relative newcomer to rock, Tony Newman, was by far the most obnoxious of the four. So I decided to single him out and make an example of him. I laid my cards on the table to see if he'd call my bluff (and it really, really, was not a bluff!).

I lunged across the aisle and loomed over the back of his seat – and my face was right in his face, livid with pent-up fury. The hearty guffawing instantly shrivelled to the sheepish titter of chastised schoolboys (or boy scouts).

"Listen, you!" I roared at the top of my voice, "Two of us can play this game – and I don't mean Kelly's bleedin' Eye! We can do this tour two ways. I could make it hard for you – really hard – or . . . we could learn to work together!"

It worked. I suppose that when my words sunk in they thought about just how unpleasant I could make their life on the road – how their post-gig sexual and chemical proclivities could be curtailed by a martinet of a road manager bent on laying down the law to the letter of their contracts. They had little option but to toe the line for a while. I'd made my point – and made my mark. Temporarily at least, I'd tamed the wildest of party animals and for the rest of the tour the Jeff Beck Group were, if not exactly model citizens, admirably civilized. They'd learnt a valuable lesson from that little contretemps – and more importantly, so had I.

That Jeff Beck tour set the tone for my future life on the road. The hassles, the chaos and the loose cannons would be the same despite the fact that in my career I've worked with a diverse range of artists that includes Led Zep, David Cassidy, Adam and the Ants and the Sex Pistols among many others. In the end, as I learnt, the musical trends may come and go but that quintessential rock 'n' roll attitude, like the song, remains the same. And long may it stay that way! Frankly, it wouldn't have been much of a challenge if I'd been in charge of a bunch of choirboys – and nor would it have been as lucrative!

The rock 'n' roll attitude was constant – and so were the hassles. They might be different in their precise nature, but I learnt to anticipate the unexpected so that in the end there wasn't much that could shock or faze me. I became an accomplished "firefighter". When things got heated I cooled the situation; when tempers blazed I extinguished them; and when bands' self-destructive urges looked like making them crash and burn I usually managed to control the fire without losing the vital spark that made these guys legendary. I think it was Neil Young who said it's better to burn out than fade away – well I'm not so sure, but I certainly got the impression that most of Zep and the Jeff Beck Group would have gone along with that philosophy! Sadly, there were to be times when I couldn't prevent a great talent from falling prey to his own volatility and unquenchable lust for excess. More of which later . . .

A perennial problem that always rankled with the acts was when greedy agents booked them into venues that were entirely unsuitable – in terms of size, access, acoustics or even sheer mortal danger for fans and performers alike. One of Jeff and the lads' gigs was a perfect example of the bookers' total lack of concern for their performers' image and style of music. To their horror they found that they'd been booked to perform at a kids' summer camp – one of those places where American parents dump their stroppy teenagers for the school holidays. Playing to an audience of 13- and 14-year-olds was not a job for serious rock musicians – that was for children's entertainers and cutesy pop performers. To say the band were unhappy would be an understatement and, when the inevitable on-stage shenanigans started and they began to treat the gig as little more than a private party, the organizers and their charges were unhappier still. Always the wild card, Tony Newman abandoned his drum kit and kept up the percussion as he staggered from tabletop to tabletop by banging his sticks on anything that would make a noise – bottles, pipes, chairs, you name it. At least he stopped short of banging out a paradiddle on a teenage head – well, at least I think he did! And then Jeff and Woodie joined in. Not to be outdone by their drummer's antics, they picked up a fire extinguisher and liberally doused the first few rows of the audience with foam. Talk about dampening the audience's spirits – sheer bloody pandemonium broke out! The organizers were evidently not amused. As they picked up the phone to call the police I realized that it was time for action. The ability to think on your feet is one of the first attributes anyone should look for in a prospective road manager – and I pride myself on the number of scrapes and brushes with the law I got my bands out of over the years. On this occasion a quick getaway was called for – my speciality! I bundled the band out of the hall and into the waiting limousine as quickly as I could and the sleek, stretched motor screeched out of the compound in a mad dash for the state line and immunity from arrest.

We made it in the nick of time – but that wasn't much consolation to my assistant, Henry (the Horse) Smith, who'd had to stay behind with the truck and all of the band's gear. When the cops arrived they didn't see the funny side. Quite the contrary, in fact, because they were determined to confiscate anything they could lay their hands on in an attempt to force the band to come back and face the music. And when you consider the vast value of a major band's touring technology, we probably would have had no alternative but to turn ourselves in and cough up the fines and/or backhanders, if not face jail sentences, to get it all back. But the appropriately named Henry had "horse" sense. He claimed that all the equipment belonged to him and that he'd simply lent it to the group for the performance and didn't expect to ever see them again. Unbelievably, the police swallowed the story and let him – and the band's equipment – go free. All we lost was Ronnie's bass guitar and a few odds and sods – not that that stopped the boys sulking about it for a day or two!

I've had better times – but few of them were entirely without some kind of incident, such as the Jeff Beck Group's gig at Schenectady Hall in upstate New York, for example. It seemed that things were really looking up when we heard that Peter Grant's latest managerial signing – Led Zeppelin – were also on the American East Coast at the time on their inaugural US tour and arrangements were quickly made for the two bands to hook up for some serious partying. Led Zep and the Jeff Beck Group – talk about an explosive combination!

Those two now legendary bands may have been volatile, but their signing was a major coup for Peter. The downside, for Peter and for me, was that great talents are notoriously hard to handle. In Beck, he had one of the world's greatest guitarists and a proven record-seller – temperamental, often stroppy but always ready to pull a rabbit out of the hat. In the end, though, it was Zeppelin that was to be Peter's biggest cash cow – and one he'd take to rich new pastures and milk for all it was worth.

Right from the off, everyone knew that Led Zeppelin were a cut above the rest of the rockers – a true supergroup in the making. Formed by Jimmy Page, one of the key songwriter/producers of his generation, from the ashes of the Yardbirds, Zep blended vintage blues and heavy rock with consummate musicianship, and made all those elements add up to something far greater than the sum of their parts. Added to Page's prodigious talents was lead singer Robert Plant. And what a find he was – an imposing, handsome, blond Viking of a man whose sex appeal was as powerful as his thunderous, yet soulful and vulnerable voice. John Paul Jones on bass was no less gifted – both at laying down the deep, throbbing basslines that melded the Zep sound together and at laying the countless women that fell willingly at his feet. And then there was Bonzo on drums. I would grow to love John Bonham dearly. He was a good – even great – man; a funny man and a great friend. He was also one of the wildest I've ever known – and I've known some very wild men in my time. I'd describe him as a playboy – but the term has too many suave and pretentious associations to sum up an irrepressible character like Bonzo. He was a walking bag of contradictions: a gentle soul who was nevertheless the epitome of the "wild man of rock" with an iron constitution capable of withstanding his prodigious and insatiable appetite for booze and drugs. His formidable drumming was the kingpin of Zep's musical direction and rightly made him a rock legend – but his offstage antics were equally hard-hitting and were to become equally famous.

Given their origins, it was almost inevitable that media interest in the band verged on the rabid – even before the release of their first album. And if the critics were a little sniffy about them at first, the live audiences fell in love with Zep at first sight and sound! America was similarly smitten, thanks largely to the heavy radio promotion of "Whole Lotta Love" (later the "Top of the Pops" theme for many years).

Anyway, Zep were coming along on the Jeff Beck Group's tour bus to the Schenectady Hall gig – but it soon became clear that they weren't just there to appreciate the performance. Richard Cole, their notorious road manager, lost no time at all in getting up to mischief, with the rest of Zep following his lead. While Jeff, Rod, Ronnie and Tony were grooving away on stage the majestic Zep boys held court in the dressing room with numerous excited females in attendance. Knowing their reputation, you'd have thought it would be John Paul, Jimmy or Bonzo who'd make the first lecherous leap on the compliant assembly of girls – but no, it was Richard Cole. When a pleasantly plump, rather innocent-looking girl walked shyly through the dressing room door in search of her rock gods, Richard lunged at her and literally swept her off her feet, spinning her upside down and rubbing his face lasciviously in her crotch. And that was just for starters. For all I know she enjoyed it – but I'm pretty sure the victims of the next little prank weren't at all happy.

One of the boys, unnoticed in a corner of the dressing room, decided to urinate into a big jug of Coca Cola – and, as you've probably guessed, he offered this foul, tainted chalice to every hapless girl who stepped tentatively into the room in the hope of having some contact with her heroes. Poor girls, I thought. It wasn't funny. Just crude. And cruel. But it wasn't the worst abuse of these innocents who threw themselves at the rock 'n' roll animals they lionized. I'd just about had enough of that kind of behaviour and had stepped outside with Peter for a breath of fresh air – both literal and metaphorical – only to walk straight into a distraught young girl as she emerged from the toilets in floods of tears. Clearly grateful to find two potential knights in shining armour, she turned to us and wailed, "There's a guy in there who's just been groping me!"

Fired up with righteous indignation, Peter and I stormed into the toilets (or should I say "restroom" since we were in America!) and immediately confronted the groper – who was about to regret the sexual assault bitterly because he, and I, were introduced to Peter's celebrated "kicking trick". This involved taking the terrified bloke by the scruff of the neck and kicking him in the shins, again and again. And then again and again. And again. And again – boot cracking against bone with a rhythmic precision that Bonzo would have been proud of. This treatment was followed up with Peter's other mode of administering punishment – namely a stiff four fingers shoved into and under the ribcage, which really takes your breath away! As I've mentioned, Peter was a whale of a man, about six foot two and weighing in at something over 300 pounds. A kicking from Peter was like one from a carthorse – and one that the groupie groper wasn't going to erase from his memory or his shins for a helluva long time! After a minute or so, which must have seemed like a lifetime to the groper, Peter finally laid off, dragged the guy's limp and crippled form to the door and hurled him through it like the sack of shit he clearly was. Unlike a sack of shit, however, he actually bounced off the floor before hauling himself painfully to his feet and wobbling off, dazed and confused, in the immortal, and accurate, words of the Led Zep song. The message came over loud and clear: urinating in a bottle was one thing, but nobody messed with Zep's fans when Peter was around, whether they were male or female.

The two bands' paths were to cross several times over the next few days as their respective tours wended their way across the States

– but it was at the Singer Bowl, a massive sports complex doubling as a concert venue just outside New York's Flushing Meadows, that things really came to a head.

Jeff and the boys were supporting America's flavour of the month, Vanilla Fudge. More significantly, as it turned out, Alvin Lee's new band, Ten Years After, were opening the star-studded bill. The Zep boys and their entourage said they'd be there to lend Jeff a bit of moral support. I thought that was quite touching to begin with – such selfless solidarity between two of the UK's best bands while they were touring on foreign turf. But of course it wasn't as simple, or as innocent, as that. Nothing ever was! Hindsight being 20:20, maybe I should have sussed that there was more to their eagerness to attend than geeing their mates along. In fact that had nothing to do with it. The Zep boys were there to get their own back on Lee for some pretty nasty remarks he'd once made about Jimmy Page – and Jeff Beck's roadies seemed happy to help them wreak their revenge, egged on, inevitably, by Bonzo and Richard Cole. Chick Churchill – one of Ten Years After's associates – was unlucky enough to be caught without backup in a locker room by a vengeful rabble of roadies who scared the crap out of him before ruthlessly stripping him of his clothes. Then they stripped him of his dignity by dumping him naked and trussed like a lamb to the slaughter in the starkly lit corridor outside.

Next it was Ten Years After's turn for the revenge of Zeppelin. Hidden in the anonymity of the shadows in a corner in front of the stage, the Zeppelin crew pelted Alvin Lee mercilessly from the moment he took the stage with anything that came to hand – including hot dogs, burgers, orange juice and probably much messier and more painful missiles. It was glorious! Lee and his band had no idea who the mysterious assailants in the shadows could be. The shower of debris stole their thunder, undermining the storming performance they'd had their hearts set on and, understandably enough, mediocrity was all they could muster.

In retrospect, Peter and Jimmy – the two partners in crime – had to be behind this. It was their way of saying, "Don't ever mess with the Zeppelin!"

If that had been the sum total of their retribution for an off-colour comment, I guess it would have been "fair dos", but they'd already planned a master-stroke that would add insult to injury. Of course, as far as the audience was concerned, Led Zep's joining the Jeff Beck Group on stage was an impromptu jamming session. I knew different! Having ruined Alvin Lee's set, a band that hadn't even been booked to play was about to steal the show. And steal the show they did. But even the Led Zep boys hadn't planned the finale that was to be the highlight of the night.

Bonzo had been at the backstage booze. Nothing unusual about that – or about the fact that, drunk as a lord, his drumming on the fast blues the galaxy of rock stars were playing was as blisteringly bang-on-the-nail as ever. What was a bit unusual was the fact that he'd suddenly decided to do a "Full Monty" while he was at it, still hitting that kick drum with mechanical, maniacal precision and venom despite the strides and underpants tangled round his ankles. For most of the audience, the sight of his private parts made public was just a bit of a Bonzo bonus to the already exciting event.

But, among the ogling crowd, some punters were less impressed at the sight of Bonzo's manhood flapping about on the drum stool. I clocked one humourless woman talking animatedly to one of the fairly heavy local police presence. Like a chill wind, the prudish outrage swept through the crowd and it was clear to see that the cops were not amused. Now, I'm not saying I'd normally think Bonzo getting his kit off was going too far. On the contrary, high spirits and outrageous behaviour like that are the all part of the sheer joy of rock 'n' roll – and long may it stay that way. A few people will always be upset by it, but when the police are among the ones with the hump, that's when the fun stops and the trouble starts. Of course, it was my job to make sure it didn't.

I could see the cops rallying together, conferring and calling for backup. I had to get Bonzo off the stage before they could arrest him. Suddenly I had a plan. I took Henry the Horse aside and told him to kill all the lights the moment the performers finished their song. He did so, plunging the stage into darkness for about ten seconds – just long enough for Richard Cole and I to grab Bonzo by the arms, pull his pants up and drag him, full-pelt, backstage. Obviously we couldn't hide him in the band's dressing area – that was the first place the cops would look for him. So we lugged him into another locker room nearby which, since it was fully equipped with shower facilities and such-like and plastered with sporting paraphernalia, I assumed was an American football players' changing room. Somewhere out there, the police were stumbling about in the darkness, their mood turning as black as the blackout we'd plunged them into.

I kicked the door shut and locked it. Hearts banging as loud as Bonzo's drumming and holding our breath in case we were heard, Richard and I set about tidying up the legless sticks-man. We waited. Bonzo, by now, was unconscious, draped lifelessly over a chair, marooned helplessly in the empty tiled expanse of the backstage changing room. The distant rumble of angry men echoed along the corridors outside – then suddenly sounded uncomfortably close. And then there was an explosion of outraged voices. At first it was an incomprehensible babble. Then it was way too close and way too clear.

"Where is the dirty motherfucker?" one loud American voice kept roaring with an authority that cut through the general furore. At least, I thought, we were safely locked in this room. No one could hear us. Bonzo was temporarily out of the game. Keep schtum and we'd be in the clear.

But then there was a thunderous banging at the door – the kind of banging that won't take no for an answer. The door burst open to reveal five or six huge cops with waists as wide as their minds were narrow. Some traitor must have given them the master key. We were outnumbered, out-muscled, outweighed and, most importantly, outlawed.

Richard and I stood in front of Bonzo in a forlorn attempt at solidarity – as if we could hide and protect him. Two of the police posse strode forward – too close for comfort, intimidating, demanding to know if this was the drummer who'd just given his public a pubic performance (not that they put it that delicately!).

"Look, he's just drunk – he's harmless,' I spluttered. "Look at him – he didn't mean any harm . . . "

The cops looked with distaste over my shoulder at the inert figure sprawled over a chair in the middle of the bleakly lit and spartan room. Neither was impressed. Their collective sense of humour bypass was obviously complete. I suppose it wasn't much of an excuse. It can't have been – because then they whipped out their batons threateningly, making it utterly clear that they meant business.

To be honest, at that point, Richard and I had given up the ghost. We were all going to get nicked and that was that. But neither we nor the cops had reckoned on a far superior authority. I'd thought the police had made a fairly impressive entrance just minutes ago. But the door through which they'd marched with such self-righteous import suddenly exploded open to admit the furious and fighting-mad figure of Peter Grant. He was always almost ludicrously huge – but fluffed up, furious and bristling with rage like a giant Mother Hen hell-bent on protecting her chicks, he almost took the door off its hinges. The door wasn't the only thing almost unhinged by his entrance: the cops clucked in panic – overshadowed and overawed and chickening out completely.

"I'm the manager of the band," Grant boomed imperiously. "Who's in charge here?"

The gobsmacked police officers silently pointed out their captain, whose eyes met Peter's and were fixed in his glare.

"You and me need to talk – alone." Peter said quietly. "Get your men out of here."

With a wave of his arm the captain dismissed his troops and Richard and I followed suit – we didn't need telling. Closing the door carefully behind us, we left Bonzo, Peter and the captain in the room and waited. And waited. And waited.

Finally, after about ten minutes that seemed a lot longer, the captain emerged, all that anger drained from his fat face, and beckoned his men to follow. Bemused, we gingerly stepped back into the locker room, where Peter greeted us with a smile.

"Well done!" he beamed. "Now, let's get Bonzo on the bus."

I didn't need to be told twice. I grabbed the still-prone Bonzo and hauled him bus-wards and within minutes Peter and Led Zep, complete with their semi-conscious drummer, were speeding out of town. No charges. No arrest. In fact, it was as if the incident had never happened. I was in awe of Peter's unique brand of diplomacy that had somehow convinced the outraged cop captain to let the matter drop. It was amazing the authority that guy commanded. Maybe it was his sheer size and physical presence . . . well, that and the sheer size and physical presence of his wallet – as I found out when I asked Peter later on the bus.

"That was a cheap get-out, Don!" he laughed heartily. "It only cost me $300!"

So now I knew how Led Zeppelin did business – and how the big man made problems just disappear. It was a lesson I'd take to heart – and which would take me to the very centre of the stellar supernova that Zeppelin were about to become.

The irony was that the quiet, understated style of getting things done that I'd developed for myself was sometimes at odds with Peter's methods. The further their balloon went up, the more money there was sloshing around – and Peter's preferred way of dealing with problems was to throw money at them. And that may have taken the edge off tricky situations, but it also brought a whole new range of complications. Despite – or maybe because of – his unquestioned authority within the rock 'n' roll sphere, Peter was drawn to people who had power of other kinds. He seemed to be influenced by anyone who was "connected", whether in government circles or in the underworld. One gentleman, although I'm not sure the term is accurate in this case, seemed to hold particular sway over Peter. Herb Elliott, that was his name. Ex CIA or FBI, he appeared on the scene after a huge US tour that Zep had just completed and he soon became instrumental in smoothing the band's way through the States. The powers that be move in mysterious ways and this Herb guy was clearly connected. As if by magic the band had police escorts on demand and incidents such as that Singer Bowl debacle were ironed out and wiped away without the need for negotiation.

One time outside the Montcalm at Marble Arch, Peter's favourite London hotel, I spotted three dodgy looking men in a car, who were definitely staking out the hotel. Naturally, I mentioned it to Peter and Herb.

"What make of car? Registration?" Herb asked in a flash.

I told him, having made a mental note of the licence plate just in case. Herb left the room purposefully and was back in ten minutes.

"It's OK. They're police – but they're looking for someone else," he said with an air of confidence that could only come from a man with some serious contacts at the highest level.

*   *   *

Maybe here's the right place for me to go back to the beginning, where, you may remember, I opened with the tragic end of John Bonham in September 1980.

"Get down to Jimmy's and take care of things," Ray had said in that awful phone call to tell me Bonzo was dead.

"OK, leave it to me," I'd replied. And I knew from long experience that Ray and Peter Grant wouldn't have called if the shit wasn't about to hit the fan. I had to get down to Jimmy Page's place sharpish. It was down to me to contain the situation, limit the damage – and that probably meant keeping the police and the press at bay.

I put the phone down, grabbed my keys and in minutes I was out of my office in the NOMIS complex in Sinclair Road, London W14, and gunning my BMW on to the A4. I sped west for Windsor, where the family of Jimmy, the prince of rock, had a palatial mansion, the Old Mill House in Mill Lane (incidentally, formerly owned by Michael Caine). It was a stone's throw from another royal household: Windsor Castle.

My mind raced faster than the car's screaming engine. John's dead. How? Was it accidental? Did he suffer? What about Pat and Jason, his wife and son? That frantic half-hour's drive was on auto-pilot as a cascade of John's larger-than-life exploits flashed through my mind – fleeting recollections that made me smile despite the Bonzo-sized hole deep in the pit of my stomach. This tragedy was the latest in a run of bitterly bad luck for the band. Whether by sad coincidence or something more sinister, the Grim Reaper had been knocking at Zeppelin's door much too often for comfort of late – as I was reminded when I stumbled breathless into the guest room at Jimmy's mansion to find Bonzo's body, lifeless, on its side. Benjy le Fevre, his personal roadie, had put him to bed after his drinking session, having taken care to prop his back with a bolster to ensure that he couldn't roll over and choke on his own vomit. The central heating had been left on but later someone had opened the windows – and it was the fresh air, I was told, that had caused the strange discolouration of his face. It was as if John's life and soul went out of the window as the fresh air blew in.

Arriving at around noon, I'd beaten the police and press to the scene. Professionals to the end, the roadies – Benjy and Rex King

– and Jimmy's manservant Rick Hobbs had already "cleaned up", by which they meant that they'd got rid of anything potentially incriminating or embarrassing to the band or John's family. The one thing even they couldn't conceal or control, though, was his blood – and whatever that contained would be revealed in the post mortem. To the uninitiated that might sound impressively level-headed and professional, but to a seasoned roadie it's pretty much standard procedure – as routine as tuning a guitar and placing the monitors correctly – especially if your man indulged heavily in all the usual extracurricular rock 'n' roll habits! And there's no denying that John Bonham indulged – in fact, he was the epitome of the wild man of rock, modelling himself on his boyhood hero, the late, great Keith Moon of the Who. It transpired that the boys had been rehearsing that day and Bonzo, characteristically, had been hitting the vodka hard – at least four quadruples, by all accounts, as well as who knows how many speedballs, the last of which was to be John's final hit. But, ironically, it wasn't that heady mix of coke and smack that killed him. Tragically, despite Benjy's diligent precautions, it was later found that John had vomited and inhaled at the same time in his deep, drunken sleep, setting up a fatal siphon effect whereby the contents of his stomach were pumped into his lungs.

Shaking off my initial shock, I took charge of my emotions – and then I took charge of the situation.

You have to be pragmatic at times like that. It was too late to do anything for John, and I could take care of his family later. Right now, damage limitation was the name of the game – and the first threat was the police. I briefed everyone in the house: keep your mouths shut and make sure the cops confine their investigation to the guest room. They must not be allowed to nose around the rest of the house! I didn't know what they might find but whatever they turned up, I was sure it wouldn't do the band any good. And once the press got wind of it they'd have a field day, especially since Bonzo was the second visitor to have died in one of Jimmy Page's guest rooms in just over a year. In fact that earlier incident served as a sort of rehearsal for this latest tragedy . . .

On 24 October 1979 Paul McCartney's company, MPL Communications, hired us to provide men to check the guest list and handle the overall security at a very prestigious award ceremony that *The Guinness Book of Records* was holding at Les Ambassadeurs nightclub just off London's Park Lane. Everybody who was anybody was there, including the press, paparazzi, liggers and jibbers (jibbers are people who blag their way into gigs, receptions or backstage without a pass or invitation), largely because Paul was being presented with a medallion cast in rhodium (which is a very hard, silvery platinum-like metal element) by a government minister. I was just checking out the members of Pink Floyd when one of my men said that there was a call for me upstairs (obviously this was a long time before the advent of mobile phones!). At the reception desk I found the call was from Ray Washbourne – and it wasn't the best of news! They'd just found one of Jimmy's guests dead at his home at Plumpton Place, Sussex. Predictably, he wanted me to get down there and take care of things.

"I think someone may have phoned for an ambulance," he said, "but that's all I know."

"Leave it to me," I said before telling Gerry Slater, my business partner, what had happened and taking off like a scalded cat.

I arrived at the same time as the police. Obviously that was because they'd been called out by the ambulance crew – which is standard procedure. Their presence meant that I couldn't clear up the way I'd have liked to. All I could do was confine their investigations to the guest room where the guy, whose name I later found out was Richard Churchill-Hale, had popped his clogs. And that annoyed the cops intensely! If I'd arrived ten minutes later they'd have been all over the house like a rash – so I was very lucky, timing-wise.

I didn't get a chance to clear up completely so they did find "substances" by his bedside. It transpired that the poor bloke had overdosed – but because he was a guest, staying in a guest room, I was able to limit the police's snooping to the room he slept in.

Anyway, going back to Bonzo, I knew that the press would hound his family pitilessly, and that simply wasn't an option. I had to keep a lid on it for as long as I possibly could, at least until Peter Grant turned up and started throwing his weight around – and, as demonstrated, that time at the Singer Bowl, that was a lot of weight to throw!

The police weren't happy about being stymied at every turn. But what could they do? It was apparently an accidental death: nothing suspicious about it. A drunken man had seemingly inhaled his own vomit – period. There was no good reason for them to snoop around, no matter how much they'd have liked to. Anyway, it was the law; they knew it and so did I. Funny how rock 'n' roll makes lawyers out of everyone involved – just like crime!

Sure enough, by the time Peter and Ray arrived and John Bonham had "left the building" for the last time in the ambulance, the road had filled with reporters and the mob was growing by the minute as the circling vultures homed in on the smell of death. The three of us discussed all the angles, analysed the kinds of problems that might ensue, made contingency plans and decided how we would box for the next few days. That resolved, Peter and Ray went off to console the boys in the band. It was only after his unusually subdued departure that it dawned on me that Peter hadn't been in his normal control-freak manager mode. Far from it – he was obviously deeply shocked by the event and, after our preliminary talk, left the whole affair to me to deal with.

At least I didn't have to worry about the rest of the band. They'd made a hasty departure minutes after John's body had been discovered and I'd arranged for more of my men to go and look after them until they were safely ensconced in secure retreats where there would be no intrusions. That may sound callous. It wasn't. It was, again, standard procedure. When there was a "death in the family" unwritten rule number one was to make sure that the band members were as far away from the action as possible. It meant fewer questions for them to answer. But, more importantly, it allowed them to grieve in private, protected from the press.

The platoons of press and police set up camp at the Old Mill House for days. So I did, too. I hardly left Jimmy's place for the following few days. Keeping the hounds at bay was a full-time job and a hard one, with the more dogged photographers climbing over the walls – and driving me and my men up the wall in the process. There were a few little incidents, but nothing I couldn't handle, and I managed to contain the situation as effectively as anyone could. Maybe I shouldn't have bothered. They'd caught the whiff of a story that was a tabloid hack's wet dream: rock star, booze, drugs and death – and if there wasn't any sex they'd find a way to work some in. So, if they couldn't get the story from the horse's mouth they'd let their imaginations – and Led Zep cuttings archives – run riot. Predictably, they added Ol' Black Magic to the lurid mix, concocting ludicrous fantasies involving Jimmy Page and his admittedly strong interest in the occult in general and Aleister Crowley in particular. For example, he owned a house that had formerly belonged to Crowley and in which there had allegedly been a terrifying catalogue of murders and suicides. The place was also apparently haunted by the spirit of a man who'd been decapitated there some 300 years earlier – all lurid grist to the newspaper mill!

Having been so close to so many famous people whose lives had been blighted and hacked to pieces by the lies and sensationalism of the gutter-press hacks, I knew exactly what they'd do to John's memory, given the chance. They didn't care whose feelings they hurt as long as they could drag up enough dirt to muddy the issue – because they know mud sticks. Any little association, any name, any snippet of gossip or unsubstantiated innuendo would do if they could cook it up into a tasty dish for their hungry public. I wouldn't mind so much if what they printed was true – but in my experience they get it wrong most of the time and hurt people more than they'll ever know. But they never, ever apologize. Worse still, they never, ever, seem to care. Luckily enough, because John was so well-liked by his friends, there were very few new revelations about him. In fact, it's a tribute to his friends' loyalty and integrity that all the press could do was dig up and rehash old stories.

Despite the press, I at least partially succeeded in controlling the way the whole tragic affair was perceived by the public by keeping a lid on everyone involved and ensuring that they didn't disclose anything. And now I faced another, far more unsettling, task: to make sure John looked his best for his swansong show for all the family and friends who wanted to pay him their last respects. To do him justice, the mortician needed to know what this vacant frame had been like in life – larger than life was what Bonzo had been. I found a photo that captured that free spirit we'd lost and made an appointment at Kenyon Morticians in Kensington – at which I duly arrived, full of trepidation.

After polite introductions in the office, I was ushered into the area where the bodies were stored, silently awaiting their burial or cremation. It was cool like . . . well, like a morgue really. I, on the other hand, wasn't just cool. I was chilled to the bone when the mortician reverently drew John out of what looked like an over-sized filing cabinet – the one where they file your life when it's no longer current. Desecrated by the autopsy and horribly discoloured, this wasn't the Bonzo I'd known and loved. John's wasn't the first dead body I'd seen and wouldn't be the last, but that didn't make that "death mask" any less horrifying. I was calmed, though, by the mortician – a kind, congenial and fascinating man. It's a tribute to his professionalism and integrity that when he looked at John's body, having talked about John with me and examined the photo I'd brought along, he saw him through my eyes. He explained the way he would use make-up and style his hair and assured me that by the time he began his quiet sojourn in the Chapel of Rest, John would look peaceful and serene – and no one would see any sign of the autopsy or the discolouration that had so disturbed me. Bonzo, peaceful and serene. That's a first, I thought.

A consummate professional in the art of sending people grace-fully to their final rest, he was just as skilled in bringing peace to the living – and, having put my mind at ease, he shared some of the intimate and touching aspects of his craft. In another "file" was another body – that of a sixty-one-year-old Greek or Cypriot woman. She was fully clothed and looked as if she'd just fallen asleep. But it had been a very long snooze because, amazingly, she'd been dead for nearly two years. Evidently her husband had requested that they kept her there, perfectly peaceful and preserved, until he died – which he apparently would be soon – so that they could make their final journey together; go home to be buried in their own country. And this wasn't a one-off. He told me he'd once kept the body of an exiled African head of state for more than six years because his family was waiting until their country's political climate changed before they could take him home and bury him in his native soil. I found myself moved by the reverence with which this gentle man accommodated people's last wishes in God's departure lounge. There couldn't have been anyone better to administer this art to John: a great and talented artist performing his art for another great and talented artist.

A few days later I returned to see his handiwork and my faith was fully justified – John had been transformed. He looked lifelike – perhaps better than he'd looked for several years. All his confusion and conflict was resolved; the stress and strain relieved. He just looked bloody handsome and, finally, the wild man of rock was completely at peace.

I phoned Peter to tell him that the funeral arrangements could go ahead and also that people could now pay their last respects. John was to be buried near his home at Rushock in Worcestershire, where he had lived with his wife Pat and Jason, his son.

My involvement in John's demise had been a tragedy in three acts. Act One: the death scene at Jimmy's house. Act Two: the Chapel of Rest. Act Three was the funeral – and again my own grief had to be put on hold because my team and I had been employed to ensure that it would be a dignified and respectful occasion, unsullied by intrusive press or fans. It was the last meaningful thing I could do for John – and I was determined to do that sad duty well, despite the irony that "quiet and dignified" were hardly what the wild man would have wanted. What he definitely would have wanted, though, was for Pat, his beloved wife, to be spared any more stress and strain than she was already suffering. And this, I would ensure – for Pat, for Jason and for John. Appropriately, my lads and I met close friends and family at John's favourite watering hole just opposite the graveyard where he was to rest, and toasted him the way he'd have wanted us to. In fact Pat made a remark that June (my wife) and I will never forget: "From his grave, John can see this pub, so he can see us celebrating his life as he would have wanted us to."

With that deeply moving thought in mind, I reluctantly left John's close family and many other friends – many of whom were my friends too – to say their final goodbyes while we prepared to fortify the church against the inevitable onslaught.

Security was just one aspect of the operation. There were more sensitive duties to deal with too and I'm proud to say that the busload of my men I brought in did an admirably discreet and respectful job, and behaved impeccably. You'd never have known that their background was in the rather less formal world of rock 'n' roll, but it was clear that their solemnity and dedication to the job was inspired by the fact that most of them had worked with Zeppelin at one time or another. They acted as ushers for the collected family and friends and were invaluable in helping to receive and lay out with due solemnity the innumerable floral tributes that poured in. Of course, I made sure that the men were strategically placed and blended in – the last thing we wanted was for them to look oppressive, like a bunch of bouncers. And to their credit they blended in with considerable diplomacy and aplomb. In the pub, and then before, during and after the service, they kept the hordes of press, autograph collectors and souvenir hunters at a respectful distance with nothing more dramatic than a wagging of fingers, a meaningful look and a shake of the head that said, "That's a no-no!" The respect with which the onlookers treated the proceedings was impressive – particularly the national press boys, who aren't renowned for their sensitivity. Mind you, they weren't behaving themselves out of any sense of decency! Just to make sure they behaved, we had quietly pointed out that if they took any liberties on that day they'd pay dearly for them in future. They knew we were the boys in charge of most major rock 'n' roll happenings they'd want to cover and took the warning to heart – as well they might – and were on their best behaviour.

That day a cornerstone of one of the world's greatest bands was lowered into the ground – and the lack of Bonzo's unbeatable beats undermined Page, Plant and Jones. Soon they announced that they felt they couldn't go on without him. It was the end of an era. Yet another rock legend had succumbed to the lethal cocktail of self-doubt, temptation and adulation that only the great stars ever sample. When you're very, very high there's a very long way to go down. John was history – and so was the band. History in the real sense of the word.

"BIG" JOE EGAN (IRELAND)

Irish Heavyweight Boxer

Introducing . . . "Big" Joe Egan

MIKE TYSON CALLED "Big" Joe Egan "the toughest white man on the planet". And he wasn't kidding. Joe was a phenomenal and ferocious boxer and by the age of twenty-four had recorded over eighty amateur wins and seven Irish titles, as well as a Golden Gloves championship title. Originally from Dublin, Joe fought a total of eleven times wearing the green vest of Ireland, going the distance with Lennox Lewis and beating future WBA champion Bruce Seldon.

On his route to becoming professional, Joe joined Mike Tyson's training camp in the Catskill Mountains, USA, and became good friends with the champion. However, Joe's dreams of becoming a world-class professional boxer were suddenly shattered following a serious car accident on the night of his second professional fight. And then his personal life hit the headlines when his fiancée, Irish model Lisa Murphy, left Joe for *Riverdance* and *Lord of the Dance* star Michael Flatley. The downward spiral continued with a new pub business venture pitting Joe against protection racketeers armed with guns, axes and machetes. Joe was shot and later charged with attempted murder.

In May 2004, after an absence from the ring of twelve years, at thirty-eight years old Joe Egan made his boxing comeback. Joe is now also an actor and author. This chapter, taken from his autobiography *Big Joe Egan, The Toughest White Man on the Planet*, briefly chronicles a number of episodes in his life as it starts to spiral out of control and he gets involve in the pub business, racketeering and crime.

HARD TIMES
By Joe Egan
Ruth

Well, when I came over to this country [the UK] first with Paddy Finn, Paddy had a man working for him, Noel Delaney; he's since dead now, God rest him. Now I'd worked in Dublin Airport with Noel's brother, Eamon Delaney, without realizing they were brothers. I knew Noel when I came over as I was introduced to him. So when I eventually came over to live in Birmingham, me and Noel became close friends and it turned out that I knew his brother.

When I moved from the Dubliner and come over to the Lyndhurst, I still was only two years in the pub trade, and I still wasn't the most knowledgeable to run a big pub. But I had ambition and enthusiasm and I had confidence that I could do it. I also had the backing of my business partner, Thomas McGeough, so we'd got the money, we'd got the muscle and we'd got the enthusiasm. But Noely was very, very knowledgeable in the running of pubs because he'd been in the pub trade so many years. He knew the ins and outs of the trade. So Paddy, fair play to him, allowed Noely to come over and work with us in the Lyndhurst as well as the Dubliner. And Noely used to come from Acocks Green, work in the Dubliner and then come over to the Lyndhurst. And Noely and myself became great friends. He was the hardest-working man I've ever seen. I've never seen a man could work as hard as that man. Unbelievable. One day his son Sean took his car and Noely cycled from Acocks Green over to Erdington. It's a good cycle. In his late sixties, and he cycled over not to let me down, to come over and work in the pub. Just an unbelievable man.

And it was through Noely that I met his and Eamon's brother John. John and Sheila are Ruth's mum and dad, and Ruth is Noel's niece.

I hadn't met Ruth yet!

It was funny when we met John. Me and Noely were after going down to get change in the Post Office and we met John there. Even though they were brothers and he only lived round the corner from the pub, Noel had never spoken to me about John. Noel used to come over to the pub, very efficient, hard working, and just get on with his work. He was my friend, one of my closest friends, but he never spoke about his personal life – so next thing I'm introduced to his brother. I said, "Well, come up to the pub, use the pub."

So John came up with his wife Sheila and I became great friends with them, and it was through them that Ruth came up to the pub. She came up one afternoon.

Ruth was working in Erdington in the Halifax. The pub had a particularly bad reputation when we took it over, but we were cleaning it up. And Ruth had heard her mum and dad talking about myself and she was looking forward to meeting me. My relationship with Lisa was over at this stage. And to start with there was nothing like that between me and Ruth; we were just friends and our families were friends.

One day I just asked her out. We went for a meal and stuff. And suddenly I'm courting her! But, at that particular time, I had all the battles with the brewery and everything else and I wasn't too well. And, fair play to her, she helped with everything, because I took very, very sick as a result of everything that happened.

My youngest brother, Connolly, had come over to help us in the pub at different times, to give us his knowledge of the trade as well and to help me. And, my youngest brother is a very good-looking bog and I actually thought that Ruth fancied him. And we joke and I still tease her about that to this day.

Desperation

The pub, the battle, the court battle, the relationship battle – everything was just coming on top. I had very, very low self-esteem, everything was just getting too much. And then I thought I was going to lose my house in Ireland that was in Lisa's name, so I was trying to hold on to the house; and I was living in England because the brewery were trying to evict me. It was just getting too much. And then it was costing me a fortune in legal fees, with a solicitor in Ireland fighting the battle with Lisa, and a solicitor in England fighting the battle with the brewery. So I was paying out any money I was making and any money that I'd saved in legal fees.

There was a barman in the pub called John O'Sullivan. He was from Cork but he'd been married to a Dublin girl called Kelsh, whose brother Patrick I knew. John had broken up his relationship in Dublin and had come to Birmingham to work for me. One day, his sister came into the pub with her boyfriend who was a car dealer, a guy called Robin Weaver. He offered me an opportunity to do some business with him. Let him conduct his business in the pub and park his cars in the car park of me and my business partner's pub.

So I thought, "Well, it'd be an extra income if he spends his money in the pub and the people he's doing business with will be spending their money in the pub." I tried to encourage as much business into the pub as I possibly could.

Then he said he was doing hooky cars, and would I mind him parking hooky cars on the car park, and he would throw me some extra money. Well, at that particular time, I was at a very low ebb. I was also in a very bad financial state. I was working eighteen hours a day, nineteen to twenty hours a day some days. I was the first up in the morning, I was the last to go to bed at night, and I was the last to get paid. And I was paying all this money out in legal fees, which I deeply begrudged paying.

Now this opportunity had come up to get involved in something I'd never done before in my life. When my back was to the wall a number of times, I'd always made ends meet. But at this moment I was very bitter, I was very sick, I was very twisted and I was very confused. And I decided to do a quick crime so I could use the money to pay legal fees, to pay Lisa to leave the house. Because I thought what she was doing to me was a bigger crime, making me pay for a house that she hadn't paid for, so my money's been paying for the house twice.

So I've gone and got involved in stolen cars.

Greed

At the time I thought, "Well, it's easy money." I thought that a legal crime was being done to me, so I'll use criminal money to pay that off. My intentions were just to pay the £19,700 – the £15,000 to Lisa, £2,700 to her solicitor and the £2,000 to my solicitor. So all I wanted to do was to get that £19,700. Anyway, getting the money was pretty easy – to tell you the truth, the cars were flying in and flying out – I suddenly realized I was breaking my heart working in the pub for sixteen to seventeen hours a day and yet I've got this £19,700 in a matter of weeks. And then the greed kicked in.

I've never been greedy in my life, but, until it actually happens to you, you can't explain. It just takes control. I'd got this £19,700 that had come so easy to me. My fortune was somebody else's misfortune and I regret it to this day and I'll probably regret to my dying day what I actually did because I'd had a car stolen off me once, and it's something that you work hard for, for somebody else to take, or for somebody else to damage. It's not nice, so for me to suddenly be involved with people taking other people's belongings, it's something I've got to live with.

And it was greed. I don't drink alcohol, I don't take drugs, I like to have full control of what I do. So at that moment in time I had full control of what I was doing. But the greed was controlling me.

I couldn't stop because of greed. It's easy money.

And I regret ever doing it. I've paid my debt to society, I've done my time. It's not nice. It's one of the seven deadly sins, and for somebody that has got great willpower and great determination, great strength of character like me to give in so easy . . . That's it.

It's deadly. And it just takes over. And it's horrible.

Fear

Seven months before, the guy that had shot me and the old man had gone missing for months. People had scoured everywhere looking for him but he'd gone off the face of the planet. Now he walked up and handed himself in at a police station. Five people went to identify him for doing the shooting because he'd no mask. He walked free after thirty-six hours.

A female police sergeant phoned me from Sutton Coldfield Court. She said, "Joe, I've bad news for you. The courts won't let us hold Jake Welch for more than thirty-six hours. We're going to have to release him. He's back. Be careful."

I said, "Thank you for your advice, sergeant."

That very week, on the Sunday the pub was busy. My fourteen-year-old nephew, my sister's boy, had come over from America and I'd gone out for a meal with him. When I got back, one of my barmaids was panicking.

"Oh, Jesus Christ, we've a fellow on the phone, he's saying, 'I'm going to kill everybody, shoot everybody.'"

I said, "Look, it's all right. If I had a pound for everyone that was going to shoot me, I'd be a rich man. It's only talk."

The phone rings again. I pick up the phone. It's Jake Welch.

Now he's the one that's already shot me, so it's not a man that's making idle threats. But now I don't want to show any weakness.

He said, "I'm going to shoot you, I'm going to blow the bollocks out of you. I'm going to blast the brains out of your skull."

"Yeah, OK, OK, bring it on," I said. "Don't talk about it, just do it. If you want to do it, come on, bring it on."

Ruth has picked up the extension in the bar and she's listening to this. When we hang up, she's panicking.

I'm saying, "It's all right, Ruth, calm down, don't worry."

So I've now got my fourteen-year-old nephew staying with me, and Ruth and me frightened, and it's a fear like I'd never gone through before. I'd been afraid before, but now I was afraid for them, whereas before I had just been afraid for myself. It was a fear I couldn't handle, plus I was weakened, I was sick. I didn't know what to do.

The police had come to the pub because they'd been called by the barmaid. She made a statement to them. Then they asked me to make a formal statement. I said, "Five people have made statements against this guy before. He walked free after thirty-six hours. Five people went to identify him. He walked free. I'd state the fact that he's a grass. He's working hand in cuff with you, so I'm not going to make a statement against him."

That was on the Sunday evening.

On the Tuesday morning, in the early hours, bosh! Straight

through the doors. The full armed police. I was in bed. They'd come up the stairs, all boiler-suited up with their machine guns and everything else, they were screaming and they were shouting. It was frightening. My nephew was up. They were searching everywhere upstairs. They had a search warrant for car documents, but they were really looking for something else. My dogs were going mad on the roof. My nephew said, "Can I take the dogs down?"

I repeated what they said: "Nobody leaves until they leave."

My cleaning staff soon arrived to clean the pub and the police made them sit downstairs, as they were searching downstairs now. They closed the door on the office and came up to call me out. Now don't forget they've got us sitting. Everywhere they went and searched upstairs, we were in their presence, but downstairs they had made me sit with two CID officers in the lounge. By now my barmaids have also arrived.

Next of all, I could hear the police screaming and shouting at the back. They brought me out and they produced a gun.

They said, "What's that?"

"A handgun."

"What are these?"

"Bullets."

"What's the gun doing under your roof?"

"It's a set-up." They hadn't found it in my presence.

They know they've fucked up. "Look," I said, "that gun's found at the back. The delivery staff, everybody, now has access to that area."

So they give me bail. But now I've rubbed them up the wrong way. They're really determined to get me now. They had a fair idea there were hooky cars being done. It didn't warrant surveillance. But, because they've fucked up on the gun, it's now personal. And I'm warned by a retired senior police officer that they're out to get me.

They've put every sort of surveillance camera on top of the flats. They produced photographs of me in cars. They put me under surveillance for months.

Eventually, they capture a guy who was delivering two cars to Ireland. He was driving one, a BMW, and another fellow was driving the other, a Jeep. Instead of going straight to the boat at Holyhead, the BMW guy's took a diversion to go and see a barmaid who used to work with me up in Wales that I had to let go because she was a bit too promiscuous, which was causing trouble! She was seeing a couple of customers and causing problems with their marriages and everything else, so I had to let her go.

He was thinking that the guy in the Shogun Jeep was going to take two hours to get to the boat, and he could do it in an hour, so he could divert and see this girl and get to Holyhead in time to catch the ferry to Dublin.

So he's spotted speeding in this 850 BMW. The registration was B1 WOW because the car was a wow. He takes the chase; they put the stingers down. He goes into the ditch.

Instead of coming out and saying that it was his stolen car, he tells the whole operation. Now not only do they have photographs of me getting in and out of cars that were hooky, but they've also got a grass.

But of course I didn't know about this.

They've hit my business partner at his house and arrested him. They've got me, and they've arrested my brother Connolly, who had nothing to do with anything.

Then they offered us a deal.

You know, when you're a kid and you're in a fight and you get somebody in a headlock and the guy goes, "I'll give you the draw," you know they'll give you the draw because you've got the win.

So, when the police offered us a deal, I said to Tommy, "No, don't take any deal. It's like the draw when we were kids. I'm not going to take the draw when I've got the win." It was a stupid childish mentality.

He said, "Take the deal."

"I'm not taking any deal."

So Tommy, my best friend, said, "I'll go with you Joe, but I think we should take the deal." If I'd fought it and I hadn't won, and he'd taken the deal he'd have felt bad. So he went with me.

And lo and behold, they produced the grass in court. They've produced photographic evidence of me getting in and out of various cars. And it was too late to take the deal.

I'd had to sell my own car – a BMW 525 turbo diesel – to pay legal fees. I sold my Jeep to pay legal fees for the battles with Lisa and with the brewery. At the time when the police hit us, I had to use a borrowed Rover Metro to go up and down to the bank because I'd sold everything that I had to pay legal fees. That's how low I was. I'd sold everything. I'd sold my eighteenth birthday watch and I'd sold my twenty-first birthday ring.

I remember the only time I'd ever seen my dad cry, we were too young to understand. We came home one day and my mum was agitated and panicking. We were only kids, and I didn't realize what was wrong. It turned out that my granddad had died, my dad's dad. We'd only met him a couple of times. I didn't really know him that well. But he was still my granddad, he was still my daddy's dad. And me and my brother were a bit panicky ourselves because my mum was agitated, she was running around like a headless chicken. When my dad had come in from work she'd said he'd better phone home. So me and my brother were sitting on the stairs and we heard my dad making the phone call. In every boy's eyes, his dad is the toughest man in the world. I remember watching my dad cry at the bottom of the stairs on the phone. I'd never felt fear like it. I was terrified because now my dad was crying, I didn't know what was going on. And I found out that his daddy had died, God rest him.

When I was found guilty in court, I looked up into the balcony and I saw my dad crying. It was eerie, as the only time I'd seen him cry before was when his dad had died. So me getting sent to prison had the same effect on my dad as his dad dying. I felt sick, sick as a man could feel.

This was before any sentencing. I was remanded straightaway and sent downstairs. The security guys were around me in the dock, I suppose to stop the prisoners jumping the dock and stuff like that. But before I went down the stairs, down to the basement, I'd seen my dad and Ruth crying.

Warwick Crown Court. We were brought back and, a couple of days or a week later, we were sentenced. Judge Coates was quite lenient with the sentencing because of my previous good record. He gave me and Tom two-and-a-half years. I was gutted for my business partner, and because my brother was innocent. My brother had only come over to help me during my illness and now they'd got him. He got two years and he did a year in prison. He hadn't been involved in anything. All he'd done was come over and help me run my pub while I was sick.

Category B

When we went for the final day of the court battle, I said to my business partner, Thomas McGeough, "Tom, you know we're going in for the last day now. It's not looking great, but we've got to go in as if we're still going to win."

So Tom said, "No, I'm going to wear my tracksuit in, because, if I'm found guilty, I want to be able to go to prison in a tracksuit. At least I can be comfortable in my tracksuit."

"Tom, if you go in a tracksuit, it looks like you're throwing the towel in. Let's go in a nice suit, a shirt and tie, and show that we still feel that we're innocent men and that we can walk out in our nice suits. But don't take it for granted that we're going to prison."

Even though Tom had been experienced in court battles and had done prison time before, I talked him out of going into court in his tracksuit. So, on the final day, we're found guilty. We were remanded straightaway, and we were brought down.

I've gone down the stairs and Tom was saying, "What am I doing in a suit?" And he's turned around to me and he pointed at me. "You told me to come in a suit. What am I doing in a suit?" And he trips and he pulls the sole of his shoe off.

So I'm laughing to myself going down the stairs and he's walking along now and his shoe's flapping. So, when they brought us from the courtroom to the prison, he's walking along with this flapping shoe. Even though I was churning inside, it gave me a little giggle inside about his flapping shoe.

We were originally sent to Blakenhurst Prison, which was a twenty-three-hours-a-day lock-up. You had an hour a day out of your cell. It was classed as a Category B prison.

When you get there, they bring you to reception. They take off your suits and stuff and they put them into a box. You sign for what you're putting in. If you've a watch or anything on, sometimes they let you keep it, depending on the value. For insurance, they only allow you to keep things of a certain value. Anyway, I had a nice watch. They took it, saying it was an expensive watch. The senior officer informs you of the rules, exactly what's going on. They take all your clothes, and they give you a prison uniform, jeans and a prison shirt. They gave us prison sneakers. They call them prison sneakers, with just two stripes, because Adidas had the three stripes. They were just like plimsolls, like a flat plimsoll, and they hadn't any laces in them. That's what we had to wear. And they hadn't got a shirt to fit me, so I'm like a deformed man in this shirt. They wouldn't let us wear our own shirt, our own clothes, so I've got this shirt that's about three sizes too small, a pair of jeans that were skin tight and a pair of slip-on plimsolls with no laces, so all the other prisoners know you're new lads and they're looking at us.

Tom got a single cell. My brother and I got a cell together, which, to my surprise, was pretty clean. The prison was clean because it was reasonably new. I was surprised because you hear about all these stories about prison conditions. So it was much cleaner than I expected. But it still wasn't very nice. And, years before, I used to watch "Porridge", and you'd hear the gates of Slade Prison on the television slamming behind you. But, until you actually hear that cell door slamming and the key locking, you don't realize it's a nightmare. The first job we got was on the prison servery, so we could get out of our cell a little bit more than the average prisoner because we had to go down to do the servery for breakfast, lunch and evening meal. So we went down, we cleaned the servery and we'd meet other prisoners that were working on the servery as well. So it would give you a little bit more freedom – just to get out of your cell for that little bit extra, whereas, apart from the hour that they would have to walk the square outside, the other prisoners would be in their cell all day. They'd come down to get their meal on their tray and bring it back up to their cell.

I heard that the prisoners used to eat together in the same canteen but then there was a bit of friction, a bit of trouble, and the prison officers couldn't control all the prisoners in one canteen. So now the different house blocks would come down in turn, get their food on to their tray and straight back up to their cell.

I was on house block 6. So from house block 6 you had to go through all the five house blocks. So we'd leave the servery. The prison officer would open the gate out of the servery, then lock the gate. We'd go down to the next house block. They would open the gate, put us through, lock the gate. We did this nearly every day, so not only was I getting my cell door locked behind me, but I'd also hear all these other cell doors and all these gates locking. And it's not a nice sound, to know that you're behind a steel door. It's not a nice feeling to hear it locking and it's not a nice feeling to know that you're stuck in there. I wouldn't recommend it to anybody. It's very degrading what you've got to go through in prison. I'm not saying they deliberately made you feel like an animal, but you do.

Most of the time, except for the hour that you were out, you were locked up. In the morning, your cell would be opened and you'd have twenty minutes to maybe go and get yourself showered before you go down and get your breakfast. Then back into your cell, locked till mid morning, till you get your lunch.

My brother Connolly had nothing to do with the crime, genuinely had nothing to do with it. The boy had come over to help me in my pub as he'd trained as a barman in Ireland. He's a little bit fragile at the best of times because, when my family were evicted in 1986, Connolly was there at the time and he was young. My mum had a breakdown in the house – the madness that was going on from these bailiffs outside, savages – and he watched her cut her wrists. Years later, he's still never really recovered from that; it plays on his mind. He's a very good-looking boy and a lovely person. But there's a distance when you look into his eyes sometimes. He's very vulnerable, very fragile; emotionally he's never been right since that eviction.

It was very hard at the time, as he was starting to get his life really together. He'd met a beautiful girl from Canada, Roisin, and she was now pregnant. So he was selling his house in Northern Ireland and he was relocating to Canada, and he'd come over to help me, say his goodbyes and to let me know that his life was going really well.

Anyway he got dragged into this for no reason. I'd rented a car for him from a friend of mine who worked for a car rental firm, and he gave me a really good discount. What I didn't realize was this guy had been doing mischief and pocketing the money from this particular rental company. Then they arrested him and charged him for ripping the company off. So, when they went through the files of cars that he'd been hiring to people without putting the money through the books, they found my name hiring one of the cars. Then they realized that this particular car had gone over to Northern Ireland.

Connolly was driving the car in Belfast with my older brother Emmet, my sister and my brother-in-law – a police officer from New York. The West Midlands Police had gone over to Northern Ireland and, with the RUC (Royal Ulster Constabulary), had stopped this car in an armed coup, like they were dealing with some sort of terrorists. All of them, including my brother-in-law the cop, were dragged out of the car and abused, guns put to them and everything else.

First of all, they held Connolly in Belfast and they put him on to the landing of Mad Dog Johnny Adair, who was the top Loyalist terrorist in Northern Ireland. Here's a young Dublin boy put on to the landing two doors away from one of the most dangerous terrorist prisoners. The boy had nothing to do with the crime. We'd proved in court that the rental car had nothing to do with this particular case, but the seeds of doubt had been planted in the jury's heads. The fact that he'd been stopped in the car in Northern Ireland, and the fact that he'd been stopped for speeding on his way to the docks in the car before then, were painted a real nasty picture.

Then they terrorized him by putting him on to the landing with Johnny Adair. Eventually, the British police brought him over to England. But he'd gone through an ordeal; he didn't want to leave his cell.

While we were in prison, the Crown Prosecution appealed against the sentencing, saying the sentencing was too light, which was rubbish. I've never been in trouble in my life before; I had an honourable discharge from the FCA in Ireland, which is the part-time army; I'd been with Delta Airlines, FAA registered; I'd been a licensee for a pub; and I had no criminal record. It wasn't a violent crime. But they tried to get us seven years. The Crown Prosecution won and ended up getting myself and Tom an extra eighteen months. They didn't go after my brother for extra time because they probably knew in their heart and souls that he was an innocent man.

I had respect amongst the prisoners due to the boxing. I was well known in the Midlands. Blakenhurst Prison is in the region, so a lot of people knew us from the pub, where I had gained respect amongst the black community as we'd stood up against the racist National Front Combat 18 scum. We also had respect amongst the honourable criminals, if there is such a thing as an honourable criminal.

The time passed quietly. It's a monitored regime, so it was very difficult – even going to the gym, you had to put your name down. Anything that you did was closely monitored. It was very, very strict – it was a prison – you're limited in what you can do. I didn't see much bullying going on. I'm sure there were bits of bullying going on, but because you're confined to your cell you don't see it.

It was monotonous and dragged out. We had a TV in our cell, which helped to pass the time. There were two newspapers per landing, so you'd get a certain amount of time to look at one. When the newspaper was given to your cell, you read every piece of it just to pass the time. You'd even read the advertisements. You had two visits a month for an hour and you weren't allowed to touch.

After about four or five months, we got shipped out to a Category D prison because our crime wasn't violent. So we ended up in Leyhill Prison, which was down in Gloucester. It was an open prison and it was nice to be able to walk around and not have a cell locked behind you. It was strange because we weren't in a cell, it was more like a room. We were even given a room key. There were rugby pitches, football pitches, tennis courts, and – as far as a prison goes – it had nice facilities, nice conditions.

But you'd earned your right to get to there: you'd conducted yourself properly in the other prisons and got your Category D, which meant that you were a low risk. It was nice to be able to be in that environment rather than being locked up twenty-three hours a day, and I appreciated that Connolly's room was next door to mine.

Air Force One

However, in Leyhill I saw a lot of bullying.

There was the rugby team in prison. Gloucester is close to Wales, where rugby is a big game, so there were a lot of Welsh prisoners in Leyhill. The Leyhill rugby team were in a league; of course, they couldn't play away games, but teams from the league would come to play them at the prison. Every couple of weeks, there was a rugby game. And it was good to go up and watch because it passed a few hours, but there was a lot of attitude amongst the Leyhill rugby squad. There was a lot of testosterone. They walked around with that "kick sand in your face" attitude. I didn't carry the same respect in Leyhill that I had in Blakenhurst because I wasn't known in the area, which is way out of the Midlands.

I was small compared to some of the rugby players. Some of them were massive men. And there was one particular rugby guy they all called "Killer" because he'd killed a man on the rugby pitch when he punched him during a row between players. He was a very, very aggressive rugby player. Obviously passionate about the game, but aggressive and that's what he was in prison for.

There was a lot of attitude within the prison but at least we were out from 7.45 in the morning to 8.45 at night. You were able to walk the grounds and had to go to your prison jobs. There was what's called a tally four times a day: at 7.45 a.m., 11.45 a.m., 4.45 p.m. and 9 p.m. you had to be in your room, they'd come round and check. Some of the rooms had televisions, but not all of them. Connolly and I were over on one side of the building. After 9 p.m., you couldn't go to the other side of the building. There were two TV lounges our side of the building and two TV lounges the other side of the building. In the day, each of the TV lounges had a designated TV channel but after 9 p.m., though, there was sometimes a bit of fraction between people who wanted to watch different programmes on the only two televisions they could watch.

I didn't go in the TV lounge much anyway because the documentaries and the soaps don't appeal to me. I'm a film man. I spent most of my time writing letters and stuff. On this particular night my brother asked me if I wanted to come down and watch this film, *Air Force One*. Gary Oldman is in the film and so is the one from *Raiders of the Lost Ark* [Harrison Ford]. So I said, "I've seen the film, Connolly, loads of times."

Anyway Connolly for some reason insisted on me coming down to watch the film. I thought to myself, "Well, he's insisting that I go down, so I'll go down." As I was on my way down to watch the film, there were a lot of lads who wanted to watch the film standing outside this TV room. They were small, insignificant guys, including one particular guy we'd nicknamed Joe 90 because that's who he looked like, but we didn't call that to his face because we didn't want to bully him.

So I walked past them and there were eight or nine of the rugby team in this particular TV room. Now, most of the time they were upstairs in the other TV room because Killer, one of the rugby guys, was on the landing upstairs and a lot of the rugby guys used to congregate around him. He seemed to have respect among the rugby players because of his rugby aggression and his passion for the game. When I walked into this particular TV room, Killer was sitting there with seven or eight other rugby players, which was strange.

So, as I walked in, I said "How's it going, Killer? Are you watching the film?"

He said, "No, the snooker's on." It was the night that Peter Ebdon was playing Stephen Hendry in the final.

I said, "Oh, there's a good movie on." And Killer looked at me and he said, "I've just told you the snooker's on."

I thought to myself, "Say nothing." I'd earned being in Category D. I'm not saying I was enjoying my sentence, but I was enjoying this particular prison a lot more than the lock-up. So I thought, "Over a TV film? No. I'll walk out." So I turned and I said, "No problem, lads."

As I'm walking out, there's the group of insignificant guys that I've come past. As I'm walking out, I could see in their faces that they couldn't understand why the big man was walking out. Connolly's obviously told these young lads that his big brother Joe was going to get the film put on for them. And he's now wondering why his brother, who in his eyes is a tough guy, is walking out. It's not like me.

So Connolly said, "What are you doing, Joe?"

"Ah, they're watching the snooker, Connolly, leave them to it."

"No, we all want to watch the film, there's a load of us want to watch the film."

"Sorry, lads, let them watch their snooker."

"Joe, the snooker's on upstairs as well. Half of them are cheering Ebdon and half of them are cheering Hendry. They've got both rooms."

"'What! They're watching the snooker upstairs as well?"

"Yeah. They've took both rooms. They've put us all out."

"Ah, I'm not having that."

So I turned and I walked back in. I walked to the television and I switched the television over. I turned and I looked at Killer. "The film's on. You got a problem with that? If you haven't got a problem, just get out. If you've got a problem, stand your ground."

And he looked and I could see the blood drain out of his face. Because I thought to myself, "If he says anything, I'll just cave his face in where he sits." Even if he'd attempted to stand up, I would have shafted him.

Whether I would have took the rest of them, I don't know, but I knew I was going to cave him in. Now this is a man that has killed a man on the rugby pitch. But I don't like bullying. He bullied me so that I had to walk out; I'd swallowed my pride and I walked out. But now I knew that he'd bullied a group of insignificant guys and my younger brother.

I'm standing over him. And I thought to myself, "If he makes even an attempt . . . " I've been in a lot of situations where I've had to look men in the eyes, and he didn't want to look; he didn't want the eye contact. He hadn't got the heart for the fight. So I'm looking down at Killer, I'm standing over him. And he's looking up at me, and then he eventually looks down. And I could see the rest of the rugby team sitting behind him and they're all waiting for him to make his move. When he looks down, I knew then he was a beaten man. I knew then the fight had gone out of him. So I stepped back. "Are you going?" I said. "Get out."

He stands up, puts his head in his chest and he walks out. I looked at the rest of them. "The rest of you out, out now." And the rest of them stood up, head on chest, and walked out single file, like a herd of sheep. Next of all, Joe 90, Connolly and all these insignificant guys filled the room and you could see them all buzzing because the bullies had been put out. They walk in and they sit down. *Air Force One* goes on. So I sit down for a couple of minutes and then I just leave them to watch the film.

After that, no problem, no problem whatsoever!

Gym Bullies

Normally, when you went to the gym, you had all these weight-lifters and power-lifters. They're the ones with first access to the weights.

I've gone up to the gym and me and my brother were training in the gym. And the weight-lifters and the rugby team seemed to have full control of the weights, the machines and everything else. So you had to sort of wait your turn for these guys to finish.

So, anyway, me and Connolly were up there and there were two of the power-lifter guys – they weren't in the rugby team, but they were the big muscle-barons. I picked up the weights that I could use, but there wasn't much left as they had most of them. They'd sets of weights all around them on a particular bench. An octopus couldn't lift the weights that they were lifting. You've only got one set of arms, so you can only use two weights at a time, but they had six sets of weights all around them. There were twelve prisoners that couldn't use anything while these muscle-barons had them. Connolly couldn't lift the weights I had picked up, as they were a bit too heavy for him. He looked across and he said, "Them ones there, Joe, I can lift."

I said, "Well, them lads aren't using them. Ask them if we can use the weights."

So Connolly walked over and he said, "Excuse me, can we use these particular weights?"

They said, "We're using them."

So he walked back.

I said, "What's wrong?"

"They said they're using them."

"They're not using the weights; they're nowhere near using the weights. They're using the other weights." They might have eventually used them, but they were not using them now. So I said, "They're not using them. Go and ask them again, can you use the weights."

So Connolly walked over. I was standing near watching. He said, "Lads, you're not using the weights, can I use them?"

"I've just told you, haven't I? We're using the weights."

So I stepped in. They're bigger than me – they're full of their muscles and their steroids. I said, "You've just told him, have you? I'll tell *you*. See you, I will rip your arms clean out of your body. I will smash you to bits with your own arms. He's using them weights, OK? You got a problem with that?"

And his balls dropped. The fact that I'd got the courage to stand up to him, his balls dropped, he didn't want to know. And he says, "No, no, no problem. I don't want any trouble."

So I said, "Connolly, take whatever weights that you want." I looked around. I said, "The rest of you lads that are waiting, you take whatever weights you want as well."

And they came in.

I said, "You pair, go over there. Stand over there and do your weights over there. These lads are all going to use this position here now."

And all the lads that were standing there waiting like sheep to use these particular weights then walked over and they used the weights. They were bullying. I didn't want any confrontation with anybody but you can't stand idly by, especially with your brother.

I'm Not Going to Vomit in Any Man's Car!

While I was in prison, one of the prison officers, Mr Higgins, had a heart attack. I'd been in the St John Ambulance and I knew a bit about first aid, so I attended to him. He was an OSG (Operational Support Grade) officer – old guys doing a bit of part-time work helping in the prisons.

I massaged his chest, kept him calm till the other officers came along, and said an ambulance was on its way. The senior prison officer said, "Right, you'll get a commendation off the governor for aiding Mr Higgins."

When I got into the open prison, I got involved with the Windsor Project which was to help the community and also get the message across that all prisoners weren't bad; how we weren't paedophiles, we weren't rapists, and that some of us were ordinary people that just turned the wrong corner and we needed a second chance. I got a commendation for the Windsor Project.

I went out to speak to Job Centres. I went out to speak to potential bosses, to give prisoners a second chance. I did OK under the work scheme, and I got my parole on the first attempt.

I served two years. The court battle went on for eighteen months because I wasn't well so I genuinely couldn't go to court. I couldn't sit for a long time. I was very, very sick, and my weight was dropping. Even though I'm big, I was gaunt and I had yellow jaundice. I was very, very ill.

While I was in prison, the doctors told me that, because I'd had abscesses cut out of me, there was a possibility that the abscesses might come back.

This day I was in the showers washing myself and I felt a lump in my back passage where I'd had an abscess cut out before. I felt sick because I thought, "Oh, Jesus, they're back." When you get the abscess cut out of your back passage, they don't stitch the wound, they kind of pack it instead. And I didn't want this again. So I was panicking.

I contacted the senior officer who was on duty. He was the same senior officer who had seen how I'd helped Mr Higgins. Straightaway he checked my medical forms on the computer and saw that there was a possibility of abscesses. He took me to the local hospital that night. When the nurse touched the abscess, I spun around, screaming "Ahhhh!" with the pain. The officer heard the scream from the other room.

She said, "Yeah, it's an abscess." She could see it sticking out.

On our way back in the car to Leyhill Prison, I said to the prison officer, "I feel sick, you'll have to stop."

It was a genuine man who took me to the hospital. I'm not just talking about a prison officer; I'm talking about a man who took me to the hospital off his own back. He knew that I was genuinely ill. He went against whatever authority; he took me of his own accord.

So there I am, projectile vomiting outside the car. I got back into the car. He said, "Thank you for not vomiting in my car."

It wasn't a prison car, it was his own car!

I said, "I wouldn't do that to any man, especially not a man that's prepared to put his neck on the chopping block to help me."

Next day, I was taken back to the hospital and it turned out that it wasn't another abscess, it was piles! But it was a relief, yeah, a very big relief.

I'm Not a Gangster's Moll!

Ruth doesn't want to be seen as a Florence Nightingale, even though she did clean up my blood, sick and shit when I was ill. She says she doesn't want to see Lisa portrayed as a glamour model and her portrayed as a skivvy!

She has got a good heart and she's a girl that has stood by me.

Before prison, when I had to get rid of the Lyndhurst pub, I put the money that I'd saved and the money that I'd got from the Lyndhurst and everything else into raking over the Moseley Arms. Now the Moseley Arms was in a derelict condition when we took it over. We spent three months gutting the place and we got the pub to where it was beautiful. At that stage, over the period of three months putting money into it, it wasn't looking good in the court battle, and it was looking like I was going to prison.

So I said to Ruth, "I can't run this pub if I'm in prison. All my money is gone. All our money has gone into this pub."

At the time, Ruth was working with the Halifax estate agents. She's a professional woman, a career woman. Her sister, Lisa, is a senior bank manager and her other sister is a senior psychiatric matron. Ruth had been with the Halifax for four-and-a-half years and was working her way up to become the mortgage adviser. Anyway, she had prospects, a career. She'd worked part-time in the pub and had also worked part-time as a barmaid in her teenage years, so she knew a little bit about running a pub. And, when I asked her, she took her redundancy from the Halifax to come and run the Moseley Arms, and she became the licensee.

And, if she hadn't, everything I put into that pub would have been gone because, nine days after opening the Moseley Arms, I was sent to prison and Ruth was thrown in at the deep end.

Not only did she have to run a business when she'd only really been a barmaid, now she was having to run a pub with her other half going to prison. So she had a nervous breakdown as a result of everything that had happened to her. Her weight plummeted from 140 pounds to below 100 pounds.

I remember the day she came to visit me in prison, and Tommy, my business partner, was also in the visiting hall. Prison visits rules were you're not supposed to move from your table, so he'd no business doing this, but he walked all the way across the visits room. A couple of prison officers were screaming at him and he came over and he gave Ruth a hug.

He looked at me and he said, "What have you done to this girl?"

And I was feeling guilty enough; I didn't need him to work it into me. But he was that concerned. And he said to her, "Come on, get yourself together. You'll be all right."

She pulled her way out. She kept it together and she ran the Moseley Arms. For the two years I was in prison, she ran and built that pub. She's got a great strength of character about her and she's a very private person. She kept the pub going, with my friends giving her a supporting hand, and the business went from strength to strength.

The Moseley Arms pub was beside a police station in Digbeth. The police used to frequent the pub regularly. But they stopped frequenting the pub and said to Ruth, "We won't come into this pub now any more because you're a front for a gangster."

And Ruth told them, she said, "How many gangsters' molls do you know that clean toilets? How many gangsters' molls do you know that scrub floors, that clean the windows? I'm not a gangster's moll, I'm a hard-working woman. And Joe's no gangster. He was a hard-working man until you caused him all those problems."

It's true. If they'd stood by me the first time round I wouldn't have had them.

I got out of prison in 2003. My parole finished in November 2004. Ruth was running the pub. I have a man's pride and ego – you know, you want to earn your own money – but my licence has gone now because I've got the criminal record.

I'd left school very young: the only thing I'd ever done was box. The only time in my life I'd ever been totally content was when I was boxing. Now suddenly, when I'm outside of boxing, everything's not going right. But every door I knocked on to try and get something for work, there was nothing happening. So I decided to make a comeback in the boxing for the first time in twelve years.

Joe, You Cut that Fine!

I had now gone from being Joe the boxer to Joe the publican to Joe the convict, and now I was back to Joe the boxer again, and it was nice for people to talk about me because of the boxing once more.

So I was out of prison, and I was training. One day, when me and my training partner, Patrick, had finished training, we went for

something to eat in this place on Broad Street that does these magnificent chicken breasts. Patrick owns a pub in Digbeth called Cleary's
and there's a guy called Lee Marshall, who is the veteran World's
Strongest Man, who sometimes does the door for him. Lee's won
over forty strongman titles. So we're getting these breasts of chicken
and Lee, who was on the door of the Rocket Club, spots Patrick and
we started chatting away. I was congratulating Lee, who had just
won his seventh world veterans title.

Les Cole, the Rocket's manager, steps out. "Joe Egan!" And he
gave me a big hug because I had just got out of prison.

"Come in, come in!"

"Les, I've just finished training; I'm just having a bit of chicken."
He started to pull my arm.

I said, "Les, I'll come up another time." I said to Lee, "Lee, I
won't even attempt to wrestle with you, you'll pull my arm out of its
socket! I will come up again. Here's my number, Les."

So, the next day, Les rang me. "Joe, we're having a medal presentation for Lee for winning his seventh world power-lifting title. The
newspapers are going to be there. Will you come to the medal presentation and be a celebrity in the photograph."

I said, "I will by all means, no problem."

So I organized a few boxing friends to come up for the photograph. The Rocket is a lap-dancing club and girls were dancing, but
there was a free bar and the Irish lads just want to have a drink. I
was standing there talking to Les, and the press were there, taking
photographs. I was having an orange juice at the bar and I spotted
Michael Flatley in the crowd.

"Michael Flatley!"

Security all came running over. "Joe, Joe, it's not Michael Flatley.
It's only his lookalike."

I walked over and I swear to God he was the spit of Michael
Flatley.

And he also *is* Michael Flatley, because he's actually changed his
name by deed poll to Michael Flatley! He drives around with his
registration on his Mercedes, Flatley. His gold card, Visa card,
driving licence – it's all been changed to Michael Flatley.

On two occasions, he had been down to Flatley's changing rooms
at Flatley's concerts, and got through all the security! He had also

been ushered into venues as Flatley because he really is the double of him.

I hadn't been aware of this guy.

So now I was in the presence of Michael Flatley's double, his lookalike. But I was looking at him and still shaking my head – is it Michael Flatley?

So I went over to talk to him.

He said, "I'm Richard from Stowport. I've changed my name – I'm not the real Michael Flatley. I've been trying to get to meet you, but you've been in prison. Paddy Finn and Mike Higgins have been trying to get a meeting on with you."

I hear his Stowport accent so I know. But I'm still in shock because it's his double.

I say, "You want to do me a favour?"

"Anything."

"Right, I'm going to walk away now, but do you see that group of lads over there?"

"Yeah."

"Go over and sit beside them. They're my friends. I won't let anything happen to you. As soon as they realize what's going on, I'll go over and I'll stop them before they do anything."

"Promise?"

"I promise."

So I stood back. The Irish lads were all laughing and drinking because it was a free bar and they all wanted the gargle. There were Patrick and Paul, and Patrick's uncle Peter, and a couple of other lads.

"Flatley" goes over and, brazen, he sat beside Patrick and looked at him. Patrick went, "Aaagghh!" He was looking at him, and all of the other lads were all looking, too. I knew that not a word was being said because no lips were moving.

Anyway, the drink's gone down. So, next of all, I see Richard "Flatley", also not saying a word. And I knew the head-butt was coming.

Then I walked over and I put my hand on Patrick's chest. Richard's face would have been smashed. I said. "It's all right, he's not the real man!"

Richard said, "Joe, you cut that fine!"

KIMBERLY WOOD (USA)

Female US Police Officer

Introducing . . . Kimberly Wood

ORIGINALLY OF IRISH decent, Kimberly Wood is the only female featured in this book. Her inclusion is not because she is nasty, violent or a criminal or because she is a world-class martial artist or boxer, but because she does one of the toughest jobs in the US – she is a policewoman.

Wood was born in 1960 on the east side of St Paul, Minnesota. Her father Frank Wood was a military police officer in the army and served in Korea. He then went on to a career in the prison service and was one of the only people in the state at the time to go from being a standard correctional officer to the highest position of commissioner of corrections. Wood's father was a big influence in her life and career, and from a very early age she wanted to follow in her father's footsteps in some way and serve her country as he did, either as a cop or as a correctional officer. She ended up doing both.

In 1979 she joined the US Army Reserves and served six years as a reservist. She received a commendation and was honourably discharged after her contract ended. Wood then decided to follow her father and so she worked for the Sheriff's Department as a police dispatcher while studying for law enforcement qualifications. After completing her training and passing, in 1995 she was hired by her first police department. Wood has since worked for five police departments covering city, rural and suburban areas, and was the first female police officer in two of those departments. In 2003 she became Deputy Chief Police Officer at the City of Milaca Police Department. After eight years as a policewoman she then decided to enter the prison service as a corrections officer and from 2004 to 2009 worked at the St Cloud Prison with some of the worst prisoners in the system. Wood is currently Mayor of Bock, Minnesota, the town in which she now lives and works.

This is her own story of her time as a policewoman on the Leech Lake Indian Reservation, one of the toughest reservations in the US.

BEYOND THE BADGE; LIFE ON THE BEAT
By Kimberly Wood

I used to drive a patrol car in Cass Lake, which is on the Leech Lake Reservation near Bemidji. The Leech Lake Indian Reservation contains 864,158 acres, including parts of Beltrami, Cass, Hubbard and Itasca Counties, and is located in north-central Minnesota, USA. As of the 2000 census, the reservation had a population of 10,205, making it the largest Indian reservation in the state by number of residents and the second-largest (to the White Earth Indian Reservation) in terms of land area. The original, much smaller Leech Lake Indian Reservation was established in 1855 and then, under the Indian Reorganization Act of 1934, the present "Greater" Leech Lake Indian Reservation was formed by the merger with three other smaller neighbouring reservations. Cass Lake itself is a glacially formed lake of approximately 25 square miles and the town of Cass Lake sits near the southwestern side of the lake and is approximately 90 per cent Native American.

I love the Native American culture, and have learned much from Native Americans and their way of life, and indeed continue to do so. To be intimately involved with the Native American community is extremely rare for a white person (and even more so for a white female) yet I have had that privilege, and I was given that opportunity by being a police officer. The community has generally been really helpful and I have asked lots of questions along the way. People know that the police officers care and we do make a difference; that's one of the many reasons for me being a female Irish cop on the reservation, as we really can help people in difficult situations, be there for them when they are in crisis, protect them, get assistance or find the resources to help them.

Our job is like no other. We wear a bullet-proof vest every day to work and, although we don't talk about it, when we leave for work we know we just might not come home at the end of the day. We work days, nights, weekends and holidays. We go to court on our days off. We work long hours and frequently – if a call has come in late in the shift – long after our shift ends (so much for the dinner, school conference or anything else that was planned after work). We have administrative tasks that have to be completed and we have classes to take, and forty-eight post credits have to be done within three years for our annual licence renewal.

Many of us generally work a rotating shift, never having the same days off. Our schedule is normally twelve-hour shifts, working day-shifts half of the month and night-shifts the other half. Many of us have pagers and cell phones, and being paged or called at home on our day off is not uncommon. Our profession is about as far from a nine-to-five, Monday through Friday job as you could possible get. Needless to say, our time off is precious and because of all of this – and more – cops need the support, love and understanding of our friends and family; most of us get that most of the time; some, well, not much at all.

I work hand-in-hand with Leech Lake Tribal Police, based on 115 Sixth Street NW, Cass Lake, which currently has a patrol division consisting of fifteen patrol officers and four patrol sergeants, and Cass County Sheriff's Department based in Walker, Minnesota. We back each other up on calls and we frequently interact with each other, passing along valuable information – sometimes while sharing a cup of coffee – and I am grateful to have worked with some of the finest officers in the state. As police officers we work closely with other departments and people, too; fire department and ambulance personnel, doctors and nurses, security guards, social workers, judges, lawyers, city council members, the mayor, business owners and many others.

Admittedly, Leech Lake Reservation does have a high crime rate for assault and domestic disturbances, as well as having stabbings, shootings, vehicle pursuits, burglary and the rest, and at the time of writing this there are eighty-four inmates currently being held in the Cass County Sheriff's Office for crimes ranging from parole violation and speeding to first-degree murder. However, I should say that even though my community has a high crime rate, readers shouldn't jump to an immediate conclusion about the typical kind of citizen living on the reservation – most residents are just like me, trying to make a living and trying to enjoy a decent life. As police officers, what we don't like to see is newspapers and the media depicting the Native American community in a purely negative light. There are, of course, negative elements in any community but there is also so much good going on in this community in which I am so proud to serve. The public needs to hear about this, too, but sadly rarely ever does.

In most cases my fellow city officers and I work alone, but we do on occasion work in pairs when we have extra officers on duty and, of course, we back each other up whenever we are called out to a situation, of which there are many . . .

Late one night my partner and I responded to an alleged domestic situation. The lights were out at the home where the abuse was allegedly taking place and so we walked around the back to see if any lights were on there. From out of the darkness an intoxicated Native American man from a nearby home came running out of his back door and opened fire with a .22.

"Police, put down the gun," my partner and I yelled. The hairs on the back of my neck stood up and in that split second I thought what in the hell am I doing this job for? And then, as he hesitated slightly, I thought to myself that I was going to have to kill this man. The man then quickly raised the gun up in the air and I began commands to him, instructing him to put the weapon down on the picnic table while getting closer, aiming my gun at his centre mass. The man placed the gun on a picnic table next to him then we converged on him, handcuffed him and took him into custody. And then to our surprise his wife came out and was visibly very upset and completely unable to understand why we were taking her husband to jail!

On another occasion, with my partners and possessing warrants, I was searching a home for a suspect. We had not found him yet and

I went down to search the basement area of the home. The basement was very bare, with no furniture and, as I looked around, I saw an unlit furnace with a little cast iron door. The door was only about eleven inches by fourteen so I thought, "Oh, what the heck," and whipped open the little door to take a look. The first thing I saw was a section of human arm; the suspect was contorted inside the furnace. "I'm getting out, I'm getting out," he yelped after I opened the door. The jail workers got their share of laughs that day as the guy was literally completely covered from head to foot in soot. I believe one of the jailers has yet to get the stained soot off his shirt patch.

Our job is bitter-sweet. One minute you can be taking an assault report; the next minute you're going to a fight in progress, shots fired. You can go from something inconsequential to something intense in seconds. And that's how our shifts usually go. We have moments of joy, laughter, sadness, hope and despair as well as high intensity and danger almost every single day we work the streets. Sometimes we see people at their best but usually when we are called out we see people at their worst: angry, violent, depressed, lonely, drunk or high, and at times defenceless and often at their most vulnerable. Being a cop is a mixed bag filled with the good, the bad and the ugly. You see things that other people don't see on a daily basis and some things that others will never see in their lifetime. However, not everyone can go to work where 99 per cent of the time they love their job and I am grateful for that. I am grateful that we are all different because I know there are some things I just wouldn't want to do for a living, just as there are some people that could never imagine being a cop, and I love being a cop.

One evening we were working a busy shift when the hospital reported a call from a man who had large gaping wounds to his leg, apparently from a pit bull dog. A little later, the same dog also viciously attacked a woman who ended up receiving more than 300 stitches. We got the identity of the owner as a "Mr Jones" and went to his home to speak to him and to arrest him on warrants. As we drew up outside his residence we saw he was standing on the top of the front steps, with two dogs chained around the steps. As my partner reached out to place "Mr Jones" under arrest, Jones shouted "Get 'em, Oscar", and from around the corner came another big black pit bull baring its teeth and looking for flesh; our flesh. As he charged towards us, my partner and I both managed to get control of the dog with mace spray and then arrested the man. The dogs were later removed from the residence by specialist dog handlers.

On another occasion on routine patrol, I stopped a vehicle with no front or back licence plates or no temporary licence sticker. When I stopped the vehicle one of the passengers bailed out and ran inside a nearby grocery store. Inside the vehicle I found a fourteen-year-old driving and his dad, who was in the back seat. The vehicle smelled of marijuana. While I was running the information with Dispatch, I could see a lot of movement inside the vehicle and could see the man in the back bending down and also reaching in the front seat. The man's license was cancelled and he was on probation. I had the boy come back to my vehicle, where I asked him, "Is there a gun in the car?"

"No," he stated.

Then I asked, "Any other weapons in the car?"

"Yes," he stated. "An axe under the front seat, a pipe next to the front seat."

I searched the vehicle and found the axe and the other weapon and asked the dad why he had the axe in the vehicle. He said, "You can't trust anyone; a man's gotta be able to defend himself."

My partner then showed up to assist me and he quickly told me that he had previously revoked the plates on this vehicle. In the end, I arrested the dad for violating his probation.

On another occasion, my partner was transporting a man to detox. Just prior to searching him, the man pulled an axe out of the sleeve of his trench coat, commenting, "Well, I don't think they will let me have this at detox, so you better take it." It seems to me that the weapon of choice lately on the reservation must be an axe! Perhaps people are comparing axes: I have this kind of axe, what kind do you have? My axe is shiny, and I sharpen mine more often than you!

On still another occasion, before sipping my coffee at the start of the day shift, I received a call about an intoxicated man assaulting people on the street with a baseball bat. When I arrived at the scene I saw three female victims, one with an apparent broken arm. My partners and I looked around for the man, who had fled the scene, and located him running on the other side of the freeway, still with the baseball bat in his hand. When the suspect saw us he dropped the bat and continued to run. My partner got hold of him and we both brought him to the ground and handcuffed him.

As cops, we put our lives on the line each and every day.

It is not all pulse-racing stuff though and we do have some really funny times on the beat, too. I remember a lady called Suzie, a very large woman at about 350 plus pounds, who would regularly get drunk and lonely and then find some reason to call the cops. I was working with a rookie cop at the time and, knowing Suzie as I did, decided to let the rookie handle it. In he went, with me following close behind, to find Suzie naked with just a sheet wrapped around her and holding a litre bottle of cheap vodka that was almost empty. Holding up the sheet around her naked body, she looked at this young new rookie officer, dropped the sheet and said, "Bet you never seen a princess before."

The rookie's jaw dropped to the floor while I was trying not to laugh too much. She told the rookie how cute he was and begged him to stay. Suzie was just lonely and decided to call the boys in blue for a bit of company.

I am the first and only full-time licensed female police officer within my department and have also been the very first female police officer in another department too. When we, as female police officers, put on our uniform and gear-up to patrol our cities, town and local communities, we often face more than the challenges of just our daily patrol. We face obstacles that our male counterparts do not; discrimination and sexual harassment. You would like to think that we live in a progressive and open society yet still there are many female police officers in many areas in the US who have to take verbal and in some cases physical abuse each and every day. It could be from the person you are arresting who spits on you, or slaps, punches or kicks you, or fellow police officers making sexist remarks. Although we pride ourselves in not taking it personally and being professional, it happens and even some of the people on the reservation and in the community we serve can be extremely prejudiced or sexist towards me as a female police officer; some just will not accept me as a competent police officer because their generation never had female police officers.

Research consistently demonstrates that the negative attitude of male officers is the most significant problem reported by female officers and in multi-departmental studies it has been shown that as many as 68 per cent of the female officers report having experienced sexual harassment, discrimination, alienation or mistreatment. Departments under-utilize female officers by not promoting them, or putting them in what is historically known as a "women's job" such as working with juveniles and in communications. A poll in *Law and Order* magazine once showed that only 9 per cent of male officers accepted females openly. I have to say, however, that there are some departments that do treat women police officers fairly and many of the people I work with are great partners who respect my professionalism and recognize that I do my job just like them. I have had many partners who are also friends and have never judged me by my gender, only by my capabilities. One of the best partners I had was when I did my field training prior to me being released on my own. He was a typical "Andy Sipowicz" type from "NYPD Blue"; a cigar-chomping Vietnam veteran who had been a cop for many years. Initially, he made it very clear he was not happy having to work with a female, but once he could see that I could do my job we actually became good working friends, and later I was invited to his wedding. That's the way it should be for everyone, but unfortunately in many cases it's not and this not only applies to female police officers, but also minority officers.

I will always remember being thanked by a woman in her eighties for investigating and eventually charging two people responsible for the burglary of her house while she was sleeping. Seeing her tears when I was able to give back some of her stolen items that had sentimental value was very heart-warming. It's those kind of moments that make the job so rewarding.

Recently a Cass County sheriff's deputy received a call about a man with a gun. I assisted him, as did a tribal officer. Earlier in the day the suspect was involved in a domestic situation and had fled the scene. He ran into a residence with the gun and was holed up in an attic space. We cleared the scene, cordoned off the area and warned the neighbours to stay away from this residence as we were now dealing with an armed suspect. An officer from the state Natural Resources Department and two state troopers came to help us. We also called the Emergency Response Team, but thankfully, before they arrived, we were able to talk the man into coming down from the attic. The stand-off was over and nobody was hurt, but it could have turned into something very different. When we searched the house, we found the gun in a pile of laundry; it turned out to be a fake that looked just like a .40 calibre Beretta.

With limited resources and manpower, we are occasionally put into circumstances and situations that other officers from larger agencies would be unlikely to have to face. Whether it's a call to a street fight at 5 a.m., a felony burglary in progress, a vehicle pursuit, a bar fight, a domestic assault, stabbing, shooting or a "shots fired" call, ultimately I know I can count on the partners I have and, although we are sometimes from different departments or agencies and we don't all wear the same uniform, we have the same mindset. In doing our jobs and handling critical calls, everyone works together for the common good and a positive outcome. Now, does this mean everyone likes each other and has the same opinions? Well, of course not but whatever our differences, when it comes to protecting a fellow officer, everything is dropped and that officer is backed up and, for a while anyway, it doesn't matter about differences of opinions; the police officers I work with would always put themselves in harm's way to protect a fellow officer. We handle many calls alone that larger agencies would normally have two or three units respond to, so it is critical that we are able to rely on each other like we do. Our lives literally depend on each other; one of these officers could be the one who saves my life, or I could be called upon to save theirs. So I'm grateful to every one of my partners.

Minneapolis Police Officer Melissa Schmidt was shot and killed while on duty. On the day of her funeral I worked patrol and, along with other officers, attended a Take Back the Night gathering in Cass Lake. Take Back the Night's motto is "Shatter the silence, stop the violence" and the first known march in the United States was organized in San Francisco, California, on 4 November 1978, by Women Against Violence in Pornography and Media. They marched through the red-light district of San Francisco in protest of rape and pornography. While the march began as a way to protest the violence that women experienced while walking in public at night, the purpose of these marches was to speak out against this violence and raise community awareness as a preventive measure against future violence. The movement has since grown to encompass all forms of violence against all persons and in the reservation citizens get together and talk about community violence and to try to come up with new ideas to help prevent further crime.

Earlier that day I was on foot patrol in my assigned district, handing out fliers, knocking on doors and talking to the members of the community about a wide range of topics. The community has seen a lot of positive growth and change recently and, aside from taking our normal police calls, part of our job as community service officers is to keep track of what is going on in our area and do a lot of proactive policing. Visiting the kids in my community is one of my favourite things and on that morning a little girl came running up to me saying, "Kim, here," and placed a small green apple in my hand.

"This is for me?" I asked.

"Yes," she replied, with a proud smile beaming from her face. A little later another couple of girls who are cousins said to me that they both want to be police officers in the community, which is wonderful to hear.

As I walked around the community that day, I had forgotten I had put a black mourning band on my badge until a teenage girl I was speaking with asked, "What is that on your badge?" I told her about Melissa's death, that her funeral was taking place that day and that the band was a symbol of mourning an officer who had lost her life. Unfortunately, I didn't have the honour of meeting or knowing Melissa but like all officers in the state that day, I wore my band not only out respect for her, but also for the Minneapolis Police Department that lost one of their own. Watching the kids running around playing at the Take Back the Night event and wearing that small black mourning band gave rise to a wide range of feelings and emotions about all our other brother and sister officers who have made the ultimate sacrifice in protecting and serving their communities, and of course about their families and partners left behind to grieve. And my thoughts were then of my own sons, my parents, friends and family; it makes me want to hold them just a little longer, a little tighter, tell them I love them a little bit more.

Unlike larger departments we don't have any specialized units and aside from incidents involving possible homicide (where we still do all of the preliminary police work), we handle almost all our calls and investigations from the beginning to the end. Our most frequent crime on the reservation is assault, and we get some very brutal assaults, some of which result in death. We are exposed to various communicable diseases like hepatitis, AIDS, tuberculosis and more, and when we are taking someone into custody and they are spitting on us or trying to bite us, these are things we must think about. We are exposed to weapons such as knives, guns, baseball bats, axes, pipes, drugs and needles almost daily. We can get injured in the course of our job; from wrestling with a person we are arresting to climbing on a roof of a business chasing juveniles. Thankfully many people are great to deal with and really do appreciate the police. But others have a great distrust or dislike of police, which is influenced by family, friends or what they have perceived as a negative contact with the police in the past. Most people don't appreciate the police until they need assistance and I would call that one of the frustrations of the job. Also, everything we do and say is under microscopic scrutiny by the public, media and the press; it is never considered that a police officer often has less than a second to react in a life or death situation. My partner once arrested a guy who didn't realize we have cameras and audio in our cars. He proceeded to tell my partner how he was going to beat his own head against the window inside the car to make it look like he was injured by the police, and then sue them for millions. There is a prayer in Cass Lake that talks about not judging your brother until you've walked in his moccasins. I can honestly say I would love to see those people who make uninformed, uneducated judgments and criticisms of cops throw on a vest and handle some of the calls we do.

As cops we see everything and can cope with most things but I was very saddened by the murder of forty-eight-year-old Darrell "Louie" Bisson, a local and much-liked blind man who was beaten to death on Second Street, just two blocks from the police department, while walking with his dog in downtown Cass Lake. Two sixteen-year-old youths were arrested on two counts each of second-degree murder. No reason is known for the attack. Two people witnessed the episode on Bisson and called 911, and when one of the witnesses confronted one of the attackers, who was using an axe handle to beat Bisson, the attacker came after him too. Around 150 family and friends attended Bisson's funeral at Christian and Missionary Alliance Church and after at his burial in Pine Grove Cemetery. After sundown about seventy-five family members, friends, Cass Lake residents and many area law enforcement officers gathered at the spot where Bisson was killed, each of us holding a candle, not only in honour of "Louie" Bisson but also as a message that violence in Cass Lake won't be tolerated.

The night of Louie's death, just prior to getting off my shift, I had the privilege of visiting him and his family. His mother had made a feast of various home-made dishes. The house was warm and filled with family who did not know that hours later their son, brother, brother-in-law, uncle or friend would be gone, forever. A life senselessly taken in a brutal, horrific attack.

During Louie's funeral, the pastor said we must try to ask ourselves "Why?" and suggested that we may in fact never really know the answer to that question. Gangs are present in Cass Lake and a lot of violence relates to drug use. Also lack of parental supervision, children fending for themselves for long periods of time, negative peer influences and alcohol are just a few more pieces of the puzzle.

However, there are more good kids than bad in Cass Lake; I see that first-hand. The majority of our youths are not involved in gangs and what needs to be focused on here is that all the youths in Cass Lake are part of the solution, not the problem. Many are involved in one of the Boys and Girls Clubs of America which "promote and enhance the development of boys and girls by instilling a sense of competence, usefulness, belonging and influence". The club in Cass Lake has a place where children can meet and play games, socialize, have fun, engage in a variety of healthy activities and contribute to the community. Some of the girls from the club took the time to make a lovely sign and leave it near the spot where Louie died. The sign read, "Darrell Louie Bisson 8-11-54 to 11-29-02; Rest in Peace; Stop Violence, Drugs and Alcohol."

We have made some great strides in building a stronger, safer community and organizations like Community Voices Against Violence, Network for Native Futures have helped make our community a better place to live. Our police department recently hired a school resource officer to be actively involved with the students and school personnel in further helping our youth in the community and as police officers we are part of the solution too; we patrol the community, we get out of the car and talk with people, we show our support at community events like Take Back the Night and we respond to a variety of calls as professionally as we can.

What are the things that make this job so gratifying? It's sometimes just the little things like the pastor who recently thanked me for arresting the person responsible for vandalizing his church with a baseball bat or the kids who wave me over just to say "hi". It's watching a kind woman approach one of my partners, apologizing to him after she accidentally set off a burglar alarm and thanking him for responding. Through rain, hail, sleet and snow, twenty-four hours a day, seven days a week, being a police officer is not just a job, it's an adventure.

MICKEY FRANCIS
(UK)

Convicted Football Hooligan

Introducing . . . Mickey Francis

O NCE ONE OF the toughest football hooligans in the UK and a
football hooligan since his youth, Mickey Francis was born in
1960 and raised in Moss Side in Manchester, England, and has
numerous convictions for violence-related offences. He has served
two prison terms and at one time he was banned from every soccer
ground in Britain.

His father was Jamaican and his mother was from Liverpool.
"My dad used to beat us badly," says Francis. "He was a big chap,
a wrestler, and we used to be scared shitless of him. Basically, he
used to beat the fuck out of us. As soon as he came into the room,
we would walk out. He was a bastard to his children and a bastard
to my mum. He used to beat her up, never treated her right and was
always fucking around behind her back."

Francis grew up on Acomb Street, about five minutes from
Manchester City's then football ground, Maine Road, and was on the
streets making money from the age of twelve. "My very first means of
collecting money was minding people's cars. People used to park up
on the street for the football match, and we would ask if they wanted
their car minded for 50p [$0.75]. If they said no, we would puncture
the fucking tyres." They had their own territory and kept to their
own streets, with other young gangs working other streets. "When
most kids were delivering papers, I was minding cars – and damaging
cars if their owners didn't pay the fee! In the end, everybody paid."

Growing up near the football ground, Francis naturally became a

Manchester City fan, and at just fifteen years old started to get involved in football violence. He loved it. His first real fight was at an away match at Wigan Football Club, about forty miles north of Manchester. "It was in the Doc Martens area," he says. "A rough area of the town, and I got knocked fucking out! This lad had banged me straight out. The police picked me up and asked me what I was doing in that area. Then they banged me in the stomach and told me to fuck off back to Manchester."

Francis started off as a little "soldier" in a football "firm" (gang) and worked his way up by showing he would always go in first and fight hard. At the age of eighteen he started to arrange fights himself and he, with about 100 others all searching for violence, would meet up at the Parkside pub near Man City football ground to arrange fights with the visiting team's supporters. Francis eventually became the head man of the "Guvnors" firm and whenever and wherever there was trouble, he would be at the front of it.

The Manchester police eventually caught up with him and set up an operation called Omega. They infiltrated the gang and watched them while they collected as much video evidence as they could. He says, "Looking back, I had an idea something was going on, but at the time I couldn't tell who the coppers were. For almost a year, I got away with murder. I could do almost anything, and I didn't get charged once, even though I was arrested twenty-eight times that year for football-related violence. They were letting me get away with it because they were building a case on me."

Eventually, when Francis was twenty-eight years old, and after dawn raids on his house, he was arrested. He was put on remand for six weeks and then let out on bail for about a year until the trial took place. He was then sentenced to prison and banned from attending any football match in the UK or Europe for ten years.

Taken from the book *Guvnors* by Mickey Francis and Peter Walsh, this is the story of his trial in 1989.

TRIAL
By Mickey Francis and Peter Walsh

"Michael, it's not looking too good. If we go through with the trial you are facing six to eight years. If you throw your hand in now, okay, the judge will take it that you are the main man. That's bad for you. But he knows that you can swing it for the other to plead guilty if you do. That will count in your favour. If you jack it in, you are looking at a lower sentence and so are the others, as they all have to get less than you. At the end of the day, I think I can get you three years if you plead guilty."

This inspiring little speech came from my barrister. He looked out of the window of the interview room in the new Liverpool Crown Court building. In the distance I could see a ferry crossing the Mersey towards Birkenhead, and the Irish Sea stretching out to the horizon.

He turned back to me. "Take a good look, Mike. The way things are, you won't be seeing it again for seven years."

Thank you very much, you bastard.

We were all pleading not guilty, but my chances of getting off were receding. The police had requested permission to give evidence while hidden behind screens. They didn't want to identify themselves, they said, because they were involved in dangerous undercover work. Naturally, I thought it was pretty sad that the justice system could let them get away with that sort of thing. They're police officers and they're getting paid to do a job. Testifying behind screens, hidden from the public gallery, gives the jury the impression that the defendants are a bunch of desperadoes.

One of these coppers was asked the question, "How would you describe Mr Francis?"

His exact words were, "He's a bully."

Not, he's tall, brown skin, stocky build, or whatever. Just "He's a bully." It's not exactly evidence, is it? They were allowed to get away with things like that and, of course, they were granted their protective screens.

There was the odd funny moment. When we were asked to plead, the court clerk went through each of us in turn.

"Michael Francis, how do you plead?"

"Not guilty."

Next.

"Not guilty"

And so on. It came to Martin Townsend. Martin has a speech impediment and we all knew he wouldn't be able to get the words out.

"Martin Townsend, how do you plead?"

Before he could open his mouth and stutter, we all shouted in unison, "NOT GUILTY!"

The whole court jumped about a foot in the air. We cracked up.

The trial began in February 1989 and was to drag on for months, a complicated mess of different defendants with different pleas. First up were two of our lads and one United fan, who admitted taking part in a fight outside Old Trafford. This was the brawl on Chester Road before Arthur Albiston's testimonial, three months after the original Guvnors arrests. Another City lad, Vincent George, a seventeen-year-old who kept a written diary of his fights entitled "War Games", went not guilty. During his trial the jury watched a three-minute black-and-white video of the fight which took place in the middle of the road as cars swerved out of the way:

A jury retired to consider a soccer hooligan case today – all twelve members also witnesses to the alleged crime.

For the six men and six women at Manchester Crown Court had seen several times over a video recording of an incident in Chester Road, Old Trafford – shot by police spy cameras – when rival supporters clashed. The confrontation left one young fan unconscious on the ground, after being kicked and stamped on.

The surveillance equipment picked up a group of City fans walking towards Old Trafford forty-five minutes after the match started. "The prosecution say their purpose was to fight – it wasn't to watch the match otherwise they wouldn't have been there at that time of day," said Mr Wright.

The group was seen by a "scouting party" of United fans and various youths were spotted picking up missiles and arming themselves with sticks, he told the jury. Then the groups clashed. Missiles were thrown, there was a large scale disturbance and one youth was left unconscious. Eventually the City fans turned and began walking away chanting and shouting.

Mr Wright said George, "had not kicked or fought with anyone but he was a member of a gang flat bent on trouble".

For Mr George, Mr John Bonney said his client accepted he

was guilty on the lesser charge of fear or provocation of violence, which carried a much lesser sentence. Mr Bonney invited the jury to consider what they had seen on the three-minute clip of video, which had shown his client had not thrown anything, kicked or stamped on anyone.

"Had he intended serious violence, he had ample opportunity to carry it out, as others did. But he didn't."

Mr Wright said that in an interview with the police Mr George had refused to identify any members of the City supporters gang "the Young Guvnors", said to be involved.

"If I did that I would probably get my head kicked in," George had told the police. (*Manchester Evening News*)

George's defence failed and he got three months for violent disorder. Rodney Rhoden, who was sixteen at the time and who jumped on a United fan's head as he lay on the floor, pleaded guilty and was sent to a young offenders' institution for six months. The video was later seen by millions when it was shown on national TV news.

Things went from bad to worse. On 15 April, ninety-four Liverpool fans died in a crush in the Leppings Lane enclosure at Hillsborough in Sheffield. The whole world was shocked and there we were about to go on trial a week later for football violence. We were fucked. By now, I was also much better acquainted with the evidence against me. It was pretty damning. At West Brom, I was caught clearly on camera having a punch-up with a couple of guys in their end. You could see me against a barrier getting caught briefly and them whacking me. Then we're on the pitch all going, "City, City" like a lithe mad army, about twenty of us, and the police take us into our own end.

Another example was a home night match against Middlesbrough. I had been getting some chips and someone smacked me on the jaw. These Middlesbrough fans had parked their van up and jumped out and we had a little kick-off. I kung-fu'd one of them in the face on the forecourt outside the ticket office. As the rest of them rushed me, I slipped and got a bit of a kicking. I read the coppers' version of this in their statements and it was absolutely spot on; they must have been right there. Although none of them had actually got to know me personally, they had clearly come pretty close.

I was concerned, though, that if I went guilty, the next person down would then be named as the main man. That meant our Chris would have been labelled the Guvnor or, if he pleaded guilty, it could have been Dave Foulkes, or Martin Townsend, or Adrian Gunning. Then they would have been hit the hardest. If you looked at the charges, in that particular season I only went to twelve games. I only picked the games I wanted to go to. But they were more or less making out that every time it kicked off, it was down to me. The Guvnors were 100–150 strong but they picked a few of us, who they thought were the main players, and a few younger lads. I didn't even go to every game but they depicted me as being a figurehead: older than everyone else, a long criminal record, a reputation, a bit of a hothead. They said, "It's got to be down to him, so make him the leader."

That was when I got the little lecture off my barrister, who was actually very good, spelling out exactly what I was facing. Seven or eight years sounded an awful long time to risk for a not guilty plea, especially as I was guilty as hell. I knew there would be little point in carrying on once the jury had seen me brawling on video. My main question became, not whether or not I was going to be convicted, but what sentence I faced. I knew I was looking at a long term because football violence was such an issue in the media and in Parliament. Everyone was saying, "Mickey, it's looking like you're the main man, you're getting slammed with it."

Fuck it. I changed my plea to guilty and so did most of the others.

On 24 April, twenty-six of us appeared before Liverpool Crown Court. Twenty-one pleaded guilty but five went not guilty on the conspiracy to riot and cause violent disorder: Adrian Gunning, aged eighteen, Dave Foulkes, twenty-five, Andrew Bennion, twenty-one, David Goodall, twenty-three, and Ian Valentine, twenty-six.

The prosecutor, David Sumner, opened the case. He said the Guvnors and Young Guvnors had about thirty key members. He went on, "There existed a hard core of people associated with this club whose sole purpose was violence for violence's sake – recreational violence. If they were meeting another particularly notorious group like Leeds it would attract them to a near organizational frenzy. They would put other member under maximum pressure to attend the games and swell their numbers."

Some of the gang never even went to the match at home games, he said.

"They adjourned to a public house and assembled again shortly after the whistle. Their purpose was to attack, intimidate and terrorise."

He said an undercover police operation against us was launched in August 1987, using officers for a specially trained unit code-named Omega.

Then one of the covert officers, referred to by the pseudonym Mr Henry in court, gave evidence from behind the screen. He claimed he was running with us for seven months going to away matches and sometimes acting as a van driver after being accepted. He said that as part of Operation Omega, he and three other detectives took on new identities, with disguises and fictional names and addresses. After each match they would return to a "safe house" to write their reports. They also used codenames for their targets: Gunning was Alpha, Foulkes was Nobby, Valentine was Heron and Goodall was Duck.

As well as trotting out the line about the Young Guvnors acting as spotter at railway stations and reporting back to us, he also said some of them, described as "baby-faced" and aged between fourteen and twenty, would position themselves next to police officers to listen in to radio messages, allowing them to find out the movement of opposing fans and so work out the best place for an attack. He said they would also watch any spectator who reacted to an opposition goal, marking him out for treatment.

The newspapers were taking a big interest. This was the *Daily Mirror*:

VIOLENT WORLD OF THE SOCCER GUVNORS
A gang of soccer thugs plotted vicious fights with rival supporters like a company ran its business, a court heard yesterday.

The gang, attached to Second Division Manchester City, had two branches, the Guvnors and the Young Guvnors, Liverpool Crown Court was told.

It was alleged that they;

Marshalled like an army, using scouts to watch the movements of rival fans;

Remained anonymous by hiding their faces from monitor cameras at grounds;

Grouped ready for attacks in pubs without seeing a second of any soccer match.

The gang was finally smashed by undercover detectives who penetrated the secret world.

And so on. Tempers occasionally boiled over. The *Manchester Evening News* was snatching pictures of everyone going in or out of the court and Adrian Gunning, who was a top lad in the Young Guvnors, lost his rag. He told the photographer to hand over his film, tried to smash his camera and apparently threatened to slit his throat. The photographer reported it to the judge, although he didn't name Adrian. The judge said he was "outraged" and said anyone else who threatened the press, who were there to report the case for the public, would be remanded until it was over. He gave a little speech, saying, "In any democracy the Press are the lamps which show justice is living. They are welcome in this court. If anyone approaches the Press they will have the full rigours of the law brought down by me. If I have a hint of it happening again, substantive periods of imprisonment will be imposed."

So Adrian was told to keep his fucking mouth shut because no one wanted to go back inside. According to a report of the trial in the *Sun*, the Young Guvnors lingered unobtrusively at railway stations to identify rival supporters to be battered in an operation of military style efficiency. The teenage "scouts" pretended to read timetables or newspapers and did not contact each other as they kept watch. Their reconnaissance was crucial to the Guvnors' campaign of violence because fans from other cities often did not wear team colours and had to be picked out by their accents.

For good measure, the prosecutor also said we had threatened the former United star Paddy Crerand at his pub in Altrincham. The boozer had been wrecked by a mob of City boys one night.

It was put over as though we were a huge, highly-organized army with everyone doing exactly as they were directed. All the stuff they raked up about us having generals and lieutenants and intelligence units was a load of bollocks. You just go to the match with your boys and if it kicks, it kicks. Rarely is anyone badly hurt.

The jury watched a film made by a police cameraman of two Leeds fans being attacked outside Maine Road. After a bit more of this treatment, four of the remaining five saw the writing on the wall and changed their pleas to guilty. Ian Valentine stayed not guilty and had all the charges dropped. Maybe we should have all done that – who knows? Many of the other hooligan cases around that time fell apart. Maybe ours would have too, but a lot of us, including myself, were frightened off by looking at seven or eight years in prison. Plus I was bang to rights on camera, there was no escaping that. The four new guilty pleas were adjourned to join the rest of us for sentence until 5 June, pending social inquiry reports.

The day of reckoning finally arrives. David Summer reprises the case. He lays it on with a trowel. He even says that one of the undercover detectives was so stressed out by the fear that he might be caught that he had a breakdown during the operation. He also reads some choice extracts from Vincent George's "War Games" diary. We all sit there in a row and I'm thinking, who the fuck is this kid Vincent George? I had never met him in my life but his little book of cuttings was helping the police to put us away.

Then it's Judge Clark's turn. I'm first up for sentencing. He goes into one about how I have tarnished the good name of English sport and how people like myself, who enjoy Saturday afternoon recreational violence, have to be stopped. He says he has no alternative but to impose custodial sentence.

And then he says, "I sentence you to twenty-one months in prison. You are banned from attending a match at any British football ground for a period of ten years."

Twenty-one months! What a result. After all that. I thought, I'm out in twelve, maximum. My family in court were upset but I was relieved. It had been a traumatic period and now at least I knew what I was getting. I could go to jail and get on with it.

The dock officer takes me down. He says, "We had a bet downstairs that you were getting six or seven years."

They put me in the cage but by now I don't care. The screws are amazed at the sentence. One says, "I'm not lying, mate, you got a right result there."

They start to bring the rest of the lads down, one by one. Chris is next.

"Eighteen months," he says.

Then the others.

"Fifteen months."

"A year."

"Six months."

Twelve of us were done that day. Seven went to jail, one went to a young offenders' institution and four of the younger lads, including Rodney, Adrian Gunning and Jamie Roberts, got community service.

The cops were praised by the judge and afterwards went round mouthing off all over the media about how marvellous they were. Nineteen people pleading guilty to affray and riot and violent disorder was a success for them. They were the heroes because they had secured convictions while a lot of similar cases were crashing. It made them look great. The main officer who ran the unit, Malcolm George, is now the national police expert on football hooliganism. Shortly afterwards, it was announced that the team that formed the nucleus of the investigations would be going to the World Cup in Italy in 1990 to keep watch on hooligans.

But the way the prison service worked then, you only served half of your sentence. With the time I had served on remand, I would be out on parole in six months. In fact I was out five months later on weekend home leave. If you think of the work that was involved in that case, six months' intelligence, lots of police expenditure, dawn raids on forty houses, sixteen months waiting to be dealt with, it must have cost hundreds of thousands of pounds. And I got twenty-one months. I often wonder if the Old Bill really were as happy with that as they made out.

After the court case, we were taken straight to Walton Prison in Liverpool. The screws were winding us up on the way, giving it loads on the coach, "They're all Scousers here, mate, they don't like Mancs. You'd better watch yourselves in the showers."

Actually the inmates were brilliant with us. We got to reception and could hear them saying, "Are you the Guvnors, are you the Guvnors? The Guvnors are here." They looked after us well. They knew all about us because the case had been in the national papers and on TV and radio. They gave us all new gear. In those days it was all uniforms, you couldn't wear your own clothes. We got new T-shirts, two pairs of underpants each, a pair of jeans, a pair of black shoes, socks. If they thought you were nothing, you got the shittiest pair of jeans that were too tight and too small for you, you got shoes with no laces in that didn't fit, you got socks full of holes. We got well boxed off. The cons dished them out, trustees, all lads who were near the end of their sentence or just model prisoners. I learned that in jail you are all in the same boat and a lot of the Manc versus Scouser stuff goes out of the window. Everyone helps each other out.

We were sent to our cells. Chris was put on a different wing and so I was on my own. I was led to my cell, opened the door and the screw said, "Welcome to your new home."

He pushed me in and shut the door. There was nothing in the room but porno pictures and a scruffy bed. Here we go. Stuck in this hole. The first thing I intended doing was cleaning the place up.

I was sharing with someone else. There were footsteps outside and I heard one Scouser say to another, "Here y'are mate, there's a fucking nigger in your cell."

I looked up and saw someone peering through the window, this kid with long hair. I thought, I've got a right cunt here. But he came in the cell and he turned out to be all right. We got on well.

The next day, we had a chance to read the headlines:

GUVNORS BANNED FOR 75 YEARS (*Daily Mirror*)
JAILED THUGS GIVEN TEN-YEAR BAN FROM SOCCER! (*Sun*)
Governors jailed as police infiltrate football gang (*Daily Telegraph*)
Guvnors' boss jailed (*Manchester Evening News*)

There were nice mug shots of me looking a right hood. Later that day, Pat Berry got fifteen months, on top of a twenty-one-month stretch he was already serving, for "leading a group of up to thirty hooligans which roamed the city centre hunting Aston Villa supporters after a match at Maine Road". Dave Goodall received a suspended sentence and a £1,000 fine. Others got community service and everyone was banned from football for various periods. Chapman, who was twenty-seven, got a £500 fine. He had confessed in his witness statement. All the lads done were from Greater Manchester, which shows how tight our firm was. No outsiders.

Many got community service because the judge said hooliganism was a community offence and so they should pay the public back. Of the whole sentencing, they gave out about twenty years, between twenty of us. I know a lad from Man United who was on a ferry when it kicked off with West Ham and he got seven years for robbing jewellery off the boat, because it was football related. He wasn't even a hooligan, he'd just gone for a snatch. That puts it into perspective. One way I did suffer though was when the *Manchester Evening News* revealed that I had worked as a stripper at ladies' parties, under the name Mickey Hot Rocks. I got ribbed for that something terrible.

It turned out there were a lot of Mancs in Walton, some of whom I knew, like Steve Bryan, who I later went into business with. I had no trouble in there at all, partly because we had a little clique and partly because of me being a big lad and the way I carry myself. If you are weak and you look weak you can get murdered. There weren't that many smackheads in jail either; they cause a lot of mither inside, always pestering people. I suppose the good news was that the week after we were sent down, City were promoted, finishing second in Division Two. Another big day I missed out on.

Jail is not as hard as it could be if you can get the things you want. If you have a strong character and put yourself about you can get pretty much anything in jail. You can get milk, decent meat, all the good stuff. You don't have to get the shit. You can bag yourself a decent job. It can be harder for your family and friends; they think you are suffering in jail when really you are getting plenty of sleep, using the gym twice a day, reading, having a break. What more do you want? If you like going to the gym and eating, it is the best way to put on weight and get yourself fit. I came out as fit as fuck, like Raging Bull. Of course, it has its downside, you can't see your family.

I was in Walton for about twelve weeks and then moved to Wymott, a semi-open prison in Leyland, Lancashire, where I shared with Chris until we both got our own cells, next door to each other. It was like going back to school. Each block is a "T" shape, with an A house, B house and C house. I was on B house. It had fourteen cells, you were allowed your own door-key and could have a stereo in your room and your own television which you could watch until

8 p.m. They would just lock the main wing door and we could have all the cells open, twenty-odd men running wild, smuggling in dope for draw parties, everyone saving their biscuits and cakes from visits until Friday night, taking your shirts off, covering the lights to make the room go blue, playing music dead loud and having a rave right there on the wing. It was wild.

One night we were in there and everyone was on the smoke. I got a bit dizzy after a few puffs because I don't smoke. They knew I'd do anything for a laugh, so one lad took a broomstick and said, "Bet you can't do this, Mickey. Get the brush, look at the light, walk round it, put it on the floor, jump over it three times and run down the corridor."

So I get this brush, go round and round, jump over it, lose my bearing totally, hit every fucking wall, smash my head open, pouring blood and collapse on the floor. I pretend I have done myself in proper. I'm lying there and they all rush round me going, "Fuckin' hell, he's done in."

"I think he's dead."

Just as they were about to call the screws I went "Yaaarg" and jumped up, and they ran for their lives.

Wymott was full of Mancs. There were a few queers about as well, although the gang rapes that you hear about in America are very rare over here. Some strange things do go on though and I think the officers are aware of it and just let it happen. On that wing, the screws knew that Chris and I were pretty game and if they looked like losing control they would sometimes say to us, "Will you sort it out for us?"

We would get extra privileges for keeping things sweet. If someone was playing up, being a cunt and ruining things for everyone else, they'd say: "If you weigh him in, Mike, don't weigh him in too badly. He needs a smacking."

They can't do it themselves because they'd get sacked, so what they try to do is manipulate you. You have to be careful you aren't used. You can't do everything they say, give someone a slap just because they don't like him. The thing is, they know what everyone is in for and it always comes out in the end. People who are in for molesting kids and that sort of stuff aren't put on rule 42, get weighed in and deserve it. Most prisons have their own little groups that run wings but they are hard places to control because once you get your feet too well in, you get moved out very quickly.

Our jailing was not the end of the firm's woes. Not long after our sentencing, eight lads pleaded guilty at Oldham Crown Court to their involvement in the Battle of Piccadilly in February 1988. They had arrested seventeen altogether, but the charges were dropped against half of them. The court was told that seventy to eighty City boys met in the early evening in the Lower Turks pub in Shudehill, where the landlord overheard them talking about attacking the Manchester United football special train that was due back from Arsenal. Then they went to Nicklebys, near Piccadilly station, avoiding London Road so the police wouldn't spot them. Eventually they moved on the station and sent in what the prosecutor called a "skirmish party" of between ten and twenty-five lads while the rest waited at the bottom of the approach, under the archway. When the scouts walked on to the platform there were only a few United boys around.

According to the report in the *Oldham Chronicle*:

A police officer ushered City fans back, an effort which met with very little resistance. Outside the station, PC Duffy was joined by two other police officers, who attempted to usher them down the approach. Mr Wright (prosecuting) said that civilian observers got the impression that the police officers were being lured away from the station. One of the officers, PC Martin, was hit on the nose after an order to send and turn was given to the mob. PC Duffy ran past and attempted, by using his truncheon, to create a safe distance between the group and the arrest. The officers were encircled by the mob, who initially attempted to free the prisoner and then attacked the police officers. Mr Wright said that PC Duffy tried to fend them off with a truncheon in one hand and his helmet in the other.

Duffy was then hit on the head with a hammer, fracturing his skull. He later spent eight months off work. A lad called David Clayton, from Oldham, was sent to a young offenders' institution for three years for using the hammer.

LUCIANO LEGGIO (ITALY)

Hitman and Enforcer

Introducing . . . Luciano Leggio

IN THIS CHAPTER written specially for this book, acclaimed writer Scott C. Lomax profiles the life of Luciano Leggio, one of the most ruthless hitmen and enforcers in modern Italian history.

Leggio was born in 1925 in the town of Corleone on the island of Sicily, Italy, and turned to crime in his teens. He saw the inside of his first prison cell when he was just eighteen years old; he was imprisoned for six months for stealing corn. Upon release, he murdered the man who had reported him to the police for the theft. In 1945, he was recruited by Mafia boss Michele Navarra as an enforcer and hitman.

Leggio became the leading figure of the Sicilian Mafia and eventually became the head of the Corleonesi, the Mafia faction that originated in the town of Corleone. Before he was finally imprisoned for life in 1974, Leggio was also infamous for avoiding convictions for a multitude of crimes, including homicide, because very few witnesses were brave enough to testify. At the time of his eventual arrest and capture Leggio was a multi-millionaire and was able to retain most of his fortune as Italian law did not yet allow authorities to confiscate criminals' illicit fortunes, although this has since changed. For a number of years he was believed to have retained significant influence as head of the Corleonesi from behind bars, but by the end of the 1970s, his lieutenant Salvatore Riina was in control of the Corleonesi clan.

On 16 November 1993 Leggio died in prison from a heart attack, aged sixty-eight.

THE MAN WITHOUT A FACE
By Scott C. Lomax

The small town of Corleone on the island of Sicily is one where the values of tradition and family honour have prevailed throughout the centuries. In most families the women are expected to stay in the home after 8 p.m. and great loyalty and respect is given to the elderly relatives, who are taken in by their young families.

Agriculture has always been the main contributor to the local economy, and today it employs 70 per cent of the workforce who grow corn, tomatoes and vines, and rural poverty is common as the town's development has been stifled by the actions of a minority of its population. Indeed Corleone does not have a cinema and only in recent years has its first supermarket opened. Its road network and infrastructure are primitive but change is taking place. Still, its land-scape has a certain beauty, without modern buildings, and this beauty has disguised the horror and masks the blood that has been shed.

Today Corleone has forty-three churches for its population of 11,000 and a statue of the Virgin Mary is present in most of the shops; its links with religion have been an important part of its history. Indeed, it was the home of Pope Leo II and it bore witness to the Holy Roman Emperor, Frederick II, driving out the Moors and colonizing Corleone with Italians.

In addition to an Arab invasion, the island has also been invaded by the Normans as part of their conquest of southern Italy. Due to its position in Sicily, Corleone, at the mid-point between the key towns of Palermo and Agrigento, has been a key strategic location in the island's battle against a long series of invaders and oppres-sors, and it became known as "Courageous Civitas" in recognition of this fact.

At one time a wall surrounded Corleone to defend it from attack. More recently its mobsters were also protected by a wall, a wall of silence; the code of *Omertà*. It is this wall, and the town's more recent history, that Corleone is most famous, or most infamous, for. A major part of the inspiration for *The Godfather* trilogy, Corleone has attracted tourists wishing to walk through the streets of the town in which the fictional Vito Corleone was born. The village's links to mafia activities are far from confined to the Hollywood blockbusters, however. Its real-life organized crime and the high-profile nature of the Cosa Nostra (the name by which the Sicilian Mafia is known) activities has led to calls for Corleone to be renamed and even a public relations exercise was undertaken, but a new name and T-shirts bearing the slogan "I love Corleone" will not allow it to escape its vile and ugly recent past. One constant reminder of that past is in the form of a grave containing the remains of one of Sicily's most violent and feared men of all time. That man is Luciano Leggio.

Leggio was born in Corleone on 6 January 1925, the day of the Epiphany in the Christian calendar, but religion never appears to have played a role in Leggio's life. He was born into a poor family, one of ten children, and only a life of crime offered him the opportunity to prosper if he was to remain in his birthplace, which was a victim of the rural poverty that was well known in many parts of Europe in the post First World War years, and this poverty has continued throughout the twentieth century.

He left school at the age of nine, unable to read or write, yet insisted in adulthood that he be called the Professor and liked to convey the impression that he was an intellectual of sorts. Of his early post-school years, little is known, but upon leaving the primitive education system he soon recognized that an honest life would be difficult to find and even if a good job was provided, it is likely that at least during his teenage years he would have chosen to turn to crime anyway.

Leggio began his criminal apprenticeship stealing cattle, which he would butcher and then he would sell the meat. In addition to livestock, he stole other products of the local farms, providing the first of many scrapes with the police.

At the age of eighteen, Leggio was to encounter the experience that would see his transition from petty thief to vicious killer. Six months of contemplation of his actions was sufficient time to allow the darkness of evil to take over what had always been a small actor on the stage of crime. It began when Leggio was caught stealing grain. He was arrested and convicted. His sentence was six months and he deeply resented the interruption to his criminal career. No doubt long before his release he began to plot his revenge on the man who had sent him to prison. Leggio's punishment had been only six months yet he sentenced the man responsible for his imprisonment to death.

Following this, the first of many murders, Leggio met the man who was to help shape his future. Michele Navarra was the boss of the Cosa Nostra in Corleone. He was a successful man who had power thanks to his association with judges, lawyers, politicians and journalists. As a doctor for the local hospital he also had the essential ability to convey a respectable image in order to hide his wicked criminal personality. Leggio was only too willing to work for Navarra as his enforcer and hitman.

In his early days working for Navarra, Leggio set his sights on a job working as a farmhand but there were no vacancies for such a position. Never one to let little trivialities such as that stand in his way, Leggio created a vacancy by shooting dead one of the hands. With a growing taste for murder and a desire to rapidly ascend the career ladder, he made the farm's owner an offer he could not refuse; he held a gun up to the terrified owner's head and told him to sign over the deeds of the farm or he would be killed. The owner complied.

As a *gabellotto* or tenant farmer, Leggio began to be accustomed to the benefits of violence in satisfying his greed. A *gabellotto* managed the land and took responsibility for it, and he also had the power to charge the already poor workers for as much rent as he wished. *Gabellottos* were a key source of revenue for the Cosa Nostra for their ability to exploit workers and secure finance for criminal activities. And when people were unable to pay what Leggio believed was only fair, then he could release his violent urges. He would obtain more land and again charge what he liked, knowing that the workers relied upon working the land for their livelihood and there was nothing they could do, or so he thought.

Regardless of the fear that Leggio instilled in the community, there were those who were willing to stand up against him and against the system that allowed him to get away with his exploitation. Placido Rizzoto was a socialist trade unionist who tried to mobilize the town's people to oppose Leggio and he began to achieve some success. It is unlikely that Rizzoto would have actually had sufficient power to undermine the work of Leggio and other *gabellottos*, especially as they were under the protection of influential men such as Michele Navarra, but his words of resistance evidently panicked the tenant farmer.

Leggio decided to try and silence Rizzoto with words of fear. With a small group of thugs he approached Rizzoto down a narrow alley but, far from afraid, the trade unionist simply picked up the killer and hung him up on a gate. The humiliated man soon realized that threats would not suffice and murder quickly came to mind.

Just days later, on 10 March 1948, as Rizzoto was walking home he was ambushed by three men. His body was later found in the bottom of a deep chasm along with the bodies of two others. He had been shot and then thrown into the fifty-foot deep void. According to several witnesses Leggio was one of the three men responsible for the murder.

Leggio's hatred for Rizzoto was well known and his arrest was inevitable, especially when witnesses came forward with evidence that implicated the young murderer. He was arrested on suspicion of murder and held in custody for two years awaiting trial, but charges were dropped when witnesses were encouraged not to testify, following immense intimidation. Leggio's two accomplices were then murdered to help ensure that the rising criminal got away with his crime without anyone being able to testify against him. In addition to witness intimidation, the only actual eyewitness was murdered. Giuseppe Letizia was an eleven-year-old shepherd who saw the crime being committed. Suffering from severe shock he was taken to the local hospital where he was treated by none other than Doctor Michele Navarra, who gave an injection to the only witness to his hitman's alleged crime. Shortly afterwards the young boy passed away. Navarra was accused of murder but there was insufficient evidence to bring about a successful prosecution. What role Leggio played, if any, in the boy's death was never established.

Although he escaped conviction, Navarra was forced into an exile that was supposed to last for five years. No doubt the doctor's absence played some role in fuelling Leggio's already growing leadership ambitions but these hopes were dashed when, due to Navarra's political connections, he was able to return to Corleone after only a few months. In spite of his boss's return, Leggio began setting up his own independent operations in cattle theft and real estate, as well as ordering the deaths of anyone who got in his way and killing people himself when it satisfied his ever growing blood lust. He was assisted by Salvatore Riina, whom he had met in prison, and another criminal named Bernardo Provenzano. Luciano Leggio saw a great deal of potential in both of them, and they were to become ruthless killers under his tutorship.

Despite the doctor having helped Leggio get away with murder, there were many grievances between the two and the feelings of loyalty which Leggio had once had for his boss began to wane. With his new, small faction he began to launch a minor war against his boss and the war would escalate until it reached a bloody climax. One of the key points in the vendetta was a dispute over Leggio's business aspirations, which he hoped would secure for himself wealth and more power. Leggio hoped to gain some work out of the construction of a controversial dam which was opposed by Navarra. The doctor was greatly angered that his pupil should have the audacity to challenge him over what was a hugely contentious issue in the town and one which had a lot of political and economic implications that would undermine Navarra's influence over the public and the regional officials. Tensions rose and Navarra, feeling threatened by what was clearly Leggio's growing ambition and determination to succeed whatever the price, decided to order a hit. Leggio was requested to meet Navarra at one of his estates in June 1958, but as he walked across a field he was greeted by the presence of fifteen men armed with guns. Somehow, due to a combination of assassins who were not of the same calibre as himself and no doubt a great deal of luck, Leggio managed to escape the farm with only an injured hand and other superficial wounds.

If the Mafia nickname had not already been given to a New York mobster, Leggio could easily have been known as Lucky Luciano following his near death experience and the way that he would escape capture and prosecution for much of his criminal career.

Any feelings of loyalty that may have lingered in Leggio's mind were now entirely crushed as he recognized that if he did not retaliate soon then there would surely be a further attempt on his life and he would not be so lucky.

And so it was that on 2 August 1958 Leggio struck and in doing so turned his vision of a Cosa Nostra family of his own into a reality. On that evening Navarra was driving home accompanied by a fellow doctor by the name of Lercara Friddi, who had no connections to the Cosa Nostra, organized crime or indeed criminal activity in any shape or form. As the vehicle travelled along a lonely stretch of road, a car blocked the way ahead and soon Navarra also found a car behind him, making a getaway impossible. No doubt he realized what was happening but was helpless to react as submachine guns began to be fired from the side of the road. His car became perforated with bullet holes and the doctor had no chance of survival. He was dead at the scene within seconds of the first shot being fired, as was his colleague whose only crime was to accept a lift home.

With the boss dead there was no stopping Leggio in his pursuit of completing his power struggle. Those who had been loyal to Navarra and those who Leggio believed to be a threat to his own regime had to be destroyed, regardless of who they were. Leggio had to gain control of the soldiers and gain their loyalty.

Unlike many Cosa Nostra bosses, including his predecessor Michele Navarra, Leggio had no problems committing murders personally. Whilst he did order the execution of a large number of mobsters, with innocent bystanders often dying for being in the wrong place at the wrong time, Leggio's early background as a hitman and enforcer appears to have created a personal interest in inflicting suffering and death that he could never abandon. Although he committed murders with guns, by strangulation and through a large variety of different methods, his preferred *modus operandi* was to stab or slash his victims. The desire for the personal contact that is associated by inflicting knife wounds, when a bullet can be fired from a distance, gives a valuable insight into the mind of this ruthless killer. Those who knew him described him as a "bloodthirsty" man who gained pleasure from killing and watching life fade from his victims.

When he was not killing personally he had little difficulty in finding "soldiers" who would kill on his behalf. In order to strengthen the Corleonesi hold on the region, it is known that brothers killed brothers, cousins killed cousins and the underlings assassinated members of other families and those from within their own ranks who posed a threat to the family or simply to further their own interests. During the mob war that followed Navarra's assassination it is estimated that 140 mobsters were killed, the majority of which were deaths caused by Leggio and his followers, and approximately fifty of whom had been followers of Navarre.

With all effective opposition either killed or too afraid, through isolation, to oppose him, the thirty-three-year-old proclaimed himself the boss of the Corleonesi and began the transition from a small family to the largest, most feared family of the Cosa Nostra. Indeed, in the days of Navarra the Corleonesi had been known as "*i viddani*" – "the peasants" – because they were based in a poor village and were felt to be an insignificant faction in the world of organized crime. Though powerful, highly respected and feared, Navarra had never been interested in accumulating great wealth, dying with relatively little to his name, or in having a presence on a regional scale. Under Leggio's leadership the Corleonesi became the main Cosa Nostra family of Sicily and Luciano Leggio earned himself the title of *Capo di tutti capi* or "Boss of all bosses".

Leggio's rise to a position amongst the leading "men of honour" was complete. He could now take his place on the Cupola or the Sicilian Mafia Commission, as it was better known when it was revived in 1970, although he never actually attended a meeting because he was in hiding on the Italian mainland at the time.

The Cupola was a body of the heads of the families of the Cosa Nostra, which was set up to decide upon matters affecting the actions of the families and to settle any disputes. Most regions of Sicily had their own Cupola and it was commonly accepted that if one family was to wage war on a second family, or if police officers, politicians, lawyers, journalists or judges were to be assassinated, the Cupola should first be consulted and give its approval, although in reality its power to enforce agreements was fairly limited, especially in its early years.

Leggio expanded the Cosa Nostra work beyond Corleone and began recruiting from nearby Palermo, which became the focus of his criminal activities. He seized control of legitimate businesses by buying out, threatening or murdering the often law-abiding bosses, and in doing so could provide an outwardly respectable image. The "honourable" businessman was able to forge new relations with other businessmen, politicians and others who would be of use to him and prove to be worthy allies. The relationships could be cemented to the point that they would be willing to help him perform his less legitimate business transactions if provided with a "sweetener".

Unlike the fictional Godfather of Corleone, the only principle that Luciano Leggio had when it came to narcotics was that they should make huge sums of money for those who controlled them and that a monopoly on drugs would provide a grip on power. Whilst Mafia families in the USA were making the majority of their money from gambling operations, in Corleone the major source of revenue was the trading of heroin which was trafficked partly within Europe, but mainly to the USA where New York Mafia bosses gained a share of the profits. In order to launder the money several seemingly legitimate businesses were founded. One of the main enterprises to provide a front for the Cosa Nostra activities was real estate, with the construction of new buildings flourishing in the early years of Leggio's supremacy.

Whilst Leggio's violence inevitably led to calls within the police force and judiciary to clamp down on what was a rapidly growing problem, his friends in high places generally prevented the police from taking effective action. So it was outside events, at least outside of the Corleonesi, which causes Leggio's circumstances to change.

On 30 June 1963, as the result of a Cosa Nostra feud, a car bomb exploded in Ciaculli, killing seven police and military officials in what had been a failed attempt against the life of the head of the Cupola. Although Leggio and the Corleonesi played no role in what became known as the Ciaculli Massacre, it caused him to panic. The murder of the police and military officers resulted in a major overt effort to target the leading members of Cosa Nostra and bring them to justice, but the actuality of the situation meant that few convictions took place. It appeared to many that the authorities only wanted to appear that they were trying to tackle the Cosa Nostra problem.

The Ciaculli Massacre forced the Corleonesi to change their ways of operating. The violence, the murders, the drug deals and other illegal operations all continued, but there was a clear recognition of the need for vigilance and discretion on a much greater level than had previously been thought necessary. Those involved had to be careful not to be caught in the face of what appeared, to the outside world, to be a determined effort to stamp out the Cosa Nostra. Yet during this whole period Leggio and his crew were still part of society, rather than fugitives in the traditional sense of the word. They did not need to make an effort to really hide their identities, which would have severely hindered their business dealings, and relied upon the fact that no one would dare testify against them or provide the police with the knowledge of their whereabouts. It is during this period that Leggio became known as "the man without a face" because of the unwillingness of those who had the ability to provide evidence against him or to assist the police in their search for the killer.

Perhaps if he had put more effort into hiding from the police, they would not have found him in the bed of a woman who had been engaged to the trade unionist Rizzoto, the man who Leggio and his accomplices killed and threw into the chasm. And so in May 1964 Leggio was to see the inside of a prison cell once again.

He stood trial in what is known as the Trial of 114 which was held on the Italian mainland due to insufficient facilities to simultaneously try such a large number of defendants, and also in an attempt to prevent witness intimidation. Nonetheless, following a year-long trial lasting from December 1967 to shortly before Christmas the following year, only ten of the defendants were convicted, with the rest, including Leggio, being acquitted. The trial had been to prosecute those believed to be responsible for a Cosa Nostra war. Leggio was not released just yet, however; he was still charged with the murder of nine of Navarra's followers.

Once again he stood in the dock in February 1969 alongside sixty-eight fellow Cosa Nostra members, this time in the town of Bari on the Italian mainland. Accused of being a member of the Cosa Nostra, Leggio denied this. He said he had never even heard of the group or of the term "Mafia". Accused of committing murder, he again denied this, alleging that he had been set up by a police officer who had asked him to pleasure his wife. Asked for the name of the police officer he responded: "Please do not ask me for names. I am a gentleman." The "gentleman" was acquitted along with his sixty-eight co-defendants, although he had admitted to having dealt on the black market during the Second World War.

It is no surprise that all were acquitted when one considers that evidence was tampered with due to the intervention of politicians, lawyers and police officers who were in the pocket of the Cosa Nostra. Furthermore, the judges presiding over the trial and members of the jury received direct threats against their lives and specific orders to acquit:

> To the President of the Court of Assizes of Bari and members of the Jury:
> You people in Bari have not understood, or rather, you don't want to understand, what Corleone means. You are judging honest gentlemen of Corleone, denounced through caprice by the Carabinieri and police. We simply want to warn you that if a single gentleman from Corleone is convicted, you will be blown sky high, you will be wiped out, you will be butchered and so will every member of your family. We think we've been clear. Nobody must be convicted. Otherwise you will be condemned to death – you and your families.
> A Sicilian proverb says: "A man warned is a man saved." It's up to you. Be wise.

Leggio walked free to recommence his criminal career. Some close aides of Leggio who became *pentiti* (the plural of *pentito*, a member of the Cosa Nostra who has testified against a boss in exchange for a lesser sentence, from the Latin for "he who has repented") claimed that Leggio's luck in evading justice was due to the corruption of senior figures in the criminal justice system. Indeed, it was argued that Sicily's Chief Prosecutor, Pietro Scaglione, took a personal interest in keeping Leggio at large. When Scaglione was shot dead in 1971 it was said that Leggio had pulled the trigger of the murder weapon, because he did not want to risk the possibilities of having someone around who knew his secrets. It has also been suggested that Leggio wished Scaglione dead because the Chief Prosecutor was assisting in the acquittal of one of Leggio's rivals. Whatever the motive for Scaglione's death, Leggio was acquitted of his murder.

In July 1969, shortly after the Bari trial, he was once again indicted for murder following a successful appeal by magistrate Cesare Terranova. In his absence in December 1970, Leggio was convicted of murdering Michele Navarra and sentenced to life imprisonment but his whereabouts were, as far as the justice system was concerned, unknown and had been since his earlier acquittal. Yet he had not been making much effort to hide, having spent the latter half of 1969 in a private hospital where he underwent treatment for Pott's disease, an ailment that had affected him for much of his life. When the police went to arrest him at the hospital in January of the following year they found he had discharged himself.

The conviction of Leggio was largely down to Terranova, who was only too aware of Leggio's brutality and was determined to keep him out of circulation. He would become even more familiar with Leggio's murderous personality when he too was assassinated in 1979, allegedly on the order of the killer who had by this time been imprisoned, though he was yet again acquitted of any involvement in the murder due to a lack of evidence.

Whilst on the run, he set up a lucrative kidnapping operation in Milan and expanded his drug-trafficking business to the northern part of the Italian mainland. In this respect his forced exile of sorts was successful in providing opportunities he might not otherwise have had. During this period he came across an old adversary by the name of Damiano Caruso, who he always suspected had killed one of his associates. Caruso disappeared without a trace. Later his girl-friend and fifteen-year-old daughter also vanished. According to several *pentiti*, Leggio killed Caruso and when his girlfriend became suspicious he raped and strangled her, and committed the same atrocity to the teenage daughter.

It was in Milan that Leggio's luck ran out. He was found on 16 May 1974 and sent straight to prison to begin his life sentence for murder. The killer was finally caged and would not be given any opportunity to kill again, at least in person.

Although convicted of only one murder – that of Navarra – there can be no doubt that Luciano Leggio was one of the most brutal, evil and murderous of the Cosa Nostra, or indeed the whole global Mafia. The number of lives he personally took are unlikely ever to be known and even the man himself probably could not keep count of them. Added to that are the lives that were taken at his request and those who were killed in murders that he, in some way, was part of a conspiracy to commit. We can be confident that this was a man who murdered a father because of suspicions which may or not have been based on fact, that he then murdered the man's girlfriend, and that he raped and gained pleasure out of strangling the distraught teenage daughter whose only crime was to be worried about where her father was.

In the case of many dangerous criminals, good and evil coexist. When he was not killing, or ordering his men to commit murder, or organizing any of his other illegal business interests, Leggio was a family man. One relative spoke about the memories of Leggio during the 1960s when the killer was at his peak: "I only met him when I was a child back in the sixties when he and a few guys would come to my house and play cards with my Dad. My Dad passed away in 1966 and I lost touch with him and his crew. He was jovial but feared. I liked him. It was family first, always! Around family was respect to and for all. I remember laughing a lot around him and at night while I was in bed, I could hear more hearty laughter, some yelling and arguing, but that was it. Boy, could he and his crew eat!"

In the end Leggio's violence and pursuit of power, regardless of the shocking cost in human life, were his undoing. He broke unwritten laws of the Cosa Nostra and shocked even hardened killers who began to think that enough was enough, especially when the net closed in around them and their eagerness for lenient sentences began to be recognized.

Leggio's reign of terror and his crime family's breach of Cosa Nostra law, which was exacerbated further by his successor Riina, led to the authorities realizing, in the face of national and international condemnation, they had to clamp down once and for all on what was plaguing Sicily. Whilst organized crime in the form of the Cosa Nostra continues (a fragmented Cupola is known to have met as recently as December 2008), it is a shadow of its former self; Leggio's ever increasing ferociousness bore witness to the beginning of the end. It is one of the greatest of paradoxes that through actions of great evil and violence, peace could begin to filter through the village and region that had experienced and lost so much.

Ironically, petty crime increased following the imprisonment of Leggio and his associates. With the top dogs out of the way, there was room for the low-level criminals to start their careers.

From his prison cell, Leggio apparently put all his efforts into attempting to maintain control of the Corleonesi before power slipped into the hands of his former student, Salvatore Riina.

Even whilst serving a life sentence the trials continued. In 1977 he was acquitted of earlier crimes following a lengthy trial, yet again due to a lack of evidence. Leggio's final court appearance was in a two-year trial known as the Maxiprocesso, or Maxi Trial, between 1986 and 1987. The trial lasted so long due to the complexities of hearing the cases of 474 defendants, although more than 100 were fugitives being tried *in absentia*. Leggio was accused of attempting to run the Corleonesi operations from inside prison and of having ordered the assassination of Terranova.

The trial was held in a court next to the prison in a bunker specifically built for such unprecedented criminal justice proceedings. Its architects were taking no risks and no flaws in the court's design could be tolerated. They built it of reinforced concrete to prevent rocket attacks and had cages for the defendants. Luciano Leggio, wearing a tailored suit, sunglasses, a Rolex watch and with a large cigar in his hand, sat in one of these cages and tried to portray himself as a man of means and a man in control. Indeed, for much of his imprisonment Leggio did live in comfortable surroundings, having been allowed to keep his extensive wealth.

In court guards were armed with machine guns and the defendants were rushed from the prison each day via underground tunnels. The trial judge, Alfonso Giordano, was accompanied by two fellow judges who would take over proceedings in the event of an "accident" or blatant assassination. Yet in the years running up to the trial police were informed, on two occasions, by an anonymous caller that Leggio had given an order to "shut the mouth" of one of the witnesses.

Leggio defended himself and accused those who had organized the trial as attempting to frame him for political reasons. Indeed, the Maxi Trial was criticized by many as it appeared to be a show trial. Despite the criticisms there were 260 convictions, though Leggio was characteristically yet again acquitted of his charge. Most of those who were convicted were later released on appeal.

He was imprisoned in Ucciardone, a maximum prison in Palermo, until 1984, when he was transferred to a prison in Nuoro, Sardinia, in an attempt to reduce his ability to influence Cosa Nostra activities on the outside. With less involvement in the criminal world, Leggio spent his time painting scenes of Corleone. An exhibition of fifty-five of his works was held in Palermo and such was the interest in the murderer's art that forty were sold within days of the exhibition opening, selling for up to $8,500 each.

The murderer turned artist may have been almost killed on several occasions but it was nature that claimed his life in the end. On 16 November 1993, at the age of sixty-eight, he suffered a heart attack and died as a prisoner in Nuoro. Yet despite his alleged crimes and murderous nature Leggio lives on in popular culture, having helped inspire many fictional mobsters including, in no insignificant way, Don Vito Corleone in *The Godfather*. He has a great number of admirers on social networking sites such as Facebook and MySpace, many of whom want to believe that Leggio was not the callous and cold-blooded criminal whose acts of evil brought terror to that small Sicilian town.

ARTHUR WHITE (UK)

London's Most Notorious Debt-Collector

Introducing . . . Arthur White

IF YOU OWED money and Arthur White was collecting, you had better pay up or find a deep, dark pit to hide in, as he was one of the most ruthless debt-collectors in London at the time.

Arthur White's own powerful, haunting, tragic yet ultimately inspirational story shows how the excesses of drugs, success, bad influence and money can quickly turn a fairly "normal" loving family man into a violent "debt-collector", and how finding a faith can turn a life back around.

One of four children, Arthur's roots are from a council estate in the East End of London and although he lived in a pretty tough area, he had a fairly normal childhood and he stayed away from petty crime and the influence of rogue teenagers. During the late 1960s and early 1970s there was a boom in the construction industry in the UK and on leaving school Arthur worked as an apprentice carpenter. On finishing his apprenticeship, he capitalized on the building boom; at the age of just nineteen he set up his own business and married his childhood sweetheart Jacqui. His business became very successful and profitable and provided him with a large house in Essex, a villa in Spain, numerous cars and the money to buy all the material things he had ever wanted.

At an early age Arthur started to train with weights. After a few years of hard training he started to compete in power-lifting competitions and eventually went on to win nine British, six European and four world championship titles. Not only was he a success in business, he was also a successful athlete.

But slowly he became obsessed as power-lifting took over his life; everyone and everything took second place. He loved his sport but it took him into a deep, dark hole he found almost impossible to get out of, and which ultimately almost ended his life. Fatigue and injuries started to plague him and he looked for ways to help. Arthur drank little, never smoked, took good care of his diet and health and never considered taking drugs. However, many men he knew in the sport were taking anabolic steroids and it wasn't long before he started taking them himself. As well as fuelling his body with steroids, he also started to take some "speed" to boost his workouts and eventually ended up on cocaine. Steroids and cocaine are a lethal mixture, but Arthur convinced himself he could control it and he justified his new habit with the premise that if others were doing it, it was okay for him to be doing it, too. But it wasn't – it was controlling him.

His life quickly spiralled out of control; he lost his business, his homes, money and eventually his marriage through an adulterous affair. The drugs were killing him. Depression led to suicide attempts and his new-found professions as a nightclub bouncer and illegal debt-collector to make ends meet and to fuel his drug habit. He soon had a violent reputation and made many enemies. His life was close to ending.

But when things were about as bad as they could get, Arthur found a faith in God and slowly turned his life around and he openly admits that his new-found faith saved him from almost certain death.

He remarried Jacqui after four years of separation, has the love and respect of his children again, and admits to having all he needs in life. He also started to compete in power-lifting again – drug free – and continued to win many more international titles until his final retirement from the sport in 2006.

Taken from his book *Tough Talk*, this is Arthur's own dark and haunting story of his time as a ruthless debt-collector, his addiction to cocaine, his dark depression and suicide attempts, and his eventual path to redemption.

TOUGH TALK
By Arthur White

"There he goes. Watch that man, he's evil."

"He's working for Joe. Keep clear of 'im."

"The guy's tooled up, he nearly killed Jimmy."

I could hear the voices of the men, as I strolled through Spitalfields fruit and vegetable market in Bishopsgate, London, coat flapped open as I looked from side to side at the different wholesale stands. I wanted to laugh. One fight, and now I was reputed to be as bad as one of the Krays.

The fight had taken place the night before, in the Gun pub, in Bishopsgate. My brother's friend Joe was a rich man, who owned a wholesale business in the market. His turnover was millions of pounds each year. He was having a problem with the market traders. He operated a credit system whereby you bought the goods, sold them and then you paid what you owed. Unfortunately, some men were unscrupulous and had no intention of paying Joe the money that they owed him. Jimmy fell into that category.

That evening, Joe was boozing away, whilst I was drinking Pepsi. I had taken some lines of coke, to keep me alert. Joe got into an argument with Jimmy, and Jimmy whacked him on the chin. Joe fell on the table and landed on the floor. He was not a fighter, and I knew that if he didn't get any help, he would be done for. So I stepped in. Grabbing hold of Jimmy, I smacked him in the mouth. A full bottle of champagne was on the bar; I hit Jimmy across the face with it. As he staggered back, I hit him again. Jimmy didn't know what was happening to him, but I wasn't finished yet – I was only just warming up! I was well aware that I had to prove myself to Joe. The whole point of meeting him that evening had been to make an agreement about being his debt-collector.

My speciality was to "throat" somebody. Being a champion "dead-lifter", my grip was like a vice: I would grab someone by the throat, which would quickly cut off their air supply, causing them to faint. Their arms would go limp, and just before they passed out, I would give them one powerful smack, which sorted them out good and proper. Jimmy experienced my technique. I dragged him through the bar doors, and continued to beat him. By now, he wasn't able to put up any resistance. I took his keys out of his pockets, opened up the door of his Mercedes car and threw him on to the front seats. Blood was pouring out of him like a leaky kettle. I told him in no uncertain terms that if he didn't pay Joe what he owed him, he would be getting more of the same, but in double doses. He paid up!

It was after 2 a.m. as I walked through Spitalfields; the tale of my exploits had already reached the market traders. Although the situation seemed comical to me, I knew that some of the punters that I would have to deal with wouldn't be easy pushovers, like Jimmy.

I needed to get tooled up.

Joe was ecstatic with my performance. Now, he was confident that he would recoup all that was owed to him, and he had his own personal bodyguard – me. Because Joe was pleased with me, he dutifully paid me £5,000, as a retainer. This money was a sort of down payment on any future worked I carried out on Joe's behalf. I felt good that, once again, I had some decent cash. The nature of the job was such that I knew that I had to kit myself out with some tools.

That very afternoon, I found a shop in Leyton, nearby where I was now renting a bedsit: it was a fishing accessories shop. I purchased a twelve-inch diver's knife. The shiny steel blade made me feel well able to deal with any punter that dared to challenge me. The knife case had two straps which, normally, divers would wear strapped to the outside of their leg. I fastened it to the inside of my forearm, with the handle pointing down to my wrist. It made access to the knife, in an emergency, easier. I got a list of names, from Joe, of the people that owed him money. My days were spent visiting various markets, collecting Joe's dosh.

I met up with one guy called Ted in the Camden Lock market. He was very reluctant to pay up and didn't like being threatened by the likes of me.

"Listen mate," he said as he pointed his finger in my face, "I know Lenny McClean, he'll sort you out."

I knew of Lenny and, shrugging my shoulders, said to him, "I'll see about that. I'll be back." Lenny McClean was known in the East End of London as the Guv'nor. He was a prizefighter who could never be beaten. People were terrified of him, and one never used his name lightly unless you were sure he was on your side. I had met up with Lenny some years previously when we were training together in a gym. I knew of his fighting skills and he knew of my strength in power-lifting. We showed each other a fair bit of respect. I never doubted for one moment that he feared me, but I knew that I couldn't cross him.

So I used my "loaf".

Lenny was working at the Hippodrome nightclub, in Leicester Square, London. I went to the club to meet him. The big bouncers on the door didn't want to let me into the club initially.

"Who are you?" they asked.

"Don't worry about who I am: I've come to see Lenny. Tell him Arthur White wants to see him."

Two of them walked off. Within minutes they returned and said, "Follow us."

They led me to a dark little office at the end of a corridor. Lenny was large as life, all of 310 pounds, in a dog's-tooth check jacket. In a very gruff voice he said to me: "Ello, son."

I told him the story about the guy from Camden Lock market threatening me with his name and filled him in on Joe's story, and the money he was owed. He agreed to come and work with me – it was an easy way for him to earn a few quid. Turning to leave, Lenny said: "That will cost yer a monkey [£500]." I paid him there and then. Lenny was now on my firm, which meant I had a lot of power.

My reputation grew in leaps and bounds. Many people thought I was Lenny's younger brother: we looked quite alike. I never dispelled those rumours; it was good for business. We were very successful in our debt-collecting. When people saw us turn up, we aroused fear, which caused them to cough up the dough quickly. It was a lucrative business. Whatever we amassed for the day's work, we creamed off our percentage first and gave Joe the rest. The following week, when I went back to see Ted, I told him Lenny was now on my firm and he paid up post-haste!

There was one guy called Johnny. He alone owed Joe a small fortune. Johnny was like a shadow – very elusive – he was hard to track down. I discovered where his office was and one day I broke into it and smashed it up. I left a message with the guy in the office next to him: "Tell Johnny that I'll be back."

Early one morning, at Spitalfields, Johnny came to Joe's stand. He didn't see me at first and I never gave him a chance to react. I pounced on him, like a cat after a mouse. I "throated" him and threw him against a pallet-load of tomatoes – 144 boxes. He and the tomatoes went flying. I kicked the squashed boxes of tomatoes out of my path to get a strong grip on Johnny again: I sorted him right out. Being a shrewd man, he settled a large part of his debt and skulked off, licking his wounds. Johnny knew that my debt-collecting was illegal and he turned up a few hours later with the police, who cautioned me. Johnny thought that once he had got the police on to me, I would back off. He didn't know me. I found out where he lived and then threatened to burn his garage down, along with his house. I was determined to win – to get him to pay up. Johnny knew I was getting too close for comfort and, eventually, he coughed up. It was a nice little earner for me.

Most of the time people paid up, but there were always one or two of them who thought they were a bit clever and could give me a knock-back. Billy was one of them. He was a wide-boy who thought he was razor-sharp. He owned a number of fruit stalls, but he was forever dodging Joe: he didn't want to pay up.

"Fancy a drive in the country, Lenny," I asked one day.

"Alright, boy," he answered.

We motored to Epping, where Billy had a large stall in the street market.

"You have owed ten grand for a long time. It's pay up time. I want the first instalment, now," I threatened.

"But, I 'aven't got it. Look, see me next week and . . . "

"No, you look. I want two grand now, and we'll talk about the rest later."

While I was busy negotiating terms and conditions, Lenny, who was standing beside me, was getting agitated. He had a lot of nervous energy building up inside him. He let out a bestial roar and, hooking his hands under the corner of the stall, he turned the lot over. The stall's contents flew through the air, spewing into the road and over the pavement. Women started screaming. Traffic was halted because oranges and apples, cabbages and potatoes were flying everywhere. Not wanting to be outdone by Lenny, I grabbed Billy by the throat and his leather belt, and turned him upside down. The contents of his pockets fell on the floor, and his money pouch emptied all over the ground.

"Put me down, put me down," he screamed.

I threw him on the floor.

"Don't hurt me, don't hurt me," he whined, as he gathered up the money which was scattered all over the street. He knew we weren't messing about. Laughing, I took the money and calmly walked off, warning, "I'll be back next week, Billy, so be ready."

Driving away, I saw in my rear-view mirror, the mess we had left behind.

"A good morning's work," I grinned at Lenny. "Ere's your monkey, mate."

The orange-flavoured "Jubbly" produced the desired effect. I thought that the triangular ice-pop would do the trick in numbing my neck, making it easier to cut, thus ending my life.

I had bought it that morning at about five o'clock from the corner shop. When I asked for it, the shopkeeper looked at me as though I was crazy. I suppose it was a strange thing for someone to request in December.

Driving through Homerton, east London, I knew it was the right time. I turned into a side road. The morning was dark and cold: it reflected how I was feeling inside. Tears ran down my face. For the last few days I hadn't slept and whenever my eyes became tired, I would lay on my bed, with a towel over them. My cocaine consumption had increased to a new high. All the money that I was earning was being snorted up my nose – I didn't care. My life was such that cocaine was my only companion. The bedsit I was renting was bereft of life and warmth. I had to push all thoughts of my life at home with my wife Jacqui and kids completely out of my mind. Even Donna wasn't very interested in me – she had turned her charms on to someone else. That's how much she cared for me!

Living no longer held any pleasure. Death was beckoning with powerful arms, waiting to engulf me. The familiar shroud of blackness, slowly, stealthily, crept over me. I welcomed it. Leaning my head back against the headrest, I tried to gain control of the battle that was raging in my heart and mind. My heart was crying out for help: help from someone – anyone – to stop me from doing what I had set out to do to myself, help from someone to sort my life out, help from someone to just help me. Yet my mind was closing the lid on my life: it's too late, there is no one, you're all alone mate. That's it. Finito. Finished. Done. Dead.

Audible sobs broke out from my lips.

'Oh Jacqui, what have I done.'

My mind jumped from the faces of my father, my mother, my siblings, my children, from people that I knew, to the people that I had given a hard time to. No one was here for me now. The Jubbly had numbed my neck. I withdrew the diver's knife from its sheath.

The dawn was breaking – it was now or never. Lifting the blade up, I looked at myself in the rear-view mirror. Those eyes that reflected back weren't mine. The blackness in them seemed to have no end. Shutting my eyes tight, I gripped the handle of the knife and placed the blade against my cheek.

Time stood still.

For what seemed like an eternity, the blade slowly opened up the skin of my cheek, sliced through my neck and down across my chest. Blood spurted out like a garden hose. With my eyes still shut, I sensed the warm stickiness of my blood, pumping out all over me. I wondered how long it would take for my heart to realize that my blood was no longer coursing around my body. I managed to replace the knife in its sheath. A heaviness weighed me down. This is it, I thought. My last few moments on earth. Fleetingly, I wondered where I was going, I hoped that it would bring the relief from this life that I desperately needed.

Dying was taking a bit of a time.

I started the car and drove deeper into the East End of London. My hope was that I would lose consciousness and crash the car. That would definitely be the end of me. I thought about other people being involved in an accident, but the truth was, I didn't care. I just wanted out of this miserable existence.

Unfortunately, the blood that, half an hour ago, was being pumped out, had now dwindled to a halt. My clotting agents were working overtime. The cut on my cheek, to my disgust, was congealing. The realization that I was going to live caused me to break down in a torrent of tears and anguish. Could I do nothing right?

Turning the car around I headed back to my bleak bedsit. Stripping off my bloodied clothes, I felt despair.

From then on, everything became an effort, but I forced myself to go to work. I didn't see any point in hanging around my flat. Maybe, I could earn enough to buy a big stash of gear and blow my brains out. Walking through Spitalfields, I noticed that people were looking at me on the sly. Nobody questioned me about the cut on my face and I let them reach their own conclusions. They probably assumed that I had been in a violent fight. They would have been right, in a way – the fight being with myself!

The hot sun was beating down on my skin with a vengeance. I was tanked up with coke and cheap wine. Tenerife.

Donna and I had decided at the last minute to hop on a plane and see some of the world. The fact that for nearly two weeks we had hardly communicated with each other didn't disturb me too much. We had gone through the motions of trying to resurrect our relationship, but I knew it was dead. Still, I tried to enjoy myself, regardless. My mood, even on holiday, was a yo-yo of confusion. One minute I would be flying high, the next I would plunge into the depths of depression.

Early one morning, I took myself off to the beach, alone. I had just called Jacqui at home and told her a pack of lies.

"I'm here on business, love."

"On business, in Tenerife. Don't take me for a fool, Arthur."

"No, no, straight up, Jacqui, I'm collecting money."

"Okay, okay," she sighed.

Replacing the handset, I knew she didn't believe me. I'd had a weird compulsion to hear her voice. Now, she was even more suspicious of me. I shouldn't have bothered.

Sitting on the beach, I watched the sun grow brighter and brighter, as the day broke forth in all its brilliance. It was difficult for me to think clearly. This was paradise – but, here was I, my mind in sheer hell and torment. The waves were gently lapping to and fro. What should have put me in a tranquil mood stirred up giant feelings of guilt, remorse, anger, sadness and loneliness, to name but a few. The motion of the waves was enticing. It was so tempting to just stand up and walk towards their beckoning call. Taking deep breaths, I was just about to walk off into a watery grave when a voice said: "You cannot take your own life."

There was no one around. It was natural for me to address the voice, looking up into the cloudless sky.

"Who are you?"

Anyone walking by would have assumed that I was a regular fruitcake and given me a wide berth when they heard me talking to myself.

The voice answered: "I am your father."

Snorting, I replied, "You're not my dad, my dad's dead."

Peering up into the sky, I waited for an answer. I thought I had glimpsed a face among the clouds, but I couldn't be sure. Shaking my head, I suddenly realized that I had finally flipped my lid.

"I'm going crazy," I said to no one. "I'm having a conversation with myself."

I forgot about topping myself. Instead, I went back to the hotel and did a few lines of coke to block everything out.

The holiday was soon over. Stanstead airport is small in comparison to the other two main London airports. Walking through customs, Donna and I probably looked like all the other sun-baked, relaxed holiday-makers. In reality that was far from the truth. At the time, I didn't notice that among the relatives and friends that were in the arrivals hall, waiting to meet their loved ones, was Jacqui.

I called her later to tell her that I was home. Lying through my teeth, I stuck to my story about being on a business trip.

"I saw you both."

Those words were like a sharp knife piercing me, right down to the bone. I would have continued to lie, but Jacqui had caught me out. I slammed down the phone.

After a couple of weeks in the sun, nothing had been resolved. Increasingly, death looked like the way out. It was either that or killing someone else and losing my liberty.

"Arthur, stop!"

I was bent over my victim, pinning him to the tarmac with my knee. My left hand was wrapped around his head, as he lay immobilized on his left side. In my right hand I held my knife. Murder was not in my mind, but teaching him a lesson was. I began to saw behind his ear lobe. My intention was to cut off his ear.

The guy that was soon to become "earless" was a stranger to me. It was through Donna that this guy was now at my mercy. My relationship with Donna was in decline. We had barely been seeing each other. Even our telephone conversations were a thing of the past. The only reason I missed Donna was because I was a lonely man at the time. I would have been happy if a smelly, old tramp had come and kept me company. I really did miss my wife Jacqui, though. It was painful to say her name, let alone think about her: that would have been torture. The flat at Leyton was never truly home to me. It was somewhere for me to rest my aching body, wash and change my clothing.

One night I was having forty winks, when the buzzer for the front door sounded.

"Arthur, it's me Donna, I need to see you."

"All right, I'll let you in."

The tone in her voice let me know that something was very wrong. How right I was. Tearfully she recounted to me the events that led her to seek me out.

"Please Arthur, please could you sort him out? No way do I want him to get away with it. He needs to be taught a lesson."

The gist of her problem was that she had had an altercation with a guy. It was drug-related. Her main concern was that she had come off worse: she couldn't live with that. That's why she had turned to me for help.

I was dressed in my jogging bottoms and a singlet. The diver's knife was strapped to my arm, as normal, on view for all the world to see! The cold February night air chilled my exposed skin. I shook myself and made my way to my car. Donna was up ahead, leading the way back to the nightclub in north London where her troubles had started. I parked my car in Tottenham High Road and we walked round the corner to the club. It was now about 1 a.m. The club's doors opened and people spilled out like sewage.

In full view of the club punters, I stood with legs apart, arms by my side and fists balled, ready for action. Rambo had nothing on me. Donna was standing just behind me. A man appeared at the door amidst a crowd of people. "That's 'im," shouted Donna.

The crowd froze. Then the guy who had had the run-in with Donna must have recognized her. He broke free from his mates and legged it. I was in hot pursuit. I hadn't taken any gear recently, but it was still in my system from the last hit. This guy was not going to get away. Adrenaline was pulsing through my body. For that moment in time, its effect was better than cocaine. I was buzzing.

The club was situated at the top of a dead-end street. At the far end of the street was a wall. The guy that I was pursuing hadn't done himself any favours by running down that street. There was no escape; he was trapped. He ran around a parked van. I had to stop him, so I grabbed the roof rack with one hand and vaulted over the top of the van, landing in front of him. The guy turned to flee. I stabbed him once in the back. He continued to run, so I stabbed him again. He stumbled and fell. I pounced on him like a tiger. In shock, the guy feebly tried to resist me. I was in my element. To keep him still I gave him a couple of punches to his body and his head. That stopped him. His right ear stood out to me, like a flashing neon light. That's when the idea of cutting it off came to me. I would have completed the job had it not been for the body-less voice.

"Arthur, stop."

I froze.

Looking around me, I was a bit spooked. There was no one there. Yet, I had clearly heard someone call my name.

The voice had broken my concentration. Not bothering to complete the job, I put my knife back into its sheath and stood up. As I turned round, I was shocked to the core. Silently, in front of me was a crowd of about two hundred people. Whilst I had been busy, doing a butcher's job on the guy, the night revellers had congregated in a mass behind me. I knew that somewhere among the crowd, would be my victim's mates. I shrugged back my shoulders. Knowing that this guy had friends in the mob ahead I guessed that I was in for a hiding. Being kicked about is no fun and I was worried that someone might have a knife.

I squared my jaw and began to walk slowly towards them. I was preparing myself for a fight. No way was I going to go down hedging for mercy. I would take it as it came and give as good as I got. Strength seemed to come from the air. As I continued to walk forward I tried to catch people's eyes, as the distance between us shortened. At the edge of the crowd, just as I was bracing myself for the first blow, something strange happened. The crowd parted and formed two sides, with a path down the middle. I hesitated. Was this a trick? Would I get half-way, only for them to close ranks – and that's the last of me? But no. As I walked through, they continued to part, until I reached the other side and safety.

My car was still in the same place. Revving the engine, it suddenly dawned on me that Donna had disappeared. I didn't worry about that for long. What was the point? Within a short time, I was home, dressed and off to work. I put the whole incident out of my mind.

My drug habit was costing me an arm and a leg. As soon as I earned a few quid, it would slip through my fingers and down my throat, or up my nose. The flat was proving too expensive to keep on so I decided to give it up. But where could I go? Jacqui didn't want me at home any more. At that point, I had left her and the children six times. She wasn't keen to take me back again and I didn't blame her. Donna had turned into a right fly-by-night, and to be honest the level of trust between us was zilch, so to stay with her wasn't an option either.

The only home in which I would be welcomed with open arms was my mum's.

"No problem son, any time."

I wondered what my mother would have thought if she had had an inkling of what I was up to. My mother was of a different era and the drugs culture was far removed from her way of life. She would have had a fit if she had known what was taking place under her roof.

The depressive, suicidal mood that I had drifted into was permanently a part of my sad life. There just didn't seem any point to anything. I took as much cocaine as I could get into my body, but I had noticed that it wasn't having the same mind-blowing effects that it used to. So, I took more and more to achieve that high.

About four o'clock one morning, after leaving work, I had snorted some coke to pep myself up for some debt-collecting. I was working alone now, which wasn't a bad way to work, though if I needed to call on Lenny, I could. Cruising along Eastway in Leyton, a car behind me tooted and flashed. Initially, I ignored the driver, but he did it a second time. Anger sprang up like a volcano erupting. I pulled over to let him overtake me. Then, I gunned the engine and tore after him. He began to drive more quickly. I flashed and tooted him. He kept looking at me in his rear-view mirror: I could sense his fear. He wanted to get far, far away from me. I wanted to pulverize him. He drove his car into a cul-de-sac. Without parking his car or turning the engine off, the guy leapt out of his vehicle like Batman and took off. He disappeared into a block of flats. I walked up to his car and shut the engine down. Taking his car keys out, I flung them down the nearest drain hole. I scanned the dark flats for any sign of life – nothing. "C'mon, show yer face. C'mon let's see how brave yer are now?" I screamed at the top of my voice. No response.

My anger spilled over into the night air, as I filled the emptiness with profane expletives. I had psyched myself up for a good fight. Now, I could only plug up the hole with more drugs.

I was trying to make amends with Jacqui. I had come to terms with the fact that my relationship with Donna was past history. I would romanticize to myself that a younger woman had an interest in me and everything was hunky-dory. But it wasn't true: I didn't want her any more. In an ideal world, Jacqui and I and the children would be reconciled and living together as one big happy family.

Real life had me still kipping at my mum's. My mother wasn't happy with my situation, but there wasn't a lot she could do. I know that she was hoping that Jacqui and I would get back together, if only for the children's sake. My mum had old-fashioned views about family life. Jacqui and I, by now, were on speaking terms. Maybe, just maybe, she might forgive me and take me back. I didn't want to push her too far, too soon. So I kept my feelings under wraps.

One Saturday morning in February all of my nice family thoughts went into oblivion. Donna would periodically call me at my mum's. We didn't have much to say to each other; it was more a case of passing the time of day. Unfortunately, this time Jacqui had chosen to pop in and see me and she overheard my conversation with Donna. It wasn't the content that troubled her; it was the fact that Donna and I were still in contact with each other. As soon as I put the phone down, Jacqui erupted. It wasn't long before we were shouting and screaming at each other. The air was thick with my lies and deception, and Jacqui was hurt.

"That's it. Never again. We are FINISHED."

She stormed out of the front door without a backward glance. It was then that it really hit me that I was alone. I suppose I should have thought about how badly I had treated Jacqui. But selfishly I was only thinking about myself. I knew then, in my heart of hearts, that this was the end of the long and turbulent road with my wife.

"No man is an island", so the saying goes, but I felt adrift from the rest of the human race. That night I went out and got hammered. I consumed so much coke and alcohol that it was amazing that I remained standing. From that point on, I went on a bender. I would try to consume as much as I could. I really wanted to kill myself but the next best thing, as far as I was concerned, was to be so out-of-it that I was only half aware of the real world.

I decided to meet up with a friend one night over the other side of the River Thames. We drank ourselves under the table and afterwards I bade him goodnight and set off in a terrible state for home. Blackheath was a distance from where my mum lived. Driving along the lonely road I noticed a road sign for Crystal Palace. I was going the wrong way. I spun the car around in one manoeuvre and headed back the way I had come.

I have no idea what happened after that – I had a complete blackout.

A cold breeze ruffled my thin silk shirt. Stirring from my "bed", I sat up. Even in my muddled state of mind, I could see that I had fallen asleep out in the open. To be more precise, I had taken refuge on a bench on Tower Bridge. The water swished beneath me. The early birds were flying up above me. How did I get there?

Dazed I looked around me. Where was my car? My tongue was like sandpaper and my head was spinning. Staggering to my feet, I wasn't sure in which direction I should head. My feet seemed to know where they were going, so I followed them.

I ended up on Westminster Bridge. The thirty-minute walk woke me up. My car was parked on the bridge, with the keys still in the ignition. I climbed in and drove home. The whole event was worrying.

Up until now, I had been able to handle whatever had happened to me. Having blackouts was another thing altogether. Where had that time gone? I realized that I needed help, and I needed it now.

In 1990, when she was thirteen years old, my daughter Emma joined a youth group at Epping Forest Community Church. She had been invited by a school friend. As the months went by, Emma became a Christian and later that year was baptized. She encouraged my wife and my son James that it would be the best thing for them, too! Neither Jacqui nor I had ever had the inclination to go to church. It had never dawned on us that we should go to church, or even send our children. Christian living was not something that we had thought about much, although if anyone had asked whether we were Christians or not, the answer would have been "yes". (That was before I went off the rails!) We, along with many others, thought that being born in England automatically gave us the right to label ourselves "Christian": after all, this is a Christian country. I didn't know much about this Christian business. In fact I didn't want to know. Christianity was for wimps, I thought. What good was it for a 270-pound heavyweight world champion power-lifter?

Vincent Wiffin was an elder of the church that my daughter Emma attended. Jacqui had recommended him to me. It was Jacqui who told me what I already knew – that I was in desperate need of professional help. I felt I had no option but to contact this Vincent guy.

When I first met Vin in 1993 I was a bit taken aback. Here, clearly, was no wimp. I was expecting him to be a bearded, long-haired, pebbly-spectacled, sandal-wearing freak. Vin was none of those. Meeting up with Vincent changed my life. It sounds a bit of a cliché, but for me it is absolutely true. Vin was no fool. He was a big guy and could clearly handle himself. I had strapped my knife to my leg: I didn't figure he would be too much trouble for me, but I wasn't taking any chances. He knew more about me than I did about him. That was a disadvantage in my book, but I kept cool and listened to what he had to say to me.

Quickly, we built up a rapport. He didn't preach to me, or bash me over the head with his Bible, or shout out "Sinner, sinner get thee hence," which I was half expecting. It would have given me a good excuse to get up and walk out.

I was a first for Vin. He confessed that he had never met anyone quite like me before and had been somewhat apprehensive about meeting me. His background was very different from mine. Living in a sleepy, middle-class village in Essex he had not been exposed to the likes of me and my lifestyle. Relating my life up until that point to Vin helped me to put my thoughts into perspective. I think it opened up a whole new world for him, too! Standing on his doorstep saying our goodbyes, Vin said a few words to me that have remained with me all my life. He said, "Arthur, you have to choose." As I walked away, his words gutted me more than anything else he had said to me at that meeting. I had to choose between Jacqui and Donna? I had to choose between my two beautiful children, or starting another family? Ultimately, I had to choose between good and evil. I had gone from a good life, with my family and job and peace of mind, to a life full of evil, drugs, violence and an immoral relationship. At this point in my life there was no peace of mind or heart. As for love: the capacity to love others, to receive their love and to love myself had gone from me. I was full of contempt for myself. Looking at others, I could see my own problems reflected in their faces: many people were selfish and so consumed with themselves that they didn't even realize that love was missing from their lives. That is a sad, sad place to be. I had thought I had reached rock bottom before but this time it was different: I felt that I was on the road of no return.

It was a cold March morning when, in Spitalfields market car park, I stood, looking up at the sky with my arms outstretched and called out, "Help me God." I didn't know if that was how one prayed but it was the best I could do in my desperation. Arrogantly, I asked God to come into my life and sort it out.

"God," I continued, "if you're so clever, you come and sort it out."

There were no angels' wings flapping, no trumpets blowing, the sky didn't open up and belch forth any weird and wonderful manifestations. Absolutely nothing. And yet a strange feeling enveloped me, soothing me, and I felt at peace with myself.

I wasted no time in making a new start. I unstrapped my precious diver's knife and threw it into a skip nearby. Back home at my mum's I took a drastic step in emptying my cache of drugs on to the kitchen table. My mum gasped in horror at the sight, taking in the fact that her darling youngest son was a drug addict.

I felt the need to share with people the new path that I had now chosen for my life. Vin was over the moon and congratulated me. He took me under his wing and showed me that following Jesus Christ was the only answer for my life, and that I would never again sink to those depths of depravity as long as I stuck close by Jesus.

I met with Vin over the weeks that followed, for marriage guidance counselling, then for Bible study and prayer. As I continued to meet with him my feelings of self-worth increased. Vin was instrumental in getting Jacqui and I back together again. Although Jacqui wasn't a Christian yet, she was well-known in the church and some of the members were apprehensive about us getting back together too quickly. They were worried that I could be using God as an excuse to get back with Jacqui. She wasn't convinced that I could change so quickly anyway.

The going was very slow and I missed my family desperately. I had a picture of them on my bedside, which I would sometimes hold tightly, sobbing my heart out, wanting so much to be back with them. The pain was awful. Jesus had now given me a new ability to love and, because I wasn't able to fully put it to use, it was causing an aching and emptiness. Out of the depth of my heartache for Jacqui and the children, I cried out: "Lord, if it's not your will for us to be together, I'll accept it. But, I will never go back to the life I once lived, and turn away from you."

I knew I had to pray that prayer: I wanted Jesus to know that I was truly His, and His alone, but I still desperately wanted my family back.

A few days later, Jacqui called me. It was 9.30 in the evening.

"Arthur, would you like to come over for a chat?"

As soon as I had put the phone down, I was up the stairs, two at a time. I showered and shaved and splashed on aftershave in what must have been record time.

We sat and talked until about three o'clock in the morning. Jacqui wanted to take things slowly, to see whether there was any truth in what I was telling her. Time would tell!

As I stood at the front door, I asked her if she still loved me.

"I have always loved you Arthur. It's just that I can't trust you. I need to be sure."

My hopes shot up a couple of notches. I believed then that God was doing something in my wife. I was hoping that soon we would be together again. However, before my hopes of Jacqui and I being together again came to fruition, I had to square things with my children. This was a painful time for me. Again, it made me realize that my selfish lifestyle had caused a great deal of hurt to many people. My fear was that my children would reject me. What would I do then?

I sat them down one afternoon and told them about my life for the past seven years. It didn't sound good even to my ears.

"Kids, I have got to tell you both that your dad was a drug addict." A lump formed in my throat making it hard for me to speak. As I recounted my sorry excuse for a life, tears flowed like a river, cascading down my face and falling into my lap. My two lovely children, unspoiled by the world, cried along with me. I had lost our beautiful house and one in Spain, not to mention the fact that I let about £150,000 slip through my fingers or, more precisely, had snorted it up my nose. I had even stooped so low as to sell my wedding ring. At that time of debauched living nothing had been precious to me. Everything was expendable.

My children were wonderful.

"Dad," my children said to me, "we're more proud of you now, than of anything that you have ever done in the past." I couldn't believe that they were so forgiving. The fact that my children had not turned their backs on me encouraged me to think that perhaps Jesus Christ wouldn't either.

Looking back on life, I have come across thousands of people from all walks of life. Many will argue against the existence of Jesus Christ, but no one can argue against the truth of my life. In the past seven years, since 1993 on that March morning when I surrendered my life to Jesus, my life has changed completely. I'm free from my eight-year cocaine addiction, my marriage has been restored, I have the love and respect of my children again, I have a decent job, I have a lovely home, my health is fully restored. And to top all that, I competed in and won another British and European power-lifting title against the same competitors – and I was drug free. On the arm of my T-shirt was printed: "The joy of the LORD is my strength" (Nehemiah 8, verse 10).

I often say and believe that I'm more of a man now than I ever was before. It takes a "real man" to be a follower of Jesus Christ in this dark, dark world. To claim that, in becoming a Christian, all your troubles vanish, you get piles of money and everything turns out great would be a lie. The truth is that no matter what your circumstances the joy of the Lord will be your strength, and Jesus will help you through them.

LIEUTENANT THOMAS A. TAYLOR (RET.) (USA)

International Bodyguard

Introducing . . . Thomas A. Taylor

M OST OF US would unhesitatingly lay down our lives for our children or for someone dear to us whom we love. It is normal and natural. But to be willing to take a bullet and ultimately sacrifice your own life for another person – a person whom you may not really know or indeed care about – must make you one of the world's toughest. There are very few people in the world willing to do exactly this, but one group of people who do this one a regular basis are professional protection specialists or bodyguards. And undoubtedly one of the toughest bodyguards working in the USA today is Thomas A. Taylor.

For thirty years Taylor was a member of the Missouri State Highway Patrol and has been a protection specialist for most of his working life. His involvement in protective operations began in 1974 when he was first assigned to the US Governor's Security Division. He has since been part of the protective details of four different governors, eventually serving as commander of the Governor's Security Division for eight years. He has acted as a survival tactics instructor, training hundreds of officers in dignitary protection and street survival tactics and, following the September 11 attacks, Taylor was named the Anti-Terrorism Coordinator for all Patrol operations. Upon retirement from Government Service, he headed a team of anti-terrorism specialists that evaluated the vulnerabilities of some of the USA's most critical assets.

Taylor was twice elected president of the National Governor's Security Association (NGSA) by the detail leaders for every governor in the USA. In that capacity, he served as the security consultant for the National Governor's Association (NGA) in Washington, DC, and helped formulate security plans for NGA events all over the nation. He has also handled many protective assignments in other countries, including Russia, Greece, Turkey, Japan, Korea, China, Ireland, India, Italy and Puerto Rico. His assignments have included protective operations for many dignitaries including the Pope, Mikhail Gorbachev, Margaret Thatcher, Henry Kissinger and every US President since Gerald Ford. He also served as detail leader for the security team that protected Arnold Schwarzenegger during his campaign to become the governor of California in 2003.

Taylor currently works as a civilian protection specialist and special projects advisor for Gavin de Becker & Associates, a California-based security consulting firm that advises and protects high-risk public figures. He is a regular instructor for the Advanced Threat Assessment and Management Academy at the UCLA Conference Centre and the Academy for Protectors. Taylor was among several top threat assessment experts in the USA chosen to serve on an advisory board to develop the MOSAIC for Assessment of Public-figure Pursuit (MAPP).

Taken from Tom's book *Dodging Bullets, A Strategic Guide to World-Class Protection* using examples of real ambushes, assassination attempts and actual assassinations, in this powerful and thought-provoking chapter Taylor describes in detail the anatomy of an ambush; what being in an ambush really means and how the professional bodyguard is trained to counter this possible deadly threat.

ANATOMY OF AN AMBUSH
By Thomas A. Taylor

How is an ambush site selected? Where and when do ambushes occur? What factors can a bodyguard rely on to avoid an ambush?

Behold a Pale Horse

"You must never neglect ambushes." So states the thirteenth-century Persian author of *The Rules of War and Bravery*. A fourteenth-century Persian work, *Principles of War*, adds that "one of the most important ruses in fighting consists in ambush, and it is impossible to count how many soldiers have lost their lives or nicked their sabres in ambushes." British historian Thomas Packenham accurately stated that "nothing concentrates the military mind so much as the discovery that you have walked into an ambush." Usually the realization of the ambush comes too late.

In 1991, the former Prime Minister of India, Rajiv Gandhi, got out of his car and was walking through a friendly crowd at a political rally. Two attractive, smiling ladies, one carrying a sandalwood garland, stood near the dais to which they knew Gandhi would come. They had been stopped at a security checkpoint but had talked their way past the guards. As Gandhi reached them, the garland lady held out the wreath to him, but an alert female constable stopped her. Gandhi intervened. "Don't worry. Relax!" he told her, and allowed the lady to place the garland around his neck. Then she knelt, as though to show respect. Gandhi reached down to help her up. The lady turned and smiled at the constable, then flipped a switch on the denim girdle around her waist. The action detonated a sash of plastic explosives around her waist, cutting her in half and killing Gandhi. In the ten-foot radius around them, seventeen others were killed and scores lay wounded. In a flash, the insidious ambush was over. Nothing left to do but hose off the street and recruit another candidate. Rajiv's refusal to learn from his mother's assassination – and go on trusting in providence rather than protection – resulted in him joining the fraternity of leaders killed before their time.

"A successful ambush screams failure at a security detail," state Gary Stubblefield and Mark Monday in their book *Killing Zone*. "The ideal ambush site restricts the target on all sides, confining him to an area, a killing zone, where he can be quickly and completely destroyed!" H.H.A. Cooper accurately states that "an impeccable, professional career, attested by the years, can be destroyed in a heartbeat by a moment's inattention, or the cruel, inexorable swiftness of the assassin's bullet, bomb, or slashing blade." The successful ambusher seldom attacks unless he is assured of winning. He follows the dictum of Sun Tzu's advice [in *The Art of War*, sixth century BC]: "Battles should always be won before the actual engagement begins." Martial arts legends refer to this concept as the "invisible fist" – landing a solid blow so that the opponent falls without ever seeing your hands. As the eighteenth-century Marshal General of France, Maurice de Saxe, points out, "If the enemy is skilful, you will see nothing!"

An ancient Chinese story is told of the general who sent a scout ahead of his army to check out a wooded area, fearing an enemy ambush. He instructed the scout to throw a stone into the woods. "If birds fly out of the woods, that means there are no soldiers there and it is safe to approach," said the general. The soldier walked up to the woods and tossed a rock into the trees. Several birds flew out, so he knew it was safe and motioned the army to approach. As they arrived, they were ambushed and killed. It seems the enemy general had instructed his soldiers to capture some birds and hide among the trees, then release the birds when the enemy scout threw a rock at the trees. De Saxe propounded that "war is a science covered with shadows in whose obscurity one cannot move with an assured step. Routine and prejudice, the natural result of ignorance, are its foundation and support."

Larry Salmon and Chris Reilly know about ambushes. They were awarded the 1996 Police Officer of the Year honours by *Parade Magazine* for their heroic actions in saving the lives of their protectees. Both men are special agents in the Diplomatic Security Service. They were on protective assignment in Burundi when an ambush hit the ambassador's motorcade on a remote mountain road. A grenade blew up and gunmen opened fire with AK-47s. Salmon, who was wounded, returned fire, allowing Reilly to escape with the ambassador. As the ambush hit, Reilly reached over the driver and put the car in reverse. He manoeuvred backward away from the attack, barely avoiding a 2,000-foot drop-off, to a place where they could get turned around. Then he shifted into drive and ordered the driver to go forward so that Salmon could trail close behind in the second car with a Burundi official. Neither protectee was injured.

Life and Death in the Kill Zone

Forty seconds. An inconsequential amount of time when you're reading a book, but when you're dodging bullets in a kill zone, it's an eternity.

The Egyptian leaders seated in the grandstand watched as the military parade passed in front of them. It was a clear day in 1981 – perfect conditions for reviewing the latest in military hardware. Everyone looked up as jets flashed by overhead. Their attention returned to the column of vehicles as a truck suddenly pulled out of line and stopped in front of the stands – probably a mechanical breakdown. A soldier stepped out of the cab and started toward the VIP area – probably to pay tribute to the president. Then they noticed a grenade arch through the air into the stands and the deadly stopwatch began. In forty seconds it would be over and President Anwar Sadat would be dead.

The terrorists – actually militant members of the Egyptian military – thought about killing Sadat at a rest house he used, but decided that it was too heavily guarded. They considered shooting down his helicopter, but Sadat utilized a shell-game defence of three helicopters and they had no way to predict which one he would use. They finally decided to carry out a bold daylight assault of the grandstand, where they knew Sadat would be sitting. As usual, success – not survivability – was the highest priority. Ironically, as part of a dress rehearsal for the parade, they were able to practise their attack, passing in front of the empty grandstand several days prior to the attack. After this reconnaissance, they were convinced that they could succeed and Sadat's fate was sealed. The only thing standing between him and death was his team of bodyguards and the plans they would formulate for his protection at the event.

As soon as the truck had rolled to a stop and the lead terrorist had jumped down to throw the grenade, another terrorist rose up in the truck bed and opened fire with an AK-47. His first shot struck Sadat in the neck, causing a fatal wound. Sadat was not wearing his bulletproof vest under his tunic that day because it caused a bulge and made him look fat. But the armour would not have saved him anyway. Another terrorist threw a second grenade, which exploded in front of the stands. An unexploded grenade would later be found under the chair next to Sadat's. The terrorist leader and another gunman made it to the railing in front of Sadat, while the other two terrorists gave them covering fire. The leader pumped round after round into Sadat's body, just in case he was wearing body armour. When the firing stopped, Sadat and seven others lay dead and another twenty-eight were wounded. Sadat was airlifted to a medical facility, but the damage was too great: two entry wounds under his left nipple; one below the left knee, exiting at the top of the thigh; and several wounds in the right arm, chest, neck and left eye. Three terrorists were wounded and taken into custody. The fourth escaped, but was captured two days later.

Politics led Sadat to discourage his protectors from standing in front of the grandstand, where they could be seen by television cameras. As the truck of terrorists lumbered out of the procession and angled toward the VIPs, his bodyguards were stationed *behind* the grandstand, approximately 60 yards from their protectee, and unable to see what was coming. The attack was thirty seconds old and Sadat lay dead or dying before they were able to return fire at the terrorists. They should have considered poet Samuel Johnson's question, "Who can run the race with Death?" Lying next to Sadat in the pile of bodies was Vice President Hosni Mubarak. He had somehow escaped injury in the attack and was named to replace the dead leader. He himself would have several brushes with death, but nothing like what he experienced on an official visit to Ethiopia in 1995.

Knowing that President Mubarak would attend the 1995 Organization of African Unity Summit, Gamat terrorists in Egypt sent a two-man advance team to Ethiopia to plan an ambush. They established residences, rented safe houses, procured additional weapons from other terrorist groups, chose the remainder of the ambush team and spent six weeks checking out possible motorcade routes. The motorcade route from Bole Airport to downtown Addis Ababa would use Bole Road, which would be lined with police and commandos. An alternate route was not even considered. An informant in Cairo called the Gamat team when Mubarak's plane departed. An observation post near Bole Airport sighted his plane when it arrived. The ambush team at the staging house was alerted by radio when the motorcade departed the airport. They readied their three vehicles and prepared for the ambush.

Mubarak's motorcade consisted of a lead motorcycle, a lead police car, Mubarak's limo (an armoured Mercedes 560), a follow-up car, three staff cars and a tail car. An Ethiopian protocol officer insisted on a seat in Mubarak's limo, which bumped the president's detail leader to the follow-up car. This left Mubarak with no security officers in his limo, and the limo could not communicate with the follow-up. Due to confusion at the airport, the motorcade departed without the tail car, which contained additional security officers. It was a series of seemingly minor mistakes that would nearly have fatal consequences.

The terrorists positioned a blue Land Cruiser and a white Volvo along the motorcade route. Three other terrorists could not start their Toyota and decided to walk to the kill zone. As the sirens approached, the Land Cruiser inched on to Bole Road. An unarmed policeman and a commando with an AK-47 approached the vehicle and ordered it to leave. Both were shot and the vehicle pulled into the road, launching the ambush prematurely.

Two terrorists, armed with AK-47s and armour-piercing rounds, began running toward the motorcade, firing on full automatic. Police and commandos returned fire. The lead motorcycle fell over. The lead car drove into the kill zone and was disabled. Mubarak's limo stopped about 90 yards from the Land Cruiser. The follow-up driver stopped 50 yards behind the limo. The Egyptian security officers in the follow-up ordered the Ethiopian driver to pull closer, but he ignored the order, forcing the officers to get out and return fire. A counter-sniper team on a nearby rooftop opened fire on the terrorists. Mubarak ordered his Ethiopian driver to make a U-turn. He backed up, crossed the median and fled to the airport. He was pursued by the follow-up car, leaving Mubarak's security force behind and forcing them to commandeer a vehicle.

Three terrorists were killed in the fire-fight, but four survived and escaped. Mubarak arrived at the airport unscathed. His limo took six hits: two in the right front door, one on the hood and three in the roof, apparently from the counter-snipers, giving new meaning to the phrase "with friends like these, who needs enemies?" Mistakes were made on both sides and Mubarak was lucky to escape alive. The Ethiopian government's intelligence operation had looked at potential problems from local threats but incredibly did not consider the possibility of a group coming in from outside their country. Soon after this incident, several changes were made in the security procedures used to protect Mubarak, and he remains alive to this day.

Fate lashed out again at President Mubarak in September 1999 while he was riding through Port Said in his armoured vehicle. As Mubarak extended his arm out his window to wave at the passing crowds, a man rushed up and cut the president's hand with a sharp instrument. Mubarak's guards quickly shot and killed the man, who was said to have been mentally disturbed. Mubarak's wound was treated with a disinfectant and he went on to deliver a speech in which no mention of the attack was made. News accounts stated that one of his guards was hit by a stray bullet and wounded, but government sources said the wound – a cut finger – occurred when the guard tried to stop the assailant from reaching the car. However, videotape footage taken after the attack showed someone pointing to a bullet hole in Mubarak's limo. It seems that Mubarak's security people had as much luck hitting the protectee's car as they did the assailants themselves. This kind of incident illustrates the risk to the protectee when friendly fire turns not so friendly.

On Dangerous Ground

World-class protective specialists understand the dynamics of ambush situations. Leo VI, the Byzantine emperor also referred to as "Leo the Wise", composed *The Taktika* (Tactics) around AD 900, in which he instructed, "When the enemy sees you making a habit of [manoeuvres], he will inevitably take the opportunity of setting a trap, into which you will fall. A single pattern of behaviour soon becomes known; he who varies his practice will embarrass his opponent and keep him in a permanent state of uncertainty."

In 1995, Macedonian President Kiro Gligorov was killed when a remote-controlled car bomb exploded as his armoured Mercedes drove by, ripping it apart. Besides Gligorov, his driver, his bodyguard and three pedestrians perished in the blast. His route to the office was well known and his car often slowed at the location of the bomb. In a way, the terrorists did not pick Gligorov's kill zone, he did!

Gary Stubblefield and Mark Monday advise: "the most dangerous area for the executive is the 200 yards around his home or office." In 1987, following the assassination of George Besse, president of the Renault car company, French police conducted an intensive investigation to capture the Direct Action terrorists who were responsible. They raided a farmhouse and discovered over sixty videotapes of Besse and other prominent French businesspeople. All the tapes showed the executives going about their daily routines around two locations: their home and their office. The terrorists were clearly looking at a group of potential targets and narrowed down the list to Besse as being the most appropriate to their cause, the most accessible and the most predictable.

Ambushes need not be elaborate or complicated to set up. In 1998, two boys of ages eleven and thirteen – dressed in camouflage and armed with rifles and pistols – waited in the bushes outside their school in Jonesboro, Arkansas, while a friend pulled a fire alarm in the school. When their fellow classmates were evacuated into the planned kill zone, they opened fire, killing four of them and one teacher, and wounding ten others.

One of the best examples of ambush tactics is the 1978 Red Brigade kidnapping of Aldo Moro, a high-profile Italian politician and former prime minister. He was considered to be a candidate for the presidency. Like many public figures, Moro was either careless or naive about his safety. He travelled the same route to the parliament each day in an un-armoured vehicle and his driver had no special training in counter-ambush techniques. Moro's chief bodyguard had served him for more than a dozen years but lacked any specific training in executive protection and served more as an aide. An un-armoured follow-up car containing three bodyguards escorted Moro's limo.

Shortly after 9 a.m., after stopping at a nearby church for communion, Moro was en route to the parliament in his dark blue Fiat 130, accompanied by his bodyguard and chauffeur. His three security guards followed in a white Alfa Romeo. He had established an easy-to-follow pattern by going to the same church every morning at the same time. As the cars approached an intersection, a car bearing diplomatic licence plates pulled ahead of the Fiat and stopped suddenly in the intersection. Moro's chauffeur applied his brakes so abruptly that the follow-up car hit Moro's car in the rear.

The driver and passenger from the blocking car got out as if to check for damage. Approaching Moro's car from both sides, they pulled out pistols and shot the driver and bodyguard, killing them instantly. Prior to this, four men dressed in Alitalia airline uniforms had been standing at the intersection as though waiting for a bus. As the action commenced, they walked to the follow-up car, pulled automatic weapons out of their flight bags and opened fire, killing two of the three officers immediately. The third officer rolled out of the car and fired three shots at his attackers before he was neutralized by a fatal shot from a sniper on a nearby rooftop. The bodyguards in the follow-up car had an automatic weapon, but it was kept in the trunk. The revolver carried by Moro's chief bodyguard was rusted shut from lack of maintenance.

The Red Brigade terrorist team consisted of eleven men and one woman, and utilized five vehicles and a motorcycle. The use of the rooftop sniper was a brilliant idea that enabled the terrorists to control the kill zone. The terrorists transferred Moro, along with a briefcase containing official documents and a briefcase containing medications, to another blue Fiat. His kidnapping took approximately forty-five seconds! When it no longer served their purpose to hold him hostage, the terrorists killed him and left his body in the trunk of a stolen car.

The Red Brigade had originally planned to kidnap the First Secretary of the Italian Communist Party, Enrico Berlinguer. However, their intelligence revealed that he regularly used an armoured vehicle and was accompanied by bodyguards in two armoured escort cars, and that his bodyguards were highly trained in counter-terrorist techniques and used different routes each day. The terrorists changed their plans and chose a softer target in Moro. Even though they were involved in a high-risk activity, they succeeded because they were able to surprise Moro's detail, because the detail members failed to take action once the ambush was launched, and because the terrorists had accurately predicted Moro's movements.

There is a warped form of math that I call the "1 + 1 = 3" Syndrome. In this twisted form of logic, the thinking goes that as nothing happened the first day of the assignment, and nothing happened the second day, nothing will happen the third day. Moro and his detail fell into the velvet-lined coffin of complacency and believed "it can't happen to me." Like many of their deceased colleagues, they fell victim to the "1 + 1 = 3" Syndrome, and it was an equation for their demise.

Lying in Wait

"Terrorism is easy to carry out if you work at it," observed Lawrence Snowden, a former Marine commander who helped investigate a 1983 series of bombings in Beirut which killed nearly 300 Americans.

> We can take measures to limit access by some people, but a real clever terrorist will study a long time before they do something. They learn traffic patterns in and out. They learn everything they need to know to carry it out. As long as we have those kind of people, it's very difficult to totally guard against and to prevent the loss of life.

"Don't have days when you are careless," states the seventeenth-century author Baltasar Gracián, explaining how the ambusher explores the weaknesses of the security team. "Sometimes luck likes to play a practical joke, and it will seize any opportunity to catch you off guard. Intelligence, prudence, courage, and even wisdom have to be ready for the test." He concludes:

> The day they [security] feel most confident will be the day they are most discredited. Caution is always most lacking when it is most needed. Those who observe us carefully use this stratagem, catching our perfections off guard *as* they scrutinize and take stock of us. They know the days on which we display our gifts; on those days cunning pays no heed. They choose the day we least expect to put us to the test. Know your unlucky days, for they exist . . . Don't risk your reputation on one roll of the dice . . . You aren't always at your best, and not every day is yours. So let there be a second attempt to make up for the first.

In 1986, Swedish Prime Minister Olof Palme dismissed his security officers for the evening and took his wife to a movie. Afterwards, while walking home, he was shot in the back and killed, and his wife was wounded. Surveillance on Palme had prompted the gunman to carry out the attack in the evening, when his security team was not present. The Swedish secret police had asked Palme to beef-up his security in 1982, but he scoffed at their suggestion. Palme should have heeded the warning of Vegetius, who wrote that "of all the precautions the most important is to keep entirely secret which way or by what route the army is to march. For the security of the expedition depends on the concealment of all motions from the enemy . . . On finding the enemy has notice of your designs, you must immediately alter your plan of operations."

The public figure attacker's most important tool is not his knife or gun, but the element of surprise. To the world-class protective specialist, surprises are never welcome outside the context of birthday parties. Since the assassin chooses the time and place of the attack, he enjoys a psychological advantage, being the only one who knows the plan. An eighteenth-century French work on guerrilla warfare stated, "The right way to fight advantageously against regular troops is the ambush. The man who lies in wait for his enemy is doubly strong, especially when he has an assured line of retreat."

In *The Art of War*, Sun Tzu placed great emphasis on the use of surprise: "Attack him where he is unprepared, *appear* where you are not expected . . . He will win who, prepared himself, waits to take the enemy unprepared . . . Rapidity is the essence of war; take advantage of the enemy's unreadiness, make your way by unexpected routes, and attack unguarded spots. If the enemy leaves the door open, you must rush in." General Waldemar Erfurth wrote an authoritative manuscript prior to the Second World War on the importance of surprise: "Luck and art must combine to catch the enemy by surprise. In war, the unexpected is the most successful. Thus, surprise is the key to victory." He added:

War should erupt suddenly, as a thunderstorm develops in the mountains or as an earthquake occurs, not preceded by warning signals . . . Surprise does not depend upon lack of care or complete ignorance on the part of the enemy. To achieve surprise, it is by no means necessary that the enemy dreams or sleeps, but that one undertakes an operation which he does not expect . . . Without giving the opponent the slightest cause for apprehension beforehand, the aggressor must strike with all his forces and with extreme violence at a previously determined day and at a pre-arranged hour. The mortal blow must be struck before the enemy even knows that war is on.

Carl von Clausewitz, who wrote *On War* in the early nineteenth century, noted that "the backbone of surprise is fusing speed with secrecy."

If the security force is properly trained, as soon as the attack is launched a barrier will pop up, blocking it, and the protectee will be simultaneously whisked away to a place of safety. But in those several seconds, fate will interject herself in a cruel display of chance, guiding bullets, jamming weapons and snagging clothing. As James Shirley (1596–1666) states in his poem *The Contention of Ajax and Ulysses:*

> The glories of our blood and state
> Are shadows, not substantial things;
> There is no armour against fate;
> Death lays his icy hand on kings.

Murphy's Law states that anything that can go wrong will go wrong, and Mr Murphy loves assassinations. Out of the uncertainties of public figure protection, one thing is certain: Mr Murphy is a mischievous lad and sometimes he plays on the side of the bodyguards and sometimes he chooses the assassin. As occurred in the shooting of President Reagan – where one of six bullets glanced off the armoured limo and passed between the door and car body at the same instant that Reagan did, striking him in the side – it is possible to hit the jackpot even if the odds are a million-to-one. The Russians have a proverb cautioning that Death carries a fat Czar on his shoulders as easily as a lean beggar. "Kings have long arms," stated Benjamin Franklin, "but misfortune longer; let none think themselves out of reach."

The Big Bang Approach

Public figures are most vulnerable when they are in or around their cars. In 1998, BMW developed a factory-produced, lightly armoured car with run-flat tyres that public figures could purchase for about $80,000. The 540i was designed to defeat the most common threats faced from small arms weapons wielded by car-jackers, kidnappers, stalkers and other criminals. But even the solid Mercedes – originally reported as being armoured – could not protect the life of Princess Diana from the devastation of a high-speed collision with a support pillar in the Alma Tunnel. Vehicle armour will allow the protectee to stay alive a few seconds longer in an ambush with small arms fire, but the person will usually not survive the blast of a well-placed bomb of sufficient force.

Four Red Army Faction terrorists, one a woman, set up a camp in a densely wooded area overlooking an intersection on a highway outside of Heidelberg, Germany, in 1981. Their target was US General Frederick Kroesen. They remained camped out for several days, planning the attack and awaiting their opportunity. Finally, they spotted the general's motorcade approaching the traffic lights at the intersection. A German civil police "sweep" car went by, but the officers didn't spot the ambush. Kroesen and his wife were riding in the back of an armoured Mercedes with a German police driver. They were followed by an unmarked car carrying two US Military Police (MP) bodyguards. As the general's car stopped at the light, the terrorists fired two RPG-7 anti-tank grenades and a burst of HK53 fire. The first grenade struck the top of the trunk and passed through, exiting the right rear side, shattering the back window and spraying the Kroesens with glass. The second grenade missed, exploding beyond the car. Four HK rounds hit the Mercedes, but didn't penetrate the armour. Four more rounds struck the MP car, but caused no injuries. The MPs jumped out with handguns, but didn't return fire. The general's driver shut off the ignition as soon as the car was hit – possibly thinking he had been struck by another vehicle – but Kroesen ordered him to drive on and they escaped with only scratches. Despite the inept reaction by all of the security forces, the vehicle armour bought them enough time to react and escape. The terrorists escaped in a stolen car.

The use of explosives in terrorist attacks is becoming more and more prevalent. Although the total number of attacks has gone down in recent years, terrorists are using bigger bombs and seeking higher casualties. They want more bang for their buck. Terrorists commonly use the "Trojan Horse" ploy, secreting the bomb in an innocent container: a package, knapsack, briefcase, U-Haul truck and so on. The bomb that blew up Pan Am 103 was secreted in a stereo cassette player. But in order to take out the protectee with a bomb, the terrorist must know what route the protectee will use and what moment in time he will use it.

In 1992, the Sicilian Mafia learned that Judge Giovanni Falcone would be flying into the airport near Palermo and motorcading to his home in the city. They used a small aeroplane to spot and follow his motorcade as it left the airport. Falcone was driving his armoured Fiat in a three-car convoy. When the motorcade crossed a drainage culvert, the terrorists set off a powerful bomb hidden in the culvert. Falcone's car was thrown 300 yards, killing him, his wife and three bodyguards. Nine others were wounded. The terrorists must have learned of his plans well in advance in order to set up the attack.

There was no more famous (or hunted!) public figure in the world than former Pope John Paul II. Terrorists and fanatics went after him as though they were big-game hunters and he was the last white rhino on Earth. He was shot in 1981 and the deadliest plots to get him were a planned sniper attack while he was in Austria in 1988, a plot to target his motorcade with a remote-controlled bomb in the Philippines in 1995 and a planned missile attack while he was in Lebanon in 1997. During the Pope's 1997 visit to Sarajevo, police discovered and defused twenty-three landmines under a bridge along his motorcade route just hours before his arrival. Many of the attempts and plots utilized plans for a bomb, but all were unsuccessful. Modern-day popes travel by motorcade all over the world. His visits are preceded by massive amounts of publicity about his arrival plans and his schedule. In many cases, there are only one or two routes available to take from Point A to Point B. So why did these attempts fail? The answer is that the papal security element maintains strict control of the route. It is cleared and swept prior to the Pope using it. The result is a splendid ballet of armoured titans in a carefully choreographed presentation. A truly secure motorcade is a work of art that precludes the opportunity of a successful attack.

In most cases, a public figure's arrival and departure plans and schedule will not be widely known. This makes it more difficult for the terrorists, so they have to conduct surveillance on the dignitary to determine his vulnerabilities. Say the mayor is observed to leave the mansion at 8:00 every morning, turn right and take the same route to City Hall. The terrorists will therefore park a car bomb along his route, follow him when he pulls out of the gate and ignite the bomb when he drives by; or they'll take him out after he parks in his reserved spot at City Hall and gets out of the car and so on.

In 1993, a roadside bomb in a tractor exploded as Saddam Hussein's black armoured limo drove by, wounding one of his bodyguards. He was en route to a secret meeting, and the only people who knew about it were members of his cabinet and his security detail. In order to place the bomb, his opponents had to know his route and when he would take it. This fact was not lost on Saddam. He may have been the leader of Iraq, but he would never have been voted Boss-of-the-Year. Questioning sixty of his own officials, he ruthlessly executed twenty of them.

Vehicle armour might discourage or defeat many kidnappers who need to take the VIP alive, but the roadside bomb is the weapon of choice for the terrorist who wants to assassinate the hard target. In 1989, Alfred Herrhausen, chairman of the Deutsche Bank, left his home in Bonn, Germany, for his routine trip to the office. He was riding in the back seat of an armoured Mercedes, escorted by two bodyguards in a lead car and two bodyguards in a follow-up car. They had travelled about 300 yards when a roadside bomb exploded at precisely the instant that Herrhausen's right door was adjacent to the bomb. The blast blew in the armoured door as though it was paper, killing Herrhausen and wounding his driver.

The precision of the attack was made possible by weeks of surveillance and planning that enabled the Red Army Faction terrorists to accurately predict Herrhausen's habits. They knew that, due to the vehicle's armour, the bomb had to be placed close to the road and had to explode at the exact instant his door went past. They posed as a construction crew near his home to observe his routines and decided to utilize a Trojan Horse device: a bicycle parked alongside the road with a child's knapsack on the luggage rack. The bag contained 44 pounds of TNT. To ensure that Herrhausen's car door received the brunt of the blast, they rigged a photoelectric cell, which would be armed by a nearby terrorist after the lead car went by. The front of Herrhausen's car then closed the circuit, firing the device on the bicycle, which was parked at the same distance from the photocell as the distance from Herrhausen's front bumper to his door. It sounds complicated and ingenious, but is hardly as difficult as figuring out the trajectory of a space shuttle mission.

What might have defeated this attack? Perhaps if Herrhausen had kept a more unpredictable schedule, the terrorists would have chosen a softer target. Perhaps if the neighbour, who was raking his leaves a week before the attack and found the firing cord running across his property, had called authorities. Perhaps if someone had questioned why a bicycle was parked alongside the road for about six weeks prior to the attack. Perhaps if a curious neighbour had called to check on the construction crew, which didn't seem to be doing much work. Without a doubt, had Herrhausen's security detail practised, at least prior to his departures and arrivals, an intensive level of counter-surveillance around his home and office – the most likely kill zones – they might have noted people and activities that were foreign to the normal environment.

Timing Is Everything

The successful ambush calls for perfect tinning on the part of the assassin. Being a few seconds too early or too late will decrease the odds of success. As Ralph Waldo Emerson stated, "In skating over thin ice our safety is in our speed." Moving makes for an elusive target. Charles de Gaulle survived dozens of attempts on his life as president of France. His small protective detail often drove him at high speed with minimal escort. This saved his life during an attack at Petit-Clamart in 1962, where the assassins' plan was to hose down his car with gunfire as he passed by. The problem arose when de Gaulle's car arrived somewhat later than originally planned, which had two effects: daylight was fading fast, and traffic was lighter than during rush hour, permitting higher speed through the kill zone. When the ambush was launched de Gaulle's car, its police follow-up car and two motorcycles were going over 70 miles-per-hour. The terrorists fired over a hundred rounds at the motorcade, using carbines, pistols and submachine guns. The six bodyguards, including the two motorcycle officers, didn't fire a single shot, but relied on the speed of the vehicles and evasive driving to escape. The un-armoured limo arrived at Vélizy-Villacoublay with broken windows and punctured tyres, but with the president and his wife unharmed.

One of the most spectacular bomb attacks on a public figure occurred in Madrid, Spain, in 1973. Four young Basque terrorists learned an interesting fact: Admiral Luis Carrero Blanco, who was the premier of Spain and General Franco's number two man, liked to go to mass at the same church every morning at 9 a.m. Their intelligence also advised that Blanco didn't use much security, making him a soft target. They began by checking out Blanco's route to church, and learned that his chauffeur used the same route each day. The terrorists studied the route, learning the surrounding area. They thoroughly checked out the church to determine where Blanco's car parked, which door he used, where he sat and when he left. They noticed that one bodyguard always accompanied Blanco into the church, while the chauffeur remained in the car. The guard always stood in the back, intently watching his protectee. The terrorists often stood right next to the bodyguard during the service, but he took no notice of them. He usually stood with his arms folded in front or with his hands locked behind him, and one terrorist fantasized about grabbing his hands and handcuffing him before he could react. Their plan was to neutralize the bodyguard and kidnap Blanco in an operation that would take no more than two minutes. They would wait until the end of mass because the bodyguard was always more alert at the beginning than the end. Two terrorists would take out the bodyguard, two would cover the entrances and six would grab Blanco, the team being comprised of ten militants with three vehicles outside. Several safe houses were planned, including one apartment that would serve as a hospital, if needed.

Suddenly, things changed. Blanco began altering his schedule. He began travelling to other areas in Spain and they rarely saw him in mass. He started using a follow-up car with additional bodyguards. Now three bodyguards accompanied him into mass when he attended. The terrorists' surveillance operation now became more dangerous. They determined that a kidnapping was now too risky and decided, instead, to assassinate Premier Blanco. They discussed different options: to machine-gun him on the street or to use a car bomb, but they wanted to keep the number of innocent victims to a minimum. The plan they chose was incredible. They rented a basement apartment on a street that Blanco regularly used to drive to work each day. The terrorists then dug a T-shaped tunnel which extended twenty-one feet out under the street, and packed the top of the "T" with three explosive charges totalling over 500 pounds. To complete the ambush, they double-parked a car to force Blanco's motorcade to drive directly over the bomb.

On the morning of the attack, Blanco left his home right on time. He was riding in his armoured Dodge Dart limo with his chauffeur and one bodyguard. They were trailed by a follow-up car, containing a driver and two more bodyguards. As they neared the ambush, a lookout signalled their approach and the double-parked car forced them into the one open lane. The triggerman on the street waited until Blanco's car was adjacent to the mark they had made on a building and set off the bomb. The tremendous blast was perfectly timed and catapulted the heavy Dodge over the roof of a five-storey church! The car hit the cornice as it went over and crashed on to a second-floor terrace in the courtyard of the church. Incredibly, the persons in the limo survived the initial blast, but all died that day. The three occupants of the follow-up car survived. The blast, which was initially thought to be from a gas explosion, ruptured sewer and water lines, and its massive crater quickly filled with water. Everyone thought Blanco's car was underwater until someone called the police to report that a car was parked on the church terrace.

Counter-Ambush Strategies

It's been said that the ultimate warrior leaves no openings, except in his mind. "The Prince must keep his secrets well so as to safeguard his room for manoeuvre and be able to avoid contradiction. If the enemy gets to know his secrets, he must at once take appropriate countermeasures." So states the thirteenth-century Persian manuscript *The Use of War*.

When Cyrus (*c*.600–529 BC), the King of Persia, conquered the city of Babylon, he became concerned about his personal safety:

> as he reflected on this, he decided that he needed a bodyguard. And as he realized that men are nowhere an easier prey to violence than when at meals or at wine, in the bath, or in bed and asleep, he looked around to see who were the most faithful men that he could have around him at such times; and he held that no man was ever faithful who loved anyone else better than the one who needed his protection.

Cyrus recognized that he was most vulnerable to ambush during routine situations. "Accordingly, he took from among [the Persians] ten thousand spearmen, who kept guard about the palace day and night, whenever he was in residence; but whenever he went away anywhere, they went along drawn up in order on either side of him."

In 1759, Major Robert Rogers (1731–1795) issued a set of guidelines to his squad of rangers. The directives became known as the "Standing Orders of Rogers' Rangers". One of the items instructed his soldiers that "when you're on the march, act the way you would if you was sneaking up on a deer. See the enemy first." The first key to avoiding an ambush situation is to maintain a high level of awareness, so as to spot the enemy lying in wait. Surveillance is the assassin's weak link. A world-class counter-surveillance operation will spot the ambush before the victim walks into it.

What is the most hazardous aspect of an activity that a public figure engages in? It's the PREDICTABILITY, stupid! Predictability leads to vulnerability. Therefore, the second key to avoiding an ambush is to be unpredictable. World-class protective specialists build spontaneity into their security plan, forcing the enemy to constantly readjust. A Yiddish proverb warns that luck without brains is a perforated sack. When Whitney Houston gets into trouble at a nightclub in *The Bodyguard*, her huge protector, Tony, fights to clear a path out the front door, the same way they came in. But Kevin Costner chooses to sneak her out the back. It is a strategy of being flexible and never leaving the same way you arrived. This scene was intended to illustrate the difference between a bodyguard and a world-class protective specialist, although Costner acts more like the former than the latter in nearly every crisis. Imagine that a celebrity is attending three high-profile functions and is accompanied by three security officers: the detail leader, who provides close-in protection; an advance agent, who has prepared each site; and a driver, who takes them to the sites and secures the vehicle. Prior to the VIP's arrival at the first event, the advance agent learns that a known threat was at the second site (a hotel) earlier, asking about the celebrity's schedule. The agent contacts the detail leader by cellular phone and warns him of the problem. The detail goes into high-alert, asking for additional assistance from hotel security, and changes to an alternate arrival point more secure than the lobby entrance. The detail maintains extra-close coverage throughout the evening, and discourages the celebrity from going into the crowds. The threat does not show up and the evening goes off without a hitch. In reality, each member of the celebrity's detail should maintain this heightened state of awareness and practise evasive tactics every day. Statistically, no one who actually intends to harm or kidnap the celebrity will be helpful enough to issue a threat first, in essence, making an appointment for the attack. What a shame that the VIP is afforded this higher, more intensive level of protection only when the perceived risk is higher, *and not every day*. Dull-witted bodyguards are often the chink in the protectee's armour that the assassin observes and then exploits.

Unfortunately, it is axiomatic that bodyguards exert more vigilance after an attack or threat than before. According to author A. Wesley Johns in *Heyday for Assassins,* the security officers who were protecting President William McKinley:

> thought that they were showing great vigilance before the President was murdered; after his assassination their circumspection knew no bounds. Their increased watchfulness was especially evident on the mild, pleasant morning of September 23 [1901] when eighty policemen, selected for their size and brawn, were assigned to guard City Hall and the courtroom

where the President's assassin, Leon Czolgosz, was to stand trial on a charge of first degree murder.

How odd that history's assassins are usually afforded more protection than the leaders they killed! Had the level of protection around prisoner Tim McVeigh been in place around the Alfred P. Murrain Building prior to McVeigh's attack – the Oklahoma City bombing of 1995 that killed 168 people – it likely would have failed or been aborted.

"Skill in the game means learning to exploit the other player's predictability, while otherwise behaving unpredictably yourself," explains physics professor H.W. Lewis in his book *Why Flip a Coin?* As an example, he uses the child's game in which one person holds out both hands with a pebble hidden in one, and the other person tries to guess which hand it's in. The one holding the stone tries to predict how the other will guess. The other one tries to predict which hand will be selected to hold the pebble. Let's say that in protective operations, the stone is the protectee, the person holding it is the bodyguard and the guesser is the assassin. Even if the assassin is an idiot and the bodyguard is an expert in quantum mechanics, the idiot will probably guess right every now and then. Imagine that you have two bodyguards – four hands – and only one assassin. Now imagine that you have three bodyguards, hiding the stone in one of six hands. As the possibilities increase, the likelihood of the assassin guessing right becomes less and less. That's why most assassins choose the most predictable place to strike: the protectee's seat at the head table, the door leading from his office, the car he rides in and so forth. These areas become what SWAT teams refer to as "fatal funnels".

"Strategic thinking is the art of outdoing an adversary, knowing that the adversary is trying to do the same to you," state authors Avinash Dixit and Barry Nalebuff in *Thinking Strategically*. Nineteenth-century German field marshal Helmuth von Moltke noted that "an attacker has a plain goal before him, and selects himself the best way to reach it. A defender must guess at the intentions of his opponent, and consider the best way to meet them." Peter Bernstein asserts that "game theory brings a new meaning to uncertainty . . . Game theory says that *the true source of uncertainty lies in the intentions of others*." The trick, he concludes, lies not in trying to guess the intentions of the opponent so much as in not revealing your own intentions.

While protecting Missouri's governors, members of my detail often found themselves standing outside the doorway of a legislator's office on the third floor of the Capitol while the governor met with the legislator inside. Almost without fail, a member of the press corps would walk up and say, "I always know when the governor is working the third floor, because one of you guys is standing outside someone's office!" This caused us to change our tactics. We began waiting inside the legislator's reception room, or using two officers to cover each end of the hallway the governor was working. It made our presence less noticeable, and made the boss a little less predictable. What we wanted to avoid at all costs was the governor saying, "The press knows I'm up there when they see you guys, so I'm going up there alone!"

Richard Marcinko, the former US Navy Seal, suggests:

If you want to win your battles, let your competition make assumptions – and then find out what they are. If you know your enemy's assumptions, you have captured the element of surprise. And if you hold the element of surprise, you can determine the rules of engagement. You can control where you engage the enemy, when you engage them, and how extensive the battle will be.

He concludes, "To the extent that you must make assumptions, you should devise alternative plans to put into action if your assumptions prove to be false. You should always have a fallback position, a Plan B."

NOEL "RAZOR" SMITH (UK)

Teddy Boy

Introducing . . . Noel "Razor" Smith

NOEL "RAZOR" SMITH was born in south London in 1960 and has spent a large portion of the last thirty years in various prisons for armed robbery, possession of firearms with intent, prison escape and grievous bodily harm. He is currently serving eight life sentences, plus eighty years in concurrent sentences. He was undoubtedly one of Britain's toughest criminals, but over the last few years has turned away from violence, taught himself to read and write and gained an A-level in law and an honours diploma in journalism. He has recently received several awards for his writing and has contributed a number of articles to the UK's *Independent* and *Guardian* newspapers, *Punch*, *Big Issue*, *New Statesman* and the *New Law Journal*, among many others.

Smith started his life of violence when he was just fifteen years old. He was among many south London kids keen to stamp their mark on the world and find an identity and a sense of belonging. Rock 'n' roll music of the 1950s had gripped his imagination and, adopting the dress, hairstyle and dance moves, a Teddy boy was born. Many of his peers followed suit and soon the Balham Wildkatz gang was formed; mob-handed, arrogant, aggressive and spoiling for a fight at every opportunity.

Life for the Balham Wildkatz was all about flying your colours, cultivating both a personal and gang reputation, claiming new turf and protecting your own patch against the enemy: the other teen subcultures based around the music scene – mods, rockers, soul boys, punks, skinheads, smoothies, rockabillies – that formed a volatile melting pot of juvenile angst waiting to explode. Clubbing, drinking, thieving and fighting became the norm and a wave of increasingly reckless and violent behaviour ensued, resulting ultimately in internecine warfare.

Smith was a veteran of that scene and former gang leader of the Wildkatz. This chapter, taken from his book *Warrior Kings, The South London Gang Wars 1976–1982*, looks at the early influence music had on Smith and his early days as a Teddy boy.

THE JOHNNY KIDD MEMORIAL NIGHT
By Noel "Razor" Smith

The Edwardian Club was a large function room situated up a wide flight of stairs at the rear of a pub called the Loughborough Hotel, at Loughborough Junction in Brixton. With its large stage and horseshoe-shaped bar it could comfortably hold around 150 people, but on Friday nights it sometimes packed in more like 250. On summer nights it got so crowded that condensation would roll down the walls like mini-rivers and pool under the tables. The Edwardian was a Teddy boy club and the creation of one of south London's most well-known original Teds, Tommy Hogan. Tommy had been a Ted since 1953 and had been at the Trocadero cinema at the Elephant and Castle on that fateful evening in 1954 when the Teds had made their name in an orgy of seat-slashing and riot. Tommy was married to an original Teddy girl named Lynne and they had five kids, all brought up to worship and respect the golden age and its idols. The oldest son, Tony, known as Bopper, was a year younger than me and well known on the Teddy boy scene. Then there was Tommy Jr, Tina, Mandy and Jimmy, who was no more than a toddler at this time. The family were rock 'n' roll through and through.

At the Edwardian Club Tommy Sr was the DJ, Lynne took the money on the door and Bopper showed his dancing talent on the dance-floor. Other people helped out as well, but it was basically a family business. Tommy's sound system was called "Edwardian Dreams" and if there was a rock 'n' roll record that he didn't have then it was one that had never been recorded. The bands who were booked were mainly the Ted bands of the day, solid four-piece rockers who could recreate the records with little deviation. The Teds didn't hold with deviations in their music, and trying to play "Tutti Frutti", for example, as a mid-tempo country tune would get them bottled off the stage. On Friday nights the club was packed and rocking and the place to be if you were a hip young retro, or an ageing Teddy boy.

It was my first real outing to a rock 'n' roll club, or any club come to that, and I was as excited as a long-tailed cat in a room full of rocking chairs. I had greased the back and sides of my hair and teased the front forward into a reasonable quiff in front of the mirror at home. My James Dean cut was growing out and starting to look like Elvis circa 1956, especially with the amount of Brylcreem I had slapped on it. I dressed in my black suit with a plain white, small-collared shirt and a dark blue slim-jim tie, which I had purchased for 10p ($0.15) at the St Bede's jumble sale, and my dad's black army shoes polished like mirrors. I finished the job with a more than liberal splash of Brut aftershave lotion. I was ready to rock at the Johnny Kidd Memorial Night.

Johnny Kidd, or plain old Frederick Heath as he had been christened, had been the lead singer with British rock 'n' roll band Johnny Kidd and the Pirates. The band had had a number 1 hit in 1960 with a song called "Shakin' All Over" and had a few more top 20 entries before the lead singer was killed in a car crash in 1963. Johnny Kidd held a special place in the hearts and memories of the original Teds because he had been one of the few home-grown exponents of rock 'n' roll music who had not "sold out" to "the establishment".

The first of the British rock 'n' rollers had been Tommy Steele who, as early as 1956, had made a clutch of recordings that could easily stand comparison with the American imports. "Rock with the Caveman", "Elevator Rock", "Build Up" and "Singing the Blues", to name but a few, were real British rock 'n' roll recordings and were guaranteed to get the Teddy boys bopping and jiving. But by 1957 Tommy Steele had ruined his rebel reputation by becoming an all-round family entertainer, going on to star in many films and variety performances and recording such songs as the "Children's Hour" favourite "Little White Bull". The Teds had a wild and dangerous reputation to uphold and Tommy Steele's comedy caperings and nicey-nice recordings just did not fit in. By the mid 1950s the Teds wouldn't even spit on Tommy Steele.

Next to take the crown as the king of British rock 'n' roll was a hip young dude named Cliff Richard. With his band, the Shadows, he burst on to the scene in early 1959 with a menacing record called "Move It", and became the Teds' new favourite. In the early days of his career Cliff made some fantastically wild rock 'n' roll recordings, some of which were still filling the dance-floors of Teddy boy clubs twenty years later. "High Class Baby", "My Feet Hit the Ground", "Livin', Lovin' Doll", "Mean Streak" and "Apron Strings" proved that Cliff and the Shadows were worthy of the Teddy boys' acclamation. But then, like a repeat of the Tommy Steele experience, Cliff too became an all-round entertainer, abandoning the guitar-jangling, foot-stomping brand of Teddy boy rock 'n' roll for more middle-of-the-road recordings like "Living Doll" and "Summer Holiday". The Teds hung their heads in sorrow.

Billy Fury was the next strong contender for the British rock 'n' roll crown. He had the looks and the attitude and his first album, the mainly self-penned ten-inch, *Sound of Fury*, contained some outstanding rock 'n' roll that was bordering on a rockabilly sound. Billy Fury could easily have taken the crown had he not been so predisposed towards ballad singing. As far as the Teds were concerned, ballads were okay for a slow dance with your bird at the end of the evening, but you couldn't bop or jive to them. Two Billy Fury recordings that did make the grade and live into the 1970s were "Turn My Back On You" and "Type a Letter", a pair of blistering boppers that were *de rigueur* at any Teds' do.

The rest of the British rock 'n' roll contingent, such as Marty Wilde, Vince Eager, Duffy Power et al. were considered to be too "soft" for the hard-core tastes of the real Teds. But Johnny Kidd was different gravy. Johnny Kidd and the Pirates were all breathless menacing vocals and nerve-jangling guitar riffs over explosive drum sounds. You could bop to Johnny Kidd records and still look as hard as nails. For a lot of Teds Johnny Kidd was the true king of

British rock 'n' roll and as such he deserved to be honoured. Hence
the memorial night at the Edwardian Club.

Personally I could take or leave Johnny Kidd. I thought his music
was okay but I was no big fan. Of all the British rock 'n' rollers Billy
Fury was my favourite, ballads and all. But the Johnny Kidd night
was to be my debut on the rock 'n' roll club scene, so I was listening
to his *20 Greatest Hits* LP on my Dansette as I was getting ready. I
ran the steel comb through my hair for the final time and winked at
my reflection in the bathroom mirror. I looked cool.

The intense heat of the day was gone but it had left the evening
comfortably warm as I headed down the three flights of stairs from
our flat to meet up with the lads on the porch of Ingle House. The
Edwardian Club had an eighteen-and-over rule, but though none of
us was over seventeen we knew we would have no trouble getting
in. Bopper had promised to take care of it and his dad was running
the club. There was me, Big Nose Eamon, Dave Wall, Peter Mayne
and Lee and John Carey, all dressed in our 1950s finery, combing
our already immaculate hair every five minutes and smoking like
James Dean, with the fag permanently hanging from the corner of
the mouth. It was around 7.00 p.m. but it wouldn't even start to get
dark until after 9.00, and there was a good and excited feeling
amongst us as we gathered around the porch chatting and practising our dance moves. Someone passed around a bottle of cider
mixed with cheap gin and I took a good drink from it. The 1970s
kids were hanging around the opposite porch and they started
shouting over to us and a bit of banter developed. They now had a
cassette player over there and the sound of Abba or the Brotherhood
of Man drifted on the summer air. I dogged out my butt and slapped
my hands together. "Fuck this shit! That music is giving me the
creeps. Let's split." Peter drained the cider bottle and launched it
into the bin chute and we moved out as a group.

Getting down to Loughborough Junction involved a bit of a
journey for us. We caught the 137 bus just outside the estate, getting
off at Streatham Hill station, and then caught a 159 bus down to the
White Horse pub on Brixton Road. Then it was a walk down to the
junction. Big Nose Eamon kept us amused on the journey with his
outrageous patter. As the 159 pulled up outside the bowling alley
on Streatham High Street we spotted three skinheads. They were

around our age and wearing the uniform of half-mast jeans, braces and boots and were standing in a group smoking. We were upstairs on the smoking deck and we all piled on to the side of the bus where we could see them and shout abuse through the windows. The skins started shouting their own abuse and giving us the wanker sign as the bus pulled away. We were all fired up and excited over it. This was the first time we had come across another teen subculture outside the estate and the instant animosity was to set the tone for all future contact.

Moving around in a group that had a distinctive look gave me a good feeling of belonging. This was my gang. We were into the 1950s and were declaring it loud and clear with our hairstyles and clothing, and if you didn't like it, well fuck you! And if you belonged to a distinctly different subculture you were an instant enemy even though I did not know you. It was strange how we all just seemed to arrive at that point at the same time; not just us, but the skinheads, soul boys and smoothies as well. Perhaps it had always been this way for teenagers, and you could certainly see the same attitude in mods and rockers of the early 1960s, but in 1976 I think the lines were being drawn more clearly. If you were not with us then you were definitely against us and that seemed to be our creed.

I was very nervous about entering the Edwardian Club for the first time and didn't know what to expect. As we walked down Loughborough Road we were passed by a big 1957 Ford Zephyr in two-tone pink and black, which seemed to be packed out with Teddy boys all hanging out of the open windows. As they passed us they sounded the horn, which played the first few bars of "Dixie", and waved to us. We didn't know them and they didn't know us, but we were fellow travellers close to the same destination so we waved back. The Loughborough Hotel was on the corner of a side street with the front of the pub facing out on to Loughborough Road. To get to the Edwardian Club we had to turn down the side street and go to the rear of the pub. When we turned the corner I was overtaken with delighted excitement. On that warm summer's evening that backstreet in Brixton looked to me exactly how I imagined it did in the 1950s. There were classic cars parked on each side of the street – Ford Zodiacs, Zephyrs and Consuls, Vauxhall F-Type Victors and Crestas, Humber Super-Snipes and Hawks

– mostly in bright two-tone paint jobs and all polished and gleaming
in the evening sunlight. There was a row of about eight motorbikes,
Triumph and BSA being the favoured marques, parked next to each
other like horses outside a Wild West saloon. And groups of
bequiffed Teddy boys and leather-jacketed rockers were standing
around as though they owned the street. As we stood there, taking it
all in like a bunch of yokels seeing the big city for the first time, a
bright pink Ford Anglia pulled up and four of the most gorgeous
girls I had ever seen got out. They were dressed up in circle skirts
with petticoats, black stockings and stiletto shoes that clicked loudly
on the pavement. I whistled softly and looked at Dave as the girls
made their way across the pavement to the club entrance. Dave
straightened his slim-jim tie and swallowed. "Wow!" he exclaimed.
And I felt the same way.

To get into the Edwardian Club you had to go up a wide concrete
staircase and on to a narrow landing. From the bottom of the stairs
we could hear the music, loud but distorted in the cavernous stairwell, as though it was coming from under water. Outside the doors
that led into the interior of the club was a table at which sat Lynne
Hogan and a couple of burly Teddy boys with hard faces. Lynne
was tall and blonde and looked very 1950s in her leopard-print
blouse and bird-wing glasses. She reminded me of one of the
Vernons Girls, the backing singers on that old 1950s TV programme
"Oh Boy!", and she had a real cockney barrow-girl charm about
her. "Hello boys," she greeted us cheerily. "Good night tonight.
We've got a decent band and plenty of Johnny Kidd on the disco. £1
each, lads." We paid our entrance fee and walked through into the
club.

The interior was dimly lit and packed with people. The bar was
right next to the entrance and we made that our first stop. As I
waited to be served in the throng around the bar, I looked around
and took it all in. The ceiling was high and domed and there were
light sconces around the walls at regular intervals above head height
but they didn't seem to give off much light. The tables and chairs
were situated around a large hardwood dance-floor with a good-
sized stage area towards the back of the room. I got my pint of light
and bitter and made my way through the crowds to the edge of the
dance-floor. I wanted to see everything. Tommy Hogan himself was

spinning the records from a set of decks in one corner of the stage and I spotted Bopper up there behind him going through a record box. The rest of the stage was set up for a band, with instruments, amplifiers and microphones all ready, though no sign of the band. The dance-floor was packed with jiving couples and bopping singles. I watched, utterly fascinated, as the jiving girls were spun around at high speed, exposing their knickers and stocking tops for a split second. I didn't yet know how to jive but I was looking forward to learning. We all did a version of the bop that we had mainly picked up from watching 1950s impersonation band Showaddywaddy on "Top of the Pops", but it was nothing like the dance I was seeing here. It looked as though my practised dance moves would need a drastic revamp if I didn't want to embarrass myself.

Big Nose Eamon sidled up to me, pint in hand and eyes glowing in the dimness. "This is fucking great!" he shouted in my ear above the music. I smiled and nodded. It was just what we had been looking for and expecting. The record that was playing approached its end and the dancers slowed down before it segued smoothly into another song and they renewed their efforts. Bopper must have spotted me from his vantage point on the stage and came down to see me. He looked immaculate, as usual, in a blue three-piece drape suit and blue creepers. He took me up on stage to meet his dad. Tommy Sr was as immaculately dressed and coiffured as his offspring and shook hands warmly with me. I liked Tommy straightaway and was impressed with the way he could work the complicated-looking decks whilst shouting encouragement to the dancers through the microphone and carrying on a conversation with me. He asked me if I had any requests I wanted playing and on the spur of the moment I asked him to play "Rave On" by Buddy Holly and to dedicate it to the Sinclair Mob. The band came on stage at 9.30 but just before they did Tommy played my request. I was made up and so were the rest of the lads. It felt as though we had finally arrived on the rock 'n' roll scene.

The majority of people at the Edwardian Club were a lot older than us and seemed to be either drape-suited Teddy boys or leather-jacketed rockers with little in between. Me and my mates were dressed in a 1950s style at least, which I think is why we were tolerated, but there wasn't a drape or a leather jacket between us, which made us stand out a bit. I made up my mind that I was going to steal enough money to get a drape suit made before I came to the club again. I wanted to immerse myself.

That night I came across a phenomenon, for the first time, that would always make me feel slightly uncomfortable in rock 'n' roll clubs. When the records were playing the dance-floor was full of dancers, but as soon as the band came on everyone would either head for the bar or outside the club for a breather, leaving only a handful of people in front of the stage. No one seemed to want to dance to the live music, only the records. I don't really know why this was because some of the better bands could produce a sound that was so close to the original as to be almost indistinguishable. It had just somehow become the tradition that no one danced to the band, but if the band were exceptional then plenty of people would gather in front of the stage to watch them perform. I sometimes felt sorry for the bands, particularly the young ones, as they gave their all for an ungrateful and undemonstrative crowd, but that was the tradition.

Around 10.30 I was feeling pretty drunk and happy. I even ventured on to the dance-floor to hop about a bit when Tommy played Johnny Kidd's "Please Don't Touch", which was my particular favourite. I noticed that Dave spent most of the evening chatting to a couple of giggling Teddy girls in one corner of the club and seemed to be getting on famously with them judging by their body language. The heat was stifling inside the club and I decided to pop outside for a couple of minutes for a bit of fresh air.

The stairwell was crowded with couples sat talking or kissing and I had to step over people to make it to the street. It was dark outside now and a bit cooler, but the street lights cast a warm orange glow over everything. I lit up a cigarette and saw Big Nose Eamon and John Carey talking to a mean-looking biker with "Road Rats MC London" on the back of his cut-down denim jacket. I walked over to take a listen and found they were talking about motorbikes. The biker was very well spoken, which seemed completely at odds with his huge straggly beard, tattoos and oil-stained denims. I was later to find that this was the case with a lot of bikers: they were not all wild-eyed criminals and some of them held down very well-paid day jobs. I was admiring the sleek lines of a jacked-up Ford Zodiac that was parked along the street from the entrance to the club when I became aware of raised voices down at the corner of the street. Three young Teds came bombing around the corner at top speed and shouting an alert. "The niggers are coming! The niggers are coming!"

Brixton was a predominantly black area and since the Notting Hill riots of the 1950s there had been no love lost between black people and Teddy boys. Having a Teddy boy club in what was essentially the heart of Brixton was a bit too much for a lot of the young black kids on the surrounding estates and sometimes there would be trouble. Bopper had told me that the week before the Johnny Kidd night a couple of Teds from Shepherd's Bush had beaten up a Rasta in one of the cab offices after leaving the club. Now it seemed there was a gang coming for revenge. I didn't know what to do. One of the Teds ran into the club and within about a minute crowds of Teds and rockers were piling down the stairs and out on to the street. I got carried along with the excitement of the crowd as we spread out across the street and began marching up towards the junction. I noticed that a lot of people had produced weapons and there was everything from sheath knives and cut-throat razors to motorbike chains and broken pool cues. I felt a bit naked without a weapon of my own but I was up for a punch-up.

There must have been about sixty or seventy of us by the time we reached the junction. I noticed Eamon, John, Lee and Peter in the crowd, faces glowing with drink and excitement, and the only one who was missing was Dave, who was still inside the club chatting up the girls. I had been in gang fights before but nothing on this scale or with this amount of weaponry on show. My heart was racing and my mouth was dry but I was eager. This was it; we were going to show these fuckers that you couldn't mess with the Teds. As we turned the corner I saw a group of about forty blacks, all armed with sticks, bats and knives, and my excitement reached fever pitch. Someone had found a plastic crate full of milk bottles outside one of the shops and was passing them out to those in our crowd who didn't have a weapon. I grabbed two bottles, one in each hand, and holding them by the necks I stood shoulder to shoulder with my people. This was what it was all about, a brother-hood, us against them; it didn't matter who the enemy was, if they weren't us they weren't anything.

The two groups stood facing each other over about twenty feet of street. A big Teddy boy, whom I later found out was called Cut-Throat John, stepped forward and shouted towards the blacks, "You fucking golliwogs! You fucking want some? Come on then!" He then ran towards the blacks with a roar and waving a cut-throat razor above his head. The Teds followed suit, roaring and running up the street towards the enemy group. The blacks hesitated for a moment and then, realizing that they were outnumbered, broke ranks and began running back the way they had come. In their panic to get away, a couple of blacks tripped and fell and were quickly swamped by kicking and slashing Teds. I heard the screams above the rest of the noise but I carried on running with the crowd. As we realized that the blacks were getting away, the crowd began to slow down. I launched my milk bottles, one at a time, over the Teds in front of me and heard them smash on the road behind the retreating blacks.

The walk back to the club was the march of a triumphant army, all back-slapping and laughter at our victory. We had "run" the Brixton blacks and that was worth savouring. Even I, novice as I was, knew that at some stage, maybe next week or next month, they would be back in even greater numbers and things might not go our way then. But for now the Teds were riding high. I noticed a pool of blood on the tarmac near the junction and knew this was where one of the black gang had been caught and battered. As I walked by, the orange street light was reflected in the blood and it made me feel slightly sick. I wondered where the owner of that blood was and how badly he had been hurt. Then I was caught up in the moment again and dismissed the blood and any thought of the victims. I caught up with Eamon, John and Peter who were in very high spirits and we all went back into the club to take the piss out of Dave for missing all the excitement.

Looking back, I realize that the Teds were what would now be described as "institutionally racist". In those days a lot of people were and, if the truth were known, a lot of people still are, and not just white people either. I think we've just got better at hiding it these days. I'm not a hypocrite and I won't sit here and pretend to have an attack of the vapours because I fought and verbally abused black gangs when I was younger. It happened, and I took plenty of stick from the other side as well. The 1970s was a pretty confused decade. You could hear the words "nigger" and "honky" on television most weeks and the National Front (NF) was openly recruiting and marching on our streets and football terraces, as was the Anti Nazi League (ANL). A lot of the Teds were NF members, and a few were members of the ANL, but I never joined any of these organizations. My reason for not joining any of the right-wing groups was because both my parents were Irish and the likes of the NF had plans to kick the "paddies" out of England as soon as they had dealt with the blacks and Asians. I had a couple of black friends and there were even a few black Teddy boys, such as Black Bill of Tooting, Olly the Cat of Streatham and Jester of the Shepherd's Bush Rebels. So, although I may have been casually racist, my loyalty was to rock 'n' roll and my hatred was for anyone outside of that sphere, whether they were black, white or brown.

The Johnny Kidd Memorial Night at the Edwardian Club will always live in my memory as a golden time. I was on the verge of getting into something to which I felt I belonged. I believed that rock 'n' roll was here to stay and that, like Tommy Hogan and the rest of the originals, I too would be bopping and jiving my way into middle age some day. I was proud to be part of it all and to have met such great characters and been accepted at face value. We all ended up pissed that night and singing rock 'n' roll songs at the tops of our voices as we made our way home. It was a great summer to be a teenager.

THE KRAYS (UK)

Notorious British Gangsters

Introducing . . . The Krays

MASSIVE HYPE AND publicity surrounded twins Ron and Reg Kray's deaths and funerals, as well as the demise of their older brother Charlie Kray. In this remarkable chapter Steve Wraith, a close friend of all three brothers, describes (with writer Stuart Wheatman) attending all three funerals of Krays – the most notorious gangsters in modern-day British history. Steve first contacted the Krays in 1990. He had sent a letter to both twins after the end credits of the film *The Krays* revealed where they were being held. Reg was the first to reply on the 14 November 1990. A second letter, from Ron, arrived shortly after. From then onwards they wrote a great many times, eventually leading to prison visits and good friendships.

Reginald "Reggie" Kray and his twin brother Ronald "Ronnie" Kray were born on 24 October 1933 in Hoxton, East London. Reggie was born ten minutes before Ronnie. Their parents Charlie and Violet Kray already had a six-year old son also called Charlie, who was born on 9 July 1927. A sister, Violet, was born in 1929 but died in infancy. In 1939 the Kray family moved from their home in Hoxton to nearby 178 Vallance Road, Bethnal Green.

The twins were to become the most famous gangsters of their generation and were involved in armed robberies, arson, protection rackets, violent assaults including torture, and the murders of Jack "The Hat" McVitie and George Cornell. During the 1950s and 1960s Ron and Reg Kray, along with their elder brother Charlie, were the foremost perpetrators of organized crime in London's East End. Although Ron Kray suffered from paranoid schizophrenia, in the 1960s they became big celebrities; the nightclub they owned attracted stars and entertainers including Frank Sinatra and Judy Garland, and they were photographed by David Bailey and interviewed numerous times on television.

At school the Kray twins showed none of their future criminal tendencies. This all started to change after their grandfather, Jimmy "Cannonball" Lee, led both boys into amateur boxing, which was at that time a popular pursuit for working-class boys in the East End. The Kray twins had then formed a gang and were achieving a degree of local notoriety for the trouble they caused. In early 1952 they were both called up for National Service in the army but deserted a number of times and on one occasion the twins assaulted a police officer who had spotted them and was trying to arrest them. They were initially held at the Tower of London (they were among the very last prisoners ever kept there) before being sent to Shepton Mallet military prison in Somerset and jailed for a month awaiting courts-martial. They ended up being given a dishonourable discharge from the army after throwing tantrums, upending their latrine bucket over a sergeant, dumping a kettle of hot tea on a prison guard, handcuffing another prison guard to the prison bars with a pair of stolen cuffs and burning their bedding.

It was during this period in military prison that Ron started to show the first signs of mental illness. He would refuse to eat, shave only one side of his face and suffer wild mood swings. Guards at the prison were convinced he was dangerously psychotic.

Their criminal record and dishonourable discharge ended their boxing careers and, as a result, the twins turned to crime. Together they bought a local snooker club in Bethnal Green, where they started several protection rackets and by the end of the 1950s the Krays were involved in hijacking, armed robbery and arson.

In 1960 Reggie Kray was incarcerated for eighteen months on charges of running a protection racket and while he was in prison, Peter Rachman, the head of a violent landlord operation, gave Ronnie Kray a nightclub called Esmeralda's Barn in Knightsbridge, London, which significantly increased the Krays' influence.

In the 1960s, they were widely seen as prosperous and charming celebrity nightclub owners and a large part of their fame was due to their non-criminal activities as popular figures on the celebrity circuit. "They were the best years of our lives. They called them the swinging sixties. The Beatles and the Rolling Stones were rulers of pop music, Carnaby Street ruled the fashion world . . . and me and my brother ruled London. We were fucking untouchable", said Ronnie Kray in his autobiography, *My Story*.

The police investigated the Krays on several occasions, but the twins' reputation for violence meant witnesses were afraid to come forward to testify.

On 12 December 1966 the Krays assisted Frank Mitchell (nick-named "The Mad Axeman") in escaping from Dartmoor Prison. Once Mitchell was out of Dartmoor, the Krays held him at a friend's flat in Barking Road. However, as a large man with a mental disorder, he was difficult to deal with and they decided that the only course of action was to get rid of him. His body has never been found and the Krays were acquitted of his murder.

Ronnie Kray shot and killed George Cornell in the Blind Beggar pub in Whitechapel on 9 March 1966. A gang war between the Richardsons – the Krays' rivals who controlled crime in south London – and the Krays had previously started when an associate of the twins, Richard Hart, had been murdered. Ronnie Kray swore to avenge Hart's death. When George Cornell was seen at the Blind Beggar, Ron took Reg's driver John "Scotch Jack" Dickson and Ian Barrie, his right-hand man, over to the pub and killed George.

In October 1967 Reggie was alleged to have been encouraged by his brother Ron to kill Jack "The Hat" McVitie, a minor member of the Kray gang who had failed to fulfil a £1,500 contract paid to him in advance by the Krays to kill Leslie Payne. McVitie was lured to a basement flat in Evering Road, Stoke Newington, on the pretence of a party. As he entered, Reggie Kray pointed a handgun at his head and pulled the trigger twice, but the gun failed to discharge. Ronnie Kray then held McVitie as Reggie stabbed him in the face, neck and stomach. McVitie's body has still not been recovered.

When Inspector Leonard "Nipper" Read of Scotland Yard was promoted to the Murder Squad, his first assignment was to bring down the Kray twins. By the end of 1967 he had built up substantial evidence against them, but still not enough for a convincing case on any one charge, mainly because most witnesses were too scared to testify. However, Scotland Yard eventually decided to arrest the Krays on the evidence already collected, in the hope that other witnesses would be forthcoming once the Krays were in custody. On 8 May 1968 the Krays and fifteen other members of their "firm" were arrested. Once the Krays were behind bars and their reign of intimidation was over, many witnesses came forward and it became relatively easy to gain a conviction. Both Ronnie and Reg were sentenced to life imprisonment, with a non-parole period of thirty years for the murders of Cornell and McVitie, the longest sentences ever passed at the Old Bailey at the time. Their brother Charlie was jailed for ten years for his part in the murders.

Ronnie was certified insane and lived the remainder of his life in Broadmoor high-security psychiatric hospital in Crowthorne, Berkshire, dying of a massive heart attack on 17 March 1995, aged sixty-one. Initially Reggie Kray was a Category A prisoner, denied almost all liberties and not allowed to mix with other prisoners. However, in his later years, he was downgraded to Category C and transferred to Norfolk's Wayland Prison. He was finally freed from Wayland on 26 August 2000, at the age of almost sixty-seven. He was released on compassionate grounds as a result of having inoperable cancer. The final weeks of his life were spent with his wife Roberta, whom he had married in July 1997 in a suite at the Town House Hotel at Norwich while in Maidstone prison.

Elder brother Charlie Kray was released in 1975 after serving seven years, but returned to prison in 1997 for conspiracy to smuggle cocaine worth £69 million (US$103 million) in an undercover drugs sting. He died of natural causes on 4 April 2000.

A few months later, on 1 October 2000, Reggie Kray died in his sleep. Ten days later, he was buried alongside his brother Ronnie, in Chingford cemetery, Essex.

FUNERALS
By Steve Wraith and Stuart Wheatman

The day started just like any other. It was 17 March 1995. I had opened the post office (in Gateshead, northeast England) as usual and went through my daily routine of serving the first few customers and then, when it was quiet again, retiring to the back-shop for a cuppa and a read of the paper. I always had the radio turned up high on Radio One or Virgin . . . as I sat down to glance at the head-lines the top news story was announced across the airways: "Former East End gangster Ron Kray has died. He had previously suffered from chest pains and has died of a suspected heart attack. He was sixty-two years old."

The news knocked me out of my routine. I was numb. I turned the dial from station to station to confirm what I had just heard. I couldn't believe it but it began to sink in. Ron had passed away at seven minutes past nine at Heatherwood Hospital, Ascot. Only a couple of days earlier I had sent him a get well card. Everyone knew of his illness. Death may be inevitable, but it is often unexpected.

It did not take long for the phone to start ringing, but for a change I was lost for words. I asked the journalists to give me a couple of hours to absorb the news before I answered their ques-tions and made comments. I needed to make some phone calls of my own first. I phoned Reg, then Charlie and then Frank and Noelle Kurylo, Janet Alsop, Gary the Gofer, Brad and Kim.

It was still sinking in the next day, when predictably the papers were full of stories about the twins. I had declined to comment to any of the major tabloids in case I was misquoted. I did talk to the locals . . . the *Journal*, the *Chronicle* and the *Gateshead Post* whose journalists I knew I could trust. During all this, my mate Ray Cann, the tattoo artist, contacted me to see if I intended to go to the funeral and that he would be willing to give me a lift there and back. I had not even thought about the funeral at this point, but agreed and thanked Ray for the offer. I had already got to know Ray well from our early involvement putting charity events together and now we were good friends. Over the next few days the newspapers carried a different headline, or a different slant, on the Kray story. It was a feeding frenzy. They ranged from Ron's alleged last words, to a statement he had made before his death that he was the evil twin and that Reg should be exonerated of all blame. For many it will have made for an exciting read; for me it simply hyped up the Kray Legend, and could only be detrimental to any plans of imminent release that Reg may have had.

Four days later Reg called me with the details for the funeral. The conversation was as follows: "Hello, Steve, Reg here, have you got a pen ? [I had] Good. The funeral is Wednesday, March 29th. Make your way to English's Funeral Parlour. I want you to make sure you get there. If you can't for whatever reason, be at St Matthew's Church for eleven. I will make sure you are on the list there as well. I'm organizing the service, so you will get in."

I told him that Ron would be proud of him for all he was doing and for being strong. He agreed, saying he was now at peace. He had others to call, so after his usual "God Bless" he was gone.

I noticed he was a lot calmer than he had been on the day that Ron died. Reg seemed to have come to terms with his brother's death and was at peace with himself for a change. He seemed to be coping well with it. I phoned Ray and let him know that Reg had asked me to attend the service. He would start making the relevant arrangements . . . time off work and use of a car for us to travel down. I then phoned Michael Russen, the taxi company owner who I knew in East London, and asked if it would be okay for us to stay at his flat overnight. No problem. He too seemed excited. Okay, I see the attention of a Kray funeral and all that goes with it . . . but to be excited about a funeral? Never mind. My next call was to a local florist. My mate Fitzy's wife, Colleen, worked for Sarah Gaskins, a florist's store in Newcastle, and said they would custom make me a wreath, whatever I wanted, for a discount price. I appreciated the gesture. I had given the wreath a lot of thought and had decided that a cruise liner was appropriate, as Ron had told me on my first visit that it was his dream to go on a round the world trip. I only wish that his dream had become a reality. But he was free now – free from the torment that had imprisoned him.

The day before the funeral Gary phoned me to organize a meeting on the day. Nine-thirty at the funeral parlour were Reg's instructions so I arranged to meet Gary fifteen minutes earlier. He did not seem too clear on the arrangements – if he was so close to Reg why did it seem that I was telling him things for the first time? I had suspicions about Gary and his relationship with the Kray family. I decided not to dwell on it for the time being. Mid afternoon, Ray picked me up in a borrowed car, and after a quick photo-shoot with the wreath for the *Evening Chronicle*, we set off on our long journey to London. We met up with Mickey Russen at Scratchwood Service Station at the end of the motorway and he drove us the rest of the way into the heart of London.

There was a lot on my mind that night. Funerals are always horrible things to have to go through, but gangland funerals will always lack that certain emotion you are used to. Gangland funerals are foremost a sign of respect by major figures from all over the country. It is a form of etiquette. All cultures have rules, the funeral marks the fact that the person had influence and people want to travel to show their support. There are different levels of intimacy . . . I knew Ron well and knew that I was there for my own reasons.

My first job the next day was to write out the card that would accompany the wreath. I wrote, "You always wanted a round the world cruise. Now you are free to enjoy it. Steve Wraith, Ray Cann, Michael Russen." Radio Newcastle had asked me to speak to them that morning on their weekly phone-in programme with presenter Mike Parr. I had done a lot of shows with Mike so was prepared for his line of questioning. His stance was, "Why mourn the death of a psychotic gangster?" I told him and the listeners back in the north-east that Ron had been a friend and that his past did not concern me. I knew him now, not as he was in the 1960s. Due to the medication, and because he had been institutionalized for so long, he was a different man to the one the public had read about. My comments apparently caused uproar with the listeners and phone lines were jammed all day with people wishing to voice their concern about that "naive, misled youngster". Radio Newcastle had never had it so good! The Krays were never going to get good publicity about anything. They are icons of underworld Britain . . . as I was mourning Ron instead of saying "good riddance", the moral majority of listeners were saying I didn't know what I was talking about. I knew more about it than most of them, so I did not let it bother me.

We left the flat at 8.45 that morning. Ray drove while Michael gave directions. I sat at the back with the wreath. As we drove through the streets of East London, I thought about the day ahead and felt honoured to be part of it. I was surprised at how quiet the roads seemed to be as it was rush hour in London . . . then we hit gridlock a quarter of a mile from Bethnal Green Road, where English's Funeral Parlour was situated. The roads that had been so good to us looked as if they were going to let us down. Somehow we managed to push our way through the traffic, and with Mick's local taxi knowledge we reached the funeral parlour with a few minutes to spare. We pulled up outside behind a police cordon and got out to lay our wreath. The first thing that struck me was the number of people gathering to witness another chapter in the Krays' storybook unfold. It was an amazing sight – like a state funeral. People pushing to get a glimpse of anything . . . reporters and camera crews . . . police all over the place. It was at this moment I realized that I had finally walked into the books that I had read all those years ago, if that makes sense. I had read every book about the Kray twins and their associates, and now I was part of one. I was not just a bystander . . . I was a family guest. The security was impressive, they were massive – all with as much jewellery as Mr T, all immaculately dressed and very mean-looking. Leading the operation was Reg's close friend Mr Dave Courtney. As we mingled amongst the who's who of the underworld, we could hear the cameras clicking across the world. Photographers were perched, balanced and clinging on for dear life from different vantage points, all trying to get the best picture for tomorrow's papers.

I laid the wreath next to Reg's floral tribute, which read, "To the other half of me". As I stood up, I shook hands and embraced Dave. There was no sign of Gary, so as Ray parked the car Mickey and me nipped to the nearest cafe for a cuppa. Once Ray had parked the car, I cleared it with Dave to allow Ray and Mick into the parlour. It was impossible to walk anywhere at a normal pace. We just had to stand in line and shuffle in as best we could. I could still not take in the numbers of people congregating. The flashguns and the clicking of shutters rattled through the air again as a prison van pulled up outside. It turned into the alley adjacent to the parlour . . . all eyes were on it, but no one emerged. God knows how many rolls of film were wasted in those few seconds. There was confusion until a dark Peugeot pulled up with Reg handcuffed to a well-dressed screw in the back. He was led quickly and quietly into English's as the crowd cheered. The authorities obviously wanted to get him in unnoticed, which was an impossible job. Reg Kray was back in the East of London once more.

We managed to get into the funeral parlour after around fifteen minutes of uncertainty and were shown to the room set aside for friends and relatives. A few familiar faces had already arrived in the shape of Frankie Fraser, Tony Lambrianou, Charlie Richardson and, of course, Charlie Kray. I also saw Alan and Janet Alsop – we were now good friends after sharing visits to Reg. I introduced them to Ray and Mickey, before I beckoned one of the funeral directors over. I asked him to tell Reg that I had arrived and within a few minutes the director reappeared and took me to see him. I was led down a small corridor to an old oak-panelled door on the left-hand side. He pushed the door open and said, "You can take as long as you like, sir."

My jaw dropped. Instead of seeing Reg, I was now alone in the room with Ron's body in the coffin. I looked back and the door closed behind me. It was no mistake. He was in a large oak coffin, his hair was swept back and immaculate, as usual. He was dressed in a crisp white shirt and silk tie. Even in death, I thought to myself, he looked dignified and dapper – every inch the well-dressed gangster. I know undertakers are experts at making the dead look good, but all the strain and mental torture which had been etched on Ron's face in his latter days had disappeared without a trace. It was like he had been wearing a mask and now it had been removed. He was free at last; he was completely at peace. I did not feel sad at seeing him in the funeral parlour. I felt sad for the fact he had died in prison. I felt sad for Reg and for Charlie, but in a way happy for Ron. I put my hand on the coffin, said my own goodbye and left for the last time. The funeral director had been waiting for me outside and led me back to another door on the opposite side of the corridor. As he opened the door Charlie Kray spun round, "Steve, good to see you mate, thanks for coming down, it's a long journey." I shook his hand, and he pulled me towards him and embraced me. Standing next to him was Reg, still handcuffed to a middle-aged prison officer.

He stepped forward, bringing the officer with him, and put his arms around me as best he could, "Steve, thanks for coming. How are you?" He seemed calm, just as he had on the phone the last time we spoke, a lot calmer than I thought he would be. English's had put on a lavish buffet for Reg but food was the last thing on anyone's mind. Reg then patted me on the head (he was always amused at my lack of hair), and asked, "Who have you come with?" I explained that I had driven down with Ray and met up with Michael and that we were staying at his place. Quick as a flash he asked, "What about Bulla Ward? Is Bulla here? Is he coming?"

Bulla and Reg had fallen out in the 1960s. Bulla was a tough bloke and laughed off one of Reg's punches one night in the Regency. There were not many men who could withstand one of his punches, so to save face Reg took out a knife and carved Bulla's face up. He regretted the fall out and had asked me to get him there to make the peace. To be truthful, with all that was going on I had forgotten to ask Mickey whether he had managed to get in touch with Reg's old mate, and whether he would be attending the funeral to pay his last respects. Mickey had claimed to know him, and had tried in vain to contact him before the funeral. I had tried as well but to no avail.

Thinking quickly I replied, "He'll be here Reg, paying his respects. Reg, I know he will." Reg smiled and then asked, "Has he forgiven me?" I didn't quite know what to say. "Yes, Reg, he's forgiven you." What else could I say on the day of his brother's funeral? "Good, good. Well thanks for coming Steve, I'd like you to go and see Ron now. I'll be in touch. In fact, you ring me later tonight, I'll let the staff know you are going to call, take care and God bless. Thanks again for coming."

He kissed me on both cheeks and embraced me. It was quite a moment, something I will never forget. Charlie repeated the farewell, saying, "I'll see you for a drink later on, Steve." The same funeral director was waiting for me outside the door, and began to lead me down to see Ron's body. "No, it's okay mate, I've already seen him," I said. He apologized before taking me back to rejoin Ray and Michael in the friends and relatives room. I think they had felt a bit out of place standing alone. I told them that I had been with Reg and Charlie and had been taken to see Ron. It was then that the whole emotion of the day hit me. I had always wanted to see the Kray brothers together, but not like this. I wiped a tear from my eye as we waited for others to pay their final respects to "The Colonel", and express their sympathies to his brothers.

By now Dave was close to having a blue fit. "I'm fighting a losing battle. I've got old blokes trying to get in here, saying they are old friends of Ron, Reg, Charlie and any old uncle you can think of. I can't let everyone in, for God's sake." I didn't envy his job one bit, but I knew that if anyone could pull off the biggest organized funeral since Winston Churchill's, then he could. Once everyone had paid their respects, the wreaths were loaded on to the horse-drawn carriage and the twenty-two limousines, which were following behind in procession. The horses were black and beautifully dressed with long black plumes protruding from their heads. We were ushered from the parlour and as we made our way outside the flashing from the cameras dazzled us once more. There was pandemonium outside. Things were beginning to happen. Dave told me to make sure I got into a car . . . it didn't matter which one. We made our way down to the eighth car; a black, six-seater, top-of-the-range limo. No expense was spared. The cars were immaculate inside and out, and each one was decked with floral tributes (our wreath remained with Reg's tribute alongside Ron's coffin throughout the day, and could be seen clearly in photographs in most national newspapers the next day). Inside our car were Ray, Michael, Janet and Alan Alsop and me. The driver started the engine and with the rest of the procession we were off on our long journey, first to St Matthew's Church in Bethnal Green, and then on to the Kray family plot in Chingford Mount Cemetery, Essex, on the outskirts of London.

It was an unforgettable journey. We had only to travel approximately three-quarters of a mile from the parlour to the church, but it took over forty-five minutes. The crowds of people were ten deep, all leaning and peering over metal fences, which had been put up by the police. I stared out at all the people. It was the sort of mania that's normally reserved for rock stars or movie idols . . . certainly not the sort of admiration the authorities would expect the public to bestow upon a notorious murderer. Cries of "We love you" and "Good on you, Ron" could be heard, whilst in the distance the clip-clop of the horses' hooves weaved their way to our first port of call. I wonder what was going through Reg's mind as we passed along roads and streets that he had not seen for the best part of twenty-five years, and how he would feel as he passed along the street where he and Ron once lived. As we neared the church, I caught a glimpse of Patsy Palmer (Bianca from the BBC soap "Eastenders") paying her respects. The East End of London had changed so much since Reg had been taken away from it, and as we finally reached St Matthew's I promised myself I would ask him how he felt about what he has seen. The scene when we reached the church was unbelievable. It was bedlam . . . simple as that. Roughly 1,200 people had gathered outside the church gates and many were chanting, "Free Reg Kray. Free Reg Kray!"

I led the occupants of our car towards the church doors. Reg had arrived about two minutes before us and was already inside. At the doors the orderly queuing system for friends and relatives had been reduced to a free-for-all. At one stage it looked like we would not get in. There was a public address system set up for those outside to hear the service, but I did not want to have travelled all that way to be stuck outside. I noticed the funeral director and luckily he remembered me . . . he ushered the five of us to the front of the crowd and into the church. The pews at the back of the church were all that was left, but I saw Dave and he waved me over.

The coffin was carried into the church by Johnny Nash from north London, Teddy Dennis from the west, Charlie Kray from the east and Freddie Foreman from the south.

Close friend Laurie O'Leary also helped take the coffin in. Frankie Fraser had originally been asked but felt his height might be a hindrance. Frank Sinatra's "My Way" played as the coffin was placed alongside Reg. The atmosphere was tense as the service began, the smell of incense hanging heavily in the air. Reg, Charlie and Dave had masterminded the day's events to Ron's specifications and it was running like clockwork. Throughout the service Reg remained handcuffed to the officer. It did not seem to bother him too much. The officer was just there with him as opposed to trying to be heavy-handed. Every so often Reg would place his free hand on top of the coffin in a moving display of affection. But why handcuff a man who had no intention of escaping? Why humiliate him? Was it a political statement by the Home Office that this man would never be free? Whatever the reasoning, to me it was inhumane. Okay, the officer was just doing a job . . . but if they wanted to they could have handled the situation differently and let him mourn without being chained to someone.

Sue McGibbon read out messages and telegrams from well-wishers. She also read out a message from Reg. It went, "My brother Ron is now free and at peace. Ron had great humour, a vicious temper, was kind and generous. He did it all his way, but above all he was a man, that's how I will always remember my twin brother Ron."

As the service ended, Ron's coffin was carried out to Whitney Houston's song "I Will Always Love You". I don't think there was a dry eye to be seen in the rows and rows of hard men. As Reg left the church he winked at our group . . . he was bearing up. It was bedlam once more as we made our way back to the car. The five of us held on to each other as we made our way through the swaying masses. It was too easy to get split up as journalists, television and radio interviewers threw questions at us. I was not interested in commenting, not today of all days. But I noticed a few others such as Patsy Manning, a close friend of the family, were willing to stop for a chat.

When we eventually made it back to the car, our driver was a little stressed, to say the least. Someone had climbed into our car and refused to move. The driver had tried to explain to him that he had the wrong car, but he would not have it. After a quiet word in his "shell-like" he left to find another car and more people to annoy. Drama over, the driver started our six-mile journey to Chingford Cemetery . . . take two . . . enter nutcase, door left. The front passenger door was pulled open and in stepped a middle-aged woman who was madder than a coach load of hatters at a magic mushroom convention. Her name was Georgina and she was armed with valium in one pocket and a half bottle of whiskey in the other (for Reg apparently). She told us a tale of woe – she was meant to marry Ron before he died and told us a few other things I can't remember. The driver looked back for some kind of assistance, but as the procession of cars had already started to move, I told him to drive on. We would have to take the unwanted passenger with us. As the car pulled away we all exchanged anxious glances in the back of the car as Georgina said, "We were going to have kids you know." This was going to be a very long six miles indeed.

This gave me another excuse to just sit back and watch the crowds. Young people, old people, hundreds upon hundreds had gathered just to catch a glimpse of the brothers. There were many memorable sights throughout the day from that limo rear window, but nothing more memorable that the sight that greeted us at the Bow Flyover. Construction work was taking place, yet the whole workforce had downed tools and were standing in a line by the roadside, hard hats off and heads bowed . . . it was one hell of a sight. I can only imagine how Reg and Charlie must have felt. As we reached Chingford, it had taken one-and-a-half hours to travel six miles, though with Georgina in the front, it felt like one-and-a-half days.

The horses pulling Ron's hearse had struggled up the steep bank leading to the cemetery gates and we followed them in. By now we were almost used to the strobe-effect lighting from the constant photographers and the pushing and pulling of the crowds. As we followed the road to the family plot, our hitchhiker decided it would be a good idea to walk the rest of the way. There were no arguments from any of us. The surrounding fence to the cemetery had a lot of holes in it and I was shocked to see people, many of them kids, clambering through. If ordinary people had made it to the graveside, we might not gain our place next to the family. I need not have worried. There were so many people around the grave, but they all kept a respectful distance as Reg first laid flowers on his mother's and father's graves, and then his wife's. He paused a little longer there, his face full of sorrow and regret.

Just then I felt a hand on my shoulder, it was Dave Courtney looking less flustered than he was earlier outside the funeral parlour. He asked me to look after Charlie for the rest of the day and make sure he wasn't hassled by anyone. I told him I'd be honoured.

We made our way to where the family had gathered directly behind Charlie and Reg. There was a tremendous feeling of grief . . . then looking around I began to wonder. It seemed a lot of people were there out of curiosity or to somehow enhance their status from their association. There were "tourists" – people just there to be part of it all – staring at Reg all the time, studying his face for reactions and to witness the London gangland boss cry. As the vicar read the last rites and Ron's body was finally laid to rest the cameras flashed en masse for the last time. Ron Kray was the centre of the world's attention again, even in death. He would have loved it. Reg threw the first piece of soil down on to the coffin and then arose, and then, one by one, we all did the same. Reg then turned, embracing Charlie, shook hands with Freddie Foreman and then out of the blue turned around to me and said, "Thanks for coming, Steve." He stretched out his hand and I grabbed it. This time it was my grip that was the strongest. Reg was finally drained of all energy. "I'll be in touch, Reg," I said. With that he was led away, pausing to say some more goodbyes.

As Reg left I stared in disbelief at people, who will remain nameless, photographing the activities at the graveside. A number of people whom I used to respect lost it that day. After one last glance at Ron's grave, we all returned to our limo. All of the wreaths lined the pathway to the grave, hundreds of them, and we paused to read as many as we could. We finally found our wreath, lying alongside Reg's. To me it symbolized how close I had become to the Kray family and was glad to see it was still next to Reg's.

The driver had been told our destination . . . the Guv'nor's public house was the venue of the wake. Without the lovely Georgina, our journey seemed to be quicker and we arrived at the wake within twenty minutes. There were already quite a few people in there, and I could see that it was soon going to be packed out. It was a typical London boozer – dim, cramped, but with wet beer and good conversation. Already there were people such as Frankie Fraser, Freddie Foreman, Charlie and his son Gary, Tony Lambrianou, Dave Courtney and, of course, Lenny McLean.

Lenny was still known as the Guv'nor of London and when I met him again at the wake I did not need to introduce myself. Lenny was the sort of bloke who would remember a name and it's always good when that happens. I never got the chance to meet up with him again before his untimely death in 1998, but followed his acting career with great admiration. The man was a real gent, a legend and someone who I was proud to call my friend.

Tony Lambrianou was a member of the Kray firm and was one of the few that stood by the twins, receiving twenty years as his "reward". I'd read his book *Inside the Firm* and got on well with him. This was the first time I had met Tony . . . soon after he introduced me to Freddie Foreman and before long I was talking with Frankie Fraser, Charlie Kray, Freddie and Tony about Ron, Reg and their memories of the old days.

Charlie Kray was the perfect host as usual, smiling and chatting to everyone who was there and thanking them for coming.

He told me it had been a great send off for his brother and that he would have loved it. As we spoke, the early evening news appeared on the large television screens. A hush fell upon the room as people watched the first pictures from the funeral. The cameras only proved what I had already thought – that Ron Kray had received a funeral normally reserved for royalty. Thinking of Charlie's words . . . it was true, he would have loved it. It was the best send off a man could ask for. There were tributes and messages from rock stars, TV stars and movie icons. The streets were full of mourners and well-wishers, people who were just dumbstruck by the whole thing, all his friends and media people from anywhere you care to mention. It was the ultimate two-fingered gesture to the authorities as Ron had the popularity to bring the nation's capital to a standstill.

As the night progressed I had my photo taken a few times, but did not really consider it appropriate at a wake. Lenny had called me over for one and there were others taken as well. I bumped into Tony Lambrianou again as he was about to leave. We wanted to make sure we kept in touch so we exchanged numbers and he promised that he would call.

By the time I had finished talking, Michael had left, Ray was bored to tears and Georgina had blagged her way in. It was late now so we had one last drink and decided to return to Newcastle. We made it back early the next day and I went straight to bed as soon as I got home. Just as I was drifting off, the phone rang – it was Reg. I was surprised but pleased to hear from him in such short space of time.

"Hello, Steve, I'm just ringing to thank you for coming down to the funeral. I was in a daze for most of the day to be honest, but I'm pleased it went well. Anyway was Bulla Ward there? He was, wasn't he? Bring him to see me, OK? My units are running out, I'll have to go. God bless."

He did not give me the chance to answer. I decided to leave it at that. He may have known that Bulla wasn't there when I told him . . . or knew he wouldn't turn up. He probably decided to leave it until the next day. I knew Reg had been through a lot lately and I had much sympathy for him. At least to hear him like this on the phone, I knew he was getting back to his old self. I'd smile to myself after such "conversations" . . . we were similar in some respects. We were both stubborn. It was as if we could not let the other have the final word on particular issues. I think he knew that I would not be enquiring about Bulla again – he just needed to make his point.

Charlie had been moved again, this time to Parkhurst Prison. He had been in Frankland prior to this and had been moved because he was suffering from chest pains and on visits he had been struggling to find his breath. He had been happy at Frankland and had made a lot of friends there through me.

The Home Office decided that Parkhurst on the Isle of Wight was the best place for him, as it was in close proximity to St Mary's Hospital. He was taken down from the high-risk prisoner status to Category B so his health could be monitored if need be. I wrote to Charlie as soon as I heard he had been moved, just to let him know that I knew his whereabouts and was thinking of him. He phoned me to let me know he was okay and that he appreciated everything that I had done for him during his stay in Frankland.

He finished by saying that he would be in touch soon, and that he would sort out a visitor form for me in the next few weeks. This was the last time I spoke to him. Charlie's health worsened further . . . when the Home Office gave permission for Reg to visit him I knew that Charlie's days were numbered.

On 4 April 2000, Charles James Kray passed away, with Diane and Reg at his bedside. He had heart problems which developed into pneumonia. He was weak and physically frail. He was seventy-three years old. Reg was devastated, he later told me that he was so overcome with guilt that he begged Charlie for forgiveness on his visit. I called Roberta to pass on my condolences and would have to sort out the arrangements for travelling down to London for what would surely be another big send off.

Ray Cann and Graham Borthwick telephoned and along with Ian Freeman we made arrangements to travel down.

I arranged the wreath for the funeral once again through Fitzy and Colly. It was in the shape of a diamond and had the work "geezer" underneath it. The local papers were on hand to get some shots of us picking up the wreath and ran a story on it. Graham drove us down to Dave Courtney's in Plumstead, south London, the night before.

There was something else on my mind other than the funeral as we made our way down; the woman from Sheffield I had a previous relationship with. She was now with someone else, a man I had met many times before and had a lot of respect for. She told her new man that I had beaten and robbed her, and that I called him an old dinosaur and that I said he was past his "sell by date". I had to laugh; this was like schoolboy stuff, but in the whole scheme of things she was trying to ruin my reputation and get me beaten up in the process. Her new man was a very well known face in London – a hard man with a fierce reputation. Through third parties I had heard threats were being made and I took them seriously. I had to. I was concerned that the matters were getting out of hand. She was telling all sorts of lies but I was powerless to shut her up. I was not frightened, but knew I would have to be a little more cautious on my trips to London, starting with the funeral. As if there wasn't enough to do and think about on a day like this, now it would be impossible for me to relax. I was concerned about a confrontation at my friend's funeral. I would keep a safe distance from him and hope he would soon see what she was doing.

The funeral had been delayed but with Reg making the arrangements you could guarantee that the day itself would run like clockwork. It was going to be a long day. I only managed a couple of hours' sleep the night before at Dave Courtney's before I was awoken with a cup of tea and a cockney, "Whey aye man ye bugger ye know!" . . . Dave had been practising his Geordie accent. Dave explained that the lads were all meeting here at 8.30 a.m. He had that sparkle in his eye so I knew he had something up his sleeve. I was sure we would all know in time. By 9 a.m. the rest of the lads were all suited and booted and ready to go.

Dave let us have his white Rolls-Royce, with his personalized number plate "BADBOY", for the day while he went with Brendan and Seymore in his new Jag. Mad Pete had the privilege of driving Dave's Roller, while Graham, Ray, Ian and myself were his passengers. Nine-thirty struck on the bright, spring, south London morning and right on cue Dave's well-rehearsed plan came into effect. The Satan's Slaves are a motorbike gang and have bases up and down the country, and all over the world. Dave knew a lot of the members of the various chapters and built up some strong friendships with them. He had arranged for six of their top men to ride as outriders to our convoy of cars, making sure we all had a safe journey all the way to Bethnal Green and English's Funeral Parlour once again.

It was a strange feeling this time round for me. Five years ago, when Ron had died, I had been naive and was still quite new to this way of life, and still meeting people and finding my feet, I suppose. Back then, if I'm honest, I was still getting a buzz from it. Now though, I felt sadness for Reg. He had seen this happen to both his brothers and each time he was the centre of attention. I never thought this was fair. It was also sad that Charlie had died a prisoner and not a free man. Regardless of his crime and his sentence – being in prison at that age ground him down immediately.

With Charlie there was still the spectacle of it being a Kray funeral. Charlie was a well-loved and respected bloke; he was also well known for his love of parties and good times: Champagne Charlie. Reg's popularity was evident at the funeral. All the up-and-coming hard men were there, the top boys from each town and city . . . something like this was an opportunity to get their name and face known; a perfect chance to gain notoriety, not criticism. I had been there, done it, and printed and sold the T-shirts. I had lived it. I had not only met the three brothers, I had become friends with them and stood by them through the years.

We reached Bethnal Green in good time with our escorts doing us proud, much to the bemusement of other traffic and the local constabulary. Outside the parlour were a lot of familiar faces, and I introduced Ray, Graham and Ian to Bruce Reynolds, Frankie Fraser, Freddie Foreman, Tony Lambrianou, Charlie Richardson and a few of the other lesser known faces. Once we had shook hands with the chaps, we put our wreaths in place and went for a drink. I had a tip-off that because of "that" woman from Sheffield, I would not be welcome at the church. Apparently she knew the people responsible for security and I would not be allowed in. I told the chaps that I would go to the church alone, but they wouldn't have it. If we were going then it was all for one and one for all. I appreciated their solidarity. We finished our drinks and made our way back out to our cars, only to be stopped in our tracks by an announcement on a megaphone by the police officer in charge. There was a gas leak on Bethnal Green Road and he wanted to limit the traffic travelling to the church by car. We would have to walk the half mile or so there and back. It was a sunny day so there was little or no complaint. We looked like a mini army, all suited and booted and crombied up, walking through the heart of East London with Dave Courtney leading the assault with what he refers to as his "Knights of the Round Table". Inspired by his fascination with King Arthur, the Knights, of whom I am proud to be one, are his best friends from different parts of the country. His house is based on Castle Camelot, and he even has the moat and the drawbridge. He has twelve seats at the round table in his dining room.

We had not been walking long and could see the church in our sights when it happened, taking us all by surprise. He had either been following us, or lying in wait for some time, silently . . . then he attacked. A Yorkshire terrier jumped out from nowhere and went straight for Ray, attempting to chew his leg off. It lightened the moment as we made our way through the already swelling crowds. Dave got us through the gates and we began to make our way past the flashing lights of the press and up the steps to the church. I saw Rob Davis on the door. I knew him well and had a lot of time for him. He knew about the "situation" I had found myself in and we were both keen to avoid any fuss. I was there simply to pay my respects. Reg had not entered the argument one way or the other, so Rob was able to make an on-the-spot decision. The church was packed to the rafters and I stood at the back of the church with Dave and Ray as I had done five years earlier for Ron. Because the church was so packed and due to the circumstances I did not get a chance to speak to Reg and let him know I was there. He was on his own now and I wanted him to know I was there and thinking of him. My mind was soon put at ease though. Ray handed me an order of service and said, "Reg thanks us for coming down." Ray had managed to slip to the front to let him know we were there. Reg shook Ray's hand, hugged him and told him to tell me thanks. I smiled inside. He knew we were there and that meant a lot to me. He knew he had friends there. We may not have been in touch so often by this time, but he knew. We were still close. The service was very much like his brother's, with the hymns "Morning Has Broken" and "Fight the Good Fight", and there were readings from Sue McGibbon and Freddie Foreman's son, Jamie. Charlie had a lot of supporters.

Charlie's body was carried from the church to Shirley Bassey's "As Long As He Needs Me" and just like the last time, all eyes were on Reg to study his reactions. We formed a line of honour outside the church as Charlie's coffin was placed back in the traditional hearse for his journey back to the family plot in Chingford, Essex. We returned to our cars and once our escorts gave us the nod we were off. Making our way to Chingford rather than following the procession of cars, we arrived in good time and took our place on a hill overlooking the graveside waiting for Reg and Roberta to arrive. Reg had seen his mother and two brothers buried while serving his time. At each one of them he'd been handcuffed to an officer . . . and each one was getting harder for him to bare. I would have thought that a few allowances could have been made for this funeral, but obviously the law is the law.

As Charlie was lowered into the ground I felt a lump in my throat. I'd had a lot of good laughs with Charlie, as I had at his trial. He was the perfect host and a gentleman, and I knew I would certainly miss him. I felt close to him because we had socialized on many occasions. It wasn't just prison visits for a few hours at a time, it was a friendship of talking on the phone and meeting up and going out together . . . and he was the best there was for a night out. Charlie was the type who would do anything for a friend. He has a tremendous lust for life and to see him die in such circumstances left a bitter taste. Everyone was outraged that he was put in prison again but realizing just how little time he had left made it worse. Our floral tribute had been the perfect words to describe him: Diamond Geezer.

As the crowds of onlookers dispersed, a man shouted out, "Three cheers for Reg Kray . . . hip . . . hip." The crowd reacted accordingly. With that, Reg shook the hands of those around him, kissed Roberta and was whisked away. That night we watched the funeral coverage on TV, and then I showed the lads around the West End as Dave and Jenny had a prior engagement at a boxing event with Ian Freeman.

Travelling back the next day I picked up the papers to see all the coverage of the funeral. As with Ron, it had taken some time for the realization to sink in. Charles James Kray was dead. When you see it in the papers and on TV like that, that's when you know it happened. On the day it's just like you are on autopilot, like it is going on but not actually real. When you see yourself and friends in that third-person situation in the media, then you know you were there and you know it did happen. The headline of one paper proclaimed, "Then There Was One" – the Krays were dying one by one, and now Reg was the last of the family line.

I had to work that night and, because of the traffic, I didn't have time to go home to rest or change clothes. I was shattered. When I finished and could finally get home I had a message from Reg waiting for me. "Hello, Steve, Reg Kray speaking. Thank you and thank your friends for taking the time to come down south to Charlie's funeral. You are a good friend. I'll ring another time, God bless." I played the message over a few times and I admit I shed a few tears. For all his faults, this man had to cope with his entire family dying whilst he was in prison. He had to deal with the despair, anguish and torment that the death of a loved one brings but he had to deal with it under different circumstances to most others. There was the build up in the newspapers as a Kray death looked imminent. Then he had to make all the arrangements and to deal with the pressures of all the media attention – being in the spotlight throughout the service only to be taken straight back immediately afterwards. Prison can be a lonely enough place, but now he really was alone. It showed more than anything how strong his character was and I, for one, hoped that he had enough fight left in him to beat the system, gain parole and spend at least a few years of freedom in the arms of the woman he truly loved.

In the year 2000, Reg had his parole hearing. To be fair, for all Roberta's hard work I could only see Reg becoming de-categorized and not on a release programme. A lot of stories had circulated about Reg's health, and I had been asked numerous times by my friends in the media to confirm he was fit and well. As far as I was concerned there were no problems. You can't always believe what you read in the papers, but there had been a lot of coverage over the last year and half of Reg's frequent trips to the hospital wings at both Blundeston and Wayland prisons were with what were described as irregular stomach complaints. Some reports suggested ulcers, others possible cancer. Reg, although admitting to pains, assured us all that it was nothing to worry about and that he had faith in the doctors he had been dealing with.

I wasn't convinced. In April, at Charlie's funeral, Reg had looked pale and it was quite noticeable that he had lost weight. A lot of observers had put this down to the worry and stress that he had endured with Charlie's illness and his parole board hearing. Our worst fears were confirmed when in September it was announced that he had been admitted to hospital in Norwich for tests. The reports at first were a little unclear and then Roberta dropped the bombshell . . . Reg had undergone exploratory surgery and a cancer had been detected. He had only weeks to live. I sat and watched the story break on the lunchtime news and still couldn't believe what I was hearing. As I watched and was taking it in, journalists started phoning me wanting some reaction to the story. I told them I was shell-shocked and that the Home Secretary should show immediate compassion and release Reg so that he could at least taste freedom before he passed away. Reg's solicitors Mark Goldstein and Trevor Lynn reiterated what I had said when they were interviewed on later bulletins. The Sunday papers carried haunting images of a frail Reg lying in his hospital bed with tubes leading from his torso, his breathing aided by an oxygen mask. It was a sad picture to have to look at. He looked very ill. He *was* very ill. He was dying and yet he was still considered to be a danger to society.

How could a Home Secretary justifiably keep this man incarcerated? My comments were carried in the *Sunday People* where I was named as Reg's surrogate son, which I found quite amusing. Pictures of Reg were all over the papers as the "exclusive" stories began to break. They were a far cry from the Reg Kray that the public remembered, which is why I thought that they would probably help his cause for support. I'd sent him a card, as had Ray, who was quite keen to visit him. I was not so sure. I had distanced myself so much from Reg in recent months I felt almost hypercritical, or like a ghoul wanting to see the last dying Kray on his deathbed. I decided against it. It would be good to catch up with Reg and see him one last time but I'd moved on since those early days. The last time I'd seen him was at Charlie's funeral. I still thought of him as a good friend – it's not that we had a falling out or decided not to speak; it's just that we had drifted apart over the years. To rekindle the past just seemed false to me. We had the sort of relationship now where we both knew we supported each other regardless of whether we were in constant contact or not.

I sent him a letter wishing him well and expressing my hope that both he and Roberta could enjoy what little time they had together. I didn't know what else to say. Have you ever tried writing a letter to someone who is dying? It's not easy.

Jack Straw, the Labour government's Home Secretary, bowed to public pressure and released Reg on compassionate grounds a few days later. But, although a free man, Reg was confined to a room in the hospital which was smaller than his prison cell in Wayland. Basically, the world knew he was dying and the government decided to let him die on the outside. The cruel irony is that he could never be free; he couldn't go out and enjoy a walk or do something he'd been longing to do for thirty years. Nevertheless, Reg was delighted at his "release" and was said to be celebrating with a bottle of Moet and some Henry Winterman cigars. Good on him, he deserved it. I phoned the hospital and left a message for him . . . I left my number and hoped now that I could speak to him for the last time.

Not a day passed without a new Kray "exclusive" in the newspapers. The tabloids in particular seemed to love the fact that the last of the Krays was dying. It was sensational in their eyes . . . Reg was a ready-made story they couldn't wait to exploit. It was sick fascination, which I found very disturbing. One particular paper carried its stories under a subheading "Death of a Gangster". Where is the respect or the dignity in that, I ask you? I suppose a lot of people would say that Reg brought it upon himself by courting the press for years, but everyone should be entitled to privacy in their dying days. I had still not spoken to Reg by the time he was considered fit enough to leave his sickbed in Norwich hospital. He was moved to a honeymoon suite in the Town House Hotel in Norwich. The room, as you would expect, was beautifully decorated with a four-poster bed and an idyllic view of the river and the surrounding countryside. It had always been Reg's wish to have a house in the country where he would be able to take long walks and enjoy the simple things in life. This hotel room would be as close as he would get to realizing this dream. It may have come at the wrong time for him but at least he was out of prison.

His condition had worsened, and as each day passed he was visited by many of his old gangland associates as well as old enemies to make their peace. Laurie O'Leary, his good friend and Kray biographer, Joe Pyle, Freddie Foreman and Frankie Fraser all paid him a visit. Reports that Reg had only six months to live were circulated, but they turned out to be wrong. I tried to contact Reg one last time by leaving a message and my telephone number with the girl on the reception at the hotel. She let me down. The message, I later learned, was not passed on, just like my other one at the hospital. Neither Reg nor Roberta was aware that I tried to contact them. The news the next day came as no great shock or surprise. On Sunday, 1 October 2000, Reg Kray, the last of the notorious Kray brothers, died aged sixty-six. Amongst those at his bedside were Freddie Foreman, Joe Pyle, Johnny Nash and Roberta. Over the next few days there were yet more rumours, this time surrounding the funeral arrangements.

The lead up to the funeral was not the set of circumstances Reg would have wanted. Some of the old chaps were adamant that Reg's dying wish was that gangland figures should be pallbearers and that his send off was to be a mirror image to Ron's. Roberta maintained a dignified silence throughout this period, refusing to be drawn into any dispute. Reg's body was taken back to Bethnal Green in prepa-ration for the funeral with Wednesday 11 October to be the day he'd be laid to rest.

The pallbearers were not to be old gangland chaps but people who Reg had grown close to through his years of imprisonment. Close friend and former cellmate Bradley Allardyce, music promoter Bill Curbishley, and Tony Mortimer, singer and songwriter from the former teen band, East 17. They had already been asked and had agreed to carry the coffin, with others to be confirmed. There would only be a handful of limos for very close friends and what was left of the family. Others would have to make their own arrangements. There was another direct snub to the old school who still maintained that it wasn't what Reg wanted. It's something I can't comment on but from what I understand Roberta was steering him away from the gangland to have the normal life he'd wanted for so many years. In fairness to the chaps, Reg was part of gangland and he always would be. They wanted to give him the best send off possible. I honestly don't know what Reg had wanted, but it would not have been for his friends and wife to start squabbling. It was appropriate that the wishes of his wife were respected.

I decided to travel down to London on the 6 a.m. train, and

reached King's Cross just after 9 a.m. I made my way to Bethnal Green via the Underground. It's hard to describe my feelings as I travelled. I'd had three hours on the train to do my thinking and I'd done a lot more prior to that. It bothered me that it had to end like this; that I would be attending just like every other "civvy". It bothered me that I was not part of it, not seeing friends and bothered by possible rumours that people may have heard that this was the case. Up and out of the station I strolled past the Bind Beggar. I stopped and paused to look at it for a second . . . the place where Ron had shot George Cornell. It felt strange. It was the first killing that led to their downfall . . . Ron had described it to me. It all seemed like a lifetime ago now.

I continued past it and reached Bethnal Green Road just after 10 a.m. I was dressed smart but casual, and had decided against a wreath. I simply wanted to pay my respects and be seen at the funeral to show any of the chaps that doubted my side of the story. I popped into a cafe for some much-needed breakfast and flicked through the *East London Advertiser*, which carried an eight-page pull-out on the East End's most notorious family. From there it was on to English's Funeral Parlour. It was unusually quiet. The faces that I was expecting to see were not there. Roberta seemed to have got her wish; the likes of Freddie Foreman and Tony Lambrianou were conspicuous by their absence. Frankie Fraser was there, as was former train-robber Bruce Reynolds with his son Nick. Billy Murray from the TV show *The Bill* was the only "celebrity" on show.

The service was at St Matthew's as it had been for his brothers. I shook hands with a few of the chaps and watched as Reg's coffin was loaded into the hearse. I had decided to walk alongside Reg to the church, quite an emotional journey as the coffin stopped at 178 Vallance Road for the last time. Although the crowds were nowhere near the same in numbers as when Ron and Charlie had been buried, they were still big enough to cause a lot of the mourners to be delayed and to miss the start of the service. It seemed to be a different affair than anyone was expecting. The church was still packed to the rafters as the vicar told of how Reg had turned to God, and the hymns which had been recited at the other two funerals were given an airing again. There was a feeling of déjà vu, maybe because it had only been a few months since Charlie had died. There were a lot of strangers in the church, which I put down to the fact that the security had failed miserably in getting the right people in. It was a lot different to how Dave had run things in 1995. Outside the church I bumped into Bruce and Nick Reynolds again. They were with Andy Jones, curator of the Crime Through Time Museum in Gloucester, and offered me a lift to the cemetery. The lift turned out to be in a beautiful red Bentley which had one previous owner; none other than Mr Terry "Eurovision" Wogan.

The journey to the cemetery was a long one. The police seemed intent in separating the cars and we ended up in a traffic jam and arrived at the cemetery just after the hearse. Outside the big gates there were people – friends of Reg – being held back by police officers. Obviously the police were only acting on instructions, but whose instructions remains a mystery to this day. To not let all his friends in seemed a bit harsh to me. I decided to go it alone and thanked Bruce, Nick and Andy for the lift and we promised to keep in touch. Both Bruce and Nick were keen to come to Newcastle when they released their books later in the year, and I told them I would only be too pleased to help them with any publicity.

As the gates finally opened, the crowd of mourners surged forward and I caught a glimpse of a bald head and cigar . . . there was only one person it could be. It was Dave Courtney with the boys; Ray, Ian, Seymour, Brendan, Christian, Wish, Welsh Bernie, Scouse John, Bulldog, Rob, Marcus, Piers and Big John. I shook hands and embraced all the lads. They were pleased to see I had not lost my bottle following the threats from my ex's boyfriend. We made our way towards the Kray plot, and we waited on the hillside overlooking the grave. Reg was carried to his final resting place as we gathered. The vicar performed the last rites and the last of the Krays was lowered down into his grave. With that, Roberta and the other close family said their thanks to those around them and they were gone. It was all very different. I think the lack of "spectators" was down to the fact that there was not another Kray brother to look at. Reg was always a crowd-puller at the other funerals just because he was Reg Kray and people wanted to say they had seen him. As far as friends go, it was apparent that there had been a falling out of some sort. Some of them had decided to stay clear, which must have been a tough decision to make. Looking around, there were plenty of new faces on the scene, just like the last two.

The wake was to be held in the heart of the East End. I decided not to push my luck and decided to travel in style with Dave and the lads in a couple of hired vintage cars back to the boozer in south London to give the last of the Krays a good old send off. My mate Gary, who made cash as a lookalike of Jaws from the Bond films, made the journey back to Newcastle with me later that night. I finished my day with a couple of swift ones on Newcastle's Quayside. I'd distanced myself purposefully to avoid a scene at my old friend's funeral. The feud with the gangland figure passed and on a later trip to London we shook hands and left the past behind us.

My Kray connection has now died along with the last brother. We had our my ups and downs, just like any friendship, but I know they all died knowing they had me as a friend. That meant a lot to me. The friends I made along the way remain friends today and I am privileged to have good memories of all three of the Kray brothers. I was proud to be their Geordie connection.

JAKE LAMOTTA
(USA)

Boxer

Introducing . . . Jake LaMotta

O NE THING IS for sure, boxer "Raging Bull" Jake LaMotta was one seriously hard bastard. In this chapter, writer Robert MacGowan gives his personal impressions of a short period in Jake's life.

Born 10 July 1921 in the Bronx, New York, Giacobbe LaMotta, better known as Jake LaMotta, is an Italian-American former boxing world middleweight champion and was the first man to beat Sugar Ray Robinson in his career, knocking him down in the first round.

LaMotta turned professional at the age of nineteen and at the end of his career compiled a record of eighty-three wins and four draws, with thirty wins by way of knockout. He won the world title in 1949 in Detroit against Frenchman Marcel Cerdan. LaMotta met two challengers, Tiberio Mitri and Laurent Dauthuille, and beat them, and then he was challenged again by Sugar Ray Robinson. The fight became known as boxing's version of the St Valentine's Day Massacre as it was held on 14 February 1951 and in the sixth round LaMotta suffered numerous sickening blows to the head. Commentators could be heard saying, "No man can take this kind of punishment!" But LaMotta did not go down. Robinson won by a technical knockout in the thirteenth round.

In the mid 1950s, LaMotta suffered from a boxing injury and took time off to recover. He was always interested in baseball and decided to form the Jake LaMotta All-Star team. After retirement from boxing LaMotta bought a few bars and became a stage actor. He appeared in over fifteen motion pictures, including *The Hustler* with Paul Newman.

RAGING BULL
By Robert MacGowan

On a stiflingly hot and humid day in the middle of July 1921, another little mouth to feed was born in Morris Park district of New York's infamous Bronx.

Little Giacobbe's first view of the world was a tenement apartment with no heating or air-conditioning and little else to make it a home. His life began in a tough area which was experiencing tough times and things were about to get a whole lot tougher. Within eight years the Great Depression would have all of America in its merciless grip and those that were poor before, like Giacobbe's family and neighbours, were suddenly much poorer.

It was a time when many entrepreneurial spirits dreamt up ever more creative and diverse ways of bringing a little extra money into the home but, try as he might, Giacobbe's father could never gather enough cash to feed, house or keep his family warm in winter, and so sank further into debt and desperation. He was a tough character though and did not give up on things easily, and this stubborn resilience certainly rubbed off on to his young son who, early in life, willingly accepted that he must do whatever he could to help support the family.

One particularly bleak day when mere survival fully occupied the thoughts of Giacobbe's parents, the peeling kitchen door creaked slowly open on to the stark and shabby room where they sat counting dimes and cents. They both glanced round absently and there stood their son with a fresh black eye, blood trickling from his nose and a lopsided grin on his little face. His mother looked at the blood spots on her linoleum floor, saw the buttons ripped from his only decent school shirt and burst into tears. His father rose to reprimand with a stern expression spreading across his swarthy countenance. But as he did so, Giacobbe opened his scuffed, grubby hand to reveal a small tangle of dollar notes. His parents stopped and stared – confused and fearful.

"Where didja get dat?" asked his father with foreboding.

"Have you stolen it?" asked his mother in a whisper.

"No, I won it!" replied the boy cheerfully.

"You won it?" she gasped. "You've been gambling?"

"No, I won it at fightin'."

"Fightin'?" demanded his astonished father.

"Fighting?" echoed his mother, her eyes drifting again to the pile of notes.

"Yeah, fightin'," continued Giacobbe, placing the money on the plastic kitchen table with the coinage already there.

"Who give you money for fightin'?"

"Dere was two older kids fightin' for money down under da bridge. It was all arranged and summa dere fadders were bettin' on who would win out."

His mother's hands flew to her face. "Never in this world!"

"Yep, so I challenged da winner and won all da dough!"

"My God," gasped his mother. "Madre mia."

"Jeez," added his father. "All da dough?"

After that Giacobbe's father took an active role in the organized scraps and made sure that his son's consistent winnings always went home in his own pocket to pay for food, rent and fuel.

"You know what?" he said to his son one day. "Giacobbe don't sound like no fighter's name. It's too Italian!"

Giacobbe watched him silently.

"I tink you should have a fightin' name. Tougher and more American soundin'."

His son remained silent, listening intently.

"Yeah, we'll shorten Giacobbe to, to . . . Jacob! No, Jake. Yeah, Jake. Your new fightin' name's gonna be Jake. Jake LaMotta."

And so the legend was born.

Fighting older, bigger opponents with longer reaches made Jake quick and ruthless. He always knew that he would have to take a few punches before he got in close enough to unload his own, and that when they did connect, every one must count. He learned how to hit hard and continually hustle forward to keep his adversary off balance, so that most of the punches coming his way did not land with their full force. When he did catch a shot, he rolled and swayed from the waist with it to further absorb and reduce its power. To conserve energy he did not move around on his feet very much, he simply shuffled forward, bobbing and weaving and taking as few punches as possible until he could unleash his own, and developed the classic style of exactly what he was – a rough, tough street-fighter. His effectiveness rapidly earned him local notoriety and he was coaxed into the amateur ring, where he clubbed down and cut through his opponents routinely.

In 1941, at the age of nineteen, he became a professional boxer and embarked on a career that would rescue his family and himself from life's doldrums, and make him world famous as he reached the very pinnacle of his chosen profession.

His "walk forward, take all and give more" style adapted well to the pro ranks and excited the fans, and soon earned him the ring name: Bronx Bull. Later, as his raw aggression carried him towards the world middleweight title, the weight division whose protagonists are known to be, at around 165 pounds, "light enough to move fast but heavy enough to hit hard", he became Jake LaMotta, the Raging Bull.

Jake never claimed to be an exceptional boxer in the classic sense; he was simply very good at taking whatever anybody had to throw at him and then bludgeoning them to defeat. This approach put him on a steady course for a world title shot but in those days and that part of the world, things were never quite so simple. In November 1947 Jake was "knocked out" by Billy Fox in a fight which was later investigated by commissioners who concluded that Jake had thrown the fight to gain favour with the New York Mafia, who then controlled much of American boxing. The mob then allowed his natural progression to continue unimpeded and less than two years later he entered the ring against the classy French-North African champion, Marcel Cerdan. Jake took the title after his rumbustious tactics caused a dislocation of Cerdan's shoulder during the contest and he was forced to retire. The ex-champion was well tipped to regain his crown but the rematch never took place, as Marcel was tragically killed in a plane crash.

LaMotta eventually admitted to "taking a dive" against Fox; it was the first and last time that Jake ever went down during a fight in his whole career. In subsequent writings he said that he lost the fight on purpose so the local Mafia could clean up on big betting odds against Fox, and he knew that he would never get an attempt at the world title without their compliance. He added, however, that losing to Fox was not as easy as he'd thought it would be and that at the start of the fight he moved around the ring pawing out a glove now and then, waiting for Billy to hit him with a punch that looked convincingly hard enough to knock him over. But that blow never came and Jake was worried that Billy was going to fall down first from one of his jabs. The resultant dive in the fourth round was not convincing, which led to the result being questioned both officially and unofficially for years afterwards.

Jake fought in the era when the middleweight ranks were ruled supremely and unquestioningly by the person who is still rated by most pugilistic aficionados as the best "pound-for-pound" boxer that has ever graced the roped square – the great "Sugar" Ray Robinson. Jake became the first man to defeat Robinson in a professional ring and disrupt his previously unbeaten string of over eighty fights, when he knocked him down and outpointed him over ten rounds in their second bout. Sugar Ray, however, was a seriously tough character as well as a brilliant boxer, and their subsequent rivalry and alternating quests for revenge took them into a total of six clashes with each other over several years. The other reason for the series was that Jake was one of very few opponents that could stretch Ray to a credible contest which would pull in the crowds. The sixth and final of their battles took place on 14 February 1951 and, considering the outcome, was perhaps unavoidably dubbed the "St Valentine's Day Massacre". After a tough struggle early in the fight it became obvious that Robinson was in better physical condition. Jake was always embroiled in some personal entanglement or other which distracted him from concentrating on giving his best in the ring, and Ray eventually took control. His lightning-fast punches thudded home into Jake's head and body and although Jake endeavoured to press home his forward march behind a prodding lead, he was gradually beaten back into defence. Near the end of the fight, during which both fighters shipped considerable punishment, almost every punch that Sugar Ray threw connected as Jake slowed noticeably. He retreated to the ropes and leaned on them for support as Ray pursued with murderous intent his anxiety to finish the contest, knowing that Jake was still dangerous even when hurt.

It should be remembered that an average professional boxer hits 50 to 75 per cent harder than an untrained "civilian" and Sugar Ray Robinson was light-years above average. He started whipping combinations in from all angles and Jake's head bobbed around on his shoulders as if it might detach at any moment and land in the time-keeper's lap. Some of his blood actually did. When Ray switched to the body, the thuds could be heard six rows back from ringside where the audience gasped in horror at the savage beating Jake was being subjected to. But he stood firm and took it all. He knew by now that he could not win and was too weak to even fight back or defend himself, so he hung on to the top rope for support and when Ray took a breather from trying to maim him, taunted through swollen, bloody lips, "Come on, Ray, you ain't tryin' hard enough. You can't put me down."

Ray restarted his assault with renewed vigour and Jake's legs twitched and trembled under the onslaught, but he did not go down. His immense strength and stubborn pride kept him on his feet until the referee mercifully, and not before time, ended the contest with Jake simply standing there like a human punchbag with his hands down by his sides. Jake's seconds led him to his corner but his still-intact pride did not allow him to stay there. He strutted across the canvas and again taunted the champion, "You couldn't put me down, Ray."

Ray looked round as if Jake was a madman let loose into society unexpectedly.

Jake's professional record shows 106 fights with eighty-three wins, only thirty of which were knockouts. It is the record of a long, hard and punishing career. He could never match the classy, athletic boxing skills of the legendary Sugar Ray Robinson, the man who even the great Muhammad Ali based his style upon. Very few, if any, could match him, but one thing is for certain and beyond all doubt – Jake LaMotta, the Raging Bull, was one seriously hard bastard.

ROY SHAW (UK)

British Bare-Knuckle Fighting Champion

Introducing . . . Roy Shaw

IN COMPLETE CONTRAST to Jamie O'Keefe's interview with boxer Dave "Boy" Green earlier in this book, in this chapter Jamie interviews Roy Shaw and highlights a completely different mindset and philosophy about what makes tough men tough.

Now in his early seventies, Shaw is undoubtedly one of the UK's best known unlicensed bare-knuckle fighters with a fight record of eleven fights: nine wins with eight knockouts, and two losses.

Shaw was born to a working-class family in Stepney, London, but later moved to nearby Bethnal Green where he spent much of his early adult life. Ever since an early age Shaw was involved in illegal activities and in 1963 he was sentenced to eighteen years' imprisonment for one of England's biggest armoured truck robberies. He allegedly fought his way out of two different holding cells at Her Majesty's Prison at Maidstone. He assaulted a number of prison guards and routinely stabbed informers, and even slashed the throat of a former best friend due to his strong belief in a code of honour amongst criminals which must not be broken.

Shaw hated the system and claimed it could never beat him. He was consistently moved to different prisons and even spent time at Broadmoor Hospital for Criminally Insane where, according to Shaw, uncontrollable prisoners were deliberately drugged up with the aim of turning them into permanent cabbages. In an attempt to control his temper, Shaw underwent experimental electro-convulsive therapy which, according to his doctor, was a complete failure and only served to make Shaw even more aggressive and unpredictable. His doctor claimed that at first Shaw came across as an intimidating yet soft-spoken gentleman, but when faced with treatment he didn't want, he became the most powerful and dangerous man he had ever tried to treat.

Once released from prison Shaw started bare-knuckle boxing in 1978, aged forty-two. He gained many infamous victories and his fights with arch-rival Lenny "The Guv'nor" McLean were described as among the bloodiest of the century and drew massive crowds.

For a series of petty crimes Shaw was sent back to prison but escaped and continued his boxing career under the alias "Roy West" until finally recaptured.

After serving the remainder of his prison sentence, Shaw stated that he had retired from both a life of crime and bare-knuckle boxing, and has since become a businessman and bestselling author.

PRIZE FIGHTER
By Jamie O'Keefe

Jamie: Roy, if I were to ask you what you feel makes tough guys tough, what would your answer be?

Roy S: Circumstances on the day, circumstances on their upbringing, circumstances on their way of life. For example, I was bullied and circumstances forced me to deal with that. Then later in life I had the same from authorities and had to deal with that. I often get young kids write to me via my website to ask me how to deal with bullying but it's not something that I can answer. How can I advise a young kid to go and smash someone's head in? It's what I think but I cannot write back to young kids and advise them to use violence so I end up not replying at all. It makes me feel sad for them because I was bullied and know what it's like but I cannot be put in that situation where I'm advising young kids on what to do. My life was pretty unique due to circumstances and I would not advise anybody to copy me.

Jamie: Can you define at least one attribute that you would attach to a tough guy?

Roy S: That they can fight or are prepared to fight.

Jamie: I believe that anyone can go to a class and learn the physical side of an art and the thinking problem-solving side, like "what to do if X happens". But I do not feel that you can learn the feelings, attitude, emotions, and values of affective learning, which I believe can only come from life's experiences, making you what you are, be it tough or soft, bully or victim, etc. What are your views on this?

Roy S: I think if you join in with some kind of group that get involved in fights then you will get the courage to have a go somewhere along the lines but I was a straight kid and wasn't involved with gangs or other groups of kids. My dad died when I was ten which was a blow for me but it still didn't make me violent or anything like that. It was only after I was sixteen and became a hard-working lad that circumstances changed things and I started robbing banks and getting in trouble with the police.

Jamie: If I was the most passive person on this planet, afraid of my own shadow, could I be converted into a tough guy, afraid of no one?

Roy S: I think it can work for some people who are not naturally tough. My grandson was only ten when he was getting bullied so I took him down the gym to teach him how to fight. After going for about nine months he could punch the bag fairly hard and could lay someone out of his own size. He has surprised me, but he still didn't go out because he was frightened of getting bullied. He needed to build up his confidence. It was exactly the same for me. I lacked confidence even though as a kid I was physically capable of knocking people out. One day I just found that I was sticking up for myself against one of the bullies and from then on it all come together and I turned into Roy Shaw the Hard Bastard somewhere along the line. Well, that's the label that some people attached to me and not one I chose myself.

Jamie: How are we to know when to choose "fight or flight"?

Roy S: The adrenaline rush chooses for you. Every time I got the rush I would fight but some people decide to not fight when it comes. It left me alone for quite a while but recently I was in this club and there was this geezer who had raped a bird. I went over to him and there were these other two lumps with him but I didn't give a fuck. I psyched myself up and let him know that I knew he was the one that had raped this girl and then knocked him spark out. I don't give a fuck if there are loads of them, like when I did four of them, when I get that adrenaline rush, nothing is going to stop me. You know how it is, you've done the same.

Jamie: Does a martial art black belt or boxing title mean someone is tough? If not, what does it mean?

Roy S: It means that they are tough as a boxer or martial artist and have the capabilities to use their art in a real situation but it doesn't mean that they automatically will. I've never done martial arts and to my knowledge never fought one so cannot really speak on their behalf.

Jamie: Can you put all the tough guys you know of into any sort of category, i.e. they are mostly from the forces, or mostly from broken homes etc.?

Roy S: I suppose the working-class breed the majority of tough guys. You don't really see royalty or rich kids boxing. The actor Mickey Rourke was someone with money that could look after himself but he was like that before he become rich and famous. When I was in France he asked me to go to America and look after him when he was in his prime as an actor but it was not for me, I didn't fancy it.

Jamie: Can you take somebody and make him or her tough? If not, what is the nearest you can get them to what you consider as being tough?

Roy S: Well, I'm a good example. When I left school at fifteen I was quiet calm and only six stone one, and had a history of being bullied. I took up boxing and soon realized that I had the gift of being able to punch and the aggression that I never had; all seem to suddenly fall in place. I had a good trainer and that can really help you to develop. Even if a trainer hasn't got street-fighting experience himself, he can still teach you and get the best from you if he understands and knows what he is talking about.

Jamie: As a young lad I had a pal, who many others and I considered to be the toughest person we had ever known. He was a brilliant street-fighter who was rarely defeated. I met him fifteen years later and he was a shadow of his former self, practically flinching if anyone came near him in a threatening manner. It was like his spirit had been broken. Do you think a tough guy can be made to be or become un-tough?

Roy S: I've never known it! People mellow with age and mature but I've never seen someone who could have a "row" suddenly not be able to do it? Maybe a personality change is possible but it's not something I've come across. Having a family kind of controls you because you do not want to bring your aggro on their doorstep. I've got a mate who was a right rascal in his younger days but now he has got a couple of kids he doesn't even go out. He just cannot be bothered with the aggro but it doesn't change the fact that he is still capable; he just can't be bothered with it all. He has got more important things in his life now.

Jamie: Do you think it is possible to sense that someone is tough just from the way they carry themselves?

Roy S: Yeah, they have an aura about them that you can sense. People like us have got it. It attracts similar sorts of people towards you and that's how you end up with a group of mates who can all handle themselves but it also attracts the mugs to you that wanna be tough.

Jamie: Is it possible to act tough without really being tough?

Roy S: Not really, you can smell out a fake or plastic gangster a mile off. They don't kid anyone but themselves. A lot of mugs try it but they get caught out. You can only act tough for so long before someone will end up doing you.

Jamie: How would you deal with a tough guy who is in your face prompting you to kick off with him?

Roy S: I don't really get it happen to me these days. People seem to be more respectful because I'm not the kind of tear up merchant that I used to be. I'm more passive in my attitude when I go out these days. However, if someone does try it on with me I will choose my reaction more wisely than I used to. I will still do them but I may bide my time to avoid witnesses and getting nicked. I had a situation at the country club last week. As I pulled up and stepped out of the cab there was a tear up going on and suddenly someone shouted "Look out, it's Roy Shaw," then the whole thing broke up!

Jamie: Is there a difference between men and women with regards to their toughness, i.e. would you be happy to let women take the place of men on the front-line of pubs and clubs etc.?

Roy S: No, women are not really fighting machines, are they? I don't even like to see them in organized boxing events. Their bodies are not made up for being punched and that. They have got boobs and have babies. They are not made to fight like men, they are too delicate. Women are to be respected, and not be beaten up or work the doors.

Jamie: What do you feel the role of martial arts, boxing, or other fighting-related arts have in making tough guys tough?

Roy S: It can help give people confidence. I did boxing so I would teach boxing to give someone confidence whereas you do it with the martial arts. I would probably teach martial arts as well had I ever studied it but I haven't.

Jamie: Do you think that regional accents have any connection to toughness?

Roy S: No, not at all. Some regional accent like the East London or Scottish accent can make you sound tough but it means nothing.

Jamie: Are you tough?

Roy S: No, but I can look after myself. A bit like you when you say that you're not tough but you are capable, well I'm not tough but I can look after myself.

Jamie: Does your current training system or method of training prepare you when confronted with a tough guy?

Roy S: The boxing has made me the person that I am.

Jamie: Is your current training system gearing you up towards toughness in any way?

Roy S: Well, I still do my weights as you know from the training session just now, plus I do my running each morning with my dogs but my knees play up a bit now from all those years of power-lifting, dead-weights and squats.

Jamie: Is there anything else you or anyone else can do to become tougher?

Roy S: If you are a weak kid then you can spend time in the fighting arts training to become tougher. It will happen over a period of time if you persevere.

Jamie: How many tough females can you name?

Roy S: None. I don't really see females as tough; I see them as lovely human beings. I don't want to see them in any other way.

Jamie: What do you think attracts people to villains, gangsters and fighters?

Roy S: I don't think many people have got the arsehole to do a bank

robbery or things like that or do the time in prison that goes with it
when you get caught. Not many could go through Broadmoor like
Frankie Fraser. People *wish* they could do the same but they can't.

Jamie: Do villains exist today as they did back in the 1960s?

Roy S: No, the "Old School" could have a row, stand up for themselves, had respect for each other, loyalty, all the things that make a
good man. People are robbing each other in business and nicking
cars and think they are gangsters. They are just paperback gangsters, wannabes. You cannot be the real McCoy without doing your
apprenticeship. Knowing people that are gangsters does not make
you one. You are what you are, no matter what you tell people. Bit
like that mug gangster that lived across the road to your old mum in
Canning Town. He couldn't kid me, your mother or Frankie Fraser
because we were all from the Old School.

Jamie: Is your life story going to be made into a film?

Roy S: Well, put it like this. We've been given £75,000 up front to
give them the option for six months with another £100,000 to come
on the first day of filming, then 6 per cent of the gross profits so I
sure hope so. It's to be called "Propaganda" and its being done by
an American company. It looks like Ray Winstone is gonna play me
in the film.

Jamie: It goes without saying that you are one of the toughest guys
in Britain regardless of if there are two, or two thousand tough
guys. Are you able to control that anger that you once had or do
you still explode? For instance, if someone spilt your beer in a pub
would you consider it something worth fighting for? Or if someone
cut you up in a car in road rage?

Roy S: I wouldn't fight over a spilt beer but I did get cut up by a guy
in a car outside my house the other week so I got out and knocked
him out. I drove up the road after and sat for a while just to give him
a chance to come round and piss off, so no police were involved.
When I come back to my house twenty minutes later he was still
spark out slumped over the steering wheel of his van.

Jamie: I would give my life for my children. What would you be
prepared to give your own life for?

Roy S: I'd fight for my two dogs, my family, a friend or anyone who
I knew was suffering.

Jamie: We often hear it said that "if anyone touches one of my kids

I will kill them" but the reality is that children do get harmed and killed but we don't see parents killing in revenge. Why do you think that is?

Roy S: Because paedophiles move away and are untraceable. If they committed a crime against a kid and stayed living locally where people could get to them then they would not last long. We would do them inside the nick if we could get to them.

Jamie: What would make you kill?

Roy S: Next question.

Jamie: What would you do if you saw somebody mugging an OAP or battering a child or animal?

Roy S: Jump them and sort them out.

Jamie: Do you think that the journey travelled, pain suffered and life you have lost is worth the wealthy lifestyle you have now?

Roy S: I wouldn't change anything but wouldn't advise anyone else to do what I've done because the cream years of my life are gone. But none of the screws that tried to make me suffer have the luxurious lifestyle that I have now.

Jamie: Many youngsters and the not so young look up to you as a hero and role model that people can triumph over disaster. This is a big responsibility to bear because you are famous now and many people aspire to be like you, so how does that make you feel?

Roy S: I would turn youngsters against following in my footsteps. I lost my life from twenty-seven to thirty-seven and would not recommend that to anyone. All that I have today is from going into the gym and training hard, not from being a gangster.

Jamie: Is there anything else that you still want to achieve before you retire?

Roy S: No, I've done the book and I'm content with that.

Jamie: What makes every day worthwhile to you?

Roy S: Everyday is nice for me. I have a successful business, I love my dogs, and I train. Life is just nice. I love Mondays, which is when I collect the rent from my properties. What more could I want?

Jamie: What is your stance on men that are violent towards women?

Roy S: Any geezer that whacks a bird is an arsehole. I wouldn't even whack a guy who was drunk and incapable of fighting. I would go back and do him the next day.

Jamie: What message or advice to young people who think it's cool to want to be a gangster or villain?

Roy S: It's not cool. In the old days there were not the opportunities to earn money like you can now honestly. You can become a millionaire from making a computer programme, writing books and ways that you could not ever imagine when I was young. We had the choice of being hard up or going out and nicking a few quid here and there. Life is much better without crime. You can live a better life on the dole these days than you could get from grafting hard in the old days. These days I get my income from my lorry park, car-site, my houses and my life story. Nothing could draw me into crime ever again.

GREGORY PETER JOHN SMITH (AUSTRALIA)

Bandit

Introducing . . . Gregory Peter John Smith

BORN IN JUNE 1952 in Melbourne, Australia, Gregory David Roberts was originally named Gregory Peter John Smith and was one seriously tough man. As a teenager Smith was rebellious and in 1969, at just seventeen years old, he became a radical political activist and one of the founding members of the Anarchist People's Liberation Army. Bright and intelligent, Smith attended the prestigious University of Melbourne but as a disaffected student leader in 1974 he occupied the university Council Chambers, and in 1975 joined the Black Week Aboriginal Activism Movement. In 1977, after the break-up of his marriage and loss of daughter in a custody dispute, Smith turned to heroin and to support his drug habit embarked on a series of armed robberies at building society branches, credit unions and shops across the region. He was eventually captured and sentenced to nineteen years' imprisonment but just two years later, in 1980, Smith escaped in broad daylight to become one of Australia's most wanted men. Helped by a motorcycle gang, Smith quickly fled to New Zealand for a short while, before fleeing to India where he became involved with the Bombay (Mumbai) mafia, smuggling drugs, gold and passports. He also smuggled guns into Afghanistan and fought with the Mujahedin against the Soviets. Wounded in action, he was evacuated to Pakistan but returned to Bombay where he was appointed controller of the mafia forgery unit and became a passport smuggler to Nigeria, Zaire, Iraq, Iran, Mauritius and Sri Lanka. After breaking up with the Bombay mafia, Smith went on freelance drug-smuggling missions to Europe but in 1990 was captured in Frankfurt, Germany, and imprisoned. He served two years in solitary confinement and four years in mainstream prison back in Australia, where he began writing his bestselling novel *Shantaram*.

Smith has had a remarkable life which is chronicled specially for this book by writer Vicki Schofield.

THE BUILDING SOCIETY BANDIT
By Vicki Schofield

There are some people who believe that Gregory David Roberts should not be a successful writer. If you are a member of the Crime Victims Support Association in Australia, your view might be that he profits from other people's misery through his writing. On the other hand, he might argue back that by sharing his experiences, he is teaching others not to go down a similar path to his. As a criminal, he was known as Gregory Peter John Smith. Whether you are sceptical or not about his intentions, there is no denying that he has a completely different life today from when he was on the run from police, when he acted as a drug smuggler for the Mumbai mafia or when he defended himself in some of the most notorious prisons in the world.

Smith has established himself as a celebrity, rubbing shoulders with some of the most famous entertainers in Hollywood. He has been an admired guest at conferences, speaking about the importance of philanthropy and respect for the common man. Even his press photos depict an image of someone who could easily be mistaken for a hippie or shaman, with his long hair plaited behind his back and his calm demeanour. When you catch a glimpse of him, you would never think that he is a hardened survivor of horrid circumstances, or that he once sparked a massive manhunt in Australia that lasted ten years. This was the man who was described as going from "one day to the next terrorizing" people.

The transition of his image is surprising, and it could be the reason he felt the need to change his name. He had travelled for years using fake passports and false identities. Perhaps this contributed to his feeling of disconnection from the person he was years before. Smith reiterates that his actions were shameful, especially those of his youth where he had threatened people with a gun to hand over money. He insists that he has written about his experiences to teach others what he has learned from falling into an underbelly world of drugs and crime. If you are one of the many people who have read his story, *Shantaram*, you may feel empathy for what he has been through, and you may wonder as to how he could have survived all that he has. His biggest regret is putting all of his effort into criminal activities, when he could have been doing what he always wanted: writing.

For a man who was considered of high intelligence by those who convicted him, how did Smith end up a hardened man in the first place? Rarely does he discuss the early years when his wayward behaviour began. On 1 June 1978, Smith was convicted and sentenced to twenty-three years in jail for a spree of armed robberies. At the time, Mr Justice O'Bryan, the presiding judge, stated firmly, "Seldom is a man presented before this court on so many serious crimes at one time." Smith's one-year run as a bandit proved impressive. He had covered a lot of ground in his short run of robberies. During his trial, he pleaded guilty to twenty-four charges of armed robbery, confessing to reaping in over AUS$32,000, collected from cinemas, shops and building societies. O'Bryan did not hold back in expressing his disapproval for Smith's disregard for a respected future. He described Smith as an appalling waste of talent, foolishly choosing to become a full-time junkie. O'Bryan reminded Smith that he could easily sentence him to a hundred years in prison within the current judicial system. But he chose to show some mercy and Smith was handed down twenty-three years instead. This was still arguably a harsh sentence for someone who carried a toy gun and was never actually physically violent towards his victims. (That would come later in life.) Smith's sentence was partly the result of bad timing as the Australian Parliament had only recently increased the maximum penalty for armed robbery to twenty-five years.

For a couple of years before Smith's crime spree, there had been a growing intolerance in Victoria for robbers and bandits. Between 1970 and 1976, an overwhelming AUS$5 million was stolen in Victoria, and Inspector Paul Delianis was becoming concerned with the increasing trend of such crimes. Local university criminologists hypothesized that it was because these acts were becoming glorified, especially for young people. As long as no one got physically hurt in the process, some youths thought that no real harm was done. It was as if the criminals were regarded in the same fashion as other victorious characters, stealing from the well off, like Butch Cassidy or Robin Hood. The press failed to help curb this idolization by branding the criminals in the media. At twenty-six, Smith was labelled "The Building Society Bandit" for his particular taste in robbery targets.

The focus on small targets such as shops, building societies and service stations concerned Inspector Delianis as much as the increase in the number of robberies. Previously, being a thief was more about getting the big payout, the one that would set you up for life or at least a long time. Usually, it would mean barging into a bank and cleaning them out for a hefty sum. But some of the bandits, like Smith, worked out that hitting the smaller targets meant that the payout was easier to get their hands on, and that the risk was minimal in comparison to banks. Less security meant less hassle. For authorities, it meant that the money was more difficult to trace and eventually recoup. This, too, was a blow to the local police.

As previously mentioned, Smith was a thief who did not physically harm anyone in the process and considered by some to be a hero. Victoria police had difficulty tracking the Building Society Bandit for a year until their luck turned and they finally caught up with him in February 1978. While attempting to pull another quick cash job in a shop, his effort was thwarted by an intolerant shopkeeper. It was a careless failure on Smith's part, but he would learn from this mistake and continue to head into a career of international crime beyond the petty money he was used to getting.

Whether or not he acknowledged it, Smith had been warming up to the idea of having brushes with the law for a couple of years preceding his sentence. Raised in a rough working-class neighbourhood, he began with good intentions, initially intending on building a life like any other average family. At eighteen, he married his girlfriend and had a daughter shortly afterwards. In order to support them, he worked in a factory during the day whilst attended university classes in the evening. He had entered the University of Melbourne with prominent grades and a talent for creative writing. Even so, Smith still exhibited a bit of deviance while being a student. He proved to have other interests than school, work and family. At five foot ten inches, with medium build, he did not appear on the outside to be a menacing figure in his youth, but years of martial-arts training had encouraged his strength and his ability to defend himself. There was certainly a sense of non-acceptance of the status quo by Smith, as he spent a lot of his time amongst activists and anarchist groups. He was often fighting for a variety of left-wing causes.

By the time he was in his early twenties, Smith had established a significant presence on the University of Melbourne campus, being elected Student Leader of the University Council in 1974. Participating in demonstrations was not satisfying enough for him. He wanted to create a new organization: the Australian Independence Group. The group began to have a negative impact on the university campus. This conflict reached its peak in the mid 1970s, when the Student Union banned the group for having some members exhibiting threatening behaviour. The university tagged them as a "bunch of thugs" attempting to use intimidation to gain power. Out of fear for what could happen to its members, the Student Council moved its headquarters to a more secure location.

While the Australian Independence Group continued to become more of a burrowing problem within the university, Smith's focus had shifted to solely concentrating on getting his next heroin hit. He admits that his immaturity got the better of him when he was faced with a personal problem he could not handle. Specifically, it was the deterioration of his marriage and the loss of custody of his daughter that proved too much. He had built a significant parental bond with his daughter, often seen by fellow classmates taking her to university and sitting in the cafe while he worked on his assignments. In retrospect, he admits he should have straightened himself out, stayed clean and put time into his writing instead. At least then he would have had a greater chance of possibility seeing her.

However, everyone has a different point of weakness and so, on the day that the decision was made about his daughter, he buckled. A friend who came to console him offered him his first hit of heroin to combat the pain and he accepted. Smith has said that he was always meticulous when using heroin; he was careful about where and when to insert the needle and left few marks on his arm. He soon discovered that the numbness would come at a hefty price and he would need some new way of funding the habit, especially as his family grew tired of him sponging money off them and began to turn him away. In the summer of 1977, Smith finally reached the conclusion that the only way he could fund his habit was to do something drastic. He figured that a movie cinema would make an easy first target. Upon arrival, he doubted himself and was unsure he could complete the task in hand. Desperation and cravings overwhelmed him, and he swallowed back any apprehension that he had left. Earlier in the day, he had attempted to obtain some methadone to treat his addiction, but discovered that it was unavailable from the usual collection point. Slumped in the men's toilets, he waited for the right moment, each sound startling him. His thoughts of retreating from the cinema were interrupted unexpectedly when a small fire erupted in one of the rubbish bins. Someone had carelessly tossed their cigarette into the trash. Smith claims that he extinguished it himself, and that the cinema ushers came and thanked him. Minutes later, he approached the counter and threatened them with a gun.

Smith was like a bumbling professor on his first robbery. His technique needed some refinement, as he made a couple of awkward mistakes. After he grabbed the bag, holding the measly bit of money from the cinema till, he sprinted out the door and collided with two police officers on the street. The money fell to the floor and he quickly snapped it up and cradled it in his arms. He was able to offer the officers a feeble excuse for his clumsiness. Smith never aroused any suspicion in them, and he was left to run free, and to continue to steal fifteen more times that year.

Although Smith has said that he was often polite to his victims and that he was nicknamed the "Gentleman Bandit", Mr Justice O'Bryan expressed different opinions of him on the day of his sentencing. Even though Smith only ever carried a toy gun, the judge was keen to point out that Smith had terrorized people to support his habit, threatened at least three women with their lives and robbed some people twice in one day. Smith retaliated by appealing his twenty-three-year sentence, with no chance of parole for sixteen years, saying that it was excessive. His attorney argued that too much emphasis was placed on his deviance from society, when more concentration should have been placed on his potential for rehabilitation. This was disregarded and Smith was sent to Pentridge Prison.

It was evident that Pentridge had a bulk of issues to deal with in the 1970s, before Smith even set foot there. It was nicknamed the Bluestone College, and it was recognized as a place where criminals developed an even harder attitude and acquired new criminal skills. Smith was placed in the H division, also known as the "high security, discipline and protection division". To inmates, it was known as the Hell division. Overcrowding and tight budgeting had raised some public concerns about Pentridge's efficiency in disciplining inmates. In 1979, not long after Smith was imprisoned, a significant riot broke out on one of the other divisions in Pentridge. Several prisoners had been drinking their own home-brew, which led to them savagely attacking officers and setting any objects at their disposal on fire. At one point, several of them managed to make it to the top of the prison roof, but were herded back towards the cells by police with batons. It sparked an outcry in the local media for a more disciplined, regulated institution.

In the H division, Smith had originally intended to wait and tolerate his sentence as best he could, but he soon believed that he would need to escape from Pentridge in order to save his life. He has claimed that he endured multiple beatings from corrupt prison guards. Even defending himself against fellow prisoners was proving to be a challenge. He used the knowledge that he acquired through experience as a well-read student to defend himself in the best way he knew.

On at least one occasion, the love of books even protected his life. Smith had encountered some tough inmates who promised him earlier that day that they were planning to kill him. He knew that like any kind of prey, there would only ever be two options: fight or flight. In this case, he knew flight was out of the question. He surveyed his cell for anything that could offer a solution and his gaze fell upon the collection of literary classics he had on the cell shelf. It seemed that destroying his prize possessions was the only option for survival, but he was still reluctant to pull the collection from the shelf. After a few moments of hesitation, he began to yank the pages from the binding. He strapped the hard covers to his mid-drift and forearms, and stuffed the pages underneath his shirt. He used any cardboard that was available within the cell to build the thickest layer he could to prevent any knives from puncturing his skin.

Miraculously, he returned from the knife fight still alive and with all limbs intact. He had defended himself using what little bit of martial arts self-defence technique he knew. But knowing that the guards could be as dangerous as the inmates, he had to dispose of any clues to what had happened. That included any sharp objects he had used, which were already inconspicuously dropped on the way back to his cell block. He tore the paper from his body and ripped it into tiny pieces. Then, he gnawed the pieces so that they were liquefied enough to flush down the toilet, watching crimson drops fall into the bowl.

Despite having developed a few enemies inside, Smith did befriend at least one inmate, Trevor Raymond Jolly, a convicted contract murderer. Jolly became his accomplice in the escape plan. He had been embroiled in the junkie world like Smith, before he was caught by police. During his contract killing trial, his defence had been that he had not intentionally killed his victim but, rather, it was self-defence. He said it was an accident in a struggle brought on when he tried to obtain the money that was owed to him for a drug deal. The Crown stated that he was contracted to kill the man for $5,000 by the victim's wife and the man she was having an affair with. At age twenty-four, Jolly ended up being sent to Pentridge only three months before Smith. Perhaps it was their age or their common heroin addiction that brought Jolly and Smith together. Either way, it caused them to form a close relationship. Both of them ended up in the prison's B division where the riot had occurred in 1979, and where long-term inmates with bad behaviour were housed. Jolly had been placed in the bad behaviour section because money was found in his possession.

After two-and-a-half years spent inside, the pair decided that it was time to take the opportunity to strike and leave Pentridge. On

23 July 1980, they were continuing to work on a concrete job they were completing just outside B division, which was often part of their routine. Unsupervised, they were able to wander away unsuspiciously from their duties into an administrative building. There, they were able to gain access to workmen's tools which had been abandoned while demolition workers had gone for their lunch. It provided a perfect time-gap for them to use the tools and cut a hole in the tin roof. Security believed it was tin snips that were used to cut the escape route, but Smith has said that they actually used a buzz saw. He described it: "We broke into the governor of security's office, and then got up to the ceiling, used a buzz-saw to cut a hole in the ceiling, got into the roof, cut through the roof with the buzz-saw."

The pair then grabbed an extension cord and took it with them up to the roof, where they walked along until they reached the front wall. Staying within security's blind spot, they dropped the cord over, and climbed it until they could let themselves go. They were finally free. Landing less than twenty metres from the front gate, they sprinted forward until they reached a small lane leading them to Sydney Road. From there, they naturally blended in, as they had ditched their work overalls earlier for normal sportswear, including football jumpers, shorts and runners. To any innocent bystander, they looked like any other pair of avid joggers.

The prison guards on duty had not seen any sign that there was trouble until 1.30 in the afternoon when they noticed the dangling power cord from the wall. One had completed a check fifteen minutes earlier and was positive that the cord had not been there then. Even then, this had not been enough to raise suspicion with the guards. They continued their shift as normal and only realized that something unlawful had happened when they completed the roll call for B division, when they found that the two inmates were missing. This occurred a couple of hours after the power cord had been seen, at approximately 4 p.m.

To Smith, the experience was exhilarating. Escaping from a maximum security prison went beyond the adrenaline he had experienced through martial arts training or any of the crimes he had committed so far. He had to have felt a pang of smugness towards the prison guards and police as he had predicted the outcome to them months earlier. Shortly after his sentence, he had mailed detectives a poem indicating his future escape plans. He was dubbed the "Chicken Man" by some because he once robbed a shop called the Chicken Inn. The poem was titled, "The Chicken from Snowy River".

There was movement at the station for the word has passed
   around
The Chicken Man was on the loose – and covering a lot of ground.
He's done some cheeky hold-ups
Every now and then
And the station men determined
To put him in the pen.

They gaoled the Chicken Man,
He couldn't turn a trick,
Now it's porridge for breakfast,
While he serves out a brick.
But the squad remains alert,
Ready again to swoop
If the Chicken Man learns to fly,
And one day flies the coop.

The local media shared this piece of writing a couple of weeks after Smith and Jolly broke free. Meanwhile, the pair was still on the loose, but they did eventually part company. Smith mingled in a few different groups shortly thereafter, including a motorcycle gang. He was able to hide for a while in New Zealand before he was smuggled into India, and settled in Bombay (Mumbai) in 1981. Jolly was not so fortunate as on 26 May 1981 he was charged with a further three years for using a firearm upon arrest, assaulting a police officer and stealing a police car.

India introduced Smith to a whole new level of crime. Originally, he began surviving on petty drug trading, particularly to foreigners visiting from abroad. But he became aware that he would need to adjust to the culture to survive in this new world. India is where he was swallowed into powerful groups of hard men, including the local mafia. At first, though, he had to adjust to living in a slum in

Bombay. Cramped in a tiny hut built with wood and rags, Smith lived in a community where around 25,000 people were squashed in a space no bigger than 800 metres square.

Smith was in his hut one day when he had heard loud screams from outside. He could see flames coming from one of the huts. He figured it would not take long for the fire to sweep through all of the community, including his own home, and it was best just to get the hell out of there. Grabbing his bag of belongings, he began to sprint as far away as he could. But, after a few minutes, he noticed the women and children glaring at him with a sense of bewilderment, and he stopped. He watched the native slum-dwellers, who were not as strong as him. They were carrying heavy buckets of water and heading into the fire to try to extinguish it as best as they could. Smith decided that he could not run this time, and that it was more important for him to help the people.

When the fire had ceased, 250 people were injured and twelve had died as a result of the crisis. Smith had a modest supply of basic first aid equipment which he used to clean the wounds and bandage up those he could. From the next day, people considered him to be a valuable doctor and would queue outside his hut for treatment from then on. It was a round about this time when Smith was given the nickname "Shantaram" or "Man of Peace".

Smith's next few years were eventful and he soon ended up back in prison. Pentridge prison had seemed like a hell, but it had only a fraction of the effect that Bombay's Arthur Road Prison had on him. Despite it only being a relatively short sentence, four months, its impact on Smith was profound. He had entered the institution weighing 90 kg, and left weighing only 45 kg. The prison had established a convict overseer system, whereby convicted murderers were able to make the decisions in the prison. They were able to control the food rations, which meant they could build on their strength while they starved the other inmates, making them much weaker. Smith, despite drastically dropping in weight from starvation, became involved in a fist fight with one of the overseers. As a result, the overseers clamped irons on his legs. They used a cramping tool to do this, tightly binding the ankles. Other prisoners would share their food rations with him, but would end up being beaten themselves. It was the boss of a local mafia who bailed him out for

US$10,000. The local Bombay mafia was a smaller unit of a larger Colombian group. As a foreigner who was obviously a survivor under harsh conditions, Smith was an asset to the mafia to smuggle passports, drugs and other illegal items between borders.

While Smith was manoeuvring between borders, the authorities were none the wiser if he was still in Australia or abroad. In 1988, the longest standing name on the top ten most wanted list for the Victorian police was Gregory John Peter Smith. Despite being on the run for so long, Smith was nervous about being caught. His fears of being recognized were justified when, in 1990, he was caught travelling from Bombay to Zurich on a false passport, carrying a stash of drugs. The authorities had previously uncovered an illegal passport operation in Bombay and had even pinpointed a specific stamp from Sri Lanka that was used in a fake passport. Any passports containing this stamp were immediately picked out by international customs officers, and it would finally land Smith in the hands of the police. To them, they had finally caught the ultimate Houdini. To take the necessary precautions, they put him in a maximum security prison in Germany, which housed the bottom-feeders of society, including terrorists. Smith was then extradited back to Australia where he ironically finished the sentence he could not bear so many years before: in Pentridge Prison.

Smith spent his second round in Pentridge compiling the short stories of his turbulent journey into a format that would make him a bestselling author. Despite his manuscript being destroyed twice by prison guards while inside, his determination would overcome any suffering he was subjected to. Although he admitted that there was the occasional opportunity to escape again and experience that thrill, he held himself back. This time, no reason to escape would be greater than his desire to see his family again. He had finished running. Since he has been published, Smith has set up charitable foundations in Mumbai, assisting the city's poor by providing healthcare coverage. He has also been approached by one of the guards who had destroyed his book years before, while he was banged up inside. The guard explained he had deep regret for committing such a deed. But Smith viewed the experience as he did so many of the hardships he endured: it had made *Shantaram* a better book in the end.

DENNIS MARTIN (UK)

One of Britain's Toughest Men

Introducing . . . Dennis Martin

A SK ANY DOORMAN on any door anywhere in the UK if there was one city where they would not want to work the doors and without doubt most would say Liverpool. Liverpool is a tough, hard, dangerous place populated by tough, hard people and is currently rated one of the most violent cities in the United Kingdom. Home of the world-famous Beatles, Liverpool is also home of some of the wealthiest gangsters in British history whose empires extend to controlling many of the clubs and pubs, and many of the doormen. If you are not tough and "known", and if you cannot "mix it" when you need to, you will not last long working the doors in this dangerous and volatile city. There was no one tougher on the doors in Liverpool in the 1970s than Sean Reich and the same goes for Dennis Martin today. Everyone knows Dennis and Dennis knows everyone. Polite, respectful, modest and well-read, Dennis is undoubtedly one of the hardest, yet humblest, doormen in Liverpool today.

LIVERPOOL'S HARDEST DOORMAN
By Barbara Preston

When you think about the term "hard bastard", what mental image comes to mind? There are a number of dictionary definitions for the term, but initially most people would probably think of a man who is perceived as being vicious or ruthless; a "big man" in his crowd, hard-drinking perhaps, and often with criminal tendencies. This stereotypical description is all wrong – at least where Dennis Martin is concerned.

Being "tough" does not mean being violent or aggressive; a "hard man" is simply someone who is able to handle difficult situations and keep his head, and, if necessary, is not afraid to fight to protect himself or others who are unable to defend themselves. Hard, tough men are also able to take a lot of physical punishment – seemingly without much effort – which takes years of dedication, training and extremely hard work.

So what has made a normally quiet, passive Dennis Martin one of the hardest men in the UK today?

Born in Liverpool, the fourth largest and one of the toughest cities in England, Dennis Martin had what he calls a "normal upbringing". He wasn't interested in sports at school but in his early teens he discovered the world of martial arts. A judo demonstration at a local fête captured his interest and there began a journey that has brought him to the pinnacle of self-defence and close protection instruction. Nowhere along the way did Dennis consciously choose the path his life took; it developed and evolved over the years and, by his own admission, his life is very much still a "work in progress".

Initially learning karate from books and television, Dennis finally heard about a karate demonstration by Masters Kase, Shirai, Kanazawa and Enoeda at the famous Red Triangle dojo in Liverpool. He was totally impressed by the dynamism and power displayed and was lucky enough to be offered a place at the dojo, which already had a long waiting list. The training was Shotokan karate and, in another stroke of luck for Dennis, Master Enoeda himself moved to Liverpool which meant that Dennis had a consistently high standard of training directly from the master himself, whom he describes as an incredibly hard trainer suiting the style of the pure Shotokan.

Martin's progression from dojo to doorman came about by accident. It was Christmas, he was eighteen years old and short of cash, and so he took a job on the door of an all-night Indian restaurant and his job was to make sure nobody left without paying. He quickly learned how to deal with drunks and aggressive groups, and shortly after he was offered occasional work on the door of the Blue Angel nightclub, where he had his first real altercation on the doors. A big guy came at him and Dennis used an ura-tsuki (a close, low, snapping punch in the ribs) to put him down.

It did wonders for his self-confidence!

Dennis continued training hard several times a week and slowly became interested in Okinawan karate; he was fascinated by the incredible power levels reached in that particular style. He wasn't a strong kicker, so the short-range traditional Goju-ryu style suited him. The term Goju-ryu actually means "hard-soft style", which refers to the closed hand techniques (hard) and open hand techniques and circular movements (soft) that comprise this martial art.

This style of karate was something that Martin would use when working on the doors because not only does it have a wide range of short-range techniques such as elbow strikes and open hand strikes, it is also very strong on conditioning – both mental and physical. Dennis met Brian Waites at a championship where Waites was giving a demonstration as he was one of the first to introduce the Goju style in England. Dennis boldy invited Waites to Liverpool for some training, which he agreed to. Also around this time, Gary Spiers, another well-known doorman and martial arts expert, moved to Liverpool and began teaching a form of "street Goju" and Dennis, of course, trained with him as well.

Through his friendship with another fellow martial artist Terry O'Neill, Dennis was taken on as a doorman at the Victoriana Club, a local hotspot for trouble. After a year on the "Vic", he moved to another nightclub further along the same road. But for Dennis, working the doors was just to make a living and pay for his passion: karate. He, O'Neill and Spiers would frequently work a Friday night, travel to London to train at a particular dojo or with a visiting master on the Saturday, then back to Liverpool to work that night, and then head off for London again to train the following Sunday.

As a doorman, Dennis quickly learned early on that the martial arts used in the dojo were not the same as were needed on the streets and the doors, and both O'Neill and Spiers taught Dennis how to modify his style and techniques for street-fighting – extremely effectively when it came to working the doors together. He also learned about dealing with people; reading them and their behaviour and getting them to do what you need them to do, preferably without a fight breaking out. He also learned about situational awareness: "I never got any of the mental side from formal martial arts. We [Dennis and Terry O'Neill] were walking through the city centre in Liverpool and I said, 'How can you remember all the guys you've smacked?' He said, 'You can't, it's impossible. You've just got to be on your guard all the time.' And I've lived by that principle ever since. I'm on my guard when I'm in public. It's what we now call situational awareness."

Ever since Dennis started martial arts training, he had an ambition to go to Japan and, after saving hard for six months, in 1973 he finally realized his dream; he spent six glorious but extremely tough months training every single day in Japan – the home of traditional karate – as well as visiting as many dojos and training in as many styles as possible. On this pilgrimage he met and trained with the very best of the best, developing himself and his skills to an extremely high level.

When Martin returned from Japan, he was almost immediately offered a job as a bodyguard for the Miss World competition – guarding Miss Israel – which he eagerly took. His evolution from hard man on the doors to a close protection officer began and he quickly set about learning the basic skills needed to become a respected bodyguard.

Martin says that close protection is one of the most interesting aspects of his career so far, and also the most fun. "It is a completely different type of security from working on the doors, with the priority on protecting the VIP rather than on self-protection. It's fast. It's mobile. While you can talk to punters on the doors to defuse situations in close protection you are moving with the VIP. You can't stop and explain politely and patiently why someone can't get an autograph," he says.

At first, as a bodyguard he had to get used to seeing things in a completely different way than when working the doors, as he was now working with the paparazzi and the media and, for his international contracts, he would be expected to know exactly what was going on in the news around the world. But as time went by he got used to it and it has now became part of the job. "Ultimately, however, you have to be prepared to use violence if necessary to protect your VIP, but only if you really have to. But as a bodyguard your objectives are ultimately to try to avoid it at all costs." he says.

For Martin, the feeling of doing a good job and being a professional is the most enjoyable thing he finds about the work and describes his world of bodyguarding as protecting people against life's predators. He says that "sometimes you have to be as hard and as devious and as cunning as the wolves that are preying on your client, so you can ultimately defeat them".

According to Martin, the skills required by a bodyguard are many, with planning operations one of the most important tasks, along with the ability to research, use information effectively and gather intelligence. Everything must be done to ensure the safety of the VIP and it's all about looking for possible trouble in advance so that it can be avoided. Fighting is the very last resort, and if it comes to that Dennis says, then the operation has failed: "The very last thing you want is to have to drag your VIP through a fire-fight."

Over the years Martin has worked on VIP protection for several Arabian royal families and international diplomatic personnel, and once he and his team looked after a client who, intelligence had informed them, had a government assassin after him. Apparently the alleged assassin was arrested at Heathrow Airport carrying an Armalite rifle and a contract from a foreign government. Martin also worked in London throughout the IRA bombings of the 1970s and had a few close shaves when venues he was attending were blown up either just before or just after his arrival.

"The most important thing for anybody working in VIP protection is to have the correct mindset. Mindset is the basis of everything," says Martin, who uses the concept called the "Vital Pyramid" as his philosophy of protection. "The base of the pyramid is mindset, everything rests on that. Mindset is about situational awareness, preparation and planning, threat evaluation. Above that are tactics, then skills and finally kit at the tip. But if you've got a good mindset you can actually avoid most problems; which is the intention of VIP protection."

Another reason why Dennis stresses so much importance on mental preparation is that close protection needs a very different attitude for self-defence. "You are no longer protecting yourself, but working to protect complete strangers, some of whom you won't even know or like. The natural instinct of self-preservation must be overcome so that if danger threatens, the VIP is protected at all costs, even if it means putting yourself in harm's way."

As a bodyguard, Martin continually trained hard and made a real effort to learn more techniques and to improve his skill-set. One of the most influential training methods which Martin learned is Neuro-Linguistic Programming (NLP), which he first learned about from Marcus Wynne while on a training course in the US. Neural-based training teaches you to develop a mental state and is highly effective in training for self-protection. Among other important techniques, which he not only mastered but has integrated into his own training programmes, are the WWII Combatives and the GUN (Grab, Undo, Neutralize) method.

After going to Japan, martial arts instruction was a natural progression and once he became involved in close protection it became important to him to be able to pass on his knowledge and skills to others working in the security business. According to Geoff Thompson, "Dennis Martin is the most credible instructor of real self-defence in the world today." He set up his own company, CQB Services, which, back in 1985, was one of the very first commercial companies to offer VIP close protection training in the UK.

CQB is a military term used to describe close quarter battle – the skills of fighting at close quarters, either armed or unarmed. In the US it is known as CQC or combatives. Martin says it is very important that all the different disciplines are trained together in order to counter attacks with a long gun, a pistol, an edged weapon, an impact weapon, a chemical weapon or bare hands. Martin says, "In the past, the unarmed combat teacher would teach one thing, the shooting instructor another, the baton instructor would teach something different and then in a real situation you had to quickly choose which technique to use. The objective of any trainer is to cut down choice which then increases reaction times and so CQB is best taught as a coherent whole – an integration of everything."

The security industry in general and door supervision and close protection in particular have changed enormously since Dennis Martin started working the doors in the late 1960s. Even though he is no longer operational in close protection he is still one of the most respected doormen in Liverpool. He continues to work the door today at a hotel in Liverpool, but now more for enjoyment as well as to keep his hand in: "If I am teaching martial arts and CQB for door staff, then I must also do the job too, to maintain credibility!" Over the years he has adapted his techniques and approach to the changes in modern society, saying, "there are now more knives and other weapons on the streets of Liverpool than there ever has been, and drugs now fuel the hot-heads as much as alcohol. And, of course, there is the danger of infection by AIDS and hepatitis though blood contact. Now neck restraint used aggressively as a "pre-emptive" manoeuvre is a more effective than a knock-out punch, which might not keep a guy down high on drugs! Today, on the doors in Liverpool, you have people off their heads on alcohol or drugs, and a large percentage of these people are predators and are not happy unless they spoil someone else's night. These people think they are hard men. And so the door crews are there to look after and protect the general public against these idiots. It's actually the door staff who are the *real* hard men!"

Martin still lives a tactical lifestyle and is always be aware of what is going on around him. He is always alert for trouble – and of ways to avoid it – and has recently spent a lot of time working and teaching in South Africa where murders, rapes and car-jackings are commonplace. "Because of the social and political situation in South Africa, the training courses which CQB Services provide are highly valued," says Martin.

Dennis Martin is hard, in the strictest meaning of the word – physically and mentally tough, durable, intense. He trains hard, he works hard, he lives hard, and teaches others how to become hard enough to deal with the modern world and work in the security industry. While over the years he has developed the techniques and skills required for working in the most high-risk areas of the world, he has never lost sight of where it all began – a karate dojo. He believes that discipline is the biggest factor in martial arts, particularly karate. It is also important in society. Training in karate does a lot for young people because whether you want to train for sport or as an art, it is great for self-development and discipline. It may not provide a skill-set you can use in daily life, but as a sport, art and for conditioning, traditional martial arts training is ideal.

Martin reckons that he will continue to work the doors and further develop his training techniques, as well as write, give seminars and, of course, keep up his own training. Add to a wide range of fighting skills the correct mindset, Neuro-Linguistic Programming, situational awareness, years of experience and the will to use everything you have as a protector rather than a predator, and you have the embodiment of a really hard bastard.

BARE-KNUCKLE FIGHTING

The Ultimate Violent Sport

GYPSY KINGS AND BARE-KNUCKLE KNIGHTS

By Tel Currie

BARE-KNUCKLE, COBBLE- OR street-fighting has been around since the year dot but is most commonly associated with the gypsy community. Of course, not all cobble-fighters are of travelling stock but travellers have settled financial and domestic disputes in this noble way for centuries. The top man in the unlicensed game has long been known as the "Guv'nor", and the travellers hail him as "King of the Gypsies".

The most common method is what is known as a "straightener" where no kicking or butting is permitted and a mutually agreed "fair play man" acts as a referee. The fair play man is usually somebody who has been a fighter themselves and has respect from everyone involved. No gloves are worn on the cobbles and commonly the fight continues until one side calls "best" (gives in) or is simply unconscious. The "all in" method is even more savage and has no rules at all. "All in" fights have been known to be fought to the death!

It goes without saying that the "all in" is the most brutal, savage form of organized street combat and is mostly saved for family versus other family disputes where pure hatred or revenge is the motivation. While unlicensed boxing is legal and includes gloves, bare-knuckle fighting is illegal so people get confused, thinking that any brawl is a bare-knuckle street fight. I have worked on the doors for many years and some doormen count a punch up with a drunk or simply slinging one out as a street fight. This is the only explanation for some of the ridiculous tallies of street fights some doormen claim. Depending on the interview, Lenny McLean claimed around 30,000 bare-knuckle fights! Sorry, but unless you are counting every drunk you turn away, that's impossible! If you have witnessed a real, organized bare-knuckle fight – a proper street fight – you will realize that these figures cannot be true.

Also, so much money is staked on these fights that with that many clean wins, McLean would have owned his own island! Trust me, twenty to thirty organized bare-knuckle fights is a lot, even in a lifetime. Lenny's unlicensed record was thirty fights, six losses, knocked out four times, stopped once in three rounds and outpointed once. That would mean he won thousands of fights against raw hard knuckle but was knocked spark out with gloves on – it doesn't add up. I intend no disrespect, but it has to be said that some of what Lenny McLean said was far from the truth, and this has now even been admitted by McLean fans such my good friend Tony Thomas, whose book *The Guv'nor: Through the Eyes of Others* is a classic read. Unlike pro boxing, you can't just look up fighters' records in unlicensed or bare-knuckle fighting, so quite often a fighter's more sensational accounts are mistakenly accepted as the truth.

I am fortunate enough to have lots of gypsy friends who are staunch, respected people, including good, solid families like the Frankhams, Stockins, Smiths, Frenches, Brazils and men like "Gypsy" Joe Carrington. These are proud people and don't leave their crap everywhere; some of their caravans are like palaces.

There are some great bare-knuckle gypsy names that run down the years including Tucker Dunn, the Gaskins, Mark Ripley, Hughie Burton, Uriah Burton (known as "Big Just"), John-John Stanley, boxer Tom Taylor, Dan Rooney, John Rooney, Ernie McGinley, Henry "The Dentist" Arab, Henry "The Outlaw" Francis, Eli Frankham, Joe-Boy Botton, Bobby Frankham, Johnny Love, Joe Smith and, one of the best fighters I have witnessed, Louis Welch from Darlington, who could well be considered the modern-day "King of the Gypsies". Mark Ripley from Kent is a man with an awesome reputation. Joey Pyle's son Joe Jr, a man who was brought up surrounded by the fight game, calls Mark "one hell of a tasty bastard". Joe Jr has seen it all and is not easily impressed. When you add that to the equation, Mark really is a bit special.

One man who you really wouldn't want to fight on the cobbles is former British light-middleweight champion Andy Till. He is simply ferocious! He is no longer a light middleweight but he is one of the hardest men I have met and I know most of them! When Andy was British champion, he was also a milkman. He would do his roadwork at around 3 a.m. and then go on his round – that would kill most people for a start off! He was a good man and took his Lonsdale belt to his kids' school to show all the children. Andy was a warrior in the ring, one of those you would have to near kill to beat.

On his milk round one day, he knocked on the door of a family with a bit of a reputation to collect the bill. For some reason, a row broke out. Then three big lumps who were brothers all sprinted halfway down the stairs and took flying leaps at Andy. Andy clumped each one right on the button while they were in mid-air. Each of the brothers thumped to the ground fast asleep after being knocked spark out. Another member of the family then went to fetch the milk bill money. If only they had done that in the first place!

Andy had some rowdy, loyal supporters as well. During a fight with a guy named Robert McCracken from Watford, the crowd tried to kill each other in one of the worst boxing crowd bust-ups ever seen. But if you want to see Andy at his best, watch the two fights against Wally Swift, a highly rated boxer, also from Watford, and you will see how hard Andy Till is. I think Andy could have been pretty untouchable on the unlicensed circuit but, although he came to a few shows, including ones I have organized, I don't know if he was interested in doing it. Andy had been fighting since a very young age, so he may have fancied a well-earned rest by then. But he's certainly not someone to take liberties with!

Without doubt one of the hardest men in a street fight is not a gypsy either but on the top rung of the "chaps" – his name is Vic Dark. Vic is a soft spoken, polite gentleman from the East End and now lives in Essex. Young Vic Dark was a member of the notorious

West Ham ICF (Inter City Firm). A lot of hard men started in the ICF, like Carlton Leach, Cass Pennant, Steve Guy and Billy Gardner. Add Vic Dark, and just those few are positively lethal!

Vic is a black belt in a number of martial arts and a heavyweight lifter. But Vic doesn't use karate or one particular fighting art, he mixes everything together into one awesome street-fighting technique so that I really don't think anyone would get near him on the street. He is also extremely respected by the top so-called gangsters. He was a pallbearer along with young Joe Pyle, Roy Shaw, Jamie Foremen (movie star son of Freddie), Freddie himself and Ronnie Nash at the funeral of the "Boss of Bosses", Joey Pyle Sr. That's how highly Vic is thought of. He was also one of Reg Kray's trusted inner circle in the nick.

Vic is someone I see as an ideal fighter. There's no shouting and roaring; he's a gentleman. He would rather have a laugh with his trusted mates than go fighting all over the place but take a liberty and God help you!

A couple of years ago, the authorities tried to get Vic put away for life after a contract killing. Every day he went to court there were guns, vans and helicopters everywhere. I wrote to Vic and gave him my support while he was on remand. When he got a not guilty verdict (quite right too!) he phoned me and sent me a message of thanks for the support. I will always support Vic Dark. A man among men!

One man from America, who has been called the "hardest man in the world", is Randy Couture, a mixed martial arts fighter who I'm sure we will hear a lot more of in the future.

The man who has been called the "King of the Gypsies" for many years is "Gypsy" Johnny Frankham. Johnny was not only a thrilling cobble-fighter, he was British light-heavyweight champion and had two blistering fights with Chris Finnegan at a packed Royal Albert Hall when the crowd and chairs became as much a part of the fight as Frankham and Finnegan. Johnny was usually asked to be "fair play man" in local fights because he had the respect of everyone and still does. As a ring fighter, he was extremely hard to hit, a bit like Kevin Paddock but, with respect to Kevin, of a lot higher calibre than the unlicensed fighters.

Another gypsy warrior who commands great respect is Les

Stevens from Reading who was also a pro and took the great John Conteh the full distance, which took some doing in those days. John Conteh was one of the most underrated fighters this country has produced. I spent a couple of great fight nights in the company of these two legends. The real deals are always gentlemen; it's the wannabes that are prats!

One ex bare-knuckle fighter stands out for various reasons; he was a decent fighter but far from the best and certainly not the worst. He was also a safe blower, that great occupation pioneered by men like George "Tatters" Chatham and wartime double agent Eddie Chapman, in the same era as the Irish charmer Peter Scott was stealing Sophia Loren's jewels and breaking into any Mayfair pad that took his Raffles-influenced fancy. But this young cobble-fighter from Sunderland turned desperately to the cobbles and gelignite just to make ends meet. As he fought and felt the pain, there was no way he could have known that one day he would buy Darlington football club and clear their £5 million (US$7.5 million) plus debt in one swoop. He is worth £300 million (US$450 million), and he went from a four-year prison sentence to the *Sunday Times* Rich List by selling chipboard and worktops. He is, of course, George Reynolds.

My Newcastle friends do make me laugh. I love them to death and they are most funny when they are being serious. It doesn't matter what you have achieved, if you are from Sunderland, which is ten miles away, they refuse to be impressed. I remember asking my late friend Harry Marsden and John "Mario" Cunningham, founders of the original "Geordie Mafia" and extremely dangerous men in their day, about George Reynolds. I said: "This guy was one of your own. He's now worth £300 million and has a football club, yacht, helicopter and Christ knows what!"

They both fixed me with a stare that blurted out MISTAKE! MISTAKE!

Harry said: "Tell man, wayya mean one of oors? He's a dirty fucking Mackem man!" It was a gem. Then he started on about them "calling us monkey-hangers" and other stuff that completely lost me. Harry wound himself up and started to punch things. Then "Mario", a man who had once escaped from Durham Prison before everything was tightened up after the John McVicar escape, piped up . . . I never mentioned Sunderland again and I still don't know what a "Mackem" is.

One of the most famous bare-knuckle fights took place between two Irishmen, Dan Rooney and Ernie McGinley, for the championship of Ireland. It turns up on every unlicensed and bare-knuckle video in circulation. There are masses of spectators all over the place, a swarm of people even sitting on their roofs for a better look. It was a bitter, brutal battle. The crowd actually became uncontrollable and the fight was a draw but it would appear Dan Rooney had the upper hand at that point.

Of the new breed, one of the best bare-knuckle fighters is an East End gypsy called Matt Attrell. A lot of people talk about Matt and it's all good. It would seem if you want to be known as a man who has fought everyone on the cobbles now, you must beat Matt Attrell, who has never ducked anyone. Danny Woolard tells how he and Matt were put in hospital after a fight in a Chinese restaurant but they took twelve of the enemy to hospital with them; the foes were full of stitches and one had lost his eye!

Danny Woolard is another man who was more than tasty on the cobbles; he has a book out and it's worth a read. In the Chinese restaurant encounter a meat cleaver was put through Woolard's head and he carried on fighting. To the credit of the Chinese restaurant, they made no statements (it goes without saying that Woolard and Attrell didn't). So many people have claimed to have been a close friend of Reg Kray in prison but Danny was, I know that for a fact, plus Reggie gave Danny Woolard a mention in his last book, *A Way of Life*.

One gypsy cobble-fighter who I had the pleasure of training and preparing for the unlicensed ring was "Gypsy" Joe Smith from West London. Joe was a brutal and fear-free cobble-fighter but just needed to brush up on boxing ring craft. I taught Joe the value of working from behind a solid jab, cutting off the ring and footwork, as well as getting him into prime fitness. We had a full gym at our disposal, as I worked in one at the time, and we would sweat it out every day. Joe's cousins Billy Smith and Jimmy Stockin also came along to a specialized boxercise circuit I set up and for some sparring. Sometimes I needed to calm them down as these boys loved nothing more than a claret-filled tear up. They were, and still are, extremely hard men. Joe, Jimmy and brother Wally Stockin were also extremely close, as I was, to Joey Pyle Sr and we would always catch up at parties. Myself and a few of the lads also did a fair bit of hair-raising debt-collecting for a very well known East End "face" and other bits and pieces.

With Joe, the first thing to sort out in training, as well as fitness, was controlling his aggression. He was used to the cobbles where fights only last about ten–twenty minutes tops and are often personal so hatred plays a large part. The boxing ring is not like that. You have to keep things under control and relax, not get wound up. You might start as first on the bill and end up last, while your opponent sits in traffic, but you must just let it ride. Getting angry is asking for defeat – why do you think Ali used to wind his opponents up so much?

At one of Joe's early unlicensed fights, when he hadn't mastered the mental side and was still thinking like a cobble-fighter, it all blew up in proper gangland fashion. It was like Eddie Richardson and Frankie Fraser at Mr Smith's club all over again. Now, it seems funny. Actually, even then it seemed funny!

I was in Joe's corner with his older brother Aaron and younger brother John. As will become clear, I will not give details of venues although I can say that this one took place near London. We were due to be second on the bill. A lot of preparation is needed on fight night; getting your man kitted out, hands bandaged up, keeping him warm on the pads and greasing him up around his eyes and face. Every time our fight slot changed, Joe had to be cooled down again, made to relax and brought back to normal thinking. Then we got a call via the promoter to say our opponent was in traffic, so we would be on fourth. Now, for some reason, nobody liked this guy we were supposed to be fighting. There were twelve fights on the bill so just how long were we going to be kept waiting was anybody's guess.

Roy Shaw, as guest of honour, had taken his place at the ringside and the place was packed. So we warmed up again. While on the pads and getting a light sweat on, another call came in: we were now on sixth. It was stand-down time again and Joe was starting to get very heated: "If this mush is not here soon, any one of 'em will do." I told him that this was normal routine in amateur, unlicensed and even pro events. So off we went again, another call and we were due on eighth but he still wasn't there, then ninth!

By now Joe's eyes were glazed over and he was pacing and staring at people. The ever reliable Steve Holdsworth of Eurosport came in the dressing room to calm him down. But now I had the old cobble-fighter on my hands and I could tell not many double jabs were going to be thrown: it was going to be a smash up!

Then the guy arrives, gets weighed in with Joe in his face, gets changed and waits in the passage near us, not a clever move. Every time Joe saw him another vein popped up in his temple. Joe walked up to him and said something that I doubt was "lovely weather" and the guy, a big, tall, gangly bloke, looked stunned.

Finally, we warmed up and were on our way to the ring. A slight touch of gloves and ding! The bell goes. But this guy did not want to punch, he wanted to come in with both arms and smother his opponent. We had been told he would do this and had prepared for it, practising stepping under the guard as it came down and smashing an uppercut into the unguarded chin. But Joe had lost it and the guy was like an octopus all over him. Then it happened; frustrated, Joe leans back and cracked his head right in the guy's face. So then the guy tried wrestling for his life and both ended up on the canvas, rolling around, kicking and punching lumps out of each other.

In the packed crowd half were for the other guy and half were hard-arsed gypsies. The crowd turned on each other with fists and chairs flying. Joe was still punching his opponent on the deck screaming, "Get these poxy gloves off me." When he got up his hand was raised because of his opponent's persistent holding and refusing to punch. As we looked back, the referee was rolling around the canvas with this bloke and had taken over where Joe left off! We all howled with laughter as fighter and ref had it out and all we could hear from the referee was: "I never liked you, you fucker!"

As a chair landed in the ring, we turned our attention to the crowd. Security had made a passageway for us through the gypsy's supporters to get us out of there and we had a few limos lined up. Then we heard what sounded like firecrackers, until one of the security guys shouted: "Fuck me! They're firing shooters." There were firecracker bangs and pings all over the place. A few of the other firm tried to punch us on the way out and we stopped and smashed them in the face with chairs!

There were a few strangers lined up with hands in pockets outside, so we made straight for the limos and drove off, pissing ourselves laughing as we went. When things had calmed down a little, Joe spluttered: "That fucking curry house I booked better still be open, I'm starving now."

They opened the restaurant as we arrived mob-handed in different limos and checking for holes in ourselves almost in their foyer! That kind of night never puts you in the mood for a jobsworth. Our waiter refused to sell beer until, that is, Aaron and "Big" John, who is about six foot seven and 300 pounds, stood up and asked him if he wanted to be put on the next day's menu – beer was served!

It was the thought of the referee battering a boxer that really got me, though, and I just couldn't get this strange picture out of my head. Joe came to my club the next day and we told everyone that we won the fight. That battle is still talked about today but there were others . . . But back to bare-knuckle fighting.

One man who rarely gets a mention but could look after himself was a man named Mark Owens (no, not the Take That bloke!). He knocked "Mad" Frankie Fraser out cold when they were in Parkhurst Prison, when Frank was at his most feared. Mark Owens obviously didn't give a toss for reputations. I think Mark and Frank became pals in the end. Also, my close friend Chris Lambrianou clumped Ian Brady and a slag called Don Barrett who turned supergrass – twice! Chris served up a nonce and a grass – instant knighthood surely!

One famous gypsy story took place in 1994. A whole army of Irish travellers in about 150 trailers headed north causing real problems for northern English gypsies who called on their Scottish allies the McPhee family for help. It was like a military invasion and the best of the McPhees travelled to meet the Irish. Both groups produced a fighter. If the McPhees won, the Irish would have to turn back but if the Irish won, the takeover of Scotland would proceed. It was like the Jacobite wars with Bonnie Prince Charlie.

The fight kicked off and the chosen McPhee was on the brink of success when suddenly the Irishman's pals joined in. No "fair play man" would have been able to handle this lot! Eventually, order was restored and the fight continued but the Scottish McPhee was now so seething with rage. He laid into the Irishman, got hold of his head, bit his nose clean off and in front of both clans . . . swallowed it!

For some reason, a month or so later the Irish tried to invade again with fresh troops, but the Scottish McPhees were ready for them and the Irish were forced to put up a fighting retreat. The domination of the northern English and their main prize, domination of the Scottish gypsies, had failed badly. No such huge "invasion" has happened since. It was like Culloden all over again but this time the Scots won!

One day, in about 1995, I met up with a few of my close mates just outside a huge roundabout, otherwise known as the town of Milton Keynes (never ask for directions in Milton Keynes!). I didn't know exactly where we were going but I assumed we were off to watch and wager on a "straightener" so I guessed it would be in the open air somewhere. For some reason a "straightener" usually takes place in the open but as we carried on, we turned into an industrial estate, tooted the horn three times and this huge metal warehouse door opened. I knew then that it was going to be an "all in" because they usually take place in built-up areas, mostly inside with the door firmly bolted. Again, it's just the way it is. There were only about twenty to thirty of us there, not a lot for the size of the place, but "all ins" are top secret as they are illegal.

One fighter was a huge Yorkshire man and the other a much smaller bloke from West London, who was the man we were supporting. The other guy was so pumped up with steroids he looked like he was about to burst and he certainly had more than a minor dose of "roid rage". As he kicked, punched and head-butted everything metal within sight of his corner, we all tried not to burst out laughing, including his opponent whom I shall call "Mark".

Now Mark was one of those guys people came unstuck with especially when he worked the doors. He was one of the smallest guys on the door but most of the hardest and respected men have been small men. People like Roy Shaw, Freddie Foreman, Frankie Fraser and even the Krays were not big men. Small, sinewy blokes with tons of bottle are by far the worst.

Somebody kicked a gas cylinder and the two were at each other, hands around each other's necks and trying to butt each other. Then there was a loud bang on the door. We all scattered and put T-shirts back on the fighters as it could only be the Old Bill.

One of the lads moved the door slightly ajar and in strutted, like the king of the world, Lenny McLean or "the Guv'nor" as he liked to be called. He sat on an old pallet and growled, "Carry on boys." I assume he had staked money and was popping in to check on his investment. I don't know who he had his money on but the fact was that Lenny was heavily into the steroid scene himself and used to jack up all the time, I'm afraid; unlike the myth, he was also a brutal bully. My guess was that he was backing "Mr Pumped Up and Roaring".

Even Lenny's own cousin and promoter Frank Warren did a magazine interview in which he described Lenny as "the very worse type of bully". He also stated that, "his book was a joke, all those bare-knuckle fights and claiming to be unbeaten in the unlicensed ring. Roy Shaw stopped him early and Cliff Field and Johnny Waldron knocked him out cold twice each. He was also beaten by a guy called Kevin Paddock. How he got away with that book I will never know, I guess people believe what they want to believe." And that was his own family!

Bob Mee, author of *Bare Fists* wrote: "The marketing of Lenny McLean's book was undeniably a success as it produced a best-seller. However, the startling claim of the first sentence of the fly-sheet – 'Lenny McLean is the deadliest bare-knuckle fighter Britain has ever seen' – is laughably wide of the mark." He added, "McLean was a tough man but had little ability outside rage, borne out of personal misery," and that McLean "could not box".

I have spoken to many people who knew or had crossed swords with Lenny McLean, but I have only left in the comments from men who would have said them whether Lenny was alive or dead, if he was standing in front of them or not. I have left out the comments from people who would say, "Lenny me old mate, great to see you!" when confronted by him in person.

A famous incident that about six different people have described to me was when a sixteen-year-old Roy Shaw fan said "Bad luck, Len" after Shaw had stopped him. McLean's response was to beat the kid senseless with a chair leg! Trust me, this is not the sort of thing you make up. I have seen him bully people with my own eyes and then slobber when a well-known North London "face" has walked in the club with his brother.

Lenny's trademark on the doors was to spread-eagle a guy's legs and punch him as hard as he could right up the groin – these were just everyday bank clerks and the like, not hard men. The idea was that the guy would wake up with huge, swollen testicles. This can now be proven, as to milk the cow even further, McLean's autobiography, *The Guv'nor*, has been followed up by a book called *The Guv'nor Tapes*. This contains everything that was too much for the original book and in it Lenny talks about this method with glee to Peter Gerrard, his ghost-writer.

Now, back in Milton Keynes Mark and the other lump were at each other once again. Mark suddenly grabbed the guy's ears, nutted him three or four times, then lifted his knee about a dozen times into the genitals. (The difference, of course, between this and the McLean story is that the fighter had agreed to an "all in" and was not just a plumber's mate!) As he did this at dazzling speed, Mark sank his teeth into the big guy's face. There was a ripping sound and a lump of meat that resembled a nose and some other bits were in Mark's mouth; he then spat them out and forced all his fingernails into the claret-filled hole of goo, blood and snot. He then ripped out yet more flesh and the bone could now easily be seen. Just before the Yorkshireman called "best" (surrender), Lenny McLean dipped his head, turned away like he was about to retch, went a bit green and said, "See ya boys, that's enough for Lenny for one day."

I assumed he had lost his money and had got used to the gloved life. Dave Courtney, who worked with Lenny for ages, says in his book *Heroes and Villains* that Lenny couldn't handle the celebrity when it came and was responsible for being "a bit of a bully". I have sparred with Roy Shaw a few times and moved around with the likes of Jimmy Stockin but they were taking it VERY easy with me. Lenny just would not have been able to do that: he would have had to knock you all over the ring, gain a victory, roar and basically take a liberty (although he would not have seen it that way).

On one occasion, a legend who was a pro (who never fought

unlicensed but was heavily involved) battered Lenny all over the ring and the guy must have been in his sixties by then! He let me use his name here but I won't, although it doesn't take much working out. This man, who was a very big heavyweight and would have beaten all the unlicensed fighters in his day, just jabbed Lenny's head off, with Lenny getting more and more wound up, throwing punches at thin air. The boxer had also sparred with Roy and found him in a far superior class; there was also a lot more mutual respect. This man had been all over the world with Joe Louis and took shit off nobody . . . including the Kray twins.

Another bare-knuckle fighter in the 1990s was called Joe Savage who claimed he was British bare-knuckle champion. He claimed forty-one wins on the trot and no losses. He was meant to take part in a fight festival in America in 1993. The fighters contesting for a grand cash prize included former heavyweights Tony Tubbs, James "Bonecrusher" Smith who had handed Frank Bruno his first defeat, Tyrell Biggs and Smokin' Bert Cooper, who replaced Mike Tyson in a fight against the Warrior himself, Evander Holyfield, in 1991. Tyson claimed damaged ribs, while some say he didn't want the fight because he knew he did not have the heart, mental power or fitness of Evander. Whatever the reason, Burt Cooper was a late replacement.

In the first round of Holyfield vs Cooper, the unthinkable happened. Cooper caught Evander with a left hook that nearly made the arena crumble and fall to the ground! If Evander was not near the ropes, he would not have got up, nobody could. Evander grabbed the ropes, his legs going in different directions. Tyson must have been kicking himself but the Warrior cleared his head and, God knows how, stopped Cooper in seven explosive rounds. After watching these guys going at each other in sparring, the undefeated bare-knuckle champion of Britain Joe Savage pulled out with a hand injury!

Talking of Tyson, one of his genuine friends (because he has a lot of "yes" men around) is "Big" Joe Egan from Birmingham via Ireland. The tongue-in-cheek title of his book is *The Hardest White Man in the World*. Joe was a very tasty boxer who admires Roy Shaw. I met Joe at a Dave Courtney party (that's about the only bit

I remember!) and I took a photo of Joe and Roy together. Joe, who is a gent and great company, is a real fighting man who can really have a proper row and by that I mean eighty wins by the age of twenty-four, a Golden Gloves Champion who went the distance with Lennox Lewis and beat Bruce Seldon. That's how good. Joe did a prison sentence and Roy's book *Pretty Boy* helped get him through it. He is a top bloke. Good on ya, Joe!

Back to Joe Savage. In April 1994, he challenged who he thought was a "shot" (burned out) Bert Cooper. Every top pro I have ever met has been keen to tell me that fighting is their full-time job. Tim Witherspoon, a gentle giant, told me he would train sometimes six to eight hours a day, six to seven days a week. They hire the best sparring partners available, top dieticians and physical conditioners. They get loads of sleep, prepare well mentally and study videos of their opponents; in short, they eat, sleep and breathe boxing. Most unlicensed fighters, unless you happen to be Roy Shaw, have full-time jobs! So, even a "shot" top fighter will nearly always beat an unlicensed or cobble-fighter. Joe Savage was way out of his depth and he knew it. Britain's undefeated bare-knuckle champion was knocked spark out in sixty-five seconds and in that time hit the deck twice. Savage retired after this fight.

One of the youngest bare-knuckle champions ever was just fourteen when he was crowned Romany champion. He was from Galway, Ireland, and his name was Billy Heaney. He won bare-fist titles again at sixteen, twenty-one and twenty-four. Not bad at all. There are a lot of real champions out there who don't do the celebrity thing, but they are the real deal.

My great friend "Welsh" Bernie Davies is an extremely hard man! Human beings are supposed to be made out of flesh and bone but Bernie is made out of pure muscle fibre. He is currently (November 2008) in prison on a firearms charge but we communicate often by letter. He is one of Wales's toughest men with his bare fists and has an "old school" manner, which means he's not a big mouth who offends people. Bernie is a friend of all the "chaps" and we all hope the powers that be have some compassion for Bernie, whose wife is extremely ill. Bernie, though, is too big a trophy for them and since when did the law have compassion?

But Bernie won't be forgotten and his brutal battles in the Welsh

Valleys shall never be forgotten either. Talking of Wales, if you think you're hard, give it large in any pub in Merthyr Tydfil and see if they are in the mood to give you your limbs back!

Lately, America has gone mad for a six foot two, thirty-four-year-old block of muscle called Kimbo Slice. His real name is Kimbo Ferguson, but, after a nasty cut over the right eye he gave to an opponent called Big D. Ferguson (obviously, no relation), he acquired the nickname Kimbo "Slice". Kimbo built his reputation on bare-knuckle brawls, or, as they say in America, "underground" fights. After an awesome reputation built in fields, barns and warehouses with his bare fists, Kimbo got bored of knocking huge men spark out on the cobbles and trained for the mixed martial arts circuit and fighting in the octagon. Recently he fought a former WBO boxing champion (famous for annihilating Tommy "The Duke" Morrison, star of *Rocky V*, and having a chin of iron!) and beat him in under three minutes.

Kimbo has become an internet legend, with sites showing his fights receiving thousands of hits. He has become a phenomenon and now has his own website where his bare-knuckle fights can be seen. I think it's hard to know whether Kimbo Slice is a true and brutal bare-knuckle warrior or a piece of American novelty and a money-spinner, the latter of course being what the Americans are so good at. Everything has to be a brand and business with a slogan or two and Kimbo is being made into a star. Kimbo can certainly have a fight, but is a touch wild and plodding. I'm not sure if he could do the business against Britain's top knuckle men or fighters like Ian Freeman. Ian is a good friend and the problem when a boxer fights a man like Ian is that, once a boxer's legs are taken away, it's game over!

If you can box and grapple, choke and hold, you are in the driving seat. Have a look at a busy street anywhere on a Saturday night at those who are drunk and get into a fight: 90 per cent will end up on the ground. So if you are strongly trained in fighting on the floor, the fight is yours. I have rarely seen two guys come out of a club or pub for a fight and both men stay on their feet like a real cobble-fighter.

In fact in 1990, when I was eighteen, two friends of mine came out of a club called the Top Hat near Ealing, London. The two lads looked good when they got into a fight, as they were both boxers and were slick, not like these idiots who have a few drinks and suddenly think they are Reg Kray and start flailing their arms like a windmill. (How many blokes do that? You almost expect their dad to come and put their hand on the guy's head as if they were a kid!) They were moving around well, when one slag ran past and, with full force, he swivelled and plunged a carving knife straight between our mate's ribs. You could actually hear it enter, crack and then a squishing sound. The knife was a kitchen knife and he must have been trying to kill my pal before legging it! This was when very few places had CCTV. When the paramedics arrived we could see a huge hole opening and closing like it was breathing! Our pal was in intensive care for two months; he only just made it.

We knew that the prick who stabbed him was one of the "firm" we were fighting and after a bit of research to find him (like torturing his mates) he spent three months in intensive care!

There are always two sides to every story. Like the rivalry between Henry "The Outlaw" Francis and Jimmy Stockin, two top gypsy knuckle men. My close, trusted Welsh pal Julian Davies, or "Juggy" as we call him, wrote a book called *Streetfighters* in which he presented Henry's version of this spiky old rivalry, so I feel I should write Jimmy's account to balance things out.

Jimmy Stockin fought 180 amateur fights – that's some going. One day at Peterborough fair, Jimmy had been on the ale all day and he was well pissed. He was well aware that his arch rival Henry Francis was at the fair. Jimmy bumped into Henry, stumbling, not in an aggressive way but just drunk. Jimmy wasn't looking to start a fight but Henry thought he was and threw a few punches at Jimmy, cutting his face. Henry was hardly affected by drink at all, unlike Jimmy, so Jim knew this was not the time. They made arrangements to fight in the morning but Henry had gone. He had left the site and gone back up north. A man called out: "Henry didn't know it was you, Jim."

"Too bad, I'm coming after him!"

The next meeting should have been in a Doncaster pub, right on Henry's doorstep. About thirty travellers from West London went along because you have to prepare for the worst. This was a bold move: this was really northerners only and a London "face" was on his way looking to fight. As they pulled up, Henry's father and brother were there but said again: "He didn't know it was you, Jim."

They were sure that Henry's mob would be in the pub and burst in through both doors to keep everyone in, but once again, no Henry Francis! They waited around for a few hours but he didn't show, so they went back south. And that was that. Now, when Henry hit Jimmy a few times, Jimmy would have been well pissed. I have seen Jimmy after a few "sherbets" many times and if he hadn't been leaning on the bar, you could push him over with your index finger. It's a very different story when Jimmy is sober, though.

Jimmy Stockin and his brother Wally (another good fighter and one of the "firm"), Joe Smith, Johnny and Bobby Frankham are certainly not bullies but I think Henry Francis was trying to make them look like a pack of wild men.

Unlike my experience of Lenny McLean, everybody has informed me that Bartley Gorman was a complete gentleman and family man. The problem again is that he was not the unbeaten superman he made out and was never the "King of the Gypsies", as he claimed in his book of that title.

Here's an example. Gorman claims that he challenged Roy Shaw, Lenny McLean, Bobby and Johnny Frankham and everyone was too scared to fight him! Now, a lot of the gypsies had not even heard of Bartley before his book came out. Bartley Gorman claims: "I challenged Johnny to a bare-knuckle fight a couple of times at Doncaster Races. I was heavier than him but he was quick and experienced. I would liked to have tested my boxing skills against his." I related this story to Johnny Frankham who nearly choked on his beer laughing! I know a hell of a lot of good gypsies and nobody had heard about these challenges!

Bartley also claims with confidence: "If Mike Tyson and Lennox Lewis were fighting in one field and I was fighting in the next field, all the gypsies would come and watch me."

What do you think?

I also personally asked Roy Shaw, Joey Pyle and Les Stevens about Bartley Gorman and no one knew who he was. If a challenge was made, Joey Pyle, who was Roy's promoter, would have known but he didn't. In Bartley's book there is a photograph of him posing, with the caption, "Taken in 1974 when I challenged Roy 'Pretty Boy' Shaw", but Roy wasn't released from prison until 1975! Bartley says he was at the Shaw vs Donny "The Bull" Adams fight in December 1975, so why didn't he challenge Roy in the ring then, or at any of Roy's fights, as this is how fights were made back then?

Bartley's book makes the "King of the Gypsies" sound like an official title given by a well-organized body. It's not, and just like "the Guv'nor" it's a very loose term. You don't fight for the title of "Guv'nor", then defend, lose or get stripped of it, and it's not an ongoing event. It's not like a pro world champion who has to first win a world title and then defend it.

"King of the Gypsies" is the same. It's not an official title as Bartley Gorman makes it sound. That's why, after all these years, John Frankham is still thought of as "King of the Gypsies" because it's to do with the type of man you are – it's more a lifetime achievement award. Otherwise, Joe Smith could lay a claim because he had nine unlicensed fights and no losses, but Joe has never claimed it because, even to him, the title belongs to Johnny. It's like Ali being called the "greatest". When Frazier and Norton beat him, they didn't become the "greatest", did they?

I remember the first time Roy Shaw ever laid eyes on Bartley Gorman and it wasn't in a field or warehouse, it was at Reggie Kray's graveside. Roy shook his hand like he has with millions of strangers everywhere. When I told Roy it was Bartley Gorman he looked at me as if to say, "Who's that?" My mate Liam, who knows every "face" because he films them all the time, can be heard on the video asking Bartley, "And who are you, mate?"

Bartley looked a bit put out and mumbled, "Bartley Gorman."

Sometime later, I showed Bartley's book to Roy. When he read the bit about him being challenged Roy went completely mental and he said: "Why the fuck is everyone lying about me just to get a gee up? It's lies and always about me just to make these slags look like something when they are nothing!" He then said: "Tel, you know every fucker there is to know, find this bloke and tell him I will fight him now! Fucking NOW!"

Those instructions were pretty clear, so I rang Joe Smith as a starting point. Joe was with his cousin Billy and mumbled something to him as if he was checking something. Then he said to me:

"Telboy, tell the Guv'nor to calm down. Bartley Gorman died a couple of months ago."

"How?" I asked.

"Cancer I think, mate."

I mumbled, "God rest him," and thanked Joe.

I told Roy the news. He was still in a rage but as soon as I told him he said: "That's terrible for his family. Did he have kids? Perhaps we should send flowers?" I respected Roy for that because the family man and the fighting man meant two different things to him. He could have said something really nasty but instead he was respectful.

A few weeks later, Roy and Joey Pyle looked through Bartley's book. They looked at the photos to try to jog their memories. Along with coppers, it's obvious that a gangster or villain has to remember names and faces – you wouldn't get very far without that skill. Neither Joe or Roy could place Bartley Gorman. When Bartley challenged Bobby Frankham, Johnny's nephew, it was clearly a publicity stunt that Bartley would not have gone through with and none of Bobby's team were contacted. Bobby himself thought it was a publicity joke. He was still in his early twenties but had assaulted a referee in a pro fight and lost his licence: his number one priority was to get his pro licence back. An illegal bare-knuckle fight on a boat was not the way to achieve this – that's obvious!

It's hard to write about the dead. I have full respect for the way Bartley conducted his life, he was a true man – the problem is purely about his claims to fights. The man commonly regarded as the "King of the Gypsies" is "Gypsy" Johnny Frankham, that's a fact.

It's also a fact that gypsies (mostly English) and "tinkers" (mostly Irish) for the most part hate each other. I know a place where one side of the street is gypsy and the other is tinker with the road being no man's land. A lot of gypsies don't even travel, they stay on a site. And I have had countless punch ups with idiots who claim to hate "pikeys". If they went into a real gypsy home, they would be in awe, especially at Johnny Frankham's. (I wouldn't get any ideas about trying to rob it though. Ha!)

Never underestimate a man just because he is not huge with bulging biceps. Billy Cribb (author of *Tarmac Warrior*) is also a rather small man but he has the heart of a lion. Most people think that the bigger the muscles in your arms, the harder you will punch; that if you pump iron like a maniac, the size of the muscle will increase and therefore so will your strength. It doesn't happen like that. What you are given naturally in terms of power is pretty much where you will stay. I used to tell people this in the gym but it usually fell on deaf ears.

Say, for example, you are doing bicep curls with heavy weights: yes, your strength will improve but ONLY on bicep curls! If you are pumping out leg extensions you will get stronger but ONLY on leg extensions. In other words, bicep curls will not make you punch harder. In fact, if you don't stretch the muscle enough after the workout (which 99.9 per cent of people do not!) you will actually decrease your power by losing range and making you more open to injury because you are so tight. Look at Ali or Sugar Ray Robinson or Joe Louis: they are loose and supple which means they can throw punches from every angle.

The key is to keep the muscles lengthened and well stretched, and to have perfect timing and accuracy. Arnie-type biceps are no substitute for a shot of speed and timing that your opponent never saw coming and carries the element of surprise. Remember heavyweight flop Bruce Seldon? He should have been able to knock a barn door off with the muscle he carried and so should Frank Bruno, but it doesn't work that way. Evander Holyfield, my particular hero, may spend an hour training his arms but he would make sure he spent an hour-and-a-half stretching them back out again.

About seven years ago, I was pure muscle because in my free time I worked out in the gym. But I was as stiff as a board and my restricted movement actually decreased my punch power! Yet I have seen many a good fighter lose a fight before it started because he has seen the size of his opponent's biceps! I have sparred with countless people and don't think I have ever been in trouble with a body-builder sort. The most painful are the tall, sinewy, snappy, natural punchers.

You can't put muscles on your chin. Bruce Seldon had huge built-up arms but no heart – it's like a lovely looking car with no engine. So never underestimate a man by his muscle or general size, it's a recipe for disaster. A man like Freddie Foreman is not a huge muscle-bound lump but he has the heart of five lions! If you want to beat him, you really would have to kill him. Now, that's a lot more useful on your firm than a steroid-filled lump who in truth is only doing that to himself to try and cover some sort of insecurity in the first place. Why else would you want to take steroids, get to mammoth size and oil your muscles? It's because you are trying to hide something or make up for the lack of something. The heart of men like Foreman cannot be trained into you, it is something you are born with.

Richy Horsley from Hartlepool fought on one of my shows and displayed all the attributes that a real fighter needs. In his second unlicensed fight he showed power, movement, mental strength and raw primitive courage. That's pure fighting instinct. It's not thinking – it's just sheer, raw, caveman-type survival. Richy has had many street fights and I can imagine has done some real damage. Richy and I didn't see eye to eye all the time but my respect for him as a modern-day fighting man is 100 per cent. There's such a very small circle of respected, staunch men left who could be so strong together and make some real money, that I do actually find it upsetting when people in such a small, trusted group fall out. It's a tragedy because you can't just replace them, they are tried and tested and it's usually misinformation or something stupid that screws up what should be a team!

On this occasion, Richy had accused me of things that must have been planted in his head because it came out of the blue and I honestly could not make sense of it. I was accused of getting him beaten on purpose. Well, only the fighter can win or lose, not the promoter, plus the fight was a classic and he lost – just! If I had wanted him beaten, I would not have put someone in who was going to struggle!

Also, I wouldn't have put him top of the bill just to have him beaten as top of the bill means "we have plans". The idea, as explained below, was for him to fight Charlie Bronson and, as Richy knows, that would have made all of us. So why would I want him beaten in his second fight? I was pretty hurt that he thought I would do that, as we had been friends before and his opponent wasn't even one of my fighters!

So I gained nothing from a Horsley defeat. But it takes a lot to lose respect for a fighter of courage and my respect for him as a fighter is still high. I hope Richy now knows the truth and that I really needed him to win! It's a shame but Richy and I have never spoken since that incident.

At the time of Horsley's fight on my show, my fighter Joe Smith was unbeaten and remains so. A lot of people asked me who would win between those two and could I arrange a fight. I could have set it up but at that time Joe was in full flight, fully fit, full of confidence and hungry, and time was on his side. Richy was still easing into the game after a very long lay-off, so it would be unfair to compare them at that time. And Joe, being a very well-liked gypsy with a huge following, would have had crowd advantage at that time. Then again, with Horsley's heart, it may not have mattered.

It looked for a little while like the infamous prisoner Charlie Bronson would be released within two or three years (this information came straight from his legal team). Richy Horsley was the man Bronson wanted to fight. I don't recall whether Bronson hated Richy or not but I know he was picked due to "disrespect", so at this time they were not the best of friends.

It may sound stupid making plans for Charlie Bronson but he had an appeal coming up. He had not been in trouble for ages, he hadn't killed or attempted to kill, and the staff at Wakefield, to a man, couldn't understand why Charlie was still in there. We knew he wouldn't get out straightaway but, if he stayed out of trouble, a three- to four-year release programme was all we needed. And knowing Charlie, if he had the fight to focus on he would have concentrated on that and stayed out of trouble. We wanted a couple of warm-up fights and then a big venue showdown with Richy. Harry Marsden, our dear pal from Newcastle, would prepare Charlie, and Richy already had a capable team around him. Now it seems like light years ago, but at the time it was a real possibility that the powers that be would give Charlie some leeway on his sentence. From then on, every letter I got from Charlie had a section about how he would destroy Richy. I remember on a visit he asked: "How is he going to deal with thirty years of rage, hurt and anger flying at him?"

Would the whole build up and atmosphere get to him so that he would crumble like Frank Bruno used to? Who knew? The problem for Richy would have been that there was bound to be an early storm – could he weather it? If he did ride it, the logical tactic would have been to let Charlie burn himself out and then open up. A stupid idea to some, but if it came off, we would be the ones laughing. It would certainly eclipse Roy Shaw vs Donny Adams in 1975.

Richy would certainly have needed to train and get strong. Richy is not a lover of training (a problem I encountered before with him) but I think he would have had enough motivation for this one. Charlie, of course, had been on the weights since his sentence started and he was as strong as an ox. It would be more difficult to guess his fitness in jail than his strength because, of course, there was not a great deal of scope for road work in Wakefield's concrete coffin. Then, a few weeks later myself, Joey Pyle Sr, Charlie Breaker and a few others made our way to the Old Bailey to hear Charlie Bronson's appeal.

On the second day, the place was full of more police with dogs and riot gear than I have ever seen in my life! By that, we knew that Charlie had been turned down on appeal. I admit, we all shed a few tears for Charlie (we had honestly forgotten about boxing in the drama of that courtroom). Charlie acted with amazing dignity and pride. His head held high, he thanked Judge Rose, who insisted on saying: "I would say to the parole board, that this is a very different man than the one who started this sentence." He didn't have to say anything but he felt compelled to tell the world that Charlie had changed. But how much longer must one man do?

ALI VS TYSON

The Kings of the Ring

HARD BASTARDS, WHAT EXACTLY ARE THEY?

By Robert MacGowan

FIRST OF ALL, when we say a man is hard and we are not talking about his readiness for sex but his fighting prowess, what do we really mean? Do we mean that he is lean, muscular and hard of body? If so, there are many such men that cannot fight at all. Do we mean that he is hard and cruel of nature? Again, that is no indication whatsoever of an able gladiator. Or, as is more likely, do we mean that he is physically robust and resilient, and can absorb heavy punishment? Those qualities certainly provide an advantage to any combatant. Conversely, though, being "hard" in that sense does not necessarily mean that a person can actually fight effectively, and there are many very good fighters who are not extremely hard men at all, though they may have accrued the reputation as such.

Let's take as an example the fearsome Mike Tyson, ex-heavyweight boxing champion of the world and reputedly at one time "The Baddest Man on The Planet".

Tyson was born on 30 June 1966, and as a child was bullied because of his lisp and high-pitched voice. His father deserted the family when Mike was two years old and his mother died when he was sixteen. That neither parent witnessed him succeeding at anything has bothered him all of his life, and he lived his early years in the shadow of his older brother, Rodney, who was relatively successful at school and in his subsequent employment. In contrast, Mike had been arrested by the police a total of thirty-eight times by the age of thirteen, and regularly drank alcohol and took drugs alongside many who were physically weaker and less ambitious than him. Mike harboured the hope from an early age of eventually making something of his life, but to fit in with his contemporaries and local gang members, he brandished weapons, robbed people at knifepoint and did not think of himself as either hard or an able fighter. Indeed, he joined the gangs mainly for protection on the mean streets of Brownsville, his hometown. Only after being remanded to a state penal youth facility, where his innate intelligence drove him to seek more from life, did he discover that he did not need weapons or a gang behind him, but could fight with his fists alone. In the gymnasium and amateur boxing ring it was found that he had exceptionally fast hands and an urgency of purpose that allowed him to finish most of his opponents well inside the scheduled distance. His early mentor, Cus D'Amato, took these natural qualities and used them to mould the youth into a bobbing, weaving, constantly moving target who, once within range, could take his opponents out with vicious left and right hooks and uppercuts delivered with every ounce of the fighter's powerful body behind them. After turning professional under Cus, he won his first nineteen bouts by way of knockout, twelve of them in the first round! Quite a start to his ring career and a change in fortune never expected by young Mike himself.

There is a theory that a man's ability to punch devastatingly hard derives from an underlying, acquired anger leading to a desire to hurt others before he himself is hurt, possibly as he was as a child. Others say that it is simply a product of perfect balance, poise, timing and execution, and, indeed, Tyson possessed all of the components in both categories. Even his height at around five foot ten, which is quite short for a heavyweight, contributed to the compact, explosive package as his crouching stance allowed him to evade many punches thrown at him before uncoiling with lightning speed and accuracy to put away all those who opposed him, with intense combination punching. His reputation grew until his mere presence and gold-toothed snarl struck genuine fear into the hearts of many experienced professional fighters, some of whom were half-beaten even before the opening bell sounded. He easily became the youngest ever heavyweight champion of the world by knocking out the then title-holder, Trevor Berbick from Canada, in round two of their contest, when Mike was twenty years, four months and twenty-two days old. His projected persona soon became that of probably the most vicious, dangerous and feared man on earth, with more than a little justification.

But was Mike really a "hard" man? In my opinion no, he was not, not within the context of world-class professional boxers who, it can be argued strongly, are as a genre the hardest men on earth and have to be able to withstand the repeated pounding to head and body their occupation entails, not only in competition but also through the many hours of necessary sparring. Mike Tyson was an exceptionally fast, well-proportioned boxer who was able to consistently land precise, effective and very hurtful punches on opponents with either hand, usually without being hit in reply – the very essence of boxing. In addition, because of his speed, power and aggression, most of his fights were over quickly with the result being that he hardly ever took any punishment. He did not need to be a hard man to be successful!

When D'Amato died the weaknesses in Tyson's mental makeup resurfaced and began to unravel the package that Cus had put together so well. As Mike fell apart as a person so did his effectiveness in the ring and eventually, on 11 February 1990 in Tokyo, Japan, he was knocked over and out by relatively light-punching Buster Douglas, who was in fact a 42 to 1 betting underdog. The defeat shocked the world and is still rated as one of the biggest surprises ever in the whole of sport. Mike Tyson's halcyon days were over. A harder man might have been able to absorb the defeat and ignominy, rally to overcome his personal difficulties and fight back with confidence to regain his former invincibility in the ring. But Mike had no hope of achieving either goal and, indeed, at every point where he needed to show the true grit and hardiness of a champion as opposed to the dynamic and electrifying fighting ability which he possessed in abundance, he failed.

He won a few fights after the defeat but aficionados of the sport could clearly see that something was gone from his persona and professional makeup. As one commentator at the time quipped whilst one of the bouts was still in progress, "Mike Tyson as we know him, has left the building."

He encountered further turmoil in his private life and rightly or wrongly (many believe the latter) was infamously jailed for a sexual assault on actress Desiree Washington.

Mike made a comeback after his release from prison three years later but ran into further trouble when his temper got the better of him in the ring and he bit off a piece of Evander Holyfield's ear in retaliation for the continual but discreet head-butts Holyfield kept landing on him. The unknowledgeable amongst us might see this as a sign of hardness whereas in fact it is a clear indication of weakness. Would not a true hard man confidently accommodate this type of illegal foul, cope with it professionally and apply an appropriate solution which brought him out on top, particularly when being paid millions of dollars and being watched by the whole world? Instead, Mike resorted to the type of action he should have left behind in his youth, an action which relinquished the moral high-ground to Holyfield whereas it should have stayed with Tyson, and lost him the fight and credibility in the whole of the sporting world. It shocked ordinary people and also boxing "experts" who did not know the real Mike Tyson or the world he grew up in, and were too slow to see the provocation to which he was bound to react. One person who certainly knew all of the above was Evander Holyfield.

Pursued relentlessly by the ever-ominous taxman and urged on by his misguided "supporters", Tyson's craving to regain the respect that he had lost drove him back to the ring several more times before being knocked out by the UK's Danny Williams in early 2005. On 11 June that year, whilst engaged in a contest with journeyman fighter Kevin McBride, Tyson quit at the start of the seventh round of what had been, until that point, a close bout. After losing the third of his last four matches Mike announced his official retirement, saying of the fight game that he no longer had "the guts or the heart any more".

So ended the career that had earned Mike Tyson over $300 million.

A previous holder of the title known as "The Richest Prize in Sport", won so emphatically and lost so disappointingly by Tyson, was Muhammad Ali, formerly Cassius Clay.

Ali is the only man ever to have been world heavyweight champion three times in an illustrious career spanning three decades. He exploded on to the professional boxing scene after winning light-heavyweight gold at the 1960 Rome Olympics, with a flashy persona, a unique line in self-praising poetry and plenty to tell the world about himself and how he was destined to become The Greatest of All Time, a destiny he arguably fulfilled, certainly amongst the heavyweights.

Ali's boxing style was completely the opposite of that of Tyson. He did a lot of his fighting on the move, flicking out long left jabs and right crosses whilst back-pedalling or dancing around the ring with long tassels flying from his dazzling white boots. He kept out of counterpunch range with his hands held at waist height, invented the "Ali Shuffle" which was basically a gimmicky fast movement of the feet designed to confuse opponents and impress the photographers, and was an all-round showman and entertainer inside and outside the roped square. He brought the fans back to professional boxing in their thousands and, eventually, in their millions via worldwide television. He took the title from Mafia-connected fearsome "hard man" Sonny Liston in Miami, Florida, in 1964 and embarked on a scintillating career which made him by far the richest sportsman and most famous person on earth.

Ali is remembered by most as a great boxer and for his ring dancing, talking and flashy showmanship, but what they tend to forget is that after he returned to the ring following the ban imposed upon him for refusing to join the army and fight in Vietnam, he fought and beat some of the hardest and most ferocious punching men in history. Ali had originally volunteered for the military but been refused on some pretext. When he eventually received the call-to-arms he had decided that he no longer wished to fight or kill any Vietnamese people as they had not done him any personal harm. Indeed, he added, if he wanted to make war on a country it would probably have to be America, as that was the country which had done him by far the most harm. He famously stated, "I ain't got no quarrel with them Viet Cong, they never called me Nigger!"

The US government did not sympathize with his philosophy and obligingly took away his living for over three years as they later did to Mike Tyson, though for a very different reason. However, the blanket-bombing campaigns, napalm sweeps and waves of young

Americans coming home in body-bags eventually rendered the Vietnam war a very unpopular one, and Ali was hailed a hero by even the non-boxing fraternity for his stand against the government which initiated it and then later backed out with red faces and massive losses.

Ali commenced his comeback in 1970 by stopping the highly rated white fighter Jerry Quarry in three rounds and this heralded his campaign for the title then held by devastating left-hooker and undefeated champion, Joe Frazier from Philadelphia.

His ensuing three-fight series with the lethal Smokin' Joe has been declared by experts to have been sufficiently physically draining on both fighters to cause lasting damage and to end the careers of most men. Of the first fight, staged at the boxing shrine of Madison Square Garden in 1971, Frazier said afterwards "I hit Ali with punches that would have brought down a building." But Ali carried on regardless and the desperate, punch-for-punch battle was described by him later as "the nearest thing to death".

He was decked in the fifteenth to suffer his first professional defeat.

The mutual damage inflicted by the three fights did effectively signal the end of Frazier's career but Ali soldiered on, winning back the title that the government had taken away from him and shipping ever more punishment. Shortly after the second Frazier fight in 1973, Ali took on Ken Norton and suffered a broken jaw, but carried on to lose a split decision. On 30 October of the following year, 1974, after several successive wins, Ali challenged again for the title now held apparently invincibly by the awesome George Foreman, who had lifted Frazier cleanly off his feet with a scything right whilst flooring him six times in four minutes and twenty-five seconds to destroy the husk that remained of him. Big George was a very hot favourite to execute Ali in similar manner in less than three rounds. Early in the fight – dubbed "The Rumble in the Jungle" as it took place in Kinshasa, Zaire, and was the fight that brought Don King to global prominence as a promoter – Ali adopted a tactic feared by the vast majority of global spectators at the time, to be absolutely suicidal against such a massively heavy-puncher as Foreman. Ali simply tucked his elbows and chin in behind his gloves, covered up as much as possible and leaned back on the ropes in what he later described as his "Rope-a-Dope" trick, as big George launched a savage attack to head and body which he sustained round after round, and during which he threw literally hundreds of punches. The ringside audience gasped and media commentators winced as Foreman's swinging punches thudded home time after time and even Ali's own supporters expected him to crumble quickly under such a savage onslaught.

But he didn't! He took the blows, withstood the pain and absorbed the punishment for seven rounds until, incredibly, Foreman punched himself out and came to a virtual standstill after trying so hard and expending every ounce of his energy on the mission to slaughter his opponent as he had so many before. But Ali was different, very different, and stood like the legend he was, unyielding and refusing to go down before Foreman's ferocity until it eventually, as Ali knew it must, began to wane. When in round eight it did and it became obvious that George was not just taking a break but tiring rapidly and struggling to co-ordinate his still-lethal punches, the crowd stilled in silent amazement as Ali peeked out from behind his defences, jabbed out a left and followed up with a series of quick left and right punches which sent the fatigued Foreman wheeling to the canvas, from where he looked up in bewilderment. He rolled on to his back and sheer exhaustion as much as anything else prevented him from rising before he was counted out by the referee. Ali had reclaimed the title for an incredible third time at the age of thirty-two.

By now Ali's ageing body had absorbed a shocking amount of blows and he was way past the point at which he should have retired for health reasons alone. But again, he didn't; he kept climbing up into the ring where he eventually met up again with a former sparring partner turned champion, Larry Holmes. Larry was a formidably fast and vicious puncher who showed little mercy to his one-time employer, who again took a serious beating. Ali finally called it quits for good on a long and punishing career after losing to upcoming Trevor Berbick, the man from whom Tyson later took the unified title, in 1981.

Ali's record shows sixty-one fights with only five defeats, four decisions and one TKO when he retired injured. From his fifty-six wins, thirty-seven were by way of knockout.

It is my humble opinion that there was a short window at the very peak of Mike Tyson's career when his predatory, crouching style, lightning hand speed and explosive punching with both hands could have beaten Ali. I base that opinion on how easily and emphatically Tyson disposed of every heavyweight around during his rise to power under Cus D'Amato, and the fact that throughout Ali's career, several men were able to get close enough to land telling punches on him. Even our own Henry Cooper floored and seriously dazed him to the point where Ali's trainer, Angelo Dundee, had to snatch more time for his man to recover at the end of the round by ripping the seam of his glove and complaining to the referee, who then had no option but to delay proceedings until it was replaced. Before and after that window though, Ali would have whupped Mike every time. When it comes to "hard men", Ali must surely have been the hardest and toughest heavyweight that the world has ever seen or will see for a very long time to come. Unfortunately, he is now paying the heavy toll on his health for that incredible physical resilience.

ACKNOWLEDGMENTS
AND SOURCES

The editor would like to thank the following for their kind permission to publish the articles and re-edited extracts indicated:

"Bouncer" © Geoff Thompson, originally published in an abridged version by *The Times*, 18 December 2003, and reproduced by permission of the author. Website: www.geoffthompson.com

"America's Most Dangerous Prisoner" © Randy Radic, reproduced by permission of the author Randy Radic

"The Doorman – Into the Fire" © Sean Reich, from the forthcoming book *A Long Walk Home*, reproduced by permission of Sean Reich

Apex Publishing Ltd for "The Lion and the Pussycat", an extract from *Loonyology* © Charlie Bronson 2008. Website: www. ApexPublishing.co.uk

New Breed Publishing for "A Champion", an extract from *What Makes Tough Guys Tough? The Secret Domain* © Jamie O'Keefe 1998. Website: www.newbreedbooks.co.uk

"A Hard Man in a Quiet Country" © Barbara Preston, reproduced by permission of the author Barbara Preston

"Sex, Money, Murder" © Randy Radic, reproduced by permission of the author Randy Radic

"Almost Out of Time" © Camille Kimball, reproduced by permission of the author Camille Kimball. Website: www. camillekimball.com

"Soviet Bodyguard" © Alexey Fonarev, reproduced by permission of the author Alexey Fonarev

"My Story" © Bob Honiball, reproduced by permission of the author Bob Honiball. Website: www.bobhoniball.lt

"Round Twelve – January 2002 to June 2005" © David Weeks, originally published in *Tyson and I: A Journey Through Life and*

Anger (Author House, 2007), reproduced by permission of David Weeks

"1963–94 Led Zeppelin" © Don Murfet, originally published in *Leave It to Me – A Life of Rock, Pop and Crime* (Anvil Publications, 2004), reproduced by permission of Lyndsey Murfet

"Hard Times" © Joe Egan, originally published in *Big Joe Egan, The Toughest White Man on the Planet* (Pennant Books, 2005), reproduced by permission of Joe Egan and Pennant Books. Websites: www.pennantbooks.com, www.bigjoeegan.com

"Beyond the Badge; Life on the Beat" © Kimberly Wood, reproduced by permission of the author Kimberly Wood

"Trial" © Mickey Francis and Peter Walsh, originally published in *Guvnors* (Milo Books, 1997), reproduced by permission of Peter Walsh. Website: www.milobooks.com

"The Man Without a Face" © Scott C. Lomax, reproduced by permission of the author Scott C. Lomax. Website: www.sclomax.co.uk

"Tough Talk" © Arthur White, Millie Murray and Tough Talk, originally published in *Tough Talk* (Authentic Lifestyle, 2000) and reproduced by permission of Arthur White. Website: www.tough-talk.com

"Anatomy of an Ambush" © Thomas A. Taylor, originally published in *Dodging Bullets, A Strategic Guide to World-Class Protection* (Institute of Police Technology and Management, 1999) and reproduced by permission of Thomas A. Taylor

Apex Publishing Ltd for "The Johnny Kidd Memorial Night", an extract from *Warrior Kings, The South London Gang Wars 1976–1982* © Noel "Razor" Smith 2008. Website: www.ApexPublishing.co.uk

"Funerals" © Steve Wraith and Stuart Wheatman, originally published in *The Krays, the Geordie Connection* (Zymurgy Publishing, 2002), reproduced by permission of Steve Wraith and Stuart Wheatman

"Raging Bull" © Rob MacGowan, reproduced by permission of the author Rob MacGowan

New Breed Publishing for "Prize Fighter", an extract from *What Makes Tough Guys Tough? The Secret Domain* © Jamie O'Keefe 1998. Website: www.newbreedbooks.co.uk

"The Building Society Bandit" © Vicki Schofield, reproduced by permission of the author Vicki Schofield

"Liverpool's Hardest Doorman" © Barbara Preston, reproduced by permission of the author Barbara Preston

Apex Publishing Ltd for "Gypsy Kings and Bare-Knuckle Knights", an extract from *Left Hooks and Dangerous Crooks* © Tel Currie 2009. Website: www.ApexPublishing.co.uk

"Hard Bastards, What Exactly Are They?" © Rob MacGowan, reproduced by permission of the author Rob MacGowan